Contemporary Corporate Strategy

With the onset of the third millennium, globalisation has become the most potent driving force for transformation in the economic, political and social lives of individuals, firms and nations. Increasing numbers of corporations around the world have been undergoing cultural and mindset paradigm shifts whilst developing corporate strategies that are increasingly attuned to the highly competitive and dynamic business realities arising from globalising national economies around the world. This book represents an eclectic collection of the latest research articles and empirical studies conducted in different parts of the world on corporate strategy, including usually neglected countries of study such as Germany, Turkey, Greece and Spain.

This book contains over 20 research papers examining various aspects of corporate strategy in different national and international settings. It is intended to equip readers with the latest knowledge to understand the complexities of corporate strategy both at theoretical and operational levels. Further, this book is specifically written with the needs of the students of strategy, both at an undergraduate and postgraduate level, who may want to gain contemporary knowledge of strategy based on empirical research.

This book will be of great interest to students and researchers engaged with corporate strategy and globalisation, as well as corporate executives in multinational enterprises.

John Saee is Professor of International Business, Corporate Strategy and Managements and Academic Director of the Doctoral Programme at the Australian Graduate School of Entrepreneurship, Swinburne University of Technology, Melbourne, Australia. His other books include *Managing Organizations in a Global Economy, Strategic Global Management, Managerial Competence within the Hospitality and Tourism Service Industries: Global Cultural Contextual Analysis* and *Global Business Handbook*.

Routledge Studies in International Business and the World Economy

First published 2007
by Routledge
2 Park Square, Milton Park, Abingdon, Oxon OX14 4RN

Simultaneously published in the USA and Canada
by Routledge
711 Third Avenue, New York, NY 10017

Routledge is an imprint of the Taylor & Francis Group, an informa business

First issued in paperback 2012

Typeset in Times New Roman By Prepress Projects Ltd, Perth, Scotland

British Library Cataloguing in Publication Data
A catalogue record for this book is available from the British Library

Library of Congress Cataloging-in-Publication Data
A catalog record for this book has been requested

ISBN13: 978-0-415-54113-8 (pbk)
ISBN13: 978-0-415-38595-4 (hbk)

This research book is dedicated to the memory of
my beloved parents

Contents

Contributors

Joaquín Alegre is at the Universidad de Valencia, Spain.

Montserrat Boronat Navarro is at the Universitat Jaume I, Castellón, Spain.

Emily Boyle is at the University of Ulster, UK.

Melih Bulu is at Yeditepe University, Turkey.

César Camisón Zornoza is at the Universitat Jaume I, Castellón, Spain.

Ricardo Chiva is at the Universitat Jaume I, Castellón, Spain.

Mariola Ciszewska is at the Leon Kozminski Academy of Management and Entrepreneurship, Warsaw, Poland.

I. Hakki Eraslan is at Bogazici University, Turkey.

Alejandro Escribá-Esteve is at the Universidad de Valencia, Spain.

Nuria González Álvarez is at the Universidad de León, Spain.

Christoph Grimpe is at the Centre for European Economic Research (ZEW), Mannheim, Germany.

Andrzej Kuśmierz is at the Leon Kozminski Academy of Management and Entrepreneurship, Warsaw, Poland.

Rafael Lapiedra is at the Universitat Jaume I, Castellón, Spain.

Jennifer Lawlor is at the Dublin Institute of Technology, Ireland.

Zahid Mahmood is at University Sains Malaysia.

Mariano Nieto Antolín is at the Universidad de León, Spain.

Krzysztof Obloj is at the Leon Kozminski Academy of Management and Entrepreneurship, Warsaw, Poland.

Francesco Perrini is at Bocconi University, Milan, Italy.

María Ripollés-Meli is at the Facultat de Ciencias Jurídicas y Económicas, Universitat Jaume I, Spain.

Angeloantonio Russo is at Bocconi University, Milan, Italy.

John Saee is at the Faculty of Business and Enterprise, Swinburne University of Technology, Australia.

Ioannis-Dionysios Salavrakos is at the University of Ioannina, Greece, and a visiting scholar at London Metropolitan University, UK.

Esther Sánchez-Peinado is at the Universidad de Valencia, Spain.

Luz Sánchez-Peinado is at the Universitat Jaume I, Castellón, Spain.

Mercedes Segarra Ciprés is at the Universitat Jaume I, Castellón, Spain.

Wolfgang Sofka is at the Centre for European Economic Research (ZEW), Mannheim, Germany.

Utz Weitzel is at the Utrecht School of Economics, The Netherlands.

Preface

With the onset of the third millennium, globalisation has become the most potent driving force for transformation in the economic, political and social lives of individuals, firms and nations. It has ushered in remarkable changes, thereby giving rise to an increasing convergence of consumer tastes for goods and services globally. Through major technological breakthroughs, it has facilitated the webs of information, resources, people and products that are electronically woven through networks of firms all over the globe. The very structures and strategies of firms and new manifestations of resources such as knowledge and information are supplanting traditional factors of production such as land, labour and capital (1; 94; 95).

In the meantime, increasing numbers of corporations around the world have been undergoing cultural and paradigm shifts. As a consequence, they have been developing corporate strategies that are increasingly attuned to the highly competitive and dynamic business realities of contemporary global economy.

This book represents an eclectic collection of research articles and empirical studies conducted in different parts of the world on corporate strategy. It is intended to equip readers with the latest knowledge to understand the complexities of corporate strategy both at an operational and theoretical level. It contains over 20 research papers examining various aspects and dimensions of corporate strategy in different national and international settings.

This research book is specifically written with the perceived needs of students of strategy both at an undergraduate and postgraduate level as well as scholars of strategy who may want to gain contemporary knowledge of strategy based on empirical research.

John Saee

Acknowledgements

I am deeply indebted to all colleagues from around the world for their encouragement, support and feedback during the compilation of this research book, including Bruce Roberts, Elian Chekroun, Terry Claque, Katrin Walz, Frank Percy, Jean-Philippe Ammeux, Pascal Ameye, Daniel Buyl, David Hayward, Dennis Ottley, Olga Muzychenko, Frank Vidal, Shirley Saunders, Henri Jolles, Veronique Lable, Wil Hamel, Heinz Klandt and Christa Vauguin. I would also like to acknowledge my students from around the world for providing challenging intellectual stimuli over the years.

1 Globalisation and the multinational enterprises' corporate strategy in the third millennium

John Saee

It has been said arguing against globalisation is like arguing against the law of gravity.

Kofi Annan, United Nations Former Secretary General, September 2000

When the world was big, we could think small. Now the world is small, we have to think 'big'.

Modern proverb

Introduction

At the dawn of the new millennium, globalisation has become the most popular agenda in the economic, political and social lives of individuals, firms and nations. When we think about globalisation, we think of the remarkable convergence of tastes in consumer goods and the pervasive culture of consumption sweeping the world. We also think of webs of information, resources, people and products; electronically woven through networks of firms spread all over the globe. We think of the political and economic transformations changing the very structures and strategies of firms, and new manifestations of resources, such as knowledge and information, replacing traditional factors of production, such as land, labour and capital. We also think of the nation-state, an institution embraced by mankind in the last two centuries, giving way to the global corporation, *the* economic transformation agent of the new century, leapfrogging firms and peoples, including those from the developing world, into market prosperity. We think of this corporation, an economic value chain loosely managed by knowledge and information webs, as perhaps the most precious productive resource known to mankind (1; 94; 95).

There has been a sea change in the world economy, with perceived far-reaching consequences on all aspects of human civilisation (75). We are moving progressively further away from a world in which national economies were relatively isolated from each other by barriers to cross-border trade and investment; by distance, time zones and language; and by national differences in government regulation, culture and business systems. We are moving towards a world in which national economies are merging into an interdependent global economic system, commonly referred to as globalisation (43).

The transformation now taking place in the global economy is unprecedented. The increasing availability of global capital, coupled with advances in computing and communications technology, is serving to speed up the processes of globalisation. Concurrently, the barriers to globalisation are increasingly disappearing in most countries of the world (22).

Meanwhile, globalisation has accelerated the process of increasing interconnectedness between societies, so much so that events in one part of the world have more and more effect on peoples and societies far away. In other words, a globalised world is one in which political, economic, cultural and social events become more and more interconnected, and also one in which they have a wider impact (11).

In this research article, an attempt is made to provide a conceptual analysis of globalisation from both historical and contemporary perspectives. Explanation is provided in terms of why firms are motivated to go global. Finally, implications emerging from the globalisation of multinational enterprises, in terms of formulating corporate strategy, are explored.

Different perspectives on globalisation

The phenomenon of globalisation means different things to different people. A review of literature suggests differing conceptualisations.

For example, viewed purely from an economic standpoint, globalisation is conceived as a process of increasing involvement in international business operations (92).

Thus, globalisation is conceived as a business trend worldwide of expanding beyond domestic boundaries, which is creating an interconnected world economy in which companies do their business and compete with each other anywhere in the world, regardless of national boundaries (17).

Within this economic conceptualisation, nations and their home firms elect to trade with each other in their attempts to increase wealth and economic prosperity for their nations, firms and ultimately their citizens.

Meanwhile, a sociological view of globalisation defines globalisation as a more pervasive force throughout the world in a sense that globalisation leads to 'the constraints of geography on social and cultural arrangements recede whilst people around the world become increasingly aware that they are receding' (91: 3).

Underlying these definitions is the belief that technological innovations in areas such as communications and transport have been the driving force behind the breaking down of national and international barriers including vast geographical distances and the presence of myriad linguistic and cultural groupings across the world. In other words, the world is increasingly becoming a 'global village'.

A more critical view of globalisation based on Marxist philosophy argues that globalisation is what people in the Third World have for several centuries called colonisation. Proponents of this school of thought maintain that the capitalist Western countries exploit raw materials and cheap labour found in the Third World countries at the enormous expense of the peoples of the Third World countries (6).

Here the question arises, is globalisation of businesses a recent development in human history?

Globalisation: a brief historical account

Broadly speaking, there is a common misconception in various academic and professional circles that globalisation, which is rapidly transforming the landscape of the world economy, is a 'new' phenomenon in human history. However, this fallacious claim is not justified in the light of historical evidence. Human societies have traded amongst themselves for thousands of years.

Let's take a look at the histories of Phonetians, Persians, Egyptians, Greeks and Roman civilisations that were evidently involved in trade and commerce, though in a different scale in terms of reach and marketplace.

Throughout the history and particularly since the establishment of agriculture as a mode of production in human civilisation, local marketplaces emerged in which farming communities traded their surplus produce in exchange for product(s) and/ or service in kind without the medium of money. This type of commercial activity was referred as the *barter system.*

With the growth of population and cities, it gave rise to new social groupings of petty bourgeois and mercantile classes, who set out on a voyage across national and then international frontiers in their attempts to maximise the rate of return for their commercial activities. Notable is the fact that there is archaeological evidence to support the notion that human society has always traded goods. A most famous example of a trade route that existed for international trade was the 'Silk Road', where caravans of merchants traversed from China via Afghanistan right through to the Middle East and Europe in their attempts to trade commodities.

Equally, it is worth noting that often governments of many powerful countries throughout history saw tremendous benefits in accessing strategically important raw materials for their growing kingdoms. But, instead of conducting trade with other governments in a contemporary transactional manner, they chose large-scale violence in conquering countries that had those vital raw materials. In many respects, it was a brutal form of international trade, which modern history condemns as sheer exploitation and oppression.

A large-scale transactional form of international trade amongst producers, middlemen and purchasers had emerged in different marketplaces, both national and international, in the eighteenth century.

In 1780s, the noted philosopher Jeremy Bentham coined the term 'international' due to the emerging reality of his day, namely, the rise of nation-states and of cross-border transactions between them. However, according to some writers, the modern onset of globalisation can be attributed to the mid-nineteenth century.

Meanwhile, there have been several precursors to globalisation, which are worthy of brief mention here (11).

First, it is argued that globalisation has many features in common with the theory of modernisation. Increasing industrialization had brought into existence a whole new set of contacts between societies, and has changed the political, economic and social processes that characterised the pre-industrialised world. Thus, modernisation is part of globalisation (64).

Second, the economic growth theory originally developed by Rostow advocated that economic growth followed a pattern in all economies as they went through industrialisation. What this has in common with globalisation is that Rostow saw a clear pattern to economic development, one marked by stages which all economies would follow as they adopted capitalism (11).

Third, there have been notable similarities between the picture of the world painted by globalisation and that portrayed in Marshall McLuhan's influential work on the 'global village'. According to McLuhan, advances in electronic communications resulted in a world where we could see in real-time events that were occurring in distant parts of the world. For McLuhan, the main effects of this development are that time and space become compressed to such an extent that everything loses its traditional identity.

Fourth, globalisation theory has several points in common with the controversial argument of Fukuyama about the end of history. Fukuyama's main claim is that the power of the economic market is resulting in liberal democracy replacing all other types of government (36).

Bearing these issues in mind, there are crucial differences between the contemporary notion of globalisation and one that was used hundreds of years ago. Globalisation today describes a far more pervasive and deep phenomenon than has never existed before. Thousands of goods, services and even ideas are manufactured globally, creating complex interconnections between states. A book, for example, can be written in Sydney, copy-edited in the USA, typeset in France, printed in Poland and then distributed globally. The advent of the Internet has made global supply chain management – including manufacturing, distribution and communication – simple and cheap.

There is another crucial dissimilarity between the ancient notion of globalisation and the modern concept of globalisation. In the ancient world large companies that could wield enormous political and economic powers did not exist, whereas in the contemporary world globalisation has led to the creation of large multinational enterprises.

Multinational enterprises and their global reach

Multinational enterprises (MNEs) have increasingly become powerful across different nations in terms of economic and political dimensions. Current statistics reveal that close to 52 per cent of world resources are controlled and owned by multinational companies. At the same time, there are 63,000 multinational corporations with around 700,000 foreign affiliates in the world today (88). Furthermore, *Fortune* magazine provides a list of a 'Global 500', which have enormous sales turnover and assets. For example, less than 30 countries in the world have a GDP that exceeds the total annual revenue of *General Motors* (5).

For the purpose of illustration, the following Table 1.1 provides a listing of the world's top twenty-five multinational companies, ranked in terms of their revenues globally.

MNEs account for most of the world's trade and investment. Indeed, the largest 500 MNEs account for over 90 per cent of the world's stock of foreign direct investment (FDI) and they themselves conduct about half of the world's trade.

Further, the 500 largest companies in the world accounted for over $14 trillion of total sales (revenues) in fiscal year 2001. The average revenues for a firm in the top 500 were $28 billion, ranging from Wal-Mart at $220 billion to Takenaka at $10 billion (72).

MNEs (also referred to as transnational corporations (TNCs)) have operations in most countries around the globe. Table 1.2 provides the top 100 MNEs that are, for example, present in a vast majority of countries around the world.

Table 1.1 The world's largest 25 MNCs, ranked by revenues, 2002

Global 500 Rank	Company	Revenues ($ millions)
1	Wal-Mart Stores	219,812.0
2	Exxon Mobil	191,581.0
3	General Motors	177,260.0
4	BP	174,218.0
5	Ford Motor	162,412.0
6	Enron	138,718.0
7	Daimler Chrysler	136,897.3
8	Royal Dutch/Shell Group	135,211.0
9	General Electric	125,913.0
10	Toyota Motor	120,814.4
11	CitiGroup	112,022.0
12	Mitsubishi	105,813.9
13	Mitsui	101,205.6
14	Cheyron Texaco	99,699.0
15	Total Fina Elf	94,311.9
16	Nippon Telegraph & Telephone	93,424.8
17	Itochu	91,176.6
18	Allianz	85,929.2
19	IBM	85,866.0
20	ING GROUP	82,999.1
21	Volkswagen	79,287.3
22	Siemens	77,358.9
23	Sumitomo	77,140.1
24	Philip Morris	72,944.0
25	Marubeni	71,756.6

Source: adapted from *The Fortune* (2002).

Table 1.2 The top 100 MNEs that have presence in the highest number of host countries in 2005

TNCs from all countries		TNCs from developing countries	
Company name	Number of host countries	Host economy	Number of host countries
Deutsche Post	103	Samsung	29
Nestlé	96	Flextronics	27
Royal Dutch/Shell	92	SingTel	21
BASF	79	CapitaLand	21
Bayer	70	LG Electronics	20
Siemens	69	Acer	19
Procter and Gamble	68	Hutchison Whampoa	15
AstraZeneca	67	Neptune Orient Lines	14
Total	65	Datatec	12
IBM	64	Hon Hai Precision Industries	12

Source: UNCTAD (2006) Investment Brief Number 5.

Motivations for enterprises to internationalise

Research has identified various sources of motivations behind the enterprises' internationalisation business strategy. They include:

- secure key supplies in various geographical locations around the world;
- access to low-cost factors of production;
- the ability to reduce costs – economies of scope and scale, together with focused production, reduce the cost of products and services;
- the ability to provide higher quality (because of economies of scope and scale);
- enhanced customer awareness and loyalty due to the interaction of three forces: global availability, serviceability and recognition;
- increased leverage over competitors by bringing resources of the worldwide network to bear on the competitive situation in individual countries;
- greater access to human skills and knowledge, because global companies can access the best people in the world, irrespective of nationality;
- increased access to financial resources and capital, including more frequent access to a variety of world stock exchanges;
- increased availability of information resources is often *the* competitive edge;
- longer and more diversified use of equipment and technology, which includes flexible manufacturing using computer assisted design and manufacturing (CAD/CAM). Communication technology is initially expensive, but has little or no maintenance costs after installation;

- broader customer base, so global companies do not rely too heavily on one market, such as the original domestic market;
- geographic flexibility offers choice regarding market and factory sites;
- bargaining power becomes enhanced because of the ability to switch production between a variety of manufacturing sites;
- cultural synergies mean that cultural diversity is seen as a major source of innovative ideas;
- enhanced image and reputation comes from the public perception that global companies 'must have' better products and services;
- opportunities for alliances and partnerships occur because greater choices are available; and
- power as a global learning organisation is closely tied in with the business goals of the company (75; 9).

MNEs' corporate strategy in the third millennium

Globalisation has brought a fundamentally different vision of strategic thinking inside the firm as well. Guided by the *global mindset*, the manager's vision is changing from coping with rapid change to driving change, from competing with rivals to collaborating with them, from planning operations to rapid execution, and from efficient resource allocation to nurturing effective customer relationships. Businesses are inventing and harvesting new technologies along global value chains and harnessing competencies for swift and effective market response. They are increasingly employing knowledge to capture increasing returns-to-scale and scope, and nurturing corporate cultures that reward ownership and empowerment of intellectual competencies. They are reaching out to cross-national market segments, sourcing worldwide, and espousing new concepts of distributing intangible assets globally (1; 91).

The evolving mindset by enterprises to develop international business strategy

Before proceeding to explore the evolving mindset by captains of enterprises in terms of international business strategy, it would merit here a brief description of what is meant by strategy with its different manifestations.

Strategy formation can be considered a conscious process through which a future plan is created and then acted upon (41; 65; 82), which is not to suggest that it is independent of strategy implementation (61; 20). Research has long since recognised that strategy formation is a process founded upon a pattern or stream of decisions (62) reflecting phases of identification, development and selection (77). Most strategy process typologies such as this (for instance, Gerbing *et al.*'s study (1994 cited in Morgan *et al.*, 65) assessing management participation in strategy formation) adopt the assumption of decisional rationality where a systematic process is followed in establishing a logical and sequential pattern of decisions, from goal formulation through to strategic choice and strategy implementation. Such a concept has been referred to as 'procedural rationality' (26). In this study, strategy formation refers to the setting of goals and the analyses that underlie the generation, evaluation and selection of strategies necessary to achieve these organisational goals. Therefore, strategy formation is concerned with both the allocation of resources and the development of organisational processes necessary to achieve the long-term goals of the organisation (91). Fredrickson (35) considered strategy formation in terms of the comprehensiveness of the processes involved and described it as the 'extent to which an organization attempts to be exhaustive or inclusive in making and integrating strategic decisions' (p. 447). Simply put, a firm's business strategy is meant to involve the optimum allocation of its resources in order to achieve a competitive advantage (37).

Business strategy plan routinely subsumes the following principles:

- has a core assignment; management of the interface between the organisation and its environment;
- involves anticipating, adapting to, and creating change both in the environment and within the organisation;
- is driven by the relentless pursuit of opportunities;
- recognising that opportunities may arise in the external environment or they may be generated within the organisation; and
- is the task of the whole organisation; it cannot be delegated to any group within the organisation.

In addition, there are three dimensions to a business strategy: *process, content and context.*

Strategy process is concerned with the how, who and when. The strategy process looks at how it is made, analysed, formulated, implemented and managed. 'Who' refers to who is involved in the strategy process and 'when' refers to when the necessary activities need to take place.

Strategy content can be looked at in terms of a product of the strategy process – this is what is, or should be, the strategy for the company.

Strategy context is the set of circumstances under which the both the strategy process and the strategy content are determined. It can be looked at as the 'where' of strategy – where being which firm and which environment.

Meanwhile, there are also three stages of strategy that can help enterprises to make use of the process more efficiently: analysis, formation and implementation. Bob de Witt *et al.* (25) argue that the foregoing are not phases, stages or elements of the strategy process that can be understood in isolation; all these separate phases are strongly interlinked and they are always overlapping.

In the strategy analysis stage, businesses identify the opportunities and threats in the environment, as well as the strengths and weaknesses of the organisation. In the strategy formation stage, business enterprises identify and evaluate strategic options that are available to them whilst choosing the one option that in their view leads to optimise chances of success. Finally, there is the implementation stage: this is when the selected strategic option is translated into a number of concrete activities that are then carried out.

A hierarchy of strategy

An enterprise normally subsumes a hierarchy of strategy. There is, first of all, a strategy for the entire company which covers all its business units and this is referred to as *corporate strategy*. There is a strategy for each separate business the company has diversified into and this is known as *business strategy*. Then, there is a strategy for each specific function unit within a business (*functional strategy*). And, finally, there are still narrower strategies for basic operating units – plants, sales districts and regions, and departments within functional areas, which are commonly called *operating strategy* (85).

The corporate, business and functional strategy hierarchy has been established as a useful framework within which to contextualise discussion of strategic issues within companies (44: 11).

Having described briefly aspects of business strategy, it is appropriate here to discuss the impact of globalisation on the mindset of leaders and managers of enterprise in terms of strategy formulations.

International mentality

Data suggests that increasing globalisation has presented unprecedented business opportunities for entrepreneurs and enterprises. At the same time, however, businesses have not always been savvy in capitalising opportunities presented internationally.

With hindsight, it can be argued that many enterprises have in the past thought of the company's overseas operations as distant outposts whose main roles are to support the domestic parent company in different ways, such as contributing incremental sales to the domestic manufacturing operations. This approach to business is referred to as *international strategic mentality* (9).

Having the international mentality means that international companies create and produce products for their domestic markets and the excesses are exported. They will build bases abroad but only to protect the domestic market. Information and decisions usually come from the parent company. Bartlett and Ghoshal (8) maintain that companies with this mentality regard themselves fundamentally as a domestic company with some foreign appendages. Decisions related to the foreign operations tend to be made in an opportunistic or ad hoc manner. The disadvantage of sticking to this mentality is that the international company will be indifferent to the desires of the consumers in its various foreign markets. In addition, the company will be inefficient in its operations as its main concern is that of supplying the home country. According to Jones (48: 22), 'international strategies based on first-mover advantages from product innovation lacked both scale and sensitivity to customer needs.' The international strategy is used commonly by US companies. However, it would be unwise to use this strategy in the fast changing world.

Meanwhile, Gibson (38) holds the view that the US company is becoming extinct. Increasingly, all companies are global, and those that succeed will glean every bit of business advantage they can from every corner of the globe.

Multinational mindset

The multinational mentality is different from the international mentality because the former exhibits sensitivity to the local markets where its subsidiaries are located. The multinational company customises its products and services to suit the needs of its individual markets. Management is decentralised and this means that the parent company gives the subsidiaries the freedom to operate as it sees fit in its respective local markets (8).

With this in mind, MNEs develop national companies that are increasingly sensitive and responsive to their local environments. These companies undertake a strategic approach that is literally multinational. Their worldwide strategy is built on the foundation of the multiple, nationally responsive strategies of the company's worldwide subsidiaries that have been typical of European MNEs. However, the problem inherent with having this kind of mentality is that since the subsidiaries are independent, operations may be inefficient due to the high possibility of product duplication. According to Jones (48), this strategy is extremely locally responsive, yet also the most risky for MNEs as well as the most expensive due to the lack of scale economies, massive duplication of activities, poor lateral communication, lack of learning mechanisms, etc. The multinational strategy also holds the greatest danger of local subsidiary management 'going native' and making decisions under the influence of local loyalties rather than with reference to the interests of the overall MNEs.

Multinational strategies are no longer practical, given their severe cost disadvantages emanating from redundancy and lack of scale.

Global mindset

The global mentality pervades the Japanese way of doing business. It aims for global efficiency. The global company produces standardised products through economies of scale as it believes that consumer preferences are more or less similar or can be made similar. Products produced are cost efficient and of high quality, thus eliminating the consumers' biases in inclinations. The management structure of a global company is that of a centralised one. This means that the final decisions come from the parent company (8).

Keys to a successful global strategy

Adapting a global strategy is not an easy undertaking, though many would aspire to apply it. There are many dimensions and environmental aspects to be considered. Various authors have developed typologies of global strategy that can be divided into three main categories.

1   Focus on the organisation's generic strategies and its competitive positioning as the sources of competitive advantage (68). According to this school it is the ability of the business to select the appropriate generic strategy for its industry, and to configure its value-adding chain in support of it, which will

generate competitive advantage. Strategic fits have to be created between opportunities and threats in the environment and strengths and weaknesses of the business itself.

2 Focus on resources, capabilities and competencies as sources sustains superior performance (25; 68). Businesses are viewed as open systems interacting with their environments to acquire resources and deliver outputs (products). Superior performance is based upon the ability of the business to develop core competences which are not possessed by its competitors, and which create perceived benefits for consumers.

3 Focus on coordination and integration of geographically dispersed operations in the pursuit of global competitiveness (8; 96). There are significant advantages to be gained from the global scope, configuration and coordination of the firm's international ctivities. According to Yip (96) the global strategy must be tailored to match each of the globalisation drivers in the industry. It is opposed to the idea of global standardasation stressing that global strategy must be flexible.

If first and second alternatives provide perspectives on the various sources of the competitive advantage generally available to all businesses, the third framework explores the issues specific to transnational or global companies. This framework will be central in our course.

According to Yip (96), there are three separate components (stages) of the global strategy:

1 developing core strategy – this is the basis for an organisation's competitive advantage;
2 internationalising the core strategy – the international expansion of activities and the adaptation of the core strategy; and
3 globalising the international strategy – integrating the strategy across countries.

Developing the core strategy

The core strategy is the basis and the main element in coming up with a competitive strategy. It states the business description, mission plan, its markets and core competencies. It is what the business is doing and what it is capable of achieving. In being aware of these, the organisation can build strategies on a solid foundation.

Taking a closer look at the elements of the core strategy, an organisation is faced by the identity and make of the business. These comprise the following:

- type of products and services that the business offers;
- types of customers that it serves;
- specific geographic markets that the enterprise covers;
- the business may have major sources of sustainable competitive advantage;

- it may have function strategy for each of the value-adding activities;
- business has a distinct competitive posture, including the selection of competitors to target, and it has a clearly formulated investment strategy (96).

These reflect the current position and standing of the organisation. It also determines the strengths and possible weaknesses the business may have. In being able to detect these characteristics, a stable core strategy can be established.

A core strategy is defined as the plan of action that is unconstrained by the location, production, management or marketing of the business. It is composed of the core values and the core purpose of the firm:

> Core values represent the essential and enduring tenets of an organisation. A small set of timeless guiding principles, core values require no justification; they have intrinsic value and importance to those inside the firm . . . The point is that a great company decides for itself what values it holds to be core, largely independent of the current environment, competitive requirements, or management fads.
>
> (21)

An insight regarding the formation of a core strategy is that it is better and more effective if it is focused on the core competencies or strengths of the business organisation (96).

The core strategy of McDonald's is to provide quality and yet low-price fast food to the general public through their outlets. That is basically what they are set to perform and they have been very successful implementing their core strategy across international borders.

McDonald's food chains are located almost everywhere in the world, in different countries with varying cultures and geographic descriptions. These include the US, France, Japan, Australia and even Russia. Their competitive advantage of being a quality fast food chain is widely accepted and recognised all throughout the world.

Internationalisation of the core strategy

This is the next step to be taken after having a good grasp of the company's core strategies.

This process involves:

- the expansion of the company geographically outside of the home country to other nations, selecting the geographic markets in which to compete; and
- the application of different strategies that would cater for various regions, adapting products.

The internationalisation of the core strategy reflects how a firm should be aware of the many influences that are inclined to affect the firm's operations.

The organisation should analyse the risks that they are exposed to in venturing outside the domestic region. A good question to ask is if the benefits earned through the adaptation of a global strategy would offset the risks taken. The advantages and disadvantages should be measured and weighed in reference to knowing the issues of trading worldwide.

Again, a clear example of this is McDonald's. In focusing on this firm, it can be observed that in all countries they offer a standard menu. However, in some countries they also offer some diverse products in addition to their standard menu. For instance, they sell chicken with rice meals in Asian countries and they have recently introduced the McOz burger here in Australia. Therefore, they are catering to the international market with just minor adjustments to keep their identity. The adaptations they make do not haze their core strategy.

Globalisation of the international strategy

The difficulties and complexity of the international strategy creates the path for the global strategy. A global strategy joins together all the different international strategies into a synergy. Globalising the core business requires:

- identification of the areas of strategy to be globalised (based on globalisation drivers); and
- integration of activities.

Global strategy levers

The global strategy levers are the options a company has to achieve different benefits and advantages in competing globally.

Global strategy levers include market participation, global products, global location of activities, global marketing, and global competitive moves. These are positioned appropriately in relation to the industry drivers and are relative to the position and resources of the business and parent company (50).

Market participation

Companies usually have a reason for setting up in a particular country, the most obvious being profit. A multilocal strategy would select a country based on the degree to which a firm believes that any market penetration there would generate success. On the other side of the scale, a firm using a global strategy would look at a country from a strategic point of view. The question is asked, 'What benefits to my overall global position would arise from a venture aimed at this country'. Even if the country is not likely to generate the greatest level of revenue, it may carry enough significance, for example, be the home base of a competitor. A multilocal approach would generally view a country with how well it would individually perform, as opposed to any globally strategic advantage it may have (96).

Products and services

A multilocal approach concentrates on tailoring a product or service that meets the needs of the country in question. A great deal of time and money can be involved in making a success of the venture as they are often involve extensive research in what the consumers from that country need and want. A global product strategy aims to have one standardised product that meets the expectations of consumers worldwide (96).

Activity location

A multilocal strategy will often place the majority of its operations in each target country, thereby setting up a number of bases that are equipped and aware enough to deal directly with local people. A global strategy will often spread its operations between numerous countries for specific advantages such as cost reduction (96).

Marketing

The multilocal strategy implies tailoring marketing to a specific country or region while the company with a global strategic approach usually has a standardised marketing strategy aimed at the whole world. This has often led to problems with global companies due to a lack of research and understanding. Many ventures have been unsuccessful as the marketing approach or brand labelling can often be confusing, misleading or downright offensive to particular consumer markets in other countries (96).

Competitive moves

Competition in the global economy is intense. Firms constantly fight and haggle for a larger slice of a lucrative market. A multilocal company will usually centre its competitive attack and defence strategy in one country at a time – perhaps one could say they prefer to protect their own shore, even if it was a shore that was invaded in the first instance. A company which uses a global strategy will often centre its competitive strategies in several markets at once. Like a great torrid of water, many countries can be infiltrated in unison. A well-known and widely used competitive strategy of both global and multilocal companies is to attack the home base of their rivals. This increased attention to a competitor's base can often lead to the competitor retracting from the market they had been in to return home to protect their own boundaries. It is paramount to have a strong global attack and defence plan (96).

Benefits of global strategy

A global approach to market participation helps a company to achieve each of the categories of global benefits: cost reduction; improved quality; enhanced customer preference; and competitive leverage.

Cost reduction

This is achieved through various means. One is through economies of scale, where a firm could reduce its cost per unit of product by manufacturing in large numbers.

Also, globalisation promotes lower factor costs, since it lessens the duplication of development and operations efforts. There is an overall department for all the regions so it avoids redundancy in purchasing and development costs (96).

An organisation could easily search the whole globe for which country be most cost effective for them, and would best serve their needs.

Improved quality of products

Since an organisation will be focusing on the manufacture of a smaller range of goods, and they have standardised the products to meet global needs, then there is greater concentration on each product line. Manufacturers do not get the inconsistencies of having to change parts and monitor the changes of production.

Enhanced customer preference

Customers would support a product or a brand more if it was available globally. It should be kept in mind that most people travel overseas nowadays. Being able to purchase or have access to a product internationally reinforces customer loyalty (79).

Having global operations and recognition sends signals to the customers that the firm is stable and one could rely on their products (79).

This is probably the key to McDonald's success internationally – a customer knows what to expect in terms of food and service in whichever branch of McDonald's they go to.

Increasing competitive leverage

Once a company is global, it is able to strategically position its operations so it can attack where it needs to. It is able to target the market of its competitors and even penetrate the home country of its rivals.

This happened in the case of Fuji film and Kodak. When Fuji started to capture portions of Kodak's market share in the US, Kodak decided to aggressively enter the Korean market, which is the home country of Fuji. This made Fuji wary of competing with Kodak.

Drawbacks of global business strategy

The problem with this kind of mindset is that the global company is not exposed to the innovations going on outside the home country. The global company cannot learn as its operations will be concentrated in one place or some places that provide cost advantages. According to Jones (48: 346), 'Global strategies, though viable in particular product markets, have proved to be too concerned with scale based efficiencies and insensitive to continuing differences in customer preferences across – and even within national markets.'

Transnational mentality

Companies have been increasingly cognizant of the shortcomings of the above-mentioned mentalities and corresponding strategies. As a result, the transnational strategy was developed in the 1990s to address the weaknesses of earlier strategic approaches. These strategies involve a combination of aspects of the three previous approaches in that product innovation, market sensitivity, and efficient production are all held as necessary to obtain competitive advantage in certain industries. The distinguishing characteristic of this approach is that the various national operations are tightly linked through information technology in order to promote lateral communication and organisational learning (see 8). Transnational strategy represents a realisation that, in many industries, globalisation in terms of a total convergence and homogenisation of consumer demand has not occurred and is not likely to manifest in the foreseeable future. Therefore, learning about local needs and operating conditions remains a key success factor in such industries. A term which captures the essence of transnational strategy is 'mass customisation', providing consumers with products tailored to their particular needs, but in the most efficient manner possible through common platforms which can be customised at low cost. In terms of spatial boundary implications, a transnational strategy would be similar to a complex global strategy, although there would more duplication of downstream activities (e.g., marketing and distribution) on a national or at least regional basis to promote local responsiveness. 'The distinguishing characteristic of this approach is that the various national operations are tightly linked through information technology in order to promote lateral communication and organizational learning'; see also (48 p.346; see also 8). An example of the application of the transnational strategy would be the American company, MTV. Martin (56) maintains that MNE in adopting a transnational strategy, tailors its channels to local cultural tastes with a mixture of national, regional and international artists, along with locally produced and globally shared programming. Being a transnational company means being flexible to the demands of the various consumers' preferences without losing the company's identity and wasting resources.

Enterprises are increasingly faced with challenges arising from both foreign and local competition. McLean (58) views that nowadays, one's patch is no longer one's doorstep – globalisation has knocked down traditional organisational boundaries and barriers and exposed organisations to a wide range of experiences and opportunities. A company has no choice but to defend itself or perish. To counteract the effects of having competition a company is forced to seek new markets because the discipline of sourcing means looking constantly across existing and potential suppliers and locations, and seeking out the right balance between quality, economics, risk, flexibility and innovation (66). Companies have to be competitive in all aspects to survive.

Company owners are forced to globalise their operations so that they will not be overrun by their competitors. 'This means that some aspects of the business will be standardised. You can't operate globally without standardised contracts and standardised work,' said Lisa Gage, director of corporate planning and strategy at General Motors (38). Standardisation can offer cost savings to a company; however, '*standardization* can do the most strategic damage by forcing *products* and practices into moulds. The resulting homogenization of business tends to undermine innovation, all the way up the supply chain. Managers become so focused on meeting tight operational targets–and stamping out exceptions – that they begin to consciously avoid the experimentation that leads to attractive new *products,* services, and processes. In the end, *standardization* erodes strategic differentiation and leads inexorably toward commoditization – and the lower growth and profitability that accompany it (69). It is all right to standardise procedures to promote uniformity and avoid confusion, but it is not all right to standardise products under the assumption that the customers' needs and wants can be generalised. A company should not force standardised products on its customers because customers' preferences vary.

Aside from standardising, companies must also adapt to the consumers' preferences. This means that a company must be aware of the preferences of its consumers in each of the local markets it caters to. Consumers are far from wanting the same things. Localisation to a certain extent is necessary.

> Localization strives to mitigate the movement towards a monolithic, undifferentiated, global consumer culture by creating a marketplace shaped by diversity, locality and responsible consumer behaviour. It leads to local self-sufficiency and resiliency while being respectful of the global context. Localization means people can diversify their own local economies, increase cohesion and resilience within their community, improving their livelihoods and protect their natural environment.
>
> (53)

It is also important for a company to localise because it 'means trying to meet basic needs from closer to home (53). This means that by being present in a local market, a company can save on shipping costs and other logistical expenses. Furthermore, a company can acquire local knowledge that can prove to be useful in its operations. Localisation can be defined as the flow of ideas, technologies, information, culture, money and goods with the end goal of protecting and rebuilding local economies worldwide. It is a form of internationalism since its emphasis is not on competition for the cheapest, but on cooperation for the best (45). It is not enough for a company to just sell products that are cheap. Quality has to go with it.

Globalisation has forced companies to switch to a transnational strategy. This means that the companies should develop global efficiency, flexibility, and world-wide learning capability simultaneously (9). To be globally efficient, companies must seek out places where they can achieve economies of scale, economies of scope, and low-cost resources leading to lower factor costs. In addition, companies must achieve the perfect combination of standardisation and localisation in order to be globally competitive. The various strategic mentalities mentioned above are only effective to a certain extent. The difficulty with the international company is that 'its resource configuration and operating systems make it less efficient than the global company, and less responsive than the multinational company' (9). With the multinational company, the problem lies in its decentralised organisation. According to Bartlett and Ghoshal (8), 'the fragmentation of activities leads to inefficiency. Learning also suffers, because knowledge is not consolidated and does not flow among the various parts of the company.' The global company suffers from being too centralised. Bartlett and Ghoshal (8) state that the central groups often lack adequate understanding of the market needs and production realities outside their home market. Moreover, global companies are unable to learn from the various local markets they serve because of their very centralised structure. The transnational strategic mentality surmounts the difficulties encountered by the previous strategies mentioned above, as it finds ways and means for the company to be globally efficient and competitive. First, it cuts cost by locating in environments where a company can achieve economies of scale and scope and lower factor costs. This means that a company establishes itself in various countries where the conditions are just right to operate in. Second, it motivates a company to be responsive to the local needs of its consumers. It motivates the company to be flexible to the demands of the global consumers. A company now adapts to the consumers' needs and wants, because consumer preferences are far from similar and can only be generalised to a certain extent. Finally, it supports worldwide learning. Since the company's operations are not restricted to one geographic location only, it encounters various technologies, cultures, and situations, which it can learn from. The company can then apply the knowledge it gains to leverage its operations.

The effect of globalisation on the existing corporate strategies can perhaps be best described by the warning of Jack Welch, chief of General Electric: 'If you can't meet a world standard of quality at the world's best price, you're not even in the game' (80).

Striking the right balance

Different industries have varying globalisation potential. Furthermore, different departments of the organisation also have varying globalisation potential (for example, the clothing industry – in terms of marketing, they would have to choose a strategy that is more multilocal, since people vary in size, shape, colour preferences etc. However, the manufacturing could promote a global approach by basing its production in one specific location). According to Prahalad and Doz (1987) cited in Porter (68), the corporate success at the international level depends on the ability of the business to coordinate (sharing information, allocating responsibility, and aligning efforts) and integrate (centralised management of geographically dispersed activities) global activities whilst at the same time retaining responsiveness to the demand of the local markets and changing circumstances when necessary.

It is possible to adapt more than one strategy in order to be effective. It all depends on the nature of the industry, the different operations involved in the value added chain, and the position and capabilities of the company. For example, Procter and Gamble applies global strategy for its disposable diaper product, but multilocal strategy is applied for detergents.

There is no right or wrong strategic mix since, like humans, organisations come with different characteristics and are faced by different situations.

Bartlett and Ghoshal (9) found that managers often oversimplify the strategic choices available to them, because of their erroneous attitude that it had to be:

- global strategy vs local responsiveness;
- centralised vs decentralised key resources; and
- strong central control vs subsidiary autonomy.

The challenges arise from the conditions that, primarily an organisation is involved with more than one country. There would be various legal, cultural and other environmental issues to consider when formulating a corporate strategy. Moreover, adapting a transnational strategy means that the company would have to become increasingly responsive to local conditions whilst capturing the benefits of global efficiency and flexibility at the same time. In addition, these dispersed resources are integrated into an interdependent network of worldwide operations (9).

Bibliography

1   Aggarwal, R. (1999) Technology and globalisation as mutual reinforcers in business: reorienting strategic thinking for the new millennium. *Management International Review* 39(2), 83–104.

2   Albrow, M. (1990) 'Introduction', in M. Albrow and E. King (eds), *Globalisation, Knowledge and Society,* London: Sage.

3   Anderson, P. F. (1982) Marketing, strategic planning and the theory of the firm. *Journal of Marketing* 46, 15–26.

4   Armstrong, J. S. and Overton, T. S. (1977) Estimating nonresponse bias in mail surveys. *Journal of Marketing Research* 14, 396–403.

5   Ball, Don and McCulloch, Wendell (1999) *International Business*, Sydney: McGraw-Hill.

6   Banarjee S. B. and Linstead, S. (2001) Globalisation, multiculturalism and other fictions: colonialism for the new millenium. *Organization*, November, 8, p. 683.

7   Barlett, D. L. and Steele, J. B. (1996) 'America: Who stole the dream?' *Philadelphia Inquirer,* September, 9.

8   Bartlett, C. A. and Ghoshal, S. (2004) *Transnational Management Text, Cases, and Readings in Cross-Border Management.* 4th edn. Singapore: McGraw-Hill.

9   Bartlett, C. A., Ghoshal, S. and Beamish P. (2006) *Transnational Management Text, Cases, and Readings in Cross-Border Management.* 5th edn. Singapore: McGraw-Hill.

10   Batra, R. (1993) *The Myth of Free Trade.* New York: Touchstone Books.

11   Baylis, J. and Smith, S. (1997) *The Globalisation of World Politics: an introduction to international relations.* New York: Oxford University Press.

12   Berkowitz, E. N., Kerin, R. A., Hartley, S. W. and Rudelius, W. (1992) *Marketing.* Homewood, IL: Irwin.

13   Bhalla S. S. (2002) *Poverty, Inequality, and Growth in the Era of Globalisation,* Washington: Institute of Economics for International Economics.

14   Borgen, F. H. and Seling, M. J. (1978) Uses of discriminant analysis following MANOVA: multivariate statistics for multivariate purposes. *Journal of Applied Psychology* 63(6), 689–97.

15   Bright, C. (1999) 'Invasive species: pathogens of globalisation', *Foreign Policy,* Fall.

16   Bull, H. (1977) *The Anarchical Society. A study of order in world politics.* London: Macmillan.

17   Burton, J. (1972) *World Society.* Cambridge: Cambridge University Press.

18   Buttery A. and Buttery E. M. (1998) *Strategic Planning for Uncertainty.* Sydney: In Focus Publishing.

19   Capon, N., Farley, J. U. and Hulbert, J. M. (1994) Strategic planning and financial performance: more evidence. *Journal of Management Studies* 31, 105–10.

20   Cespedes, F. V. and Piercy, N. F. (1996) Implementing marketing strategy. *Journal of Marketing Management* 12, 135–60.

21   Collins, J. C., Porras, J. I. (1996) Building Your Company's Vision, *Harvard Business Review,* September–October 1996, 65–79.

22   Cullen, J. B. (1999) *Multinational Management: a strategic approach.* Cincinnati, Ohio: South-Western College Publishing.

23   Czinkota, M. R. and Ronkainen, I. A. (1998) *International Marketing.* 5th edn. Orlando, Florida: Harcourt Brace & Company.

24   Czinkota, M. R. and Ronkainen, I. A. (2001) *Best Practices in International Business,* Florida: Harcourt College Publishers.

25   De Wit, B., Meyer, R. (1998) *Strategy Process, Content, Context. An International Perspective.* 2nd edn. London: International Thomson Business Press.

26   Dean, J. W. and Sharfman, M. P. (1993) Procedural rationality in the decision making process. *Journal of Management Studies* 30(4), 587–610.

27   Dess, G. G. and Davis, P. (1984) Porter's (1980) generic strategies as determinants of strategic group membership and organizational performance. *Academy of Management Journal* 27, 467–88.

28   Dollar D. and Kraay A., (2001) *Trade, Growth, and Poverty,* World Bank working paper, June. New York: World Bank.

29   Dunning, J. (1988) *Explaining International Production.* London: Unwin Hyman.

30   Eisenhardt, K. M. (1989) Making fast strategic decisions in high velocity environments. *Academy of Management Journal* 32, 543.

31   Fahey L. (1994) *Strategic Management: Today's Most Important Business Challenge, The Portable MBA in Strategy,* New York: Wiley.

32 Fitzgerald, K. R. (2005). Big savings, but lots of risk. *Supply Chain Management Review* 9(9).

33 *Fortune* (2002) *The 2002 Global 500: The World's Largest Corporations.*

34 Fraser, J. & Oppenheim J. (2001) in M. R. Czinkota & I. A. Ronkainen, *Best practices in international business*, Florida: Harcourt College Publishers.

35 Fredrickson, J. W. (1984) The comprehensiveness of strategic decision processes: extensions, observations and future directions. *Academy of Management Journal* 27, 399–423.

36 Fukuyama, F. (1992) *The End of History and the Last Man.* New York: Free Press.

37 Fulop, L., Linstead, S. (1999) *Management. A Critical Text.* National Library of Australia. South Yarra: Macmillian Education Australia Pty Ltd.

38 Gibson, S. (2006) Going Global. *eWEEK* 23(15).

39 Goldsmith, J. (1996). 'The winners and the losers' in J. Mander and J. Goldsmith, *The Case Against the Global Economy*, The Sierra Book Club, San Francisco.

40 Hambrick, D. C., Korn, L. B., Federickson, J. W. and Ferry, R. M. (1989) *21st Century Report: Reinventing the CEO.* New York: Korn/Ferry and Columbia University's Graduate School of Business, p. 27.

41 Hart, S. and Banbury, C. (1994) How strategy making processes can make a difference. *Strategic Management Journal* 15, 251–69.

42 Hellriegel D. and Slocum J. (1996) *Management.* 7th edn. Cincinnatti, Ohio: South-Western College Publishing.

43 Hill, C. (2000) *International Business: competing in the global marketplace.* 3rd edn. New York: McGraw-Hill Higher Education.

44 Hill, C. W. L. and Jones, G. R. (1998) *Strategic Management: an integrated approach.* Boston, MA: Houghton Mifflin.

45 Hines, C. (2003) Time to replace globalisation with localization. *Global in Global Environmental Politics* 3.

46 Hoogvelt, A. (1997). *Globalisation and Postcolonial World.* MacMillan Press, London.

47 Hughes, A. (1999) 'Fernz crosses Tasman in global growth quest', *Sydney Morning Herald*, 20 September, p. 32.

48 Jones, M. T. (2002) Globalisation and organizational restructuring: a strategic perspective. *Thunderbird International Business Review*, 44(3), 325–51.

49 Koslow, L. E., and Scarlett, R. H. (1999) *Global Business.* Houston, Texas: Cashman Dudley.

50 Kotler P., Armstrong G., Brown L., Adam S. and Chandler P. (1998) *Marketing*, 4th ed., Prentice Hall, Australia Pty. Ltd.

51 Lane, H. W. and di Stefano, J. J. (1992) *International Management Behaviour: From Policy to Practice*, 2nd edn, Boston: PWS-Kent.

52 Lovelock, C. H. (1999). Developing marketing *strategies* for *transnational, Journal of Services Marketing*, [online], 13 (4/5).

53 Lucas, C. (2003) Localization – an alternative to corporate-led globalisation. *International Journal of Consumer Studies*, 27 (4).

54 Mahoney, D., Trigg, M., Griffin, R., and Pustay, M. (1998) *International Business: a managerial perspective.* Melbourne: Addison Wesley Longman.

55 Marquardt, M. J. (1999). *The Global Advantage: how world-class organizations improve performance through globalisation.* Houston, Texas: Gulf Publishing Company.

56 Martin, D. (2006). Rebuilding brand America: corporate America's role. *Journal of Business Strategy* 27 (3).

57 McGuinness, A. and Morgan, R. E. (2000) Strategy, dynamic capabilities and complex science: management rhetoric vs reality. *Strategic Change*, in press.

58 McLean, J. (2006). Globalisation is here to stay. *British Journal of Administrative Management* 53.

59 McTaggart D., Finlay C., Parkin M. (1996). *Economics.* 2nd edn. Sydney: Addison-Wesley Publishing Company.

60 Mintzberg, H. (1990). 'Strategy formation: school of thought', in J. W. Frederickson (ed.), *Perspective on Strategic Management*, New York: Harper Business.

61 Mintzberg, H. (1990) The design school: reconsidering the basic premises of strategic management. *Strategic Management Journal* 11, 171–95.

62 Mintzberg, H. and McHugh, A. (1985) Strategy formation in an adhocracy. *Administrative Science Quarterly* 30, 160–97.

63 Mintzberg, H. (1987) The Strategy Concept II: Another Look at Why Organisations Need Strategies. *California Management Review* 30(1), 25–32.

64 Modelski, G. (1972). *Multinational Corporations and World Order.* Beverly Hills: Sage Publications.

65 Morgan R. E., McGuinnes T. and Thorpe E. R (2000) The contribution of marketing to business strategy formation: a perspective on business performance Gains, *Journal of Strategic Marketing* 8, 341–62.

66 Morgan, R. and Bravard, J.-L. (2006) How globalisation alters your world. *Computer Weekly*, 13 June

67 Murphy, T., Schreffler, R., and Diem, W. (2006) Better Off Abroad. *Ward's Auto World*, 42 (5).

68 Porter, M. E. (1990). *The Competitive Advantage of Nations.* New York: Free Press.

69 Rigby, D. K. and Vishwanath, V. (2006) Localization, the revolution in consumer markets. *Harvard Business Review,* 84 (4).

70 Robbins, S., Millett, B., Cacioppe, R. and Waters-Marsh, T. (1998) *Organisational Behaviour, Leading and Managing Australia and New Zealand.* 2nd edn. Prentice Hall, Australia Pty. Ltd.

71 Ross, Donald G. (1999) *Export Finance.* Waratah Export Finance Services Pty. Ltd, Sydney.

72 Rugman, A. M., Verbeke, A. (2004) A perspective on regional and global strategies of multinational enterprises. *Journal of International Business Studies*, 35(1), 3–18.

73 Sachs, J. (1998) International economics: unlocking the mysteries of globalisation. *Foreign Policy*, Spring, 97–109.

74 Saee, J. (1998) Intercultural competence: preparing enterprising managers and entrepreneurs for the global economy. *Journal of European Business Education* 7(2).

75 Saee, J. (2005) *Managing Organizations in a Global Economy.* Ohio, USA: South Western-Thomson Learning.

76 Salvatore D. (1998). *International Economics.* 6th edn. Englewood Cliffs, New Jersey: Prentice Hall Inc.

77 Schwenk, C. (1995) Strategic decision making. *Journal of Management* 21(3), 471–93.

78 Shelly G., Cashman T. and Serwatka J. (1998). *Business Data Communications; Introductory Concepts and Techniques.* 2nd edn. International Thomson Publishing.

79   Shiffman L., Bednall D., Watson J. and Kanuk, L. (1997) *Consumer Behaviour*, Prentice Hall, Australia Pty. Ltd.
80   Simon, H. (1996) *Hidden Champions: Lessons from 500 of the World's Best Unknown Companies*, Boston: Harvard Business School Press.
81   Slavatore, D. (1998), *International Economics.* 6th edn. New Jersey: Prentice Hall.
82   Slevin, D. P. and Covin, J. G. (1997) Strategy formation patterns, performance and the significance of context. *Journal of Management* 23(2), 189–209.
83   The Australian Bureau of Statistics (1997) Available at www.abs.gov.au
84   Thomas, J. B., Gioia, D. A. and Ketchen, D. J. (1997) Strategic sense making: learning through scanning, interpretation, action and performance. *Advances in Strategic Management* 14, 299–329.
85   Thompson and Strickland (1996) *Strategic Management.* 9th edn. Irwin, Sydney: Times Mirror Higher Education Group.
86   Bostone, T. (1997) 'The Digital Drucker'. www.dgsys.com/~tristan/technodrucker.html.
87   UNCTAD (2000). *World Investment Report 2000: Cross-border mergers and acquisitions and development.* New York and Geneva: United Nations.
88   UNCTAD (2002). *Statistics: Foreign Direct Investment Inflows in Country Groups.* New York and Geneva: United Nations.
89   Vasques I. (2002) Globalisation and the poor. *Independent Review* 7(2), 197–207.
90   Vorhies, D. W. (1998) An investigation of the factors leading to the development of marketing capabilities and organizational effectiveness. *Journal of Strategic Marketing* 6, 3–23.
91   Waters, M. (1995) *Globalisation.* London: Routledge.
92   Welch, L. S. and Luostarinen, R. (1999) 'Internationalization: Evolution of a concept'. In P. J. Buckley and P. N. Ghauri (eds), *The Internationalization of the Firm: a reader.* 2nd edn. London: International Thomson Business Press.
93   World Trade Organisation (2002) *Trade Statistics 2002.* Geneva, Switzerland: World Trade Organization.
94   Yaprak, A. (2002) Book Review in *Thunderbird International Business Review*, 44(2), 297–302.
95   Yaprak, A. and Tutek, H. (2000) Globalisation, the multinational firm, and emerging economies. *Advances in International Marketing*, 10, 1–6.
96   Yip, G. S. (1995) *Total Global Strategy: Managing for Worldwide Competitive Advantage.* New Jersey: Prentice Hall.

2 Growth and innovation strategies in global competition

Utz Weitzel

Introduction

Intensive competition forces multinational enterprises (MNEs) to constantly scrutinise every subsidiary's performance. However, for the creation of truly global competitive advantages, MNEs need a growth and innovation strategy that effectively utilises and channels the interplay between subsidiaries, divisions, corporate headquarters and holdings. Such a strategy must be flexible and open enough for local excellence without losing too much of its global reach and sustainability. While previous approaches, such as the core competence framework, emphasise commonalities between business units, contemporary concepts in strategic management explicitly focus on an MNE's centre of global coordination and analyse how well its strategies and skills fit the needs and opportunities of various subsidiaries and divisions. Successful headquarters (HQs), irrespective of whether they coordinate a specific division or the whole corporation, do not only create more value than they cost, they also create a competitive advantage and more stakeholder value than any of their rivals. To accomplish this, four ways are identified: direct influence on each subsidiary as an entity; promotion of lateral linkages within the MNE; provision of functional leadership; and corporate (portfolio) development. The more productivity pressures force MNEs to disperse their activities throughout the world and the more competitive pressures impel close coordination of these operations, the more global growth strategies play a pivotal role in the success of the whole company.

Empirical studies found that the coordination of research and development (R&D) portfolios and projects is not only highly complex and demanding, but also offers high potential returns to well-defined global growth and innovation strategies (Campbell *et al.*, 1995a; Buchanan and Sands, 1994). Since the objective of this chapter is to analyze the impact of such strategies it is useful to focus on the various mechanisms of global R&D coordination and their impact on MNE growth and performance in international competition.

To achieve this objective a number of obstacles must be overcome: first, there is the need to survey the international management literature and develop a robust framework for the analysis of different growth strategies. Second, a theoretical base encompassing organisational and managerial aspects of multinational R&D has to be developed. Here, a behavioural innovation model is suggested as conceptual foundation for the analysis of MNEs' coordination of R&D. Since the complexity of the research problem makes it virtually impossible to obtain analytical solutions, a simulation model is used. Third, the dynamic dimensions of both the HQ's growth strategy and corporate R&D, and their combined influence on the innovation-led growth of MNEs, must be considered. Although the 'process school' of international management emphasises some of these aspects (Doz and Prahalad, 1981, 1984; Bartlett and Goshal, 1987, 1989; Hedlund, 1986), 'despite the label of the school, the process orientation in the theoretical body of the school is undeveloped' (Melin, 1992, p. 111). However, in a purely national setting, there do exist some process-oriented simulation models of innovation-led firm growth (Nelson and Winter 1977a,b). Therefore, in analysing the dynamic advantages of MNEs, this chapter merges two disparate strands of research: a solid theoretical base explaining national firm growth and the primarily static analysis of MNEs in global competition.

The chapter is structured as follows. In the first section two elementary dimensions of multinational coordination are derived from the literature, which are then employed to advance six coordination types for further analysis. In the second section a simulation model of MNE growth and R&D coordination is developed. The third section presents the simulation results and a discussion of their strategic significance for HQ-subsidiary interactions and multinational R&D coordination. The chapter concludes with a short summary and some implications for theory and management.

Developing a theoretical framework

Adopting Porter's (1986) well-known distinction between the configuration and coordination of international operations, it is argued that MNEs in technologically competitive markets cannot afford to neglect foreign location advantages (like centres of excellence) and therefore tend to geographically disperse their innovation process (Pearce and Singh, 1992; Cheng and Bolon, 1993). The following analysis assumes such a decentralised configuration and, within this framework, focuses entirely on the HQ's coordination and integration of multinational R&D.

Extent and scope of multinational R&D coordination

In search for a conceptual approach to multinational R&D management a review of the relevant literature suggests the following differentiation into HQs' extent and scope of coordination.

The first of these two dimensions, that is, the extent of international coordination and control, is closely connected to the more traditional centralisation versus decentralisation approach. This notion typically assumes dyadic parent-subsidiary relationships and focuses on the overall degree of centralisation and local autonomy in decision-making. The MNE is perceived to optimise a clearly defined trade-off between national responsiveness and international efficiency by seeking a balance between centrifugal forces, which pull R&D decision-making into decentralised labs and centripetal forces, which tend to centralise the articulation, implementation and coordination of innovation programmes. While a minority of firms solve this trade-off by choosing an extreme extent of international coordination (i.e., absolute centralisation or total local freedom), most firms favour a joint R&D coordination with either HQ or subsidiary as ultimate decision-maker (Behrman and Fischer, 1980a,b). Furthermore, data indicates that many MNEs, instead of pursuing a constant policy across all subsidiaries, choose to inversely relate their coordinative efforts to the size and success of their labs (De Meyer and Mizushima, 1989; Pearce and Singh, 1992; Dunning, 1993). This case-dependent variation of local autonomy results in a wide array of heterogeneous subsidiaries, ranging from strongly controlled support units to world product mandates (Ronstadt, 1978; Hood and Young, 1982; Pearce, 1989).

Turning from the traditional concept of dyadic trade-offs to a more expanded network approach in R&D management, a second dimension must be added to the one identified above.

This second dimension, that is, the scope of coordination, potentially captures the strategic value of operating labs in different countries by embodying the importance with which subsidiaries' local advantages and interests are considered in the HQs' formulation of a global strategy. Scope of coordination thus represents an MNE's market orientation or its mentality along the lines of Perlmutter's (1969) classic ethnocentric, polycentric and geocentric conceptions. The more recent process school extensively elaborated these conceptions. Therefore, the proposed dimension of scope also constitutes an important element in contemporary MNE models, like Bartlett and Goshal's (1987, 1989) 'transnational' and Hedlund's (1986) 'heterarchy'. All of these concepts go beyond the traditional parent-subsidiary dichotomy by emphasising lateral information flows and technology transfers between interdependent subsidiaries as idiosyncratic characteristics of integrated networks – an aspect which many empirical studies confirm to be crucial for a globally effective innovation process (Pearce and Papanastassiou, 1996; Pearce and Singh, 1992; De Meyer and Mizushima, 1989; Goshal and Bartlett, 1988).

Typology of MNEs' central coordination

Table 2.1 shows six different HQ types that can be derived from respective combinations of the two dimensions, extent and scope of international coordination.

The operative HQ, as the name implies, intensively coordinates its subsidiaries along a centrally articulated program. However, it is the scope or contents of this program that determines the specific role of the HQ. While the geocentric HQ tries to integrate the interests and local market characteristics of its subsidiaries into a globally balanced strategy, the rather ethnocentric HQ focuses on home market issues and a hands-on style of management. Although the close involvement of the operative HQ offers competitive advantages in synergies and economies of scale,

Table 2.1 Types of HQ

Scope of international coordination	Extent of international coordination		
	High	*Low*	*Case dependent*
Home market	Operative HQ (domestic)	Financial HQ (domestic)	Flexible HQ (domestic)
World market	Operative HQ (multinational)	Financial HQ (multinational)	Flexible HQ (multinational)
	Ethno- or geocentric	Polycentric	Case dependent

it also bears the downside of biased interferences and little local responsiveness. The more geocentric HQ, in contrast, motivates and evaluates local managers on more flexible financial and strategic criteria. It thus encourages lateral relations and local initiative, but runs the risk of striking the wrong balance and losing potential competitive advantages.

The financial HQ coordinates a federation of loosely linked entities, where local managers (much like in diversified conglomerates) are given considerable autonomy to meet their budget and profit targets. Since this highly decentralised decision-making overrides the HQ's scope of coordination, MNEs with either type of financial HQ are primarily polycentric and differ only marginally due to their domestic or multi-domestic orientation.

The flexible HQ, as discussed in the previous subsection, adapts its extent of coordination and control to local subsidiaries' size and performance. While successful subsidiaries gain more (polycentric) autonomy, those with poor results lose some of their independence to the (ethnocentric or geocentric) parent. Due to this case-dependent influence of the parent, a homogeneous strategic orientation within the MNE is unlikely.

On the basis of this framework several questions can be asked: do competitive advantages due to a global growth and innovation strategy exist? In a heterogeneous and dynamic world, how do the different HQ types perform and which provides most competitive advantages in R&D coordination? What sort of strategic advantages can be identified and how do they originate in MNEs?

In order to answer these questions the following section develops a simulation model of MNE growth. This instrument is then used to experimentally analyse the different parent types in a dynamic setting of global competition.

Modelling global growth and innovation strategies

The following model of international firm growth allows the simulation of a maximum of $L=3$ countries (indexed l), each of which is able to function as home market and location of the HQ for not more than $U=2$ MNEs (indexed u). As shown in Table 2.2, the entire population of firms consists of up to six MNEs (with a total of 16 subsidiaries) which compete against each other, both globally (as multinational entities u) and locally (as subsidiaries l,u).[1] Depending on the configuration of worldwide operations, subsidiaries may innovate, produce and/or market local

Table 2.2 The 'global market' in the simulation model

MNE/locat.	$u = 1$	$u = 2$	$u = 3$	$u = 4$	$u = 5$	$u = 6$
$l\triangleleft\triangleright=\triangleleft\triangleright 1$	HQ 1,1	HQ 1,2	Subs. 1,3	Subs. 1,4	Subs. 1,5	Subs. 1,6
$l\triangleleft\triangleright=\triangleleft\triangleright 2$	Subs. 2,1	Subs. 2,2	HQ 2,3	HQ 2,4	Subs. 2,5	Subs. 2,6
$l\triangleleft\triangleright=\triangleleft\triangleright 3$	Subs. 3,1	Subs. 3,2	Subs. 3,3	Subs. 3,4	HQ 3,5	HQ 3,6

products, while the main function of their HQ is to coordinate these activities. The subsections below will present these areas of responsibility in order.

Innovation process

In this model, all economic activity is seen to result from an innovation process. For this an idealised R&D process is simulated: scientific inventions from the research phase are transformed into marketable technologies (indexed c) in the development phase, which finally serve as a basis for the construction and market introduction of single products (indexed r) during the design phase.[2] The following primarily focuses on a subsidiary's research phase as an exploratory example for all three stages in global R&D.

Equation 2.1 shows that there are three different sources for the locally attainable research output I^F in period t: first, own research activities Ω^F; second, spillovers from local competitors Γ^F; and third, research done by other subsidiaries in the same MNE. The last right-hand term assumes that active subsidiaries (whose pointer $FL_{i,u}$ define i as their research location) engage in intra-MNE networking by exchanging their local research results Ω^F with sister-laboratories in other countries ($i \neq l$). However, in the international information transfer a share of κ^F is lost. The intuition behind this technology transfer parameter κ^F is twofold: it can be interpreted as a demand side parameter, which determines the extent of research in one country accepted by customers in another. In this case, κ^F serves as a measure of heterogeneity in global demand. Alternatively, it can be seen as a supply side parameter, which captures inefficiencies in the communication and coordination of global R&D.

$$I^F_{l,u,c,t} = \Omega^F_{l,u,c,t} + \Gamma^F_{l,u,c,t} + \sum_{i=1}^{L}\left(b\cdot\Omega^F_{i,u,c,t-1}\right)$$

$$\text{with } b = \begin{Bmatrix} 1-\kappa^F \\ 0 \end{Bmatrix} \text{ if } FL_{i,u} \begin{Bmatrix} = \\ \neq \end{Bmatrix} i \text{ and } i \begin{Bmatrix} \neq \\ = \end{Bmatrix} l \quad \text{and } 0 \leq \kappa^F \leq 1$$

(2.1)

As shown in equation 2.2, a firm's own research, Ω^F, is typically seen as a long-term process which requires stamina and commitment in the form of continuous periodical investments, K^F.[3] Hence, the average budget over the duration of research project c in t (with the last period ψ^F of project c-1 as starting point) is calculated.[4] This average is normalised over a minimal investment $K^{F,min}$ and allows for economies of scales β^F.

$$\Omega^F_{l,u,c,t} = \left(\frac{\displaystyle\sum_{i=\psi^F_{l,u,c-1}}^{x} K^F_{l,u,i}}{x-\psi^F_{l,u,c-1}} \cdot \frac{1}{K^{F,\min}} \right)^{\beta^F} \tag{2.2}$$

$$\text{with } x = \left\{ \begin{matrix} t-1 \\ \psi^F_{l,u,c} \end{matrix} \right\} \text{if } t \left\{ \begin{matrix} \leq \\ > \end{matrix} \right\} \psi^F_{l,u,c} \text{ and } \beta^F \geq 1$$

In line with the growth model of Nelson & Winter (1977a,b), it is assumed that a firm's success does not solely depend on internal R&D, but also on technological spillovers Γ^F from its local competitors (see equation 2.3). If a firm wants to gain such external results, first, its output Ω^F has to be lower than the corresponding output $\Omega^{F,max}$ of the technological leader and, second, the country-specific diffusion rate α has to be strictly positive to allow for information to spill over at all. An industry-specific dialogue parameter ι determines to what extent own R&D is needed to profit from competitors' research. In order to understand, exchange and utilise external information (provided $\iota>0$), a firm must first invest in its internal technical know-how or 'dialogue capability'.

$$\Gamma^F_{l,u,c,t} = \alpha_1 \cdot \left((1-\iota_l) + \frac{\iota_l \cdot \Omega^F_{l,u,c,t}}{\Omega^{F,max}_{l,c,t}} \right) \cdot \left(\Omega^{F,max}_{l,c,t} - \Omega^F_{l,u,c,t} \right) \tag{2.3}$$

$$\text{with } \Omega^{F,max}_{l,c,t} = max\left\{ \left(\Omega^F_{l,u,c,t} \right), u=1,2,...,U \right\} \text{and } \alpha_1, \iota_l \in [0,1]$$

At this point the research phase of the simulated innovation process is fully defined. With the exception of the following differences, equations 2.1 to 2.3 analogously apply to the development and design stage: For the determination of firm's output in the development phase, equation 2.2 does not look at an average, but an accumulation of periodical investments. Thus, in contrast to research, the development output increases with each period, reflecting the notion that the distinct nature of this stage is one of learning by trial and error.[5] The main difference between (technological) research and (product) design is the relatively short and manageable time horizon of the latter. Here, equation 2.2 considers a simple time-cost trade-off, which a firm chooses for each new design project (see Weitzel, 1996).

Production process

Total production costs are split into a variable part $K^{P,var}$ and a fixed part, $K^{P,fix}$. In equation 2.4, the latter is primarily a function of fixed unit costs $k^{P,fix}$ and local production volume V in $t-1$.[6] Fixed costs are investment decisions made in the past. So, for simplicity, the production volume V in $t-1$ is used to calculate the fixed costs in t. The final right-hand term in equation 2.4 represents experience effects which are positively influenced by the cumulative amount of produced goods and a learning rate λ. (The total variable costs $K^{P,var}$ are determined analogously to equation 2.4 with the distinction that they are linked to the current volume V in t.)

$$K^{P,fix}_{l,u,c,r,t} = k^{P,fix}_l \cdot V_{l,u,c,r,t-1} \cdot \left(\sum_{i=1}^{t-1} V_{l,u,c,r,i} \right) \qquad (2.4)$$

Diffusion process

A firm's total sales are calculated on the basis of the Bass diffusion model (1969). Due to its widespread recognition, the following only briefly discusses how the concept is utilised in this chapter, that is, how a selection of firm-specific parameters labelled 'marketing package' influences the purchase behaviour of consumers. Since potential demand M is divided into ϕM venturesome 'innovators' and $(1-\phi)M$ risk averse 'imitators', each product of each firm has two corresponding marketing packages.[7] For innovators, who are disposed to trying a new product (mainly because of its novelty), the most important influence to buy is the extent of R&D incorporated in the innovation.[8] Low prices certainly have a positive effect, but their weight in the marketing package is comparatively small.[9] However, for imitators, who buy in later stages of the product life cycle, the opposite weighting is assumed. Furthermore, since imitators typically purchase tried products, the most important factor in their marketing package is the number of previous sales of the product as a proxy for perceived quality and word of mouth. Once all marketing packages are fully described by the elements above, the impact of competition is taken into account by determining, for each market segment, the relation of a firm's product-specific marketing package to all corresponding values in the industry.

Coordination process

Up to this point the model provides little indication, whether the local innovation, production and diffusion processes discussed above should be interpreted as isolated activities in autonomous subsidiaries or as integrated activities in a tightly coordinated network. In the latter it is the responsibility of the HQ to develop and implement a global growth strategy. Since R&D is a major source of corporate growth, the model focuses on the renewal and expansion of product ranges when formulating local and global growth strategies. According to the satisficing principle (Cyert and March, 1963) and as shown in equation 2.5, it is assumed that a firm plans to introduce a new product, as soon as its actual growth rate W falls below a certain aspiration level, or critical growth rate Λ.[10] Given this impetus to innovate, the urgency of the new project (i.e., the length of its design phase τ) is determined in equation 2.6, where $\vartheta \in [0,1]$ represents an MNE's inertia to change. In equations 2.5 and 2.6, W^H, Λ^H and ϑ^H represent the global values of the HQ whereas W^S, Λ^S and ϑ^S stand for the local growth and strategy values of the subsidiary. Their relative influence in an MNE's coordination process is determined by the centralisation parameter $z \in [0,1]$. If $z=0$, subsidiaries act totally autonomous, if $z=1$, the whole MNE is centrally managed by the HQ, and if $0<z<1$, growth strategies are more or less joint decisions.

$$z_u \cdot W^H_{u,t} + \left(1-z_u\right) \cdot W^S_{l,u,t} < z_u \cdot \Lambda^H_u + \left(1-z_u\right) \cdot \Lambda^S_{l,s} \tag{2.5}$$

$$\tau_{l,u,c,r} = z_u \cdot \vartheta^H_u \cdot W^H_{u,t} + \left(1-z_u\right) \cdot \vartheta^S_{l,u} \cdot W^S_{l,u} \tag{2.6}$$

While z defines the extent of central coordination, a second strategic parameter, Δ, specifies the scope of central coordination, that is, the proportion with which subsidiaries' local strategies and foreign market conditions are integrated into an MNE-wide growth strategy. As shown in equation 2.7, the integration parameter Δ determines to what extent the HQ (located in the MNE's home country, where pointer $HQ_{l,u}$ equals l) considers the local growth W^S of its subsidiaries abroad ($HQ_{l,u} \neq l$) when calculating W^H for its global strategy. For simplicity, it is assumed that the critical growth rate Λ^H and degree of inertia ϑ^H are calculated analogously.

$$W^H_{u,t} = \frac{1}{1+\Delta_u \cdot \left(L-1\right)} \cdot \sum_{l=1}^{L} b \cdot W^S_{l,u,t}$$
$$\text{with } b = \left\{ \begin{matrix} \Delta_u \\ 1 \end{matrix} \right\} \text{if } HQ_{l,u} \left\{ \begin{matrix} \neq \\ = \end{matrix} \right\} l \quad \text{and } 0 \leq \Delta_u \leq 1 \tag{2.7}$$

Results and discussion

An advantage of simulation models is that they are able to analyse complex situations. A disadvantage is that no analytical optimum can be achieved. However, if the complexity of a problem excludes analytical solutions, rather than change the assumptions and analyse the wrong model, an accumulation of simulation runs and a numerically approximated optimum is preferred. In light of this, a large number of simulation runs (collectively over two million) were conducted to obtain results as exact as possible.[11]

In order to examine the HQ types developed from the literature (see Table 2.1) the maximum configuration of six MNEs in three countries (see Table 2.2) and the parameter specifications displayed in Appendix 2A are used. The operative HQ as well as the financial HQ are described by combinations of exogenously given high and low values for the centralisation parameter z (extent of coordination) and integration parameter Δ (scope of coordination). In MNEs with a flexible HQ, the degree of a subsidiary's autonomy is endogenously determined by the ratio of its local revenues (used as a proxy for the subsidiary's size and success) to the global revenues of the whole MNE.[12] Apart from these differences in the coordination of international innovation processes, all six MNEs are endowed with identical parameter settings (see Appendix 2A). This ensures that the HQ's management style is the only possible origin of local or global competitive advantages. With regard to international demand, variations of the technology transfer parameter κ and the share of innovative buyers ϕ are used to simulate several world markets, each with a different degree of heterogeneity in local product preferences and a distinct risk attitude towards innovations.[13] Such diversity in global demand not only guarantees a comprehensive analytical spectrum, but also generates sufficient 'management pressure' upon the HQ to prove their coordination skills.

MNE performance

Since we analyse the growth and innovation strategies in a globally competitive environment, the most interesting aspect in the simulations is not the absolute performance of a single firm, but rather the relative success of MNEs when compared to the performance of their global competitors. The present analysis therefore ranks the cumulated revenues of all MNEs in each simulation run and then examines the frequency with which each of the six different MNEs reach a certain position or rank in the market.[14] While all the basic results can be seen in Appendix 2B, the following attempts to first explain them along the lines of the two dimensions of coordination before it moves on to a more detailed discussion.

Scope of international coordination

As far as the scope of coordination is concerned, Figure 2.1 shows that the market orientations of the HQs do have a substantial impact on the relative performance of MNEs. It also shows that HQs with a geocentric approach are generally more successful than their ethnocentric counterparts – not only in terms of market lead-

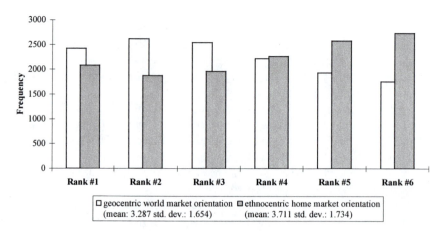

Figure 2.1 Global performance by scope of coordination[15]

ership (rank #1), but also with respect to their mean position relative to their competitors (see legend of Figure 2.1). Apart from these anticipated findings, the most striking results are the markedly different 'slopes' of the frequency distributions.

As for ethnocentric MNEs, the convex shape of their distribution clearly reveals the HQs' strong focus on domestic issues. From an extreme perspective, the intensive coordination along a distinctly articulated growth strategy provokes an 'all-or-nothing' outcome: depending on the heterogeneity and risk attitude of global demand, the high specialisation on international synergies either creates a significant competitive advantage, or it simply inhibits local as well as global flexibility and destroys potential value added. In the first case, the fit between the HQ and its subsidiaries frequently leads to market leadership (see Figure 2.1). In the second case, the lack of fit does not only result in the MNE falling well behind its geocentric competitors (rank #5 or #6), but also causes a remarkably high number of bankruptcies (see Appendix 2B).

Although this result is consistent with Campbell *et al.*'s (1995b) theoretical and empirical findings about HQs' double-edged influence on subsidiaries, Figure 2.1 shows that it is only valid for certain HQ types and therefore needs to be qualified. In fact, the concave frequency distribution of the more geocentric MNEs tells a completely different story: in contrast to the 'all-or-nothing' approach, which mainly relies on dyadic hub-and-spoke relations between the ethnocentric HQ and its subsidiaries, the geocentric scope of coordination encourages lateral linkages and network interaction. By doing this, it introduces an additional management goal that could be described as 'finding a global middle ground'. This includes the development of a global innovation strategy that tries to balance subsidiaries' local concerns – specifically, their plans for the expansion and renewal of national product ranges. The dominance of geocentric HQs in Figure 2.1 can thus be attributed to comparative advantages of network flexibility.

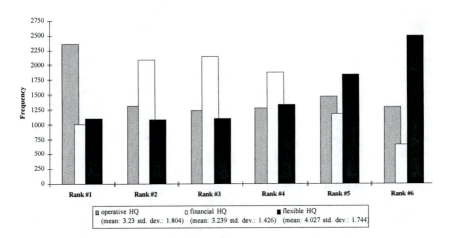

Figure 2.2 Global performance by extent of coordination[17]

Extent of international coordination

Turning from the scope to the extent of coordination, the simulation results in Figure 2.2 shows that the geocentric orientation represents a necessary, though not sufficient condition for the global success of MNEs. Especially the high frequency of market leadership for the operative HQ makes it clear that superior MNE growth also depends on the HQ's ability to decisively implement a centrally articulated innovation program throughout the corporation.[16] If the latter dimension of coordination is of little concern to the HQ, as in the case of the financial HQ, the chances of reaching the top rank in the competitive field are more than halved (see Figure 2.2). This is mainly due to the insufficient teamwork by the subsidiaries and a subsequent lack of synergies in the international innovation process. However, in exchange, the high local responsiveness of the decentralized units prevents a greater number of bankruptcies (see Appendix 2B). While flexibility alone is not sufficient for strong market leadership, it does contain enough growth potential for second- and third-best positions.

The most interesting result in Figure 2 is the remarkably poor performance of MNEs with a flexible HQ. It is highly counter-intuitive, as this type of HQ explicitly rewards successful subsidiaries by granting them more autonomy, and, because it pushes less successful subsidiaries by intensifying the pressure from central management. Nevertheless, the drawback of this 'carrot and stick' approach lies in the unstable and myopic coordination of local product ranges: while successful subsidiaries are increasingly allowed to focus on their own R&D and thereby detach themselves from international innovation projects, the less successful, centrally coordinated rest of the MNE is left behind with little mutual support. Further, the worse the collective performance of this group, the less potential synergy effects there are in international R&D, and the less local flexibility is left for the subsidiaries to at least partially offset their low product quality. Once such a polarity between successful and unsuccessful subsidiaries has developed within the MNE, even the more autonomous subsidiaries experience difficulties in global competition, given that they basically operate as locally isolated firms. Hence, they often end up in the same vicious cycle of centrally reinforced decline. This long-term argument specifically explains why the flexible HQ has the highest bankruptcy rate of all HQ types (see Appendix 2B).

Concluding this subsection, a combined analysis of the figures above and the results in Appendix 2B show that, in a heterogeneous and dynamic world, the geocentric operative HQ dominates all other HQ types – not only along the two dimensions of coordination but also in terms of its individual market leadership. Furthermore, both the ethnocentric operative HQ and the multinational financial HQ are found to be considerably stronger and more competitive than either of the flexible HQs (see Appendix 2B).

As all simulated MNEs differ only in their type of HQ, the diversity in their growth patterns provides evidence of the existence and importance of strategic advantages. However, despite this finding, it remains unclear which specific aspects of the model lead to superior performance. The following subsection examines this issue.

Identification and characterisation of strategic advantages

A closer look at the reasons for the dominance of the geocentric operative HQ reveals two central advantages. Both are based on dynamic arguments.

Strategic advantage #1: economies of stability

The first strategic advantage hinges on the existence of economies of stability in MNE growth. In order to gain these economies, two conditions must be met: MNE growth has to be stable not only over time but also across geographical markets. While stability over time focuses on the smooth local growth of individual subsidiaries, geographical stability emphasises a globally balanced growth path for the entire MNE.

One advantage of stability over time is that subsidiaries with few fluctuations in local growth build up higher financial reserves and thus face a lower risk of bankruptcy. Conversely, as equation 2.4 shows, unstable growth results in frequent production overheads. Another even more important advantage of stability over time lies in avoiding a disproportional investment in new technologies and products. As discussed in connection with equation 2.2, one of the most discriminatory features of the innovation process is the time horizon of individual R&D stages. Since unstable growth and local crises induce subsidiaries to specialise on short-term instruments of success, such as the design and introduction of incremental innovations, they tend to neglect long-term commitment in research. Thus, persistent growth fluctuations are found to lead to an investment gap that causes significant disadvantages with respect to future core competencies.

As for the flexible HQ, a globally unbalanced growth strategy may cause a polarisation between subsidiaries and thereby impair corporate competitiveness and performance. However, diminishing synergies within the MNE are not the only reason for the importance of geographical stability. Next to this internal motive there is also a strong external argument for an internationally stable growth path. According to equation 2.3, subsidiaries with limited or irregular R&D are less able to receive or utilise local technological spillovers, because they have a poor capacity to understand external information or, in the case of joint ventures, little of their own information to return. It does not help to establish only sporadically active windows or observation posts in other countries. In order to ensure a continuous dialogue capability and to obtain external R&D results, 'one must be a player, not a spectator' (Bartlett and Goshal, 1986, p. 91). To be part of technological developments around the world, MNEs must commit to continually invest into a network of foreign R&D labs. The more geographical stability in terms of internationally balanced growth, the more such a global innovation strategy is supported.

Figure 2.3 illustrates the general importance of an effective R&D network by simulating the extreme case of a two-country / two-firm setting, where one MNE centralises its R&D in the home market while the other invests into a decentralised configuration.[18] With the variation of economies of scale in R&D (represented by β) and market heterogeneity (technology transfer parameter κ), two classic factors

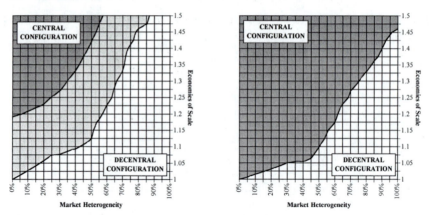

Figure 2.3 Optimal multinational configuration of R&D

of configuration are used to establish a framework for the following analysis.[19] As the base case on the left of Figure 2.3 shows, cumulated revenues of the decentralised MNE are higher than those of its centralised competitor whenever market heterogeneity is high and economies of scale are low.[20] In a second simulation run, the global diffusion rate α is increased from 5 per cent in the base case to 10 per cent. As the enlarged white area on the right of Figure 2.3 shows, a higher degree of technological spillovers forms a strong incentive for more decentralised R&D. In an additional simulation, the introduction of a third country with a local centre of excellence curtails the central MNE's range of superior performance by the light grey area.[21] This significant reduction of the dark grey area (over all simulations) supports the above argument for the construction and maintenance of an international R&D network. As well as providing support for economies of scale and market heterogeneity, the results reveal the importance of other exogenous factors, like technological spillovers and foreign know-how agglomerations.

After the analysis of the advantages of local stability over time and global stability across geographical markets, these two positive effects can be used to explain the different performances of MNEs' growth and innovation strategies. As for the financial HQ, the high autonomy of its subsidiaries ensures a stable local growth, but at the same time impedes the coordination of a globally balanced development. Conversely, the ethnocentric HQ emphasises a centrally stabilised MNE growth, but tends to neglect its subsidiaries' concerns and thus causes local crises and fluctuations. Only the global growth policy of the geocentric operative HQ combines both components into economies of stability. It thereby successfully creates a strong strategic advantage over all other coordination types.

Strategic advantage #2: global learning

The second strategic advantage is based on the ability of the whole MNE to learn from the local successes of individual subsidiaries. To accomplish this, an HQ must ensure that national advantages are perceived, communicated and appropriated throughout the corporation. Learning is therefore understood as geographical learning, where local success factors of demand and supply are integrated into a global growth strategy, which then is implemented in all subsidiaries.[22]

For demand side factors, such as consumers' attitudes towards risk, the argument runs as follows: subsidiaries react to high risk levels in local markets (increased share of innovative buyers ϕ) by accelerating their R&D and expanding their product range. As Figure 2.4 illustrates, this has a positive effect on their innovation rate and growth. If the HQ's coordinative efforts support a global learning process, the increased innovation rate is transferred to subsidiaries in less challenging markets.

For supply side factors, such as firms' aspiration levels, a similar argument can be made: subsidiaries often try to compensate for disadvantages in foreign countries by pursuing a more aggressive innovation strategy (higher critical growth rate Λ) than their local competitors. As depicted in Figure 2.5, such focus on the frequent introduction of new products generally results in stronger growth. Additionally, the continuity of innovations tends to stabilise the subsidiary's development, as demonstrated by a comparison with the highly fluctuating and crises-induced growth path of the lowest aspiration level ($\Lambda = 0.8$). Again, with global learning, it is generally possible to transfer these innovation incentives to less sensitive subsidiaries and thereby enhance MNE performance.

Altogether, the general predominance of the geocentric operative HQ hinges on the fact that it simultaneously satisfies both conditions for global learning: the integration and implementation of local advantages. While the financial HQ fails to properly enact its central strategy and therefore violates the second condition, the ethnocentric operative HQ does not meet the first condition, because it is too involved with domestic issues.

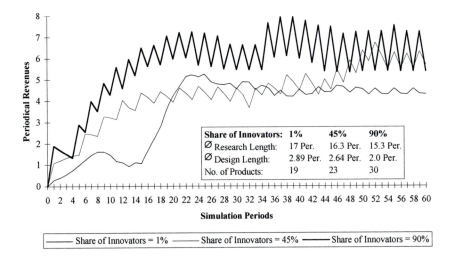

Figure 2.4 Local growth by share of innovators

a If two MNEs reach the same amount of cumulated revenues they are both denoted the same rank (e.g. #4) while the following rank (#5) is omitted. However, the MNE with the lowest cumulated revenues is still ranked last (#6). As the results show, this system can lead to slight differences in the total number of ranks denoted to all MNEs.

b The total number of 4500 simulation runs is put together as follows: 100 combinations of two demand parameters (with a ten step variation each) multiplied by 45 'world market combinations' of MNE home countries and possible configurations of local competitors. Proof for the existence of 45 world market combinations: for homogeneous world market combinations (all countries are identical) it can be shown that there exist $A^3_{hom} = 15$ different configurations for six MNEs (with two HQs in each of the L=3 countries), because of:

$$A^N_{hom} = \prod_{j=1}^{N}(2j-1) \text{ [proof by complete induction]}.$$

Heterogeneous world market combinations can be described by $2N-k$, $k=1,...,2N-1$ homogeneous combinations of the order $N-1$:

$$A^N_{het} = \sum_{k=1}^{2N-1} k \cdot A^{N-1}_{hom} = N \cdot (2N-1) \cdot \prod_{j=1}^{N-1}(2j-1) = N \cdot A^N_{hom}$$

Hence, with three different national markets, which all represent home countries for exactly two MNEs, altogether 45 world market combinations have to be considered ($A^3_{het} = 45$).

Notes

1 The grey areas in Table 2.2 mark the MNEs' home countries.

2 Since both research and development of a technology c are conducted in a parallel fashion, inventions are not indexed separately.

3 The periodical research budget K^F is determined by an exogenously given percentage of total revenues in $t-1$.

4 The total research length $\psi^F_c - \psi^F_{c-1}$ for technology c is a decreasing and convex function of I^F (see Weitzel, 1996).

5 In other words, the longer and the more intensively a development team tests and improves a new technology the safer, easier to handle and more comfortable it eventually is for the customer.

6 Note that the production volume V is not restricted to local sales only. Depending on the global configuration of production capacity, it can also be the volume of a world scale plant.

7 To avoid the so-called 'bass trap' the market is split a priori (see Weitzel, 1996).

8 In the marketing package the extent of R&D is represented by output I (see equation 2.1).

9 Prices are endogeneously determined (with a mark-up on unit costs) and account for experience effects. For a more detailed disussion see Weitzel 1996.

10 Both growth rates, W and Λ, refer to the (actual or targeted) quotient of firms' revenues in $t-1$ and t.

11 Since it is impossible to show all experimental data in this chapter, the following displays a selection of the most representative results. A copy of the program (written in Borland Turbo C++™) is available from the author.

12 The extent of coordination or centralisation parameter z is therefore determined by $1-R^S/R^P$, where R^S represents the subsidiary's and R^P the MNE's revenues.

13 Since κ and ϕ are both varied in ten steps (between 0 and 1), 100 different parameter combinations or world markets are simulated altogether.

14 The same was done with respect to MNEs' cumulated profits. However, the corresponding rankings were so similar to those derived from the global revenues that it seems appropriate to restrict the results as described above.

15 This figure compares the rank-specific aggregates of all shaded columns in Appendix

2B (world market orientation) with those of the non-shaded columns (home market orientation).

16 This theoretical finding about the dominance of operative HQs (high extent of coordination) is strongly supported by several empirical studies, which inter alia show that R&D is one of the most centralised functions in MNEs and that there is a general tendency in MNEs towards more centralised decision-making (for an overview see Martinez and Jarillo, 1989 and Dunning, 1993).

17 This figure compares the rank-specific aggregates of the first pair of columns in Appendix 2B (operative HQ) with those of the second (financial HQ) and third pair (flexible HQ).

18 Apart from these changes to the previous simulation, all parameter values remain the same (see Appendix 2A).

19 See equations 2.2 and 2.1, respectively. For empirical evidence on the importance of these two determinants in R&D configuration see Pearce and Singh, 1992.

20 White areas in Figure 2.3 represent a ratio of centralised to decentralised cumulated revenues smaller than 1. Grey areas represent a ratio greater than 1.

21 For the simulation of a foreign centre of excellence a purely national firm with a *ceteris paribus* doubled R&D intensity was specified.

22 For the first aspect of integration see equation 2.7, for the second aspect of implementation see 2.5 and 2.6.

23 Critics of the eclectic paradigm claim that ownership-specific advantages should not be considered separately, for they stem from either localisation or internalisation advantages (Itaki, 1991). Of course, it is also possible to adapt the elements of the model to this line of argument (Dunning, 1995).

References

Bartlett, C. A., & Goshal, S. 1986. Tap your subsidiaries for global reach. *Harvard Business Review,* 64(6): 87–94.

Bartlett, C. A., & Goshal, S. 1987. Managing across borders: New organizational responses. *Sloan Management Review,* 28(1): 43–53.

Bartlett, C. A., & Goshal, S. 1989. *Managing across borders: The transnational solution.* Boston, MA: Harvard Business School Press.

Bass, F. M. 1969. A new product growth model for consumer durables. *Management Science,* 15(5): 215–227.

Behrman, J. N., & Fischer, W. A. 1980a. *Overseas R&D activities of transnational companies.* Cambridge MA: Oelgeschlager, Gunn & Hain.

Behrman, J. N., & Fischer, W. A. 1980b. Transnational corporations: Market orientations and R&D abroad. *Columbia Journal of World Business,* XV(3): 55–60.

Buchanan, R., & Sands, R. 1994. Creating an effective corporate centre: The influence of strategy on head office role. *European Business Journal,* 6(4): 17–27.

Campbell, A., Goold, M., & Alexander, M. 1995a. The value of the parent company. *California Management Review,* 38(1): 79–97.

Campbell, A., Goold, M., & Alexander, M. 1995b. Corporate strategy: The quest for parenting advantage. *Harvard Business Review,* 73(2): 120–132.

Cheng, J. L. C., & Bolon, D. S. 1993. The management of multinational R&D: A neglected topic in international business research. *Journal of International Business Studies,* 24(1): 1–18.

Cyert, R. M., & March, J. G. 1963. *A behavioral theory of the firm.* Englewood Cliffs, NJ: Prentice-Hall.

De Meyer, A., & Mizushima, A. 1989. Global R&D management. *R&D Management*, 19(2): 135–146.

Doz, Y., & Prahalad, C. K. 1981. Headquarters influence and strategic control in MNCs. *Sloan Management Review*, 23(1): 15–29.

Doz, Y., & Prahalad, C. K. 1984. Patterns of strategic control in multinational corporations. *Journal of International Business Studies*, 15(2): 55–72.

Dunning, J. H. 1980. Toward an eclectic theory of international production: some empirical tests. *Journal of International Business Studies*, 11(1): 9–30.

Dunning, J. H. 1988. The eclectic paradigm of international production: A restatement and some possible extensions. *Journal of International Business Studies*, 19(1): 1–31.

Dunning, J. H. 1993. *Multinational enterprises and the global economy.* Wokingham, England: Addison-Wesley.

Dunning, J. H. 1995. Reappraising the eclectic paradigm in an age of alliance capitalism. *Journal of International Business Studies*, 26(3): 461–491.

Goshal, S., & Bartlett, C.A. 1988. Creation, adoption, and diffusion of innovations by subsidiaries of multinational corporations. *Journal of International Business Studies*, 19(3): 365–388.

Hedlund, G. 1986. The hypermodern MNC – a heterarchy?. *Human Resource Management*, 25(1): 9–35.

Hood, N., & Young, S. 1982. US multinational R&D: Corporate strategies and policy implications for the UK. *Multinational Business*, 2(1): 10–23.

Itaki, M. 1991. A critical assessment of the eclectic theory of the multinational enterprise. *Journal of International Business Studies*, 22(3): 445–460.

Martinez, J. I., & Jarillo, J. C. 1989. The evolution of research on coordination mechanism in multinational corporations. *Journal of International Business Studies*, 20(3): 489–514.

Melin, L. 1992. Internationalization as a strategy process. *Strategic Management Journal*, [Special issue]. Winter 13: 99–118.

Nelson, R. R., & Winter, S. G. 1977a. Simulation of Schumpeterian competition. *American Economic Review*, 67(1): 271–276.

Nelson, R. R., & Winter, S. G. 1977b. Dynamic competition and technical progress. In B. Balassa & R. R. Nelson (eds), *Economic progress: Private values and public policy*: 57–101. New York, NY: North-Holland.

Pearce, R. D. 1989. *The internationalization of research and development by multinational enterprises.* London, England: Macmillan.

Pearce, R. D., & Papanastassiou, M. 1996. R&D networks and innovation: Decentralised product development in multinational enterprises. *R&D Management*, 26(4): 315–333.

Pearce, R. D., & Singh, S. 1992. *Globalizing research and development.* London, England: Macmillan.

Perlmutter, H. V. 1969. The tortuous evolution of the multinational corporation. *Columbia Journal of World Business*, 4(1): 9–18.

Porter, M. E. (Ed.). 1986. *Competition in global industries.* Boston, MA: Harvard Business School Press.

Ronstadt, R. C. 1978. International R&D: The establishment and evolution of research and development abroad by seven U.S. multinationals. *Journal of International Business Studies*, 9(1): 7–23.

Weitzel, U. 1996. *Dynamics of innovative firms in global competition: A simulation model.* Discussion paper No. 96–87, J.L. Kellogg Graduate School of Management, Northwestern University, Department of Management and Strategy, Evanston, IL.

3 Determinant factors of the entry mode choice in diversification moves

An integrative framework

Luz Sánchez-Peinado, Artina Menguzzato-Boulard and María Ripollés-Melia

Introduction[1]

In general, three dimensions define a diversification strategy: degree, type and mode. Degree of diversification constitutes a firm characteristic while diversification type and mode represent two important firm decisions: the choice of the new business and the choice of the entry mode.

The first decision, related to the type of diversification, is associated to the choice of a particular business and its familiarity with the firm core business, and has attracted the attention of past research. The second decision, related to the mode of diversification, determines the resource commitment and the control assumed by firms in the new business. Previous studies have highlighted the importance of type of diversification, considering that relatedness may explain firm performance. However, the success or failure of diversification moves also depends on the right choice of entry mode. In spite of this, researchers have systematically neglected to study this aspect.

In this sense, there is relatively little theoretical and empirical research examining the extent to which pre-entry conditions influence the choice of entry modes. Analysis of the entry mode choice has traditionally focused on the role of entry barriers and the entrant's ability to breach those barriers (e.g. Yip, 1982a,b). However, competitive conditions determine a new framework where firm decisions are being influenced, directly or indirectly, by multiple factors of a different nature, such as characteristics of the destination industry, profile of the entering firm (i.e. entrepreneurial posture, experience on international markets, etc.), the value and relevance of the resources held by the entering firm or its motives for entry. In addition, past research on this topic has focused exclusively on the study of internal and external growth as ways of entering new businesses, without considering the existence of hybrid forms such as strategic alliances, which have experienced an important growth.

Thus, the importance of the decision on the mode of entry in explaining the outcome of diversification, and the scarce past research on the issue requires new studies to cover this major gap in the literature. We therefore consider it is necessary, first, to identify the ex-ante factors that influence this decision in order to build a theoretical framework to study diversification mode, and second, to introduce the study of cooperation strategies as an alternative to the traditionally considered entrance options.

Our study assumes the challenge of examining in depth the entry mode choice and its determinant factors, and analysing the use of firm cooperation within the framework of diversification process.

Entry mode choice in diversification moves

In general, academics have considered the choice between internal development and acquisitions as alternative methods of diversification. Internal development gives the firm complete control of operations and implies higher resource commitments in the new business and consequently it is a higher risk alternative. On the other hand, acquisitions also provide a high degree of control to the diversifying firm and offer the fastest means of building a sizeable presence in a new business, but they are fraught with risks of overpayment, inability to fully assess the value of acquired assets, and post-acquisition challenges including problems related with cultural integration.

However, as market dynamism increases and the need for flexibility becomes more important, firms are seeking shared-control modes to implement their growth strategies. Thus, interfirm cooperation has become a habitual practice in strategic management, as it is a strategic response to growing competence and the need to access a wider range of technologies and capabilities (Escribá *et al.*, 2003a,b). In fact, several studies point out that strategic alliances were the most widely employed strategic options in the 1980s (Ghemawat, Porter and Rawlinson, 1986; Morris and Hergert, 1987; Menguzzato, 1992; García Canal, 1992; Hageedoorn, 1993). In spite of this, academics traditionally have not included their analysis in the study of the diversification process (Yip, 1982a). This may be explained by the fact that this strategy could be considered as a mix between internal and external growth. However, recognition is gradually being made of the potential of cooperative agreements to undertake corporate diversification (Killing, 1982; Roberts and Berry, 1985; Pennings, Barkema and Douma, 1994; Dussauge and Garrete, 1999). In effect, interfirm cooperation is a way to draw on the resources of an incumbent firm and to minimise entry risk, but it also raises problems concerning partners' divergent interests. In this way, alliances in related diversification strategies allow firms to collaborate with other organisations, which offer complementary products, without the need to develop resources internally (Freije-Uriarte *et al.*, 1994; Grant, 1996; Mitchell and Singh, 1996). Familiarity facilitates the integration between internal and external resources and their application in the new environment (Kogut and Zander, 1993). Moreover, complementary resources may lead to higher operational synergies in strategic alliances. In contrast, possibilities of learning in non-related diversification strategies are fewer than in related ones (Hamel, 1991; Luo, 2002), although alliances allow firms to share cost and risks, as well as complementary assets and skills with host partner firms (Contractor and Lorange, 1988).

Therefore, the increasing use of alliances between firms and their potential to implement diversification processes justify their inclusion in the analysis of the entry mode choice. The interest lies in determining the circumstances that favour the use of cooperative agreements over internal development or mergers/acquisitions. Due to the scarcity of theoretical and empirical studies about this topic on diversification research, we will present other theoretical perspectives which analyse how transaction related-factors, firm's strategic orientation or other economic factors may influence the entry mode choice. The development of these perspectives will allow us, firstly, to have a more holistic view about our research topic, and secondly, to present an eclectic model focused on the determinant factors of the entry mode choice. Specifically, we will develop an integrative framework to study the real complexity of the modal decision, based on some internationalisation theories[2] (eclectic paradigm, Uppsala model and global strategic model) and other general perspectives (transaction cost theory, entrepreneurship perspective and resource-based view).

Theoretical perspectives: an overview

Traditionally, the choice of entry modes into new businesses has focused on the study of entry barriers and the possibility of reprisals from incumbent firms (see, e.g., Chatterjee, 1990; Chatterjee and Singh, 1999; Yip, 1982a,b). Furthermore, the entry mode decision has also been studied from other theoretical perspectives, which analyse how other economic and strategic factors may influence on such decision.

From an economic view, the choice of entry modes is based on efficiency criteria,because it is the result of a cost-benefit analysis of different alternatives. Specifically, under the transaction cost theory, the decision criterion is based, mainly, on the minimisation of transaction and production costs. It is considered that the possession of excess resources, specific to the firm, and whose sale to other firms is subject to high transaction costs, justifies firm diversification (Teece, 1982). The specific entry mode chosen will depend on the characteristics of the new competitive environment. In this way, when environmental conditions encourage the investment on the business (e.g., because demand uncertainty is low), the firm may choose higher resource commitment modes to enter it. In contrast, if entry costs exceed benefit prospects, the firm may decide not to enter into the new business or enter it by low resource commitment modes.

However, academics have highlighted the importance of complement efficiency and economic considerations with more strategic arguments because firms may prefer to improve their competitive positions, sacrifying cost advantages, for example (Harrigan, 1985; Porter, 1980). In this sense, the global strategic model (Hill, Hwang and Kim, 1990; Kim and Hwang, 1992) considers three groups of variables in the entry mode choice in international markets: transaction-specific variables (value of specific know-how and tacitness), strategic variables (global concentration, synergy and strategic motives) and external variables (external uncertainty, familiarity, demand uncertainty and nature of competence).

From our point of view, the global strategic model may also explain the entry mode choice in diversification moves, but it is necessary to adapt some theoretical arguments. With regard to external variables, we should only consider demand uncertainty because external uncertainty (or country risk) is controlled in entries into new businesses located in the domestic market. On the other hand, familiarity should be equivalent to the relatedness between the new business and the core activity of the firm, so that the lower the relatedness between the businesses, the higher the perceived entry risk and, consequently, the higher the preference for lower resource commitment modes. Finally, the strategic variables should refer to the possibility to obtain synergies between businesses and the firm's strategic objectives for diversification moves (e.g., to be present in strategic businesses with high potential growth, to face up to more diversified competitors, etc.).

From other strategic perspectives, such as the Uppsala model, the entry mode choice may also be analysed under a dynamic perspective, considering the influence of past experience and accumulated knowledge of the firm (Johanson and Vahlne 1977, 1990). Specifically, the entry mode choice may be considered as an incremental process, in which the firm gradually increases its resource commitment as it gains experience and knowledge of the markets.

The sequential model developed to explain the internationalisation process of the firm may also be used to explain the process followed in diversification moves. In this sense, when a firm enters a new business, it starts with a small investment into a related area and, then, they increase gradually its resource commitment in less related businesses (Chang, 1996). Over a series of entries, firms accumulate experience that can be used to undertake new entries by direct methods.

Therefore, firm knowledge limits not only the degree of resource commitments in new businesses but also the direction of the diversification strategy. The firm will search for industries where it can apply and share its technological and marketing know-how. That is, it will search for related business. But the experience in entering and operating in different businesses will allow the firm to acquire new knowledge to use it in subsequent entries (Chang, 1996).

This gradual process implies that the experience accumulated in other businesses provides firms with greater capacity to assess the potential fit with the new business. This capacity should reduce the risk of failed entry. Likewise, past experience into new businesses allow firms to acquire necessary skills and knowledge that will enhance the likelihood of the success of future entries.

Other arguments based on the importance of firm resources and capabilities indicate that the entry mode choice is limited by firm resources and past experiences (Madhok, 1997, 1998). For this reason, the resource requirements of the new business and the firm knowledge base determine the choice of entry modes (Madhok, 1997, 1998). But, contrary to the economic arguments, which are focused on the exploitation of resources, this new perspective highlights also the possibility to access new resources and capabilities to renew the firm knowledge base. Therefore, this perspective proposes a balance between firm resource limitations and new resource requirements when firms choose an entry mode.

From our point of view, the fact that each theoretical perspective has focused on different aspects to explain the entry mode choice is due to the complexity of the phenomenon. Hence, an integrative framework, which includes different theoretical perspectives, should offer a wider view to study the modal decision. In this sense, we have verified in our theoretical overview the existence of four groups of factors: external factors, firm-related factors, strategy-related factors and transaction-related factors. The external factors refer to the height of entry barriers and the incumbent reactions arising from entries into new businesses. The firm and strategy-related factors encompass the type of diversification strategy followed by the firm and its capacity to face up to the challenges of new entries. Finally, the transaction-related factors determine the dissemination risk arising from knowledge transfer and the possibility of opportunistic behaviours.

Determinant factors of the entry mode choice

External, internal (firm- and transaction-related factors) and strategic factors constitute the base of our integrative proposal presented above.

Industry factors[3]

Structure variables measure the strength of the standard set of conceptual barriers: differentiation, capital requirements and incumbent reactions (Porter, 1980, 1985; Yip, 1982a,b; Sharma and Kesner, 1996). Traditionally, incumbent reactions are represented by both market concentration and market growth rate (eg. Porter, 1980; Yip, 1982a,b; Chatterjee, 1990), whereas height of barriers is directly represented by R&D and marketing intensity.

The vast majority of academics advocate the use of swift methods, such as acquisitions or strategic alliances, to enter rapidly growing sectors, because the long lead time of internal development will lead to an opportunity cost in high growth markets (Hennart, 1991; Hennart and Park, 1993; Hennart and Reddy, 1997; Chang and Rosenzweig, 2001).

In our opinion, additional explanations exist to support this theoretical argument. Sectors with high growth rates are usually new and emerging industries, characterised by high levels of uncertainty and instability (Porter, 1980). Under these structural conditions, firms will tend to limit their resource commitment and prefer more flexible methods (Menguzzato and Renau, 1991; Menguzzato, 1994). Thus, we may expect that in a rapidly growing industry, opportunity costs of slower entry and uncertainty are high, so cooperative agreements will be preferred over internal development and acquisitions.

Regarding industry concentration ratio, some authors consider that entries by internal development are likely to threaten the existing price structure and competitive positions of incumbents because this option implies additional capacity in the industry (Caves and Mehra, 1986; Zejan, 1990; Hennart, 1991). The incumbent firms can resist the marketing efforts of new entrants by taking measures such as aggressive advertising or lowering prices. In contrast, the purchase of an incumbent firm would be less likely to touch off a destructive battle since no new productive sources of supply are introduced to threaten their positions (Caves, 1982; Kogut and Singh, 1988b; Zejan, 1990; Hennart, 1991; Hennart and Park, 1993; Anand and Delios, 2002). For other researchers, both strategic alliances and acquisitions allow entering firms to avoid retaliation from incumbents in a concentrated sector because total productive capacity in the entered industry remains unchanged (Chang and Rosenzweig, 2001). However, concentrated sectors should also, by definition, offer fewer acquisition candidates, increasing the premium paid for this type of operation and, thus, discouraging an acquisition. Hence, higher levels of concentration should, therefore, favour entry by a strategic alliance (Yip, 1982a,b; Kogut and Singh, 1988a).

On the other hand, marketing and R&D intensity represent the level of product differentiation in the industry and, thus, the expenditure that entering firms should make in order to obtain the necessary assets to compete in a new environment. Thus, both variables represent industry-specific costs[4] and may erect important market barriers (Bain, 1956; Porter, 1980; Kessides, 1986).

Advertising intensity enhances consumer brand loyalty and therefore renders more difficult any attempt by new entrants to induce brand switching (Porter, 1980). Indeed, high levels of marketing intensity indicate the presence of differentiated products and, thus, the existence of several advantages related to brand recognition, reputation, design and control of distribution channels (Bain, 1956). These advantages should create strong barriers to entry and important switching costs, so acquisition of an incumbent firm should allow entering firms to overcome them (Yip, 1982a,b).

International management literature has also analysed the impact of marketing intensity on the entry mode choice. In general, researchers defend acquisition of a local firm as the best way to access marketing capabilities and market knowledge (Caves and Mehra, 1986; Kogut and Singh, 1988a,b; Anand and Kogut, 1997; Anand and Delios, 2002). Entry by slower methods, such as internal development, may require long time horizons to build up a brand or reputation that alters the existing loyalty patterns (Gatignon and Anderson, 1988; Gomes-Casseres, 1990; Capron and Hulland, 1999; Petrick *et al.* 1999; Anand and Delios, 2002). On the other hand, any purchase of brands is subject to transactional problems (Caves, 1996), while hiring local managers to build marketing capabilities is difficult due to their firm-specific nature and uncertain imitability (Ekeledo and Sivakumar, 1998; Chen and Hu, 2002). Hence, given the inseparability of capabilities from owners, the acquisition of incumbent firms remains a suitable choice (Anand and Delios, 2002).

However, acquisitions are not the only way to access marketing competencies of incumbent firms. The establishment of cooperative agreements should facilitate access to these competencies and overcome barriers arising from high levels of marketing intensity (Chen and Hennart, 2002). Nevertheless, firms established in advertising-intensive industries are generally reluctant to cooperate with unknown firms in an attempt to protect their brands and marketing investments (Kogut and Singh, 1988b). In these cases, the reputation of the entering firm is relevant when establishing an alliance with an incumbent firm because it is an indicator of its quality (Stuart, 2000).

Empirical evidence is not conclusive. Some studies confirm the use of acquisitions to overcome differentiation barriers (Anand and Kogut, 1997; Anand and Delios, 2002), but others do not confirm the influence of marketing intensity on the choice of entry mode (Yip, 1982a,b; Caves and Mehra, 1986; Kogut and Singh, 1988b; Chen and Hennart, 2002).

On the other hand, R&D intensity also represents a differentiation barrier. Studies that analyse the impact of this variable on the entry mode choice stress the importance of relying on the support of an incumbent firm to access technological opportunities, either by acquisitions (Anand and Kogut, 1997; Anand and Delios, 2002; Belderbos, 2003) or by cooperative agreements with an incumbent firm (Kogut and Singh, 1988a,b; Kogut and Chang, 1991; Anand and Kogut, 1997; Mutinelli and Piscitello, 1998; Chen and Hennart, 2002; Belderbos, 2003). It is evident how researchers advocate the use of cooperative agreements and particularly joint ventures to enter R&D-intensive sectors. The higher product differentiation and continuous technological changes that characterise this type of sector lead firms to adopt flexible forms to enter them (Mutinelli and Piscitello, 1998; Reuer, Zollo and Singh, 2002).

Firm characteristics

The literature has also focused on the importance of firm characteristics as determinant factors in the entry mode decision, since they represent the accumulated firm experience and the resources and capabilities available to undertake future diversification moves. Firm size and degree of diversification have been the main characteristics considered in studies focused on this topic.

Firm size is the best indicator of firm capacity to face up to entry costs (Yip, 1982a,b). However, the importance of this variable contrasts with the scarcity of empirical studies that include it in the analysis of the mode of diversification. In general, larger firms may diversify by internal development since they possess greater resources and capabilities to directly overcome entry barriers (Yip, 1982a,b). But, at the same time, larger firms possess greater financial resources and thus a higher capacity to finance acquisitions (Yip, 1982a,b; Chatterjee, 1990; Chang and Singh, 1999).

The existence of contradictory arguments and the scarcity of empirical evidence hinder the analysis of the impact of firm size on the choice of entry mode into new areas.

International management literature provides more clarifying explanations for our analysis. Small-sized firms suffer from financial and managerial constraints and lack of complementary assets to undertake growth. These constraints leave them with few means of entering new businesses and force them to seek cooperative agreements with incumbent firms, which enjoy access to distribution channels and industry-specific assets (Stopford and Wells, 1972; Contractor and Kundu, 1998; Mutinelli and Piscitello, 1998; Tsang, 1998).

In contrast, larger firms prefer to enter by methods that involve higher re-source commitment and operational control since they possess the capacity to internalise new operations without sharing the control of activities (Kogut and Singh, 1988a,b; Gomes-Casseres, 1989; Erramilli and Rao, 1993; Mutinelli and Piscitello, 1998; Tan *et al.*, 2001; Barbosa and Louri, 2002).

Empirical evidence about the influence of firm size on entry mode choice is not conclusive. Some studies show that larger firms are more likely to enter new busi-nesses by acquisitions (Caves and Mehra, 1986), whereas other studies conclude that firm size favours internal development (Kogut and Singh, 1988b). Other stud-ies do not confirm a significant influence of firm size on entry mode choice (Yip, 1982a,b; Azofra and Martínez-Bobillo, 1999; Chang and Rosenzweig, 2001).

Based on the existing theoretical arguments, we advocate for the use of meth-ods that involve greater resource commitment and degree of control between larger firms due to their greater financial and managerial capacity to undertake a diversification strategy.

A further characteristic of the firm is its degree of diversification. This attribute indicates previous experience in entering new businesses (Yip, 1982a,b; Chang and Singh, 1999). In this sense, less diversified firms start with small investments in new areas and increase their resource commitments in subsequent movements as they gain experience and knowledge of the diversification process (Chang, 1996).

This sequential approach to diversified entry, developed by Chang (1996), has not been contrasted empirically. The only study to include the impact of degree of diversification on the entry mode choice is that carried out by Yip (1982a,b). Re-sults show a greater tendency to use acquisitions between more diversified firms. In contrast, Chang and Singh (1999) include degree of diversification as a control variable, but their results indicate that more diversified firms are more likely to use internal development. Thus, existing empirical evidence leads us, once again, to focus on international management literature.

Numerous studies include the effect of degree of diversification on entry mode choice when going into international markets.[5] The vast majority defend and confirm a positive relationship between degree of diversification and use of ac-quisitions to enter new markets or businesses (Wilson, 1980; Yip, 1982a,b; Caves and Mehra, 1986; Zejan, 1990; Brouthers and Brouthers, 2000). More diversified firms have developed complex organisational structures, generally divisionalised ones, and sophisticated management control systems that allow managers to con-trol quasi-independent subsidiaries or divisions (Caves and Mehra, 1986; Hennart and Park, 1993). This advantage favours the integration of other firms into the organisational structure and, thus, increases the probability of choosing acquisi-tions to enter new businesses (Barkema and Vermeulen, 1998).

In contrast, other authors propose an inverted U-shaped relationship between degree of diversification and the propensity to use internal development (Figure 3.1) (Barkema and Vermeulen, 1998). Low and moderate levels of diversification are associated to an increasing tendency to use internal development over acquisi-tions, but this propensity diminishes and even becomes inverse for higher levels

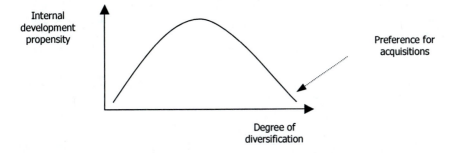

Figure 3.1 Curvilinear relationship between degree of diversification and internal development propensity (Barkema and Vermeulen, 1998)

of diversification. Increasing levels of diversification imply greater accumulated experience in entries to new businesses and, thus, the possession of sufficient resources to undertake a new entry by internal development. However, as previous researchers have argued (see Penrose, 1959), if the number of a firm's businesses becomes too large, the cognitive limits of its management team will prevent internal growth in the firm. This constraint could force firms to enter by acquisitions.

From our point of view, the inverted U-shaped form proposed by Barkema and Vermeulen (1998) to explain the relationship between degree of diversification and the propensity to use internal development is valid if we only consider acquisitions and direct entry as alternative methods to undertake corporate diversification. In this way, we can expect that less diversified firms and, thus, firms with less experience in diversification moves will be more likely to use acquisitions with incumbent firms. However, the consideration of strategic alliances in the study of mode of diversification provides a new way for firms to avoid entry uncertainty without committing greater resources to the new business. For this reason, without calling into question the validity of the arguments exposed by Barkema and Vermeulen (1998), we support the hypothesis of incremental commitment with experience and, therefore, degree of diversification.

In sum, we assume that more diversified firms have accumulated knowledge about different businesses and entry modes, so they will perceive less risk in their subsequent entries. Under such circumstances, these firms will show a greater tendency to increase their resource commitment in their diversification process. In addition to this, the accumulated experience in management and control of different businesses and the divisional structure adopted by diversified firms facilitate the acquisition and, thus, the integration of a new firm.

Firm strategic attitude

There are other factors related to firm strategic attitude that will also favour the establishment of strategic alliances in diversification moves. Factors such as type of diversification or firm entrepreneurial orientation could offer additional explanations of how firms choose entry modes when expanding into new businesses.

With regard to the type of diversification, the literature indicates that firms entering a related business can transfer and leverage their current resources and capabilities and develop new ones by internal development. Moreover, entries via related acquisitions are more likely to involve the purchase of unwanted assets since such acquisitions entail the purchase of redundant resources that come with the acquired firm, increasing bureaucratic costs for diversifying firms (Hennart and Reddy, 1997; Chang and Singh, 1999). On the other hand, familiarity between the new activity and the firm core business exposes firms to an important opportunistic risk from partners who could try to erode firm competitive advantage by appropriating strategic assets. Transaction costs emerging from the establishment of property protection clauses lead firms to the internalisation of the transaction by internal development.

In contrast, firms entering a non-related business will find more difficulties in transferring existing organisational routines and their resource excesses to the new business and, thus, they should acquire an incumbent firm in order to access desired resources and capabilities (Yip, 1982a,b; Wernerfelt, 1984; Caves and Mehra, 1986; Chatterjee, 1990; Harrison *et al.*, 1991; Hennart and Park, 1993; Chang and Singh, 1999; Brouthers and Brouthers, 2000).

Although empirical studies focused on diversification strategy have not included cooperative agreements as a way to enter new businesses, we consider that these strategic options could present an important potential for non-related diversification moves since they allow firms to access market knowledge and share risks with other partners. We also consider that cooperative agreements could be more efficient methods than acquisitions due to the post-integration problems and costs arising from the purchase of a firm pertaining to a different sector.

In this sense, Balakrishnan and Koza (1993) point out that joint ventures are more desirable than acquisitions when acquirers do not know the value of the desired assets. Joint ventures are efficient vehicles for reducing information asymmetries and providing flexibility in cases of higher uncertainty because they make it possible to gather additional information on the value of the partner's assets and to rescind the relationship at relatively low cost (Woodcock, Beamish and Makino, 1994; Hennart and Reddy, 1997). Hence, we could expect firms to favour cooperative agreements over acquisitions in non-related moves because they have little knowledge of other partner's business (Balakrishnan and Koza, 1993).

Based on these arguments, we advocate for (a) a higher use of internal development to enter related businesses because familiarity encourages deployment of excess resources and protection of firm-specific assets; and (b) a higher use of cooperative agreements over other methods to enter non-related businesses because they allow firms to avoid information asymmetries and costs associated to the integration of firms coming from very different sectors.

A further strategic factor that influences entry mode choice is firm entrepreneurial orientation. A close examination of past research on firm-level entrepreneurship reveals two main research streams that complement each other: the first is concerned with the analysis of the content of the entrepreneurial act, which corresponds to Miller's conceptualisation of the 'entrepreneurial orientation' (Miller,

1983), and the second is directed to focus on the study of the entrepreneurial management process developed mainly following on from the seminal work of Stevenson and Gumpert (1985). Miller (1983) defined 'entrepreneurial orientation' from the interrelation of three basic characteristics: the innovative attitude, willingness to take on controlled risks and proactiveness.[6] He also developed a scale which enabled this orientation to be measured, and which was subsequently further extended by Covin and Slevin (1989) and has had far-reaching repercussions in the specialised literature, since it provides a base from which situations that may be considered entrepreneurial can be identified.

The second one has focused on the analysis of entrepreneurship as a management process. This study has essentially centred on two interrelated processes: the entrepreneurial opportunity recognition process and the process of resource acquisition to exploit these opportunities – all these processes are characterised by flexibility (Stevenson and Gumpert, 1985; Stevenson and Jarillo, 1990; Shane and Venkataraman, 2000).

Based on the above literature, researchers have stressed the potential of strategic alliances to satisfy the growth objectives of entrepreneurial firms (Cooper, 2001). Alliances allow firms to identify potential business opportunities and access information, resources, markets and even technologies needed to exploit those opportunities (Anand and Khanna, 2000; Dussauge *et al.*, 2000; Cooper, 2001; Hitt *et al.*, 2001). Moreover, alliances concede the necessary flexibility to maintain innovation levels that characterise entrepreneurial firms (Miller, 1983).

On the other hand, strategic alliances allow firms to mitigate risk emerging from entrepreneurial activities and increase their knowledge base in order to exploit future business opportunities (Dess *et al.*, 2003). In addition to this, the rapidity associated to these agreements provides entrepreneurial firms with the possibility of taking advantage of detected opportunities.

Transaction-specific factors

From transaction cost theory, researchers have proposed other variables related to the transaction that determine the most efficient governance structure for the firm. We refer to the value of contributed assets, the tacit component of transferred know-how and specificity of investment (Anderson and Gatignon, 1986; Hill and Kim, 1988; Hill, Hwang and Kim, 1990; Kim and Hwang, 1992; Madhok, 1998). Value and tacitness represent the dissemination risk faced by firms in transactions, whereas specificity represents opportunism risk.

When the nature of specific know-how transferred by a firm is tacit, it is by definition difficult to articulate and codify (Nelson and Winter, 1982). It is also personal know-how and specific to the context in which it has been generated (Nonaka, 1994). Its transmission implies important transaction costs because certain types of knowledge are difficult to patent, exposing the firm to more dissemination risk (Anderson and Gatignon, 1986). Hence, when transferring tacit know-how, firms are more likely to select high control modes such as internal development or acquisitions (Kim and Hwang, 1992; Madhok, 1998; Luo, 2001).

Moreover, the difficulty of transferring tacit know-how to other firms with different organisational routines favours the use of internal development over acquisitions.

On the other hand, the value of contributed assets also represents a dissemination risk faced by diversifying firms. When firms transfer their own specific advantages, they are transferring intangible assets with high proprietary content. As a result, a high control entry mode is more efficient than share-control modes. More valuable assets for firms' competitive advantage are technological and commercial knowledge (Ekeledo and Sivakumar, 1998; Chen and Hu, 2002). Transfer of these assets implies higher transaction costs due to market imperfections (information asymmetries) and dissemination risk, so, under these circumstances, a high control mode is more efficient (Anderson and Gatignon, 1986; Hill and Kim, 1988; Hill, Hwang and Kim, 1990; Hennart, 1991; Agarwal and Ramaswami, 1992; Kim and Hwang, 1992; Chang and Rosenzweig, 2001; Luo, 2001).

Furthermore, some authors argue that firms transferring valuable assets to new businesses could prefer to develop them internally due to their specificity compared with other firm resources (Hennart and Park, 1993; Brouthers and Brouthers, 2000).

Hence, we consider that firms transferring tacit know-how and valuable intangible assets to new businesses will tend to prefer internal development over acquisitions and strategic alliances due to their proprietary content and firm-specific nature.

On the other hand, transaction cost theory stresses the importance of the specificity of investment to explain entry mode choice (Williamson, 1975, 1985). Specific assets are investments (in physical and human assets) that have value only in a limited number of transactions, in other words, specialised assets that are employed in one or very few uses (Williamson, 1985).[7]

If entry in a new business implies a specific investment in a particular use, this investment could not be easily employed in alternative uses without loss of value (Williamson, 1991). Hence, the firm faces important exit barriers and loss of flexibility due to switching costs and restricted range of suppliers available to the firm (Williamson, 1985). These circumstances increase firm vulnerability to opportunistic behaviour and, thus, increase transaction cost associated with low-control modes (Madhok, 1998).

Hence, according to transaction cost theory, we consider that the greater the specificity of the investment in the new business, the greater the probability that firms will favour an entry mode with high control such as internal development or acquisitions.

Conclusions

This chapter offers an integrative framework to analyse the entry mode choice in diversification moves through the consideration of four groups of factors: industry characteristics, firm characteristics, strategic variables and transaction factors. We also offer the first theoretical analysis of the determinant factors of mode of diversification including cooperative agreements as a vehicle for expansion into new businesses. Our theoretical analysis provides support for the important role that strategic alliances may play as a way to overcome market barriers and to learn how and where to diversify. In this sense, our chapter highlights the potential of cooperative agreements to avoid reprisals from firms established in concentrated sectors or to overcome entry barriers related to differentiated products.

On the other hand, we point out that cooperative agreements are a valid option for small- and medium- sized firms with a diversification strategy. And we also indicate the utility of cooperative agreements in implementing non-related diversification strategies, since they allow firms to access market knowledge and share risks with other partners. Furthermore, these agreements allow firms to avoid information asymmetries and costs associated to the integration of firms coming from very different sectors.

Regarding the degree of diversification, we advocate for an incremental resource commitment in new businesses as the firm becomes more diversified. Firms with a low degree of diversification and, thus, less experience in diversification moves, perceive higher uncertainty and risk in the entry, being more likely to use modes involving low resource commitments. As firms acquire experience in new businesses and, thus, increase their degree of diversification, they prefer to control operations in future entries. The experience and knowledge acquired in previous entries allow firms to successfully enter new businesses without sharing the benefits gained with other firms.

Finally, dissemination risk associated to the transfer of valuable assets and tacit know-how and the difficulty of applying it in different contexts discourages the use of cooperative agreements. On the other hand, investments in specific assets increase transaction costs due to the need to protect them from opportunistic behaviours and, hence, favour the use of more integrated methods, such as internal development or acquisitions.

Our analysis has some important theoretical implications for future research endeavour. First, it defends the need to take advantage of different strategy frameworks with the aim to enrich the study of entry mode choice. Second, our chapter defends the complementarity between different theoretical perspectives to explain a firm decision. We consider that academics and researchers can better understand the managerial process by adopting an integrative perspective. Finally, the study of cooperative agreements to diversify constitutes an emerging topic on diversification research.

Notes

1 The authors wish to acknowledge the funding received from the Spanish Ministry of Science and Technology through the SEC2002–01878 project.
2 We consider that the choice of entry mode in new markets or new businesses may be influenced by similar factors related to firm characteristics or industry conditions. Therefore some theoretical arguments made in the context of the firm internationalisation process can be adapted to the study of the diversification process.
3 By industry factors, we are referring to characteristics of the destination industry.

4 Kessides (1986) points out that the investment in media marketing needed to successfully penetrate the market leads to an unrecoverable entry cost in the case of failure, thus advertising creates a sunk cost barrier to entry.

5 Wilson (1980); Caves and Mehra (1986); Kogut and Singh (1988a); Zejan (1990); Hennart and Park (1993); Barkema and Vermeulen (1998); Brouthers and Brouthers (2000); Chang and Rosenzweig (2001); Harzing (2002).

6 Lumpkin and Dess (1996) maintain that the concept of proactiveness, as understood by Miller (1983) or Covin and Slevin (1989), is ambiguous and includes a dimension which measures the firm's competitive orientation.

7 Following Williamson's (1985) work, specificity can be related to four types of assets: location, physical assets, human assets and contributed assets. For our analysis, the specificity of investment is related to location, physical and human assets whereas specificity related to contributed assets is included in the concept of value of contributed assets and explains the risk of dissemination of firm-specific advantages.

References

Agarwal, S. and Ramaswami, S. N. (1992) 'Choice of foreign market entry mode: impact of ownership, location and internalization factors', *Journal of International Business Studies*, 23(1), 1–27.

Anand, B. N. and Khanna, T. (2000) 'Do firms learn to create value? The case of alliances?', *Strategic Management Journal*, Special Issue, 21(3), 295–315.

Anand, J. and Delios, A. (2002) 'Absolute and relative resources as determinants of international acquisitions', *Strategic Management Journal*, 23(2), 119–134.

Anand, J. and Kogut, B. (1997) 'Technological capabilities of countries, firm rivalry and foreign direct investment', *Journal of International Business Studies*, 28(3), 445–465.

Anderson, E. and Gatignon, H. (1986) 'Modes of foreign entry: a transaction cost analysis and propositions', *Journal of International Business Studies*, 17(3), 1–26.

Azofra, V. and Martínez-Bobillo, A. (1999) 'Transaction costs and bargaining power: entry mode choice in foreign markets', *Multinational Business Review*, 7(1), 62–75.

Bain, J. S. (1956) *Barriers to new competition*. Harvard University Press. Cambridge, MA.

Balakrishnan, S. and Koza, M. (1993) 'Information asymmetry, adverse selection and joint ventures: theory and evidence', *Journal of Economic Behavior and Organization*, 20(1), 99–117.

Barbosa, N. and Louri, H. (2002) 'On the determinants of multinationals' ownership preferences: evidence from Greece and Portugal', *International Journal of Industrial Organization*, 20(4), 493–515.

Barkema, H. G. and Vermeulen, F. (1998) 'International expansion through start-up or acquisitions: a learning perspective', *Academy of Management Journal*, 41(1), 7–26.

Belderbos, R. (2003) 'Entry mode, organizational learning, and R&D in foreign affiliates: evidence from Japanese firms', *Strategic Management Journal*, 24(3), 235–259.

Brouthers, K. D. and Brouthers, L. E. (2000) 'Acquisition or Greenfield start-up? Institutional, cultural and transaction cost influences', *Strategic Management Journal*, 21(1), 89–97.

Capron, L. and Hulland, J. (1999) 'Redeployment of Brands, Sales Forces, and General Marketing Management Expertise Following Horizontal Acquisitions: A Resource-Based View', *Journal of Marketing*, 63(2), 41–54.

Caves, R. E. (1982) *Multinational Enterprise and Economic Analysis*. Cambridge: Cambridge University Press.

Caves, R. E. (1996) *Multinational Enterprise and Economic Analysis*. 2nd edn. Cambridge: Cambridge University Press.

Caves, R. E. and Mehra, S. (1986) 'Entry of Foreign Multinationals into US Manufacturing Industries', pp. 449–481 in Porter, M. (ed), *Competition in Global Industries*. Boston, MA: Harvard Business School Press.

Chang, S. J. (1996) 'An evolutionary perspective on diversification and corporate restructuring: entry, exit, and economic performance during 1981–89', *Strategic Management Journal*, 17(8), 587–611.

Chang, S. J. and Rosenzweig, P. M. (2001) 'The choice of entry mode in sequential foreign direct investment', *Strategic Management Journal*, 22(8), 747–776.

Chang, S. J. and Singh, H. (1999) 'The impact of modes of entry and resource fit on modes of exit by multibusiness firms', *Strategic Management Journal*, 20(11), 1019–1035.

Chatterjee, S. (1990) 'Excess resources, utilization cost, and mode of entry', *Academy of Management Journal*, 33(4), 780–800.

Chatterjee, S. and Singh, J. (1999) 'Are tradeoffs inherent in diversification moves? A simultaneous model for type of diversification and mode of expansion decisions', *Management Science*, 45(1), 25–41.

Chen, S-F. S. and Hennart, J-F. (2002) 'Japanese Investors' Choice of Joint Ventures Versus Wholly-owned Subsidiaries in the US: The Role of Market Barriers and Firm Capabilities', *Journal of International Business Studies*, 33(1), 1–18.

Chen, H. and Hu, M. Y. (2002) 'An analysis of determinants of entry mode and its impact on performance', *International Business Review*, 11(2), 193–210.

Contractor, F. J. and Kundu, S. K. (1998) 'Modal choice in a world of alliances: analyzing organizational forms in the international hotel sector', *Journal of International Business Studies*, 29(2), 325–358.

Contractor, F. J., Lorange, P. (1988) *Cooperative Strategies in International Business*. New York: Lexington Books.

Cooper, A.C. (2001) 'Networks, alliances and entrepreneurship' in M. A. Hitt, R. D. Ireland, S. M. Camp and D. L. Sexton (eds), *Strategic Entrepreneurship: Creating a new integrated mindset*, Oxford: Blackwell.

Covin, J. G. and Slevin, D. P. (1989) 'Strategic management of small firms in hostile and benign environments', *Strategic Management Journal*, 10, 75–87.

Dess, G. G., Ireland, R. D., Zahra, S. A., Floyd, S. W., Janney, J. J. and Lane, P. J. (2003) 'Emerging Issues in Corporate Entrepreneurship', *Journal of Management*, 29(3), 351–378.

Dussauge, P. and Garrette, B. (1999) *Cooperative Strategy. Competing Successfully Through Strategic Alliances*. London: John Wiley & Sons.

Dussauge, P., Garrette, B., Mitchell, W. (2000) 'Learning from competing partners: outcomes and durations of scale and link alliances in Europe, North America, and Asia', *Strategic Management Journal*, 21(2), 99–126.

Ekeledo, I. and Sivakumar, K. (1998) 'Foreign market entry mode choice of service firms: a contingency perspective', *Journal of The Academy of Marketing Science*, 26(4), 274–292.

Erramilli, M. K. and Rao, C. P. (1993) 'Service firms' international entry mode choice: a modified transaction-cost analysis approach', *Journal of Marketing*, 57(3), 19–38.

Escribá, A., Menguzzato, M. and Sánchez, L. (2003a) 'Are cooperative agreements a strategy for everyone?', Competitive Paper, EURAM Conference, 3–5 April, Milan.

Escribá, A., Sánchez, L. and Sánchez, E. (2003b) 'Nueva Evidencia sobre el uso de la cooperación entre empresas en España en el periodo 1994–1999: características y evolución', *Información Comercial Española*, 809, 189–207.

Freije-Uriarte, A., Rodríguez, S., Freije-Obregón, I. and Freije-Obregón, A. (1994) 'Alianzas estratégicas en diversificación horizontal (modelo de concreción de este tipo de alianzas)', *Boletín de Estudios Económicos*, XLIX, 152, 205–238.

García-Canal, E. (1992) 'La cooperación interempresarial en España: características de los acuerdos suscritos entre 1986 y 1989', *Economía Industrial*, 314, 113–122.

Gatignon, H. and Anderson, E. (1988) 'The multinational corporation's degree of control over foreign subsidiaries: an empirical test of a transaction cost explanation', *Journal of Law, Economics, and Organization*, 4(2), 305–336.

Ghemawat, P., Porter, M. E. and Rawlinson, R. A. (1986) 'Patterns of international coalition activity', pp. 345–365 in M. E. Porter (ed.), *Competition in Global Industries*. Boston, MA: Harvard Business School Press.

Gomes-Casseres, B. (1989) 'Ownership structures of foreign subsidiaries: Theory and evidence', *Journal of Economic Behavior and Organization*, 11, January, 1–25

Gomes-Casseres, B. (1990) 'Firm ownership preferences and host government restrictions: an integrated approach', *Journal of International Business Studies*, 21(1), 1–22.

Grant, R. M. (1996) 'A knowledge based theory of inter-firm collaboration', *Organization Science*, 7, 375–387.

Hagedoorn, J. (1993) 'Understanding the rationale of strategic technology partnering: interorganizational modes of cooperation and sectorial differences', *Strategic Management Journal*, 14(5), 371–385.

Hamel, G. (1991) 'Competition for competence and interpartner learning within international strategic alliances', *Strategic Management Journal*, 12, Special Issue, 83–103.

Harrigan, K. (1985) *Strategies for Joint Ventures*. Lexington: Mass. D.C. Heath & Co.

Harrison, J. S., Hitt, M. A., Hoskisson, R. E. and Ireland, R. D. (1991): 'Synergies and post-acquisition performance: differences vs similarities in resource allocations', *Journal of Management*, 17(1), 173–190.

Harzing, A-W. (2002) 'Acquisitions versus greeenfield investments: international strategy and management of entry modes', *Strategic Management Journal*, 23(3), 211–227.

Hennart, J-F. (1991) 'The Transaction Costs Theory of Joint Ventures: An Empirical Study of Japanese Subsidiaries in the United States', *Management Science*, 37(4), 483–497.

Hennart, J-F. and Park, Y. R. (1993) 'Greenfield vs Acquisition: the strategy of Japanese investors in the United States, *Management Science*, 39(9), 1054–1070.

Hennart, J-F. and Reddy, S. (1997) 'The choice between mergers/acquisitions and joint ventures: the case of Japanese investors in the United States', *Strategic Management Journal*, 18(1), 1–12.

Hill, C. W. L. and Kim, W. C. (1988) 'Searching for a dynamic theory of the multinational enterprise: a transaction cost model', *Strategic Management Journal*, special issue, 93–194.

Hill, C. W. L., Hwang, P. and Kim, W. C. (1990) 'An eclectic theory of the choice of international entry mode', *Strategic Management Journal*, 11(2), 117–128.

Hitt, M. A., Ireland, R. D., Camp, S. M. and Sexton, D. L. (2001) 'Strategic entrepreneurship: entrepreneurial strategies for wealth creation', *Strategic Management Journal*, 22, 479–491.

Johanson, J. and Vahlne, J. E. (1977) 'The internationalization process of the firm: a model of knowledge development and increasing foreign commitments', *Journal of International Business Studies*, 8(1), 23–32.

Johanson, J. and Vahlne, J. E. (1990) 'The mechanism of internationalization', *International Marketing Review*, 7(4), 11–34.

Kessides, I. (1986) 'Advertising, sunk costs and barriers to entry', *Review of Economics and Statistics*, 68(1), 84–95.

Killing, J. P. (1982) 'How to make a global joint venture work', *Harvard Business Review*, 60(3), 120–127.

Kim, W. C. and Hwang, P. (1992) 'Global strategy and multinationals' entry mode choice', *Journal of International Business Studies*, 23(1), 29–53.

Kogut, B. and Chang, S. J. (1991) 'Technological capabilities and Japanese foreign direct investment in the United States', *The Review of Economics and Statistics*, 73(3), 401–413.

Kogut, B. and Singh, H. (1988a) 'Entering the United States by Joint Venture: Competitive Rivalry and Industry Structure', pp. 241–251 in F. K. Contractor and P. Lorange (eds), *Cooperative Strategies in International Business*. Lexington, MA: Lexington Books.

Kogut, B. and Singh, H. (1988b) 'The effect of national culture on the choice of entry mode', *Journal of International Business Studies*, 19(3), 411–432.

Kogut, B. and Zander, U. (1993) 'Knowledge of the Firm and the evolutionary theory of the multinational corporation', *Journal of International Business Studies*, 24(4), 625–645.

Lumpkin, G. T. and Dess, G. G. (1996) 'Clarifying the entrepreneurial orientation construct and linking it to performance', *Academy of Management Review*, 21(1), 135–172.

Luo, Y. (2001) 'Equity sharing in international joint ventures: an empirical analysis of strategic and environmental determinants', *Journal of International Management*, 7, 31–58.

Luo, Y. (2002) 'Product diversification in international joint ventures: performance implications in an emerging market', *Strategic Management Journal*, 23(1), 1–20.

Madhok, A. (1997) 'Cost, value and foreign market entry mode: the transaction and the firm', *Strategic Management Journal*, 18(1), 39–61.

Madhok, A. (1998) 'The nature of multinational firm boundaries: transaction costs, firm capabilities and foreign market entry mode', *International Business Review*, 7(3), 259–290.

Menguzzato, M. (1992) *La cooperación empresarial: Análisis de su proceso*. IMPIVA, Valencia.

Menguzzato, M. (1994) 'La relevancia de las Alianzas Estratégicas en las Relaciones Interempresariales Este-Oeste', *Revista Europea de Dirección y Economía de la Empresa*, 3(1), 9–14.

Menguzzato, M. and Renau, J. J. (1991) *La dirección estratégica de la empresa. Un enfoque innovador del management*. Editorial Ariel, Barcelona.

Miller, D. (1983) 'The correlates of entrepreneurship in three types of firms', *Management Science*, 29(7), 770–791.

Mitchell, W. and Singh, K. (1996) 'Survival of businesses using collaborative relationships to commercialize complex goods', *Strategic Management Journal*, 17, 169–195.

Morris, D. and Hergert, M. (1987) 'Trends in international collaborative agreements', *Columbia Journal of World Business*, 22(2), 15–21.

Mutinelli, M. and Piscitello, L. (1998) 'The entry mode choice of MNEs: an evolutionary approach', *Research Policy*, 27(5), 491–506.

Nelson, R. and Winter, S. E. (1982) *An Evolutionary Theory of Economic Change*. Cambridge, MA: Belknap Press.

Nonaka, I. (1994) 'A dynamic theory of organizational knowledge creation', *Organization Science*, 5(1), 14–37.

Pennings, J. M., Barkema, H. and Douma, S. (1994) 'Organizational learning and diversification', *Academy of Management Journal*, 37(3), 608–640.

Penrose, E. (1959) *The theory of the growth of the firm*. New York: John Wiley.

Petrick, J. A., Scherer, R. F., Brodzinski, J. D., Quinn, J. F. and Ainina, M. F. (1999) 'Global leadership skills and reputational capital: Intangible resources for sustainable competitive advantage', *Academy of Management Executive*, 13(1), 58–69.

Porter, M. E. (1980) *Competitive Strategy*. New York: Free Press.

Porter, M. E. (1985) *Competitive Advantage*. New York: Free Press.

Reuer, J. J., Zollo, M., Singh, H. (2002) 'Post-formation dynamics in strategic alliances', *Strategic Management Journal*, 23(2), 135–151.

Roberts, E. B., Berry, C. A. (1985) 'Entering new businesses: selecting strategies for success', *Sloan Management Review*, 26(3), 3–17.

Shane, S. and Venkataraman, S. (2000) 'The promise of entrepreneurship as a field of research', *Academy of Management Review*, 25(1), 217–226.

Sharma, A. and Kesner, I. F. (1996) 'Diversifying entry: some ex ante explanations for postentry survival and growth', *Academy of Management Journal*, 39(3), 635–677.

Stevenson, H. H. and Gumpert, D. G. (1985) 'The heart of entrepreneurship', *Harvard Business Review*, 85(2), 85–95.

Stevenson, H. H. and Jarillo, J. C. (1990) 'A paradigm of entrepreneurship: entrepreneurial management', *Strategic Management Journal*, 11, 17–27.

Stopford, J. M. and Wells, L. T. (1972) *Managing the multinational enterprise*. New York: Basic Books.

Stuart, T. E. (2000) 'Interorganizational alliances and the performance of firms: a study of growth and innovation rates in a high technology industry', *Strategic Management Journal*, 21(8), 791–811.

Tan, B., Erramilli, K. and Liang, T. W. (2001) 'The influence of dissemination risks, strategic control and global management skills on firms' modal decision in host countries', *International Business Review*, 10(3), 323–340.

Teece, D. J. (1982) 'Towards an economic theory of the multi-product firm', *Journal of Economic Behavior and Organization*, 3, 39–63.

Tsang, E. W. K. (1998) 'Motives for strategic alliance: a resource-based perspective', *Scandinavian Journal Management*, 14(3), 207–221.

Wernerfelt, B. (1984) 'A resource-based view of the firm', *Strategic Management Journal*, 5(2), 171–180.

Williamson, O. E. (1975) *Markets and Hierachies: Analysis and Antitrust Implications*. New York: Free Press.

Williamson, O. E. (1985) *The Economic Institutions of Capitalism*, New York: Free Press.

Williamson, O. E. (1991) 'Comparative economic organization: The analysis of discrete structural alternatives', *Administrative Science Quarterly*, 36(2), 269–296.

Wilson, B. (1980) 'The Propensity of Multinational Companies to Expand Through Acquisitions', *Journal of International Business Studies*, 11(1), 59–65.

Woodcock, C. P., Beamish, P. W. and Makino, S. (1994) 'Ownership-based entry mode strategies and international performance', *Journal of International Business Studies*, 25(2), 253–273.

Yip, G. S. (1982a) *Barriers to Entry. A Corporate-Strategy Perspective*, Lexington, Massachusetts and Toronto: Lexington Books.

Yip, G. S. (1982b) 'Diversification entry: internal development versus acquisition', *Strategic Management Journal*, 3(4), 331–345.

Zejan, M. C. (1990) 'New ventures or acquisitions. The choice of Swedish multinational enterprises', *The Journal of Industrial Economics*, 38(3), 349–355.

4 A meta-analysis of organisational innovation

Moderator effects of internal and market variables[1]

César Camisón Zornoza, Montserrat Boronat Navarro and Mercedes Segarra Ciprés

Introduction

Organisational and environmental factors have been considered as determinants of innovation in organisations. However, innovation literature offers a diversity of results about the relationship of innovation and some of these theoretical variables. Therefore, the main issue of this chapter is to evaluate the extent to which these theoretical variables produce heterogeneity between results of innovation studies. So we propose a meta-analytical review of organisational innovation, which includes potential moderator variables belonging to the internal environment of the company and others related with the market in which the organisation is immersed.

A wide range of organisational characteristics have been studied as predictors of organisational innovation. Particularly, the importance of studying the effects of organisational size has given rise to a large number of studies aimed at determining the influence of size on innovation (Camisón *et al.*, 2004; Damanpour, 1992; Audretsch and Acs, 1991; Hitt *et al.*, 1990; Moch and Morse, 1977). However, innovation literature presents contradictory findings about the direction and the intensity of the relationship between organisational size and innovation. On the one hand, there are studies that point out the existence of a positive relationship and argue that size is the best predictor of innovation (Aragón-Correa and Cordón-Pozo, 2000; Sullivan and Kang, 1999; Damanpour, 1992; Dewar and Dutton, 1986; Ettlie *et al.*, 1984; Kimberly and Evanisko, 1981; Moch and Morse, 1977; Aiken and Hage, 1971). On the other hand, other studies defend a negative relationship (Wade, 1996; Aldrich and Auster, 1986; Hage, 1980). Finally, some studies suggest that no relationship exists (Aiken *et al.*, 1980).

Some previous studies based on the meta-analytical review have found that these contradictory results may be somehow conditioned by differences or errors in measuring the key variables. For instance, Damanpour (1992) and Subramanian and Nilakanta (1996) show that the multi-dimensional character of innovation is one of the factors affecting the direction and intensity between innovation and size. Also, Camisón (2001) argues that the effect of organisational size on performance is explained by the way the organisational size is measured.

In the first part of the chapter we suggest a conceptual framework for analysing the effects of internal and market variables on innovation. Then, we develop a meta-analytical review. Finally, the conclusions and limitations drawn from the meta-analysis are presented.

Conceptual framework for the meta-analyisis of innovation

The present chapter is an extension of a previous meta-analytical review (Camisón *et al.*, 2004) in which we analyse the relationship between size and innovation. In this previous study, we show that there is no solid empirical evidence on the relationship between size and innovation. On the one hand, larger organisations have more complex and diversified resources and capabilities (Damanpour and Evan, 1984) and greater technical know-how, which enable them to adopt a higher number of innovations (Nord and Tucker, 1987). In addition, large organisations are better able to bear the losses brought about when innovations are not success-ful (Damanpour, 1992; Hitt *et al.*, 1990). Kimberly and Evanisko (1981) point out that increased size makes it easier to adopt innovations, but they also defend that the effects of size may vary according to the kind of innovation involved.

On the other hand, some empirical studies emphasise the existence of a nega-tive relationship between size and innovation. So, the inherent disadvantages of greater size inhibit innovatory behaviour, since larger organisations are character-ised by a more formalised structure and there is a more bureaucratic environment within the firm. These have a negative effect on the culture that fosters innovation, resulting in a decrease in management commitment toward innovation (Hitt *et al.*, 1990). In addition, the flexibility of small- and medium-sized enterprises allows them to adapt and improve more easily, and accept and implement changes more readily (Damanpour, 1996).

In order to explain the heterogeneity of the findings, Camisón *et al.* (2004) confirm the existence of a significant and positive correlation between size and innovation, and explain that the contradictory results of previous studies are due to divergences in the way the variables analysed are measured. Some authors as-sume that the divergence of results between organisational size and innovation is based on methodological rather than theoretical reasons. These comments emerge in studies that justify the little coherence in a negative relationship between these variables (Subramanian and Nilakanta, 1996; Damanpour, 1992). Damanpour (1992) points several moderating effects on this relationship: type of innovation, type of organisation, stage of adoption of innovations, measurement of size vari-able and scope of innovation. Along these lines, this work points out the existence of other theoretical variables that have a moderating effect on the relationship, such as organisational attributes and some factors relating to the environment and the strategy of firm.

Therefore, we present a conceptual framework for the meta-analysis of or-ganisational innovation in Figure 4.1 in order to evaluate the moderating effects of internal and market variables, as well as types and measurements of innova-tion. We then consider that the control of these theoretical and methodological

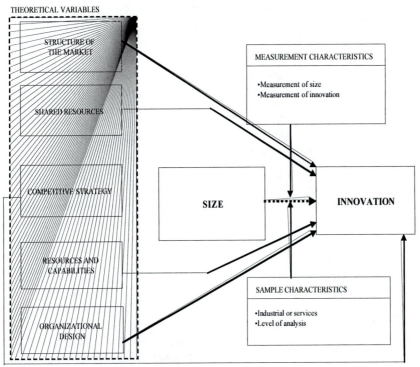

Figure 4.1 Conceptual framework for the meta-analysis.

variables contributes to explaining the heterogeneity between results of innovation studies.

According to other previous meta-analytical studies (Szymanski *et al.*, 1993; Damanpour, 1991), we propose the analysis of some theoretical moderator variables, such as external and internal organisational characteristics, that we classify in five groups: (a) variables relative to the market structure, such as industrial concentration or entry barriers; (b) variables relative to shared resources, externalities or agglomeration economies; (c) variables that make reference to the competitive strategy; (d) variables relative to resources and capabilities; and (e) variables that refer to organisational design.

We then make subgroups within these five groups in order to develop the meta-analytical procedure. In the first group relative to the structure of the market, we include three types of variables: variables that aim to increase? the opportunities of the market, the growth of the market, or the changes in the market (Banbury and Mitchell, 1995; Sengupta, 1998); industrial concentration variables (Amit and Wernerfelt, 1990; Greve, 1999); and variables relative to the intensity of the expenditures in the industry (Sharma and Kesner, 1996).

Concerning the second group, relative to shared resources, we do not make more subgroups because of the similar nature of the variables used in primary studies. Within this group, we include variables such as number of strategic alliances or cooperation agreements works (Hitt *et al.*, 1997; McMillan *et al.*, 2000).

Competitive strategy variables are subdivided in variables relative to the options followed in marketing or R&D areas (Ettlie, 1983; Ettlie *et al.*, 1984; Chang and Hong, 2000; Buzzell and Wierserma, 1981). Another subgroup refers to diversification strategy (Hitt *et al.*, 1991; Baum *et al.*, 2000).

Resources and capabilities variables are classified in different subgroups of variables relative to the experience, professionalism, abilities and attitudes (Zmud, 1984; Dewar and Dutton, 1986; Damanpour, 1987; Cardinal, 2001).

Finally, we make different subgroups with respect to organisational design variables: centralisation, specialisation, formalisation or functional differentiation (Damanpour, 1987; Dewar and Dutton, 1986; Baldridge and Burnham, 1975).

Meta-analytical procedure

Methodology

We applied meta-analytical procedure following Hunter and Schmidt (1990). This methodological technique allows quantifying the results reached in other studies that analyse the same research topic. Meta-analysis applies statistical procedures to integrate results of a set of primary studies (Sánchez-Meca, 1999)

Therefore, results from previous studies with the same subject become inputs for making this meta-analytical work. Nevertheless, in order to integrate these results is necessary to have a common unit of measurement that allow us comparing them. In our case, we use the correlation coefficient; so the average effect size of a set of studies is the mean correlation interstudies. This procedure was developed by Glass (1976), Hunter *et al.* (1982), and Hunter and Schmidt (1990).

After obtaining the mean correlation interstudies, we analyse if the observed variability is caused by certain statistical artefacts or by the presence of other theoretical variables that exert a moderating effect on the relationship. So we come to analyse and to value if these methodological and conceptual variables, which are present in empirical studies, could affect results.

The first step in the meta-analytical procedure involves reviewing the literature in order to select the primary studies that have certain requirements. In the present work we cover the time span between 1970 and 2001, which becomes the first condition to accomplish by primary studies. Another requirement is that primary works are empirical and include statistical information necessary to meta-analytical procedure; we refer to Pearson's r correlation coefficient, or any other statistical information transformable according to the statistical formulas used in meta-analysis.

In accordance with these criteria, the total sample that we obtained in the first meta-analysis, already cited about the relationship between size and innovation (Camisón *et al.*, 2004), included 53 primary studies. Nevertheless, we should select those that included the correlation between innovation and theoretical variables, previously mentioned, to be able to make our present research.

The process of codification implies the definition of the criteria followed in the meta-analysis. In our case the following indications are considered: in studies with multiple independent samples the correlations for each one were included; for studies that included different ways of measuring innovation the correlations from all the combinations between different measures of innovation and theoretical variables were taken into consideration; we included different types of innovation and also different ways of measuring innovation (number of innovations, R&D expenditures); and the sample size taken into consideration was the number of firms used in the primary studies.

Type of innovation includes: administrative versus technical innovations, product versus process innovations, and radical versus incremental innovations. In the case of the way of measuring innovation, in addition to the number of innovations, which is the measure that is most often used in primary studies, other measures were found: R&D intensity, defined as the ratio between investment in R&D and sales; R&D expenditures; and the innovation to sales ratio, where we can find in the numerator the number of patents, while the denominator contains the average sales of new products.

Results

In this section, we analyse the effect of theoretical variables and the measurement of innovation variable on the results of innovation studies. We observe the mean correlation from each theoretical variable and innovation (Table 4.1), and then we make different subgroups attending to variables that are in each one of these groups (Table 4.2) and then attending also different measures of innovation.

We then study if the percentage of variance explained by the sampling error in these subgroups exceeds 60 per cent. In this case it is not necessary to search for other moderating variables. Otherwise, if a group does not meet this percentage, it is necessary to introduce more subgroups or search other variables, and test if a difference between groups still exists. Following Hunter and Schmidt (1990), the total observed variance consists on the variance of the population S_ρ^2, plus

Table 4.1 Moderator effects of the theoretical variables

Moderator theoretical variables	k	Total sample	Mean correlation	Observed variance	Sampling error variance	75% rule	95% confidence interval
Market structure	24	6241	0.0724	0.0177	0.0038	21.5033	0.0247
Shared resources	5	1010	0.1303	0.0425	0.0048	11.3029	0.0607
Competitive strategy	41	10,271	0.0171	0.0239	0.0040	16.7055	0.0193
Resources and capabilities	44	4333	0.1199	0.0320	0.0099	31.0848	0.0295
Organisational design	75	5225	0.1515	0.1232	0.0139	11.2835	0.0266

Table 4.2 Sub-group meta-analysis of moderator effects

	k	Total sample	Mean correlation	Observed variance	Sampling error variance	75% rule	95% confidence interval
Market structure							
Opportunities of the market	9	1573	0.1075	0.0276	0.0056	20.3942	0.0490
Market concentration	11	3152	0.0813	0.0163	0.0035	21.1954	0.0347
R&D intensity	4	1516	0.0175	0.0062	0.0026	42.8593	0.0504
Competitive strategy							
Technological strategy	7	598	0.2534	0.0253	0.0104	40.9866	0.0754
Marketing strategy	13	5712	0.0393	0.0020	0.0023	100	0.0259
Diversification	21	3961	−0.0504	0.0418	0.0053	12.6865	0.0311
Resources and capabilities							
Attitude toward change	8	338	0.2581	0.0447	0.0211	47.2704	0.1007
Professionalism	16	820	0.2528	0.0182	0.0174	95.6236	0.0647
Experience	12	2401	0.0529	0.0232	0.0050	21.5415	0.0400
Managerial tenure	9	774	0.1270	0.0277	0.0114	41.1244	0.0697
Organisational design							
Centralisation	24	1623	−0.1462	0.0497	0.0144	28.9212	0.0480
Specialisation	21	1768	0.4083	0.0510	0.0083	16.3528	0.0391
Formalisation	19	868	−0.0321	0.0781	0.0223	28.6127	0.0672
Functional differentiation	10	966	0.3468	0.0813	0.0081	9.9560	0.0558

the variance due to the sampling error, S_e^2. We then checked to see whether the observed variance is mainly due to the error variance or to the variance of the population. If the variance caused by the sampling error does not account for 75 per cent of the total observed, then we cannot accept the hypothesis of homogeneity among empirical correlations and will have to look for other moderating variables that affect the correlations. This procedure has been called the '75 per cent rule' and it is based on corrections for three artefacts (sampling error, error of measurement and range variation). In situations in which only the sampling error is being considered, the limit can be reduced to 60 per cent (Gooding and Wagner, 1985). It is possible to compare groups that employ different methods of measurement of innovation variable. This process tests whether there are significant differences between the mean *r* (*t*-test), thus enabling us to confirm the existence of intergroup homogeneity.

Relationship between innovation and structure of the market

The group as a whole (Table 4.1) presents a positive and significant mean correlation ($\bar{r}=0.072\pm0.025$), because this interval does not include zero, which means that the correlation coefficient is significant. Nevertheless, the variance due to the sampling error accounts for only 21.50 per cent of the total variance, indicating a high heterogeneity between the correlations and the existence of moderating variables.

Studies included in our sample have allowed only observing three subgroups (Table 4.2) and we observe a potential moderating effect of the attractiveness of the market, industrial concentration and intensity in expenses in R&D. Nevertheless, when we make more subgroups, attending types of innovation and ways of measurement of innovation (Table 4.3), the lack of data, due to some subgroups having only two studies or not enough pairs of subgroups to compare, has prevented having to test this moderating effect.

Relationship between innovation and shared resources

We cannot find different subgroups relative to shared resources, because the measurement of this variable only refers to the number of alliances or agreements between firms. In addition, the analysis of the relationship between innovation and shared resources has not been tested, because the number of studies that include this variable is low (Table 4.1). The mean correlation between shared resources and innovation is not high ($r=0.130\pm0.061$) but it is significant. The rule of 75 per cent only reaches 11.30 per cent, showing that it should search other moderator variables.

Table 4.3 Combined moderator effects: market structure and innovation

	k	Total sample	Mean correlation	Observed variance	Sampling error variance	75% rule	95% confidence interval
Opportunities of the market							
Product innovation	3	420	0.2330	0.0164	0.0064	39.1834	0.0908
Technical innovation	4	651	0.2497	0.0111	0.0054	48.9698	0.0723
Number of innovation	4	657	0.0865	0.0024	0.0060	100	0.0761
Market concentration							
R&D intensity	2	1124	0.0991	0.0008	0.0017	100	0.0579
Number of innovation	2	320	0.0040	0.0009	0.0063	100	0.1099

Relationship between innovation and competitive strategy

This relationship is positive but not significant ($\bar{r}=0.017\pm0.019$) and the heterogeneity is high (Table 4.1). This is showed by the lower percentage of the total variance explained by the measurement error (16.71 per cent).

Within this set of studies we can differentiate (Table 4.2) between a first subgroup that gathers the strategies in technological and production matter followed by the company, a second subgroup that refers to the commercial strategies, and a third subgroup with variables relative to the degree of diversification of the firm.

In our analysis we verify the moderating effect of types of innovation with diversification (Table 4.4). The subgroups that we have made (product/process, technical innovation) have intragroup homogeneity; due to the existence of differ-

Table 4.4 Combined moderator effects: competitive strategy and innovation

	k	Total sample	Mean correlation	Observed variance	Sampling error variance	75% rule	95% confidence interval
Technological strategy							
Radical innovation	2	110	0.5349	0.0000	0.0094	100	0.1346
Incremental innovation	2	110	0.3396	0.0004	0.0145	100	0.1668
Process innovation	4	220	0.4373	0.0097	0.0121	100	0.1079
Product innovation	2	110	0.2349	0.0000	0.0165	100	0.1782
Number of innovation	6	330	0.3698	0.0156	0.0138	88.4277	0.0940
Marketing strategy							
Number of innovation	3	162	0.1067	0.0142	0.0184	100	0.1537
Innovation to sales	9	4302	0.0307	0.0017	0.0021	100	0.0299
Diversification							
Product innovation	2	306	0.0338	0.0025	0.0066	100	0.1123
Process innovation	3	362	0.1670	0.0020	0.0079	100	0.1006
Technical innovation	5	668	0.1060	0.0066	0.0074	100	0.0753
R&D expenditures	4	367	−0.0327	0.0325	0.0110	33.7911	0.1028
Number of innovation	5	792	0.1663	0.0255	0.0060	23.5852	0.0679
R&D intensity	5	1820	−0.2234	0.0086	0.0025	28.8023	0.0437

ences in the correlation coefficients between process and product innovations, it could be said that type of innovation exerts a moderating effect in this case. With regard to the measures of innovation (Table 4.4), we do not observe intragroup homogeneity. But in this work, we do not introduce more moderating variables because of the impossibility of making other classifications. Nevertheless, we point out that different types of diversification can affect this relationship.

In the variables concerning commercial, technological and production strategies (Table 4.4), subgroups are homogenous. But due to lack of data, we cannot verify the moderating effect. With regards to this, it is worth emphasising that differences between types of innovation (product/process, radical/gradual) exist. Mean correlation is comparatively strong with process than with product innovation, and also strong with radical innovations than in gradual innovations. Therefore, it seems that the type of innovation moderates the relationship between the two variables, although this fact cannot be confirmed with test *t*, due to the reduced sample of primary studies.

Relationship between innovation and resources and capabilities

We observe in Table 4.1 that the correlation between innovation and resources and capabilities is also positive and significant ($\bar{r}=0.120\pm0.030$), but the percentage of total variability due to sampling error variance is only a percentage of 31.08, so we must continue looking for moderating variables.

In the set of selected empirical studies we formed different subgroups relative to different characteristics of resources and capabilities as such: managerial attitude toward change, professionalism, age of the organisation or experience, and possession of a managerial position (Table 4.2).

When we make different subgroups attending types and measures of innovation (Table 4.5), we only test the moderating role with the professionalism variable. In this case, the intragroup homogeneity is tested in all subgroups, but the differences between radical and gradual innovations are not significant, and we could not test the moderating effect between product and process innovations because of the lack of studies. However, in the comparison between technical ($\bar{r}=0.279$) and administrative innovations ($\bar{r}=0.175$), significant differences exist ($t=1.81$, significance$=0.10$), so this classification of types of innovation exerts a moderating effect. The mean correlation between technical innovation and professionalism is higher than between administrative innovations and the variable, as in other studies (Damanpour, 1987; Zmud, 1982, 1984).

Nevertheless, we could not find a moderating effect in managerial attitude toward change, organisation experience and managerial abilities subgroups (Table 4.5).

Relationship between innovation and organisational design

First, we observe (Table 4.1) a positive and significant correlation between the organisational design and innovation ($\bar{r}=0.152\pm0.027$). However, the variance

Table 4.5 Combined moderator effects: resources and capabilities and innovation

	k	Total sample	Mean correlation	Observed variance	Sampling error variance	75% rule	95% confidence interval
Attitude toward change							
Radical innovation	3	122	0.1945	0.0087	0.0233	100	0.1729
Incremental innovation	3	122	0.1847	0.0113	0.0235	100	0.1735
Technical innovation	3	127	0.2604	0.0719	0.0210	29.2207	0.1641
Process innovation	3	127	0.2604	0.0719	0.0210	29.2207	0.1641
Professionalism							
Radical innovation	3	139	0.2990	0.0193	0.0183	94.7742	0.1530
Incremental innovation	3	139	0.2086	0.0253	0.0202	79.7732	0.1608
Technical innovation	8	410	0.2785	0.0208	0.0169	81.3587	0.0902
Administrative innovation	3	171	0.1751	0.0020	0.0168	100	0.1466
Product innovation	2	114	0.1500	0.0169	0.0171	100	0.1810
Process innovation	3	145	0.2738	0.0030	0.0181	100	0.1521
Number of innovation	9	503	0.2461	0.0197	0.0161	81.6991	0.0828
Experience							
Technical innovation	4	758	0.1104	0.0314	0.0052	16.4715	0.0705
Administrative innovation	2	441	0.0738	0.0169	0.0045	26.7251	0.0930
Product innovation	3	400	−0.0322	0.0367	0.0075	20.5510	0.0983
Number of innovation	6	1205	0.0189	0.0199	0.0050	25.0706	0.0566
Managerial tenure							
Technical innovation	5	348	0.0561	0.0033	0.0145	100	0.1055
Administrative innovation	3	298	0.0625	0.0075	0.0101	100	0.1137

explained by the sampling error accounts for only 11.28 per cent of the total variance. So, heterogeneity between the groups exists, since the rule of 75 per cent is not reached. We then look for moderator variables.

The variables related to organisational design, which we identify in our sample of empirical studies, appear in Table 4.2. Because the groups are still not internally homogeneous (75 per cent rule), we study the moderator effect of types of innovation and of measures of innovation (Table 4.6). Only in the case of specialisation (Table 4.6) we test internal homogeneity in a pair of innovations (process/product), but we cannot confirm the moderator effect because differences between two groups are not high. Neither in the case of centralisation, formalisation, and functional differentiation could we test the moderating effect of type of innovation (Table 4.6).

With regards to measures of innovation (Table 4.6), we only find one measure in these studies (number of innovations), so we cannot test its moderating role, even if there is internal homogeneity in some cases (formalisation and functional differentiation).

Conclusion

In order to compare results obtained from innovation studies, we should pay attention to the types of innovation, as well as the variables belonging to the internal environment of the company and variables related with the market. If the empirical studies control these variables, the heterogeneity between results of innovation studies can be lowered. Thus, the use of meta-analysis is particularly recommended in cases where the academic community does not agree on a matter, particularly on the direction and intensity of the relationship between some core variables analysed in primary studies.

The meta-analytical results suggest that centralisation is an inhibitor factor for the innovation, because the concentration of decision-making authorities makes it difficult for innovative solutions, and the dispersion of power is necessary for innovation (Thompson, 1965). On the other hand, the correlations between specialisation, functional differentiation and professionalism with innovation are positive. A higher degree of professionalism is explained by the existence of a great variety of specialists (Kimberly and Evanisko, 1981) and an increase in the generation of new ideas (Aiken and Hage, 1971). Moreover, when we study the relationship between innovation and professionalism, it is necessary to differentiate between types of innovation, because it influences this relationship.

Results offer empirical evidence about competitive strategy. Thus, the unrelated diversification strategies encourage the short-term position, which inhibits the investment in R&D (Williamson, 1975). By contrast, related diversification strategy is connected with long-term decisions, and this promotes the investment in innovation.

The main limitation of this work is with the fact that primary studies do not facilitate common characteristics, and this information is necessary for evaluating the moderator effects of the theoretical variables on innovation. Another limitation refers to the inability to correct statistical artefacts, because a lack of information is very common in studies involving meta-analysis (Damanpour, 1992; Gooding and Wagner, 1985).

Table 4.6 Combined moderator effects: organisational design and innovation

	k	Total sample	Mean correlation	Observed variance	Sampling error variance	75% rule	95% confidence interval
Centralisation							
Radical innovation	5	234	−0.0516	0.0329	0.0217	66.0113	0.1292
Incremental innovation	5	235	−0.0671	0.0374	0.0215	57.6044	0.1287
Process innovation	7	308	−0.0660	0.0549	0.0231	42.0114	0.1125
Product innovation	3	170	−0.1008	0.0948	0.0176	18.5689	0.1501
Technical innovation	13	788	−0.2078	0.0679	0.0679	22.6258	0.0674
Administrative innovation	5	396	−0.1132	0.0464	0.0125	26.8472	0.0979
Number of innovation	10	702	−0.1177	0.0373	0.0141	37.6270	0.0735
Specialisation							
Radical innovation	3	153	0.6408	0.0194	0.0069	35.7380	0.0943
Incremental innovation	3	153	0.5375	0.0023	0.0101	100	0.1138
Process innovation	5	211	0.5122	0.0210	0.0132	62.7462	0.1007
Product innovation	3	170	0.6435	0.0087	0.0062	71.1492	0.0889
Technical innovation	14	1128	0.5242	0.0233	0.0066	28.3220	0.0426
Administrative innovation	5	546	0.2088	0.0402	0.0085	21.0068	0.0806
Number of innovation	10	875	0.4476	0.0255	0.0074	28.9866	0.0533
Formalisation							
Radical innovation	4	195	−0.0794	0.0724	0.0207	28.5588	0.1409
Incremental innovation	4	195	−0.0234	0.0812	0.0209	25.7645	0.1417
Technical innovation	9	442	0.1042	0.0730	0.0203	27.8661	0.0932
Administrative innovation	4	186	−0.0692	0.0465	0.0218	46.8606	0.1446
Product innovation	3	170	0.1713	0.0603	0.0169	28.0524	0.1472

	k	Total sample	Mean correlation	Observed variance	Sampling error variance	75% rule	95% confidence interval
Process innovation	4	210	0.1777	0.0456	0.0182	39.9557	0.1322
Number of innovation	6	278	−0.2011	0.0302	0.0203	67.2050	0.1140
Functional differentiation							
Technical innovation	4	373	0.4107	0.1490	0.0075	5.0268	0.0848
Administrative innovation	4	373	0.2831	0.0534	0.0092	17.1810	0.0939
Number of innovation	3	225	0.2967	0.0070	0.0112	100	0.1200

Note

1   The present study is part of a wider research, which has received financial support by grants from the Spanish Ministry of Science and Technology, and FEDER (European Fund for Regional Development) (SEC2003–01825/ECO) and the Instituto Valenciano de Investigaciones Económicas (WP-EC 2002–15).

References

Aiken, M. and Hage, J. (1971) The organic organization and innovation. *Sociology* 5, 63–82.

Aiken, M., Bacharach, S. B., French, J. L. (1980) Organizational structure, work process, and proposal making in administrative bureaucracies. *Academy of Management Journal* 23(4), 631–652.

Aldrich, H. E. and Auster, E. (1986) 'Even dwarfs started small: liabilities of age and size and their strategic implications', in L. L. Cummings and B. B. Staw (eds), *Research in Organizational Behavior*, Greenwich, CT: JAI Press.

Amit, R and Wernerfelt, B. (1990): Why do firms reduce business risk?. *Academy of Management Journal* 33(3), 520–533.

Aragón-Correa, J. A. and Cordón-Pozo, E. (2000) La influencia del tamaño, las dimensiones estratégicas y el entorno en la implantación de innovaciones en la organización: internet en las pequeñas y medianas empresas. *Investigaciones Europeas de Dirección y Economía de la Empresa* 6(2), 91–110.

Audretsch, D. B. and Acs, Z. J. (1991) 'Innovation and size at the firm level'. *Southern Economic Journal* 57(3), 739–744.

Baldridge, J. V. and Burnham, R. A. (1975) Organizational innovation: industrial, organizational and environmental impact. *Administrative Science Quarterly* 20, 165–176.

Banbury, C. M and Mitchell, W. (1995) The effect of introducing important incremental innovations on market share and business survival. *Strategic Management Journal* 16, 161–182.

Baum, J. A. C., Calabrese, T., Silverman, B. S. (2000) Don't go it alone: alliance network composition and startups' performance in Canadian biotechnology. *Strategic Management Journal* 21, 267–294.

Buzzell, R. D and Wierserma, F. D. (1981) Modelling changes in market share: a cross-sectional analysis. *Strategic Management Journal* 2, 27–42.

Camisón, C. (2001) La investigación sobre la PYME y su competitividad: balance del estado de la cuestión desde las perspectivas narrativa y meta-analítica. *Papeles de Economía Española, Papeles de Economía Española* 89/90, 43–87.

Camisón-Zornoza, C., Lapiedra-Alcamí, R., Segarra-Ciprés, M., Boronat-Navarro, M. (2004) A meta-analysis of innovation and organizational size. *Organization Studies* 25(3), 331–361.

Cardinal, L. B. (2001) Technological innovation in the pharmaceuical industry: the use of organizational control in managing research and development. *Organization Science* 12(1), 19–36.

Chang, S. J. and Hong, J. (2000) Economic performance of group-affiliate companies in Korea: Intragroup resource sharing and internal business transactions. *Academy of Management Journal* 43(3), 429–448.

Damanpour, F. (1987) The adoption of technological, administrative, and ancillary innovations: impact of organizational factors. *Journal of Management* 13(4), 675–688.

Damanpour, F. (1991) Organizational innovation: a meta-analysis of effects of determinants and moderators. *Academy of Management Journal* 34(3), 555–590.

Damanpour, F. (1992) Organizational size and innovation. *Organization Studies* 13(3), 375–402.

Damanpour, F. (1996) Organizational complexity and innovation: developing and testing multiple contingency models. *Management Science* 42(5), 693–716.

Damanpour, F. and Evan, W. M. (1984) Organizational innovation and performance: the problem of organizational lag. *Administrative Science Quarterly* 29, 392–409.

Dewar, R. D. and Dutton, J. E. (1986) The adoption of radical and incremental innovations: an empirical analysis. *Management Science* 32(11), 1422–1433.

Ettlie, J. E. (1983) Organizational policy and innovation among suppliers to the food processing sector. *Academy of Management Journal* 26(1), 27–44.

Ettlie, J. E., Bridges, W. P. and O'Keefe, R. D. (1984) Organization strategy and structural differences for radical versus incremental innovation. *Management Science* 30, 682–695.

Glass, G. V. (1976) Primary, secondary, and meta-analysis of research. *Educational Researcher* 5, 3–8.

Gooding, R. Z. and Wagner, J. A. (1985) A meta-analytic review of the relationship between size and performance: the productivity and efficiency of organizations and their subunits. *Administrative Science Quarterly* 30(4), 462–481.

Greve, H. R. (1999) The effect of core change on performance: Inertia and regression toward the mean. *Administrative Science Quarterly* 44, 590–614.

Hage, J. (1980) *Theories of Organizations*, New York: Wiley.

Hitt, M. A., Hoskisson, R. E., Ireland, R. D. (1990) Mergers and acquisitions and managerial commitment to innovation in M-form firms. *Strategic Management Journal* 11, 29–47.

Hitt, M. A., Hoskisson, R. E., Kim, H. (1997) International diversification: on innovation and firm performance in product-diversified firms. *Academy of Management Journal* 40(4), 767–798.

Hitt, M. A., Hoskisson, R. E., Ireland, R. D., Harrison, J. S. (1991) Effects of acquisitions on R&D inputs and outputs. *Academy of Management Journal* 34(3), 693–706.

Hunter, J. E. and Schmidt, F. L (1990) *Methods of meta-analysis.* Newbury Park: Sage.

Hunter, J. E., Schmidt, F. L and Jackson, G. B (1982) *Meta-analysis: Cumulating research findings across studies*. Beverly Hills, CA: Sage.

Kimberly, J. R. and Evanisko, M. J. (1981) Organizational innovation: the influence of individual, organizational, and contextual factors on hospital adoption of technological and administrative innovations. *Academy of Management Journal* 24(4), 689–713.

McMillan, G. S., Hamilton, R. D., Deeds, D. L. (2000) Firm management of scientific information: An empirical update. *R&D Management* 30(2), 177–182.

Moch, M. K. and Morse, E. V. (1977) Size, centralization and organizational adoption of innovations. *American Sociological Review* 42, 716–725.

Nord, W. R. and Tucker, S. (1987) *Implementing routine and radical innovation*. Lexington, MA: Lexington Books.

Sánchez-Meca, J. (1999) Metaanálisis para la investigación científica. In F. J Sarabia (ed.), *Metodología para la investigación en marketing y dirección de empresas*. Madrid: Pirámide.

Sengupta, S. (1998) Some approaches to complementary product strategy. *Journal of Product Innovation Management* 15(4), 352–367.

Sharma, A. and Kesner, I. F. (1996) Diversifying entry: some ex ante explanations for postentry survival and growth. *Academy of Management Journal* 39(3), 635–677.

Subramanian, A. and Nilakanta, S. (1996) Organizational innovativeness: exploring the relationship between organizational determinants of innovation, types of innovations, and measures of organizational performance. *Omega* 24(6), 631–647.

Sullivan, P. and Kang, J. (1999) Quick response adoption in the apparel manufacturing industry: competitive advantage of innovation. *Journal of Small Business Management* 37, 1–13.

Szymanski, D. M., Bharadwaj, S. G., Varadarajan, P. R. (1993) An analysis of the market share-profitabiliy relationship. *Journal of Marketing* 57(3), 1–18.

Thompson, V. A. (1965) Bureaucracy and innovation. *Administrative Science Quarterly* 10, 1–20.

Wade, J. (1996) A community-level analysis of sources and rates of technological variation in the microprocessors market. *Academy of Management Journal* 39(5), 1218–1244.

Williamson, O. E. (1975) *Markets and Hierarchies: analysis and antitrust implications*. New York: MacMillan Free Press.

Zmud, R. W. (1982) Diffusion of modern software practices: Influence of centralization and formalization. *Management Science* 28(12), 1421–1431.

Zmud, R. W (1984) An examination of 'push–pull' theory applied to process innovation in knowledge work. *Management Science* 30(6), 727–738.

5 Global ethical challenges and multinational enterprises strategic responses

In search of a new world ethics

John Saee

There will be no survival of our globe without a global ethic.

Hans Kung

Introduction

There has been a sea change in the world economy, with perceived far-reaching consequences on all aspects of human civilisation. This dramatic transformation is largely precipitated by the phenomenon of globalisation.

The transformation now taking place in the global economy is unprecedented. The increasing availability of global capital, coupled with advances in computing and communications technology, is serving to speed up the processes of globalisation. Concurrently, the barriers to globalisation are increasingly disappearing in most countries of the world (11). As a consequence, the word 'globalization' is in daily use throughout the world: *mondialisation* in France, *Globalisierung* in Germany and *Quan qui hua* in China.

Multinational enterprises (MNEs) and entrepreneurs alike are increasingly capitalising on unprecedented business opportunities around the world which are spawned due to globalisation of national economies.

With that in mind, MNEs and entrepreneurs need to exercise due diligence in conducting their businesses in a socially and ethically responsible manner internationally, as unethical business practices are not going to helpful to the sustainability of business enterprises strategically. Ethical behaviour of businesses has become a major issue throughout the world; when a business behaves unethically it is widely publicised by the media to concerned citizens.

Examples of unethical business behaviour that are widely condemned include poor working conditions; low wages; enforced overtime; harsh, sometimes brutal, discipline and corporal punishment; bribery; patent or copyright infringements; lying and deceit about product performance and safety; deliberate use of harmful substances; intentional environmental pollution; discrimination; and violation of promises.

Enron is a prime example of a multinational with serious ethical dilemmas.

It has been dubbed 'one of the worst corporate frauds in history'. But how did they get away with it for so long? In part, flaws in the American legal system are to blame. Enron had the means to audit its own information and its own pension funds, and the opportunity to employ its own auditors/accountants. Personal greed and the need for power were also to blame. Executives covered their tracks by cooking the books and by acquiring many firms, in order to make it seem like the company was booming. But could it have been prevented? Prior unethical behaviour within the firm was uncovered after the bankruptcy. White-collar crimes were not harshly punished in those days, and didn't serve as a deterrent for unethical behaviour (73; 74).

In this research article, an examination is made of ethical practices and propensities across nations that have considerable implications for MNEs and global entrepreneurs.

The world is becoming more and more interdependent due to the increasing globalisation of world economy, mass migration, tourism and worldwide application of information technology, coupled with increasing regional and worldwide cooperation. Thus, MNEs, including entrepreneurs, are now operating within different socio-cultural environments involving people of culturally diverse backgrounds. This can also give rise to many ethical problems facing MNEs and global entrepreneurs and international firms operating in different countries. Some ethical dilemmas may include bribery, deceit/false information, anti-competitive behaviour, discrimination, environmental issues and social responsibility.

Ethical dilemmas in business practices around the globe

Bribery

This is a typical phenomenon facing businesses around the world. Shaw and Berry (62) defined bribery as remuneration for the performance of an act that is inconsistent with the work contract or the nature of the work one has been hired to perform. European law contains measures against corruption exercised within European countries, but unethical behavior of European businesses overseas is not covered within European laws. Moreover, many countries, such as France, Belgium, Greece, Germany and Luxembourg, allow their firms to deduct foreign bribes as business expenses from their taxable income. Multinationals from these and several other countries can actually itemise costs on their tax forms as 'bribes' or 'extortion payments'. In Germany, this particular item of tax deduction is called *nuetsliche ausgaben*, or 'useful expenditure'. These laws give a degree of legitimacy to bribery and extortion and many leaders feel that corruption does not originate in their societies as much as outsiders bringing corruption to their societies (37).

On the other hand, American executives found guilty of bribery outside the USA have been fined heavily and frequently sent to prison (67).

Despite American regulations against bribery, many parts of the business world consider it to be an acceptable or normal practice, regardless of whether it is considered legal or not. A recent report issued by the US Commerce Department estimates that since 1994 foreign firms have used bribes to edge out US multinational companies on some US$45 billion of international deals (34).

Bribery seems to be more extensive in developing nations. There is a prevalence of bribery in most Asian, African and Middle Eastern nations, regardless of its legality. In a number of African nations bribery is such a strong and common norm that it overrides the law (62). In developing countries, government workers have low salaries. High-ranking officials become wealthy or can supplement their salaries through widespread bribery, which appears to be a common and acceptable practice (43).

Even individualistic countries such as Canada and the USA differ among themselves as to the manner in which they view and condone bribery. For example, Canadian law permitted Exxon and General Motors to make large political contributions that are considered illegal in the USA (9).

Bribery in Japan is an open kind of activity that is culturally accepted (12).

Overall, it is estimated that approximately US$85 billion is involved in bribes from developed countries to developing nations.

Universally, bribery is not accepted as an immoral, illegal or unethical business practice despite the American government's desire to level the playing field and assert a universal ethical approach to replace all forms of bribery internationally with competition based solely on merit of the products and services offered by nations (18).

For the purpose of illustration, the following Table 5.1 provides a list of the ten least and ten most corrupt countries in the world.

Table 5.1 Ten least and ten most corrupt countries in the world (ranked by Transparency International Corruption Perceptions Index)

Top ten least corrupt countries		Bottom ten most corrupt countries	
Rank	*Country*	*Rank*	*Country*
1	Finland	81	Mozambique
2	Denmark	82	Kenya
3	New Zealand	82	Russia
3	Sweden	84	Cameroon
5	Canada	85	Angola
6	Iceland	85	Indonesia
6	Norway	87	Azerbaijan
6	Singapore	87	Ukraine
9	Netherlands	89	Yugoslavia
10	United Kingdom	90	Nigeria

Source: adapted from www.transparency.de/documents/cpi/2000/cpi2000.html

False information

Another related issue is the question of deceit/false information facing international trade. One serious detriment to the expansion of international business is the degree to which various nations condone the practice of falsifying information. Lying is a particularly complex phenomenon: the person lying must intend to deceive the person with whom he or she is communicating (1).

In the area of advertising, nations seem to differ in their reactions to deception. In collectivist cultures such as Hong Kong and Malaysia, managers tended to view deceptive advertising as acceptable. On the other hand, the managers in the individualistic cultures (UK and US) did view it as a major problem (56). In Venezuela, however, fraudulent advertising is considered a very grave problem in the business world but not highly unethical when compared to the ranking of other ethical issues (54).

Falsifying reports, according to Hong Kong managers, is a highly unethical practice. Malaysian managers also consider falsifying reports as highly unethical. In Canada, many corporations stress the integrity of books and records (45). Furthermore, abuse of one's expense account was considered more of an ethical issue among employees of American firms than of UK firms even though both nations are classified as highly individualistic. Padding one's expense account was considered by Hong Kong Chinese and Malaysian managers as one of the highest ranked unethical practices (48).

Dealing with competitors

The manner in which companies compete with one another in the international market is a vital issue. If companies feel that some nations do not provide a level playing field for all competitors, they are less inclined to do business there, even with all other things being equal. Two overriding concerns are violation of patents and copyrights and obtaining information about competitors.

Outright violations of patents and copyrights that occur in some nations tend to impede international trade. The International Trade Commission estimated that the US alone loses US$40 billion annually in sales and royalties from the theft of intellectual property (43). Asia, which is a collectivist culture, has been accused of the most serious offences of software piracy. Piracy is still considered legal in Indonesia and Thailand, although software copyright protection legislation has been passed in Japan and the Philippines. Despite the legal aspects against piracy in Japan, a high tolerance level still exists for software piracy activities in this country (63).

Another concern of international companies is the degree to which various nations condone industrial espionage or obtaining information about competitors. Millions, or perhaps billions, of dollars may be lost as a result of such illegal activities.

There are, however, many ways for obtaining information about competitors, some of which are not overtly criminal even though they may well be unethical. These include the following:

- milking potential recruits who have worked for competitors;
- picking brains at conferences;
- conducting a phoney job interview;
- hiring people away from competitors to obtain information;
- interviewing competitors under false pretences;
- debriefing design consultants who have served with competitors;
- grilling suppliers;
- infiltrating customer business operations;
- studying aerial photographs of a company's plant; and
- taking a plant tour (28).

Gaining information from competitors is an ethical grey area and the managers from different countries seem to accept such practices as a fact of doing business in a fast-paced and fast-changing world. Thus, gaining competitors' information is considered ethical behaviour by Hong Kong Chinese managers and Malaysian managers (48) and not a problem for US and UK employees (56).

Environmental and ecological concerns

One of the most pressing and thorny international management problems is the ecological impact of industrialisation around the globe. To protect the environment and the people from the unintended consequences of industrialisation, most developed countries have established numerous regulations and enacted specific environmental legislation. Today, because of the increased knowledge about the environmental impact of industrialisation, there are worldwide pressures and demands to curve the damage to the environment (27).

A study (8) found that there were varying degree of attitudes amongst French, German and American managers when it came to environmental pollution caused by industries. For example, managers from France and Germany believed that the pollution would not harm the environment; on the other hand, US managers would not approve of actions that posed a threat to the environment or released illegal pollutants.

As can be seen, there is a variety of perceptions of ethics in the business world in terms of what constitutes business ethics. However, inquiries into ethics suggest that it is all about right and wrong conduct based on a societal moral standard (58; 59). It is concerned with human relationships, duties and obligations: how we think about and act towards each other, and the consequences of our decisions and actions in terms of human outcomes as opposed to mere profit. Ethics is an important dimension of international management because ethical behaviour in one country is sometimes viewed as unethical in another country. The complexity and interdependency involved in international business management also spills over into the area of social responsibility. While the impact of obligations and the responsibilities of a domestic business are limited to its home environment, those firms involved in international business create a web of interdependent and often conflicting responsibilities that are not easily resolved. For international management there is a wider area of potential misunderstanding, disagreement and dispute.

Society allows organisations to operate within certain parameters and business is expected to operate in a manner consistent with societal interest. The uncertainties are due to differences in the moral philosophies underlying norms and value systems of various cultures (27).

Moral philosophies and their relevance to business ethics

A moral philosophy is conceived in terms of a set of principles or rules that people use to decide what is right or wrong (64). Moral philosophies help explain why a person believes that a certain choice among alternatives is ethically right or wrong (55).

There are several moral philosophies that help shape ethics around the world that have considerable implications for the operations of business enterprises globally.

The leading moral philosophical thoughts can be classified into four categories, which have considerable implications for the business world:

- teleology;
- deontology;
- theory of justice; and
- cultural relativism (55).

Teleology

Teleology tends to advocate that a behaviour or action is acceptable in a society for as long as it produces desired outcomes, such as a promotion at work or a bigger market share for a product or service. Teleological philosophy is often referred to as *consequentialism* by moral philosophers because of the emphasis placed by such philosophies on evaluating the morality of an action mainly by examining its consequences (55).

There are two key teleological philosophies that may have implications for contemporary management practices: *egoism* and *utilitarianism*.

Egoism

Egoism is primarily based on the pursuit of individual self-interest and can be seen as the determinant of individual behaviour. In other words, any action taken by an individual in order to further his or her self-interest is ethically justified. Thus from an egoistic perspective, an act contrary to one's self-interest is an immoral act (35).

Given individual differences, self-interest naturally varies among individuals. For example, for some individuals, money is the most important goal in life but for others it may be acquisition of power and prestige. However, when confronted with choices, an individual would seek out those option(s) that would maximise his or her personal self-interest, and that is in line with the philosophical school of thought based on egoism.

Utilitarian view

The utilitarian approach, initially advanced by the noted English philosopher Jeremy Bentham, tends to argue that decisions are made solely on the basis of their outcome or consequences. It further maintains that the goal of utilitarianism is about maximising the greatest good for the largest number of individuals. John Stuart Mill objected to this, claiming that Bentham's utilitarianism failed to take into account the difference between an honest and a dishonest act that produce the same result (51). Another critique of utilitarianism is that while it insists that total good be maximised, it tells us nothing about the distribution of this good (35).

Meanwhile, Jackson notes, the problem with this school of thought is the question of justice: 'It is perfectly justifiable, using these principles, to persecute the minority in the interest of the majority' (39: 279). This brings us to the notion of morality, which is embedded within the theory of deontology.

Deontology: the theory of rights

Deontology (derived from the Greek word *deon*, meaning 'duty') is an ethical theory holding that acting from a sense of duty rather than concern for consequences is the basis for establishing our moral obligation (51). The noted German philosopher Immanuel Kant, who pioneered this school of thought, believed in a universal moral philosophy, which he referred to as *categorical imperative*. All morality depends on a single categorical imperative that is applied across the entire range of human behaviour. People have capacity to will, they have will-power and it is free. Therefore, humans are able to regulate their own behaviour in accordance with their own law, which is moral law. We demonstrate our freedom when we act in accordance with our moral law. The basis of moral law is formulated in categorical imperative. Formulations of imperative, according to Kant (42) include:

- One should only act on a principle that one can will to be universal law.
- One ought always to act so as to treat humanity, in oneself or in another, as an end in itself, and not as a mere means. Individuals should be treated with respect and dignity as an end in itself; they should not be used as the means to reach the end. A person should not be done harm even if the end aim is good.

Deontology, as promulgated by Kant, is all about 'doing the right thing' as a universal moral duty, which is a lot easier to follow both in business and personal life. On the other hand, teleology, in particular egoism, is problematic in the sense that it ultimately advocates that any means justifies the end. Egoism advocating for self-interest can be closely attributed to the controversial Machiavellianism school of thought that propounds, amongst other things, application of deceit and ruthlessness in the pursuit of self-interest.

Given the heightened awareness and expectations of sound ethical business behaviour among modern consumers, corporate behaviour based on egoism can no longer be justified. In fact, one can argue that it doesn't make business sense for any contemporary organisation to pursue an egoistic corporate behaviour. This is due to the fact that there is a myriad of competitors in today's marketplace who are too keen to satisfy consumers' needs and expectations by making product and service offerings in a responsible manner. Businesses that conduct themselves unethically will be the ultimate losers.

Theory of justice

There are three fundamental guiding principles that the *theory of justice* provides to managers in terms of ethical decision-making:

- be equitable;
- be fair; and
- be impartial (55).

The theory calls for managers to establish standard rules that are equity-based and transparent. At the same time, these rules should be administered to all employees in the same way, thus no individuals should be held responsible for action(s) over which they have no control (i.e. those actions which may fall outside the clearly defined and delegated responsibilities of individual workers).

Cultural relativism in ethical decision-making

According to Donaldson (25), all cultures are different and no culture is any better or worse than any other, they are simply different. It is therefore correct to accept the culture and its values for what they are and not to be judgemental about them.

According to cultural relativism, there is no single right way; therefore, people should not impose their own standards and values on others. For the relativists, nothing is wrong. However, cultural relativism is a flawed concept (69: 29). Norms and practices may indeed vary from society to society, but the prevailing norms and practices in one culture do not themselves determine what actions are ethically right or wrong. Even within a specific cultural context, this is a matter for critical analysis, judgement and debate. It is illogical to infer that because a certain state of affairs exists, it is necessarily right or wrong or the things should remain that way. There is room for moral reform in most societies. Fulop and Linstead argued that the official morality may primarily serve the interests of a ruling minority (for example, in classical Chinese ethics), the ritualistic principles of 'li' justify the need for unquestioning loyalty to rulers and the unequal privileges afforded to these rulers.

The strongest argument against cultural relativism is that the teachings of every religion (Buddhism, Christianity, Confucianism, Hinduism, Judaism and Islam) subscribe to the 'golden rule': do as you would be done by (29).

Business ethics defined

Although business ethics is primarily shaped by societal ethics, however, scholars on business ethics have conceptualised business ethics in a number of ways including:

- business ethics is considered a non-mandatory system of certain standards of behaviour (15);
- business ethics is commercial behaviour guided by a slowly accumulated set of guidelines, which have been found to be necessary for the continuous conduct of commercial relationships (24);
- business ethics is the standards for conduct perceived as right and moral by individuals within an enterprise, taking into account the human welfare of those affected by decisions and behavior (36); and
- 'Business Ethics is applied ethics: it studies the relationship of what is good and right for business' (35: 1).

On the other hand, Grace and Cohen (30) defined business ethics as a complex issue, which covers the interactions between firms, individuals, industries and society.

Why is business ethics needed?

For enterprises to exist in contemporary global markets, it is necessary to incorporate ethical behaviour into their practices. The major reasons behind ethical business practices are:

- to prevent businesses from abusing the rights of the general public. For example, some business practices can cause harm to consumers through the production of defective products – it is the ethical responsibility of these companies to recall such products;
- to protect employees from being subjected to unethical practices. For example, sales representatives should not be given quotas that may induce them to partake in unethical dealings;
- to ensure businesses remain economically viable by complying to the value system of a society in which they operate. That is, for businesses to be successful they must abide by the established ethics of society;
- to protect business itself from unethical practices of employees. For example, if a business has its own set of ethical guidelines, employees will be unable to harm the good name of the business. Such ethical guidelines also provide security against unethical competitors; and

- to act as major motivator for ethical employees to achieve a high degree of productivity (i.e. employees will be proud to belong to a company where sound ethical behavior is the prevailing norm (41).

An international study by Becker and Fritzche (8) found evidence that French, German and American managers overwhelmingly agreed that in the long run sound ethics was good for business. A business cannot afford to have a reputation for *not* behaving ethically, which can in turn be damaging to its business interests.

With these issues in mind, modern organisations are better served by developing sound ethical guidelines for their managers to abide by.

According to De George (19), the following ethical guidelines should be observed by MNEs and global entrepreneurs/managers operating overseas, particularly in Third World countries, if they want to want to be seen to be conducting themselves ethically:

- do no intentional harm. This includes respect for the integrity of the ecosystem and consumer safety;
- produce more good than harm for the host country;
- contribute by their activity to the host country's development;
- respect the human rights of their employees;
- to the extent that local culture does not violate ethical norms, MNCs should respect the local culture and work with and not against it;
- pay their fair share of taxes;
- cooperate with local governments in developing and enforcing just background (infrastructure) institutions (laws, governmental regulation, unions and consumer groups) that serve as a means of social control (19: 3–4).

Equally, it is important for entrepreneurs to strictly adhere to local laws while making every effort for them to be seen to be truthful in the conduct of their business affairs. Moreover, for them to be respected by the host culture they need to show respect for the people and the environment in which they operate. Finally, MNEs and global entrepreneurs need to practise the golden rule: 'do as you would be done by'.

Concluding remarks

In this chapter, a number of perspectives dealing with ethics were discussed that have important implications for MNEs, global entrepreneurs and modern enterprises. It can be concluded that the MNEs, global entrepreneurs and international organisations of today not only have an obligation to abide by sound ethical considerations, but also to preserve the ecological well-being of the planet, respect the host culture, and discharge their social responsibility consistent with a socio-economic view.

While there are no comprehensive guidelines for the conduct of international organisations, some scholars have, however, specified certain behaviour deemed as appropriate for the conduct of businesses globally. De George has suggested that global entrepreneurs/ multinational firms should take the following six steps to act with integrity in their dealings with the people of the world:

- The firm should act in accord with its own self-imposed values, which cannot be less than an ethical minimum, but may well exceed this. For example, a firm may neither give nor take bribes.
- In addition to satisfying the basic moral norms applicable everywhere, the firm should uphold other equally obvious moral rules.
- The firm should enter into business agreements by building on these rules. Business agreements should be fair and benefit both sides.
- Because developing countries are poor in infrastructure, international organisations have special obligations towards them.
- The firm should consider ethical dimensions of its actions, projects and plans before acting, not afterwards. This means that the ethical dimensions should be an integral part of strategic planning.
- Each person should be given his or her due. The MNEs and global entrepreneurs should be open and receptive to complaints from those affected and address their claims with justice (19).

The need for a comprehensive, cohesive and universal code of conduct for entrepreneurs and organisations doing business internationally is paramount. The increase of world trade among global partners and the increase of foreign direct investment mandate that everyone work towards a better understanding and a common ground of precepts upon which to base decisions can help foster and further business and social contacts around the world. The result should be a facilitation of trade, increase in profit and a heightened standard of living (72).

Bibliography

1   Agar, M. (1994) The intercultural frame, *International Journal of Intercultural Relations* 18(2), 221–237.
2   Amba-Rao, S. C. (1993). Multinational corporate social responsibility, ethics, interactions, and Third World governments: an agenda for the 90s, *Journal of Business Ethics,* 12.
3   Baker, B. N., Murphy, D. C. and Fisher, D. (1983) 'Factors affecting project success', pp. 669–685 in D. I. Cleland and D. R. King (eds), *Project Management Handbook*, New York: Van Nostrand.
4   Ball, D. and McCulloch, W. Jr. (1996) *International Business: the challenge of global competition.* Chicago: Irwin.
5   Barnhart, C. and Barnhart, R. (1989) *The World Book Dictionary.* Chicago: Field Enterprises Educational Corporation.
6   Baumhart, R. (1968) *An Honest Profit: what business men say about ethics in business.* NY: Holt, Rinehart and Winston.

7   Becker, H. and Fritzche, D. (1987) 'Business ethics: a cross-cultural comparison of managers' attitudes', *Journal of Business Ethics*, 6, 289–290.

8   Becker, H. and Fritzsche, D. (1987) 'A comparison of the ethical behavior of American, French and German managers', *Columbia Journal of World Business* 22, 87–95.

9   Benson, G. (1992) *Business Ethics in America*. Lexington, MA: Lexington Books.

10 Bourdeau, P. (1988) 'Viva la crise! For heterodoxy in social science', *Theory and Society* 17(5), 773–787.

11 Buller, P. F., Kohls, J. J. and Anderson, K. S. (2000) *Managing Conflicts Across Cultures, Organizational Dynamics*. vol. 28, issue 4, p. 52

12 Caroll, S. J. and Gannon, J. M. (1997) *Ethical Dimensions of International Management*. California: Sage Publications Inc.

13 Carroll, R. (1988) *Cultural Misunderstandings: the French-American experience* (trans. C. Volk). Chicago: University of Chicago Press.

14 Collins, R. and McLaughlin, Y. (1996) *Effective Management*. 2nd edn. North Ryde, NSW: CCH Australia.

15 Crawford, J. W. (1974) *Advertising*. Boston: Allyn and Bacon Inc.

16 Cavanagh G. F., Dennis J., Moberg D. J. and Velasquez, M. (1981) 'The ethics of organizational politics,' *Academy of Management Review* 6(3), 366.

17 Davidson, J. and Cooper, G. (1993) *European Women in Business and Management*. London: Paul Chapman.

18 De George, R. (1986) *Business Ethics*. 2nd edn. New York: MacMillan.

19 De George, R. T. (1993) *Competing with Integrity in International Business*. New York: Oxford University Press.

20 De Mente, B. (1981) *The Japanese Way of Doing Business: the psychology of management in Japan*. Englewood Cliffs, New Jersey: Prentice-Hall.

21 De Mente, B. (1988) *Korean Etiquette and Ethics in Business*. Lincolnwood, Illinois: NTC Business Books.

22 De Mente, B. (1990) *Chinese Etiquette and Ethics in Business*. Lincolnwood, Illinois: NTC Business Books.

23 De Mente, B. (1991) *Japanese Etiquette and Ethics in Business*. Lincolnwood, Illinois: NTC Business Books.

24 Dirksen, C. J. and Kroeger, A. (1973) *Advertising Principles and Problems*. 4th edn. Georgetown: Richard D. Irwin.

25 Donaldson, T. (1989) *The Ethics of International Business*. New York: Oxford University Press.

26 Eyles, Miltenyi, Davis Pty Ltd (1989) *English in the workplace – a shrewd economic investment*. vol. 1. Canberra: AGPS.

27 Fatehi, K. (1996) *International Management: a cross culture and functional perspective*. New Jersey: Prentice Hall.

28 Flax, S. (1984) 'How to snoop on you competitor', *Fortune*, 14 May, 28 –33.

29 Fulop, L. and Linstead, S. (eds) (1999) *Management: a critical text*. South Yarra: Macmillan Education.

30 Grace, D. and Cohen, S. (1998) *Business Ethics: Australian problems and cases*, 2nd edn, Melbourne: Oxford University Press.

31 Heidegger, M. (1962) *Being and Time*. New York: Harper and Row.

32 Hellriegal, Jackson, and Slocum, J. W., Jr (1999) *Management*. 8th edn. Nuremburg: ITP Publishing.

33   Hitt, W. D. (1996) *A Global Ethic: the leadership challenge*, Columbus, Richland: Battelle Press.

34   Hodgetts, R. M. and Luthans, F. (2000) *International Management.* New York: Mc-Graw Hill Inc.

35   Hoffman M. and Moore, J. (1990) *Business Ethics*. 2nd edn. New York: McGraw Hill.

36   Holt, D. H. (1998) *International Management*. London: The Dryden Press.

37   Holt, D. H. and Wigginton K. W. (2002) *International Management*. 2nd edn. Orlando, FL: The Dryden Press.

38   Ivancevich, J., Olekans, M. and Matteson, M. (1997) *Organizational Behavior and Management.* Sydney: McGraw Hill.

39   Jackson, T. (1993) *Organizational Behavior in International Management.* London: Butterworth Heinemann.

40   Jackson, T. (1995) *Cross-cultural management.* UK: Butterworth Heinemann.

41   Jefkins, F. (1973) *Advertising Made Simple.* London: Howard and Wyndham Ltd.

42   Kant I. (1964) *Groundwork of the Metaphysics of Morals* (trans. H. P. Paton). New York: Harper and Row Publishers.

43   Kohls, J. and Butler, P. (1994) Resolving cross-cultural ethics conflict: exploring alternative strategies, *Journal of Business Ethics,* 13, 31–38.

44   Kumar, B. N. and Steinmann, H. (1998) *Ethics in International Management*. Berlin, New York: De Gruyter.

45   Lefebvre, M. and Singh, J. (1992) The context and focus of Canadian code of ethics, *Journal of Business Ethics* 13, 31–38.

46   Mahoney, D., Trigg, M., Griffin, R. and Pustay, M. (1998) *International Business: a managerial perspective*. Melbourne: Addison Wesley Longman.

47   Mayer, D. and Cava, A. (1993) Ethics and the gender equality: Dilemma for US multinationals, *Journal of Business Ethics* 12, 701–708.

48   McDonald, G. and Zepp, R. (1988) Ethical perceptions of Hong Kong Chinese business managers, *Journal of Business Ethics* 7, 835–845.

49   Mead, R. (1998) *International Management: cross-cultural dimensions*. Cambridge, MA: Blackwell.

50   Mead, R. (2000) *International Management: cross-cultural dimensions*. 2nd edn. Cambridge, MA: Blackwell.

51   Mill, J. S. (1957) *Utilitarianism.* New York: Bobbs-Merrill.

52   Mullins, L. J. (1996) *Management and Organizational Behavior.* 4th edn. London: Pitman Publishing.

53   Payne, D., Railborn, C. and Askvik, J. (1997) A global code of business ethics, *Journal of Business Ethics,* 16, 1727–1735.

54   Perdomo, R. (1990) Corruption in business in present day Venezuela, *Journal of Business Ethics* 9, 555–556.

55   Phatak, A. V. (1997) *International Management: concepts and cases.* Cincinnati, OH: South-Western College Publishing.

56   Robertson, D. and Schlegermilch, B. (1993) Corporate institutionalization of ethics in the US and Great Britain, *Journal of Business Ethics* 12, 301–312.

57   Rodrigues, C. (1996) *International Management: a cultural approach.* New York: West Publishing Company.

58   Saee, J. (1993) Culture, multiculturalism and racism: an Australian perspective. *Journal of Home Economics of Australia* 25, 99–109.

59   Saee, J. (1994) Fundamental challenges of social responsibility, ethics, consumerism and the law confronting the world of advertising. Paper presented at the ANZAM conference, New Zealand, 7–10 December.

60   Sanyal, R. (2001) *International Management: a strategic perspective.* New Jersey: Prentice Hall.

61   Sartre, J. P. (1969) *Being and Nothingness: an essay on phenomenological ontology* (trans. H. Barnes). London: Routledge.

62   Shaw, W. and Berry, V. (1989) *Moral Issues in Business.* 4th edn. Belmont, CA: Wadsworth.

63   Swinyard, W., Rinne, H. and Kau, A. (1990) The morality of software piracy: a cross-cultural ethics analysis, *Journal of Business Ethics* 9, 655–664.

64   Taylor, P. W. (1975) *Principles of Ethics: an introduction to ethics.* 2nd edn. California: Dickenson.

65   'Thousands in Pakistan call for end to child labor', *The Philadelphia Inquirer*, 26 April 1995, p. A8.

66   Velasquez, M. G. (1992) *Business Ethics: concepts and cases.* 3rd edn. New Jersey: Prentice Hall.

67   Vogel, D. (1992) The globalisation of business ethics: why America remains distinctive, *California Management Review*, 30–49.

68   Weber, M. (1930) *The Protestant Ethic and the Spirit of Capitalism.* London: Alen and Unwin.

69   Wellman, B. (1992) Which types of ties and networks provide what kinds of social support?, *Advances in Group Processes*, 17(2), 28–45.

70   Weir, D. and Schapiro, M. (1981) *Circle of Poison,* Institute for Food and Development Policy, San Francisco, p. 22.

71   Scholte, J. A. (1996) 'Toward a critical theory of globalisation', pp. 43–57 in Eleonore Hoffman and Gillian Young (eds), *Globalisation: Theory and Practice,* London: Pinter.

72   Payne, D., Railborn, C. and Ashvik, J. (1997) A global code of ethics, *Journal of Business Ethics* 16(18), 1727–1735.

73   Wikipedia, 'Enron'. Available at http://en.wikipedia.org/wiki/Enron

74   Wikipedia, 'Sarbanes-Oxley Act'. Available at http://en.wikipedia.org/wiki/Sarbanes-Oxley_Act

6 Strategic alignment of information systems development

Rafael Lapiedra, Joaquín Alegre and Ricardo Chiva

Introduction

Despite the many well-known success stories of the use of Information Technology (IT) to deliver benefits to organisations, there is considerable evidence that the implementation of information systems (IS) can be hazardous. The success of IS is widely accepted throughout IS research as the principal criterion for evaluating information systems. However, theorists have not agreed on the constructs that best represent IS success. The problem lies in the ambiguity of the concept. DeLone and McLean (1992) construct a model that seeks to establish a unifying taxonomy that can be applied in the selection of IS success constructs for study.

It has long been argued by both practitioners and researchers in the field of IS that the contribution made by large-scale IS deployment to superior business performance is predicated on the dynamic alignment of business and information technology strategies, and the underlying architectures and systems that support strategy execution.

This chapter attempts to analyse one aspect that may play a part in helping the successful strategic alignment of the IS development. We will focus on the analysis of user participation during the development process. The introduction to this chapter is followed by a literature-guided framework, which includes a brief review of the construct of strategic IS alignment. We then identify the users of information systems and analyse the process of acceptance of a new system. Later, we put forward some suggestions that could contribute to a positive participation of users in the development process.

Theoretical background

The concept of strategic alignment between IS and business strategies has already been analysed in the IS literature (Henderson and Venkatraman, 1991; Chan *et al.* 1997, Van der Zee and De Jong, 1999; Reich and Benbasat, 2000; Chan, 2002). Managers should ensure a clear link between business goals and the IS/IT strategies that support them in order to gain some significant value from investment in IT.

Strategic alignment between business and IT is largely influenced by social constructs such as the level of communication between business and IT executives, the level of connection between business and IT planning processes and the level of domain knowledge shared between business and IT executives (Reich and Benbasat, 2000). The difficulties involved in attaining strategic IS alignment may be due to several factors including organisational inertia, gaps in knowledge between IS and business managers, split responsibilities and a tendency to underestimate the problems that are associated with effecting IT-enabled organisational change (Hirschheim and Sabherwal, 2001).

Strategic IS alignment is an extremely complex objective to achieve in practice because IT is often deployed primarily to solve pressing functional and technical problems without regard to overall strategic considerations. Too often, managers fail to anticipate the broader implications for organisational change that the implementation of a new information system generates.

DeLone and McLean (1992) synthesised a six-factor taxonomy of IS success from the diversity of IS success measures used in the literature. The categories of the taxonomy are system quality, information quality, IS use, user satisfaction, individual impact and organisational impact (Figure 6.1).

DeLone and McLean (1992) see use as an IS success variable. They label IS use as the consumption of IS output, which they consider to be a precursor of individual impact. In this model, IS use is required to have a significant impact on achieving system benefits. Although DeLone and McLean did not mention perceived usefulness in their taxonomy, we assume that perceived usefulness is included in the taxonomy category of user satisfaction. Perceptions of usefulness derive from personal valuations of an IS.

We may consider that an IS fails when the output it provides does not match its expectations, when it cannot be developed under given budget constraints, or when users show resistance to the system or simply do not use it. Information systems researchers have documented widespread failures in the implementation of IS (Bostrom and Heinen, 1977; Joshi, 1991).

Laudon and Laudon (2000) estimate that, on average, around 75 per cent of IS fail to achieve the objectives that were initially planned. It would be interesting

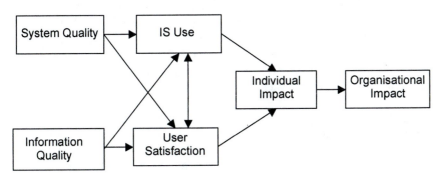

Figure 6.1 Information systems success model (DeLone and Mclean, 1992).

to analyse the reasons for that high failure rate. Although we may find different kinds of reasons that exert an influence on the failure or success of the IS, such as lack of support from top management (Newman and Sabherwal, 1996), poor management practices in the creation of new procedures and roles to adapt to the new information system (Davenport, 1998), and deficiencies in managing its implementation (Smith, 1999), in this chapter we will focus on the lack of user participation during the process of IS development.

IS users

In business, managers are trained to consider the needs of their customers. IS may be considered to be a 'business within a business' and, as such, they must be developed to bear in mind their 'customers', who are the users of the system. They must be considered as important inputs within the process of IS development (McLean, 1979; Panko, 1989).

Land and Hirschheim (1983) have identified different types of users in an organisation:

1   the individuals or group who request the new system;
2   managers or supervisors;
3   individuals and groups whose jobs are locked into the computer system; and
4   individuals and groups outside the organisation who have relationships with the organisation.

It is widely accepted that information systems must be designed to match the needs of their 'customers', that is to say, of 'those whose responsibilities or jobs are supported by the system and then it is reasonable that these people will need to be involved in the establishment of requirements, controlling development and in day to day running' (Avgerou and Cornford, 1998, p. 219).

IS users' satisfaction

Before a system is designed and implemented the future users must know how it is going to affect their jobs. The implementation of an IS may be considered a political process where users' acceptance of the new system will play an important role in its success. Management Information System (MIS) researchers recognise users' acceptance of systems as a major objective of systems implementation (Ginzberg, 1981). We can analyse the process of users accepting a new IS from an equity theory perspective, the applicability of which has already been recognised in the organisational literature (Greenberg, 1982).

Equity theory suggests that individuals are concerned about their inputs, outcomes and the fairness of an innovation or change that is going to be implemented. Individuals are also constantly comparing themselves with others in their reference group to assess whether the relative gains are the same (Adams, 1963). If the individual perceives that the new IS will lead to a decline in their net gains, or inequity compared to others, then they will not accept the new system. On the other hand, if the individual perceives an increase in their equity, they are likely to welcome the new IS.

At this point, a new question could arise, namely, does end-user involvement in the development process ensure that they will perceive an increase in their equity? Like any good question, it does not have a good answer. Nevertheless, we can say that the early involvement of the user in the development of the IS may provide a clear understanding of the consequences it may have for them, and this will eliminate, or at least reduce, the feelings of distrust stemming from the unknown. And, if the new system is going to bring an increase in their equity, they will have a more positive predisposition and will be motivated to work hard on the development of the new IS.

User participation will allow them to gain an understanding of the thinking behind the strategic IS plan and, consequently, resistance to change will be reduced. There must be a trade-off in the number of people who are to be involved in the plan, since the more people you involve, the longer the planning takes to conclude. However, it is also true that the more people you involve, the greater the understanding and support for the plan will be.

User participation

We cannot say that getting users to become willing to participate in the development process will be a panacea. Once we achieve this predisposition we have to see if it is going to be possible for them to participate and if it is going to bring benefits to the process output. Land and Hirschheim (1983) reviewed the problems that may arise from involving users in the process of IS development. They identified problems ranging broadly from political problems concerning competing user groups to more operational ones, such as the difficulty involved in developing system specifications that users can understand.

Thus, user participation in systems development is believed to have positive effects on user acceptance, but it does not guarantee that the process will enjoy positive benefits that will help to make the implementation of the new system successful. And, as Gallivan and Keil (2003) say, it could even be dangerous 'to assume that user participation necessarily leads to successful project outcomes' (p. 39).

Newman and Sabherwal (1996) consider that user participation in software development is beneficial because it improves the process of determining requirements and keeps users informed about the progress being made. These two reasons may lead users to perceive a greater equity leading to higher levels of user satisfaction and system usage. The benefits of user participation, however, will be moderated by other factors, such as the generally assumed fact that there will be effective communication between users and software developers in order to identify the system requirements. In order to obtain the benefits of user participation in the development process it will be necessary to have effective communication between both parties. 'Effective user-developer communication does not occur, either because information is not transmitted between the two groups or because information that is transmitted is somehow misleading or distorted' (Gallivan and Keil, 2003, p. 42). Land and Hirschheim (1983) pointed out the difficulty involved in developing system specifications that are understandable to users as one disadvantage that arises from implicating users in the design process.

Gallivan and Keil (2003) propose a process model that defines four stages for communication between users and software developers:

1 Users become aware of the message they want to communicate to developers.
2 Transmission of messages through one or more communication channels.
3 Developers receive and interpret messages from users.
4 Developers set priorities and take action.

This model suggests that software developers have to look further ahead and read the information content provided by users between the lines. User participation is a generally desirable condition for successful project outcomes, but their mere involvement is not a 'magic bullet' technique that is able to overcome the high failure rate. It must be properly managed to ensure that there will be effective communication between users and software developers in order to identify the system requirements that will allow the strategic alignment of the new IS.

Guidelines for strategic alignment of IS development

When developing an IS, companies all too often think they are merely installing a computer system and they do not spend enough time on analysing the strategic implications of the new system. Neither do they realise that their IS can have significant implications for the way the company is organised and the day-to-day culture of the organisation. To make matters even worse, they often make simplistic assumptions about how the system will change the culture as if by magic (Davenport, 2000).

Effective IS implementation seems to be associated with firms that have superior capabilities for orchestrating the design, deployment, management and use of the required system.

(a)   Ensure the organisational climate

It is essential that those who will by affected by the change share values and visions. The greater the extent of the change, the more important it is that values and visions are shared. With strategic IS planning the focus is on articulating a vision of the role of IS in the organisation and on developing a strategic envelope that defines the parameters for the strategic application of IT systems. Strategic IS planning should be constructed as a dynamic process. Traditional top-down IS planning is no longer suitable. IS/IT planning processes must become more iterative, goal-oriented and evolutionary, and involve a continuous process of organisational learning (Van der Zee and De Jong, 1999).

In many companies, the IS plan is developed by a small number of people, often from the IT department, and some consultants. The plan is then presented to the organisation and, unsurprisingly, it runs into immediate resistance. People do not understand the thinking that went into the plan. A better approach is to involve not just several more IT staff and managers, but also the business managers and their employees who will become the main users of the new system being developed.

There are a number of actions that may contribute to generating the right organisational climate, such as:

- establishing mechanisms for collaboration within the organisation;
- use of participative methods in planning, requirements in elicitation, design and implementation;
- including quality of working life and job satisfaction as specific design objectives for the new system;
- identifying sources of friction and trying to eliminate them. Friction is all too often the result of poor communications; and
- being prepared to share the pay-off from the new system with the workforce. A policy based on equity rather than market forces can transform a hazardous situation.

(b)   Ensure the understanding of all stakeholders

The introduction of a new information system is hampered by uncertainty. A typical reaction to the uncertainty engendered by change is anxiety accompanied by actions aimed at resisting the change. Some of the information required to help all stakeholders to understand what is going on is related to the following:

- the reasons and motivations for the change;
- what pay-offs can be expected from the change, even if these are negative for the stakeholder in question; and
- the process of change, including the role the stakeholder is expected to carry out, the new skills required, and the training that will be followed.

There are a number of actions that may contribute to a better understanding, such as:

- establishing a help and counselling service for the duration of the change;
- arranging group meetings in order to define expected pay-offs and disseminate mission statements;
- providing training to stakeholders at the right time; and
- establishing control mechanisms to identify gaps in understanding through questionnaires and surveys.

(c)   *Set up organisation to manage change*

It is important to identify the obstacles which may hold back the implementation of the project. Obstacles usually come from the poor ability of the organisation to absorb the changes required by the new system. The organisation must be prepared to handle the change that the new IS will entail. In order to manage change, it is recommendable to establish channels throughout the organisation which enable stakeholders at any level to communicate their concern and knowledge. Resistance to change usually arises from the non-availability of communication channels.

It is also highly recommended that charismatic leaders within the organisation are identified and legitimised to guarantee their support for the project.

Implications for managers

Achieving alignment between business and IS/IT is no trivial task. Senior executives should articulate a comprehensible vision and strategy for IT within the business. This will provide the central reference point for all decisions about IS/IT investments. Senior executives should not only articulate the vision but also need to take the steps necessary to ensure that the vision is disseminated throughout the organisation. Managers should also make sure that business and IT are dynamically aligned at both the strategy and execution levels (Grant, 2003). In order to achieve this, both business and IT must form effective collaborative partnerships at all levels. Managers must be willing to bring about the complex organisational changes necessary to facilitate the appropriate deployment and effective use of the systems and the information they produce.

Concluding remarks

For organisations to derive significant value from investment in IT, managers have to ensure there is a clear link between business goals and the IS/IT strategies that support them. The literature reveals a high percentage of failure in the implementation of IS. Lack of user participation in the development process is one of the factors that may cause a system to fail. Early involvement of users in the IS development process will allow them to understand the thinking behind the strategic IS plan and will thus help reduce resistance to the changes that a new IS would bring to the organisation.

User participation is a generally desirable condition for successful project outcomes, but their mere involvement is not a 'magic bullet' technique that is capable of overcoming the high failure rate. It needs to be properly managed to ensure that there will be effective communication between users and software developers that allows identification of the system requirements.

References

Adams, J. S. (1963) Towards an understanding of inequity, *Journal of Abnormal and Normal Social Psychology* 67, 422–436.

Avgerou, C. and Cornford, A. (1998) *Developing Information Systems. Concepts, Issues and Practice.* Basingstoke: Macmillan Press Ltd.

Bostrom, R. P. and Heinen, J. (1977) MIS problems and failures: a socio technical perspective, *MIS Quarterly* 1(3), September, 17–32.

Chan, Y. E. (2002) Why haven't we mastered alignment: the importance of the informal organization structure, *MIS Quarterly Executive*, 1(2), 97–112.

Chan, Y. E., Huff, S. L., Barclay, D. W. and Copeland, D. G. (1997) Business strategy orientation, information systems orientation and strategic alignment, *Information Systems Research* 8(2), 125–150.

Davenport, T. (1998) Putting the enterprise into enterprise systems, *Harvard Business Review*, July–August.

Davenport, T. (2000) The future of enterprise system-enabled organizations, *Information Systems Frontiers* 2(2), 163–180.

DeLone, W. H. and McLean, E. R. (1992) Information systems success: the quest for the dependent variable, *Information Systems Research* 3(1), 60–95.

Gallivan, M. J. and Keil, M. (year?) The user-developer communication process: a critical case study, *Information Systems Journal* 13, 37–68.

Ginzberg, M. J. (1981) Early diagnosis of MIS implementation failure: promising results and unanswered questions, *Management Science* 27(4), 459–478.

Grant, G. G. (2003) Strategic alignment and enterprise systems implementation: the case of Metalco, *Journal of Information Technology* 18, 159–175.

Greenberg, J. (1982) 'Approaching equity and avoiding inequity in groups and organizations', pp. 389–436 in J. Greenberg and R. L. Cohen (eds), *Equity and Justice in Social Behavior*, New York: Academic Press.

Henderson, J. C. and Venkatraman, N. (1991) Understanding strategic alignment, *Business Quarterly* 55(3), 8–14.

Hirschheim, R. and Sabherwal, R. (2001) Detours in the path to strategic information systems alignment, *California Management Review* 44(1), 87–108.

Joshi, K. (1991) A model of users' perspective on change: the case of information systems technology implementation, *MIS Quarterly* June, 229–242.

Land, F. and Hirschheim, R. (1983) Participative systems design: rationale, tools and techniques, *Journal of Applied Systems Analysis* 10, 91–106.

Laudon, K. C. and Laudon, J. P. (2000) *Management Information Systems. Organizations and Technology in the Networked Enterprise.* London: Prentice Hall International.

McLean, E. R. (1979) End users as Applicant Developers, *MIS Quarterly* 3(4), 9–21.

Newman, M. and Sabherwal, R. (1996) Determinants of commitment to information systems development: a longitudinal investigation, *MIS Quarterly* 20 (1), 23–54.

Panko, R. R. (1989) 'Directions and issues in end-user computing', pp. 23–40 in R. R. Nelson (ed.), *End-user Computing. Concepts, Issues and Applications.* New York: John Wiley & Sons.

Reich, B. H. and Benbasat, I. (2000) Factors that influence the social dimension of alignment between business and information technology objectives, *MIS Quarterly* 24(1), 81–114.

Smith, H. L. (1999) A study of strategic information systems design in home health agencies, *Journal of Computer Information Systems* 39)3), 57–68.

Van der Zee, J. T. and De Jong, B. (1999) Alignment is not enough: integrating business and information technology management with the balanced business scorecard, *Journal of Management Information Systems* 16(2), 137–156.

7 Effective global negotiation strategies for corporate managers and leaders in the third millennium

John Saee

Introduction

The twenty-first century is witnessing a spectacular growth in globalisation of trade across national boundaries, made possible through the exporting of products and services, offshore operations, strategic alliances/joint ventures, mergers and acquisitions, and licensing and distribution agreements.

In early 2006, Luxembourg-based steelmaker Arcelor, which had successfully lured Canada's Dofasco away from Germany's ThyssenKrupp the previous year, became itself the acquisition target of Mittal Steel, an Indian-controlled firm headquartered in the Netherlands. During the same period, US-owned Boeing sold 27 787-Dreamliners to Air India and finalised a supply contract with Japan's Toray for the carbon fibre needed to produce the aircraft. In China, Google Inc. (US) negotiated with government authorities over regulatory conditions for operation of their Internet search engine. These are but a few examples of the millions of international business (IB) negotiations that occurred during early 2006. These were the headline grabbers, but less prominent actors also negotiated across borders. All told, the amount of IB negotiation worldwide seems to have exploded in recent years and shows no signs of abating (34).

Meanwhile, much of the global trade which occurs around the world involves face-to-face negotiations amongst entrepreneurs and representatives of firms who are engaged in making business deals, literally on a daily basis. Arguably, successful negotiators display a highly developed intercultural communication competence – an essential criterion to conduct successful negotiation across the globe.

International negotiation is very complex and difficult because it involves different laws, regulations, standards, business practices and, above all, cultural differences. Most of the difficulties in international negotiations, however, are due to cultural differences. That is why negotiation today is considered one of the single most important global business skills. The saying 'when in Rome, do as the Romans do' is an indication of our awareness that to succeed in international negotiation we need to suppress our ethnocentric tendencies. To successfully conclude a business deal, labour agreement or government contract with foreigners, who are in most respects different from us, requires a considerable amount of communication skill. To successfully manage such negotiations, businesspeople need to know how to influence and communicate with members of a culture other than their own (3). It is, therefore, important to understand the cross-cultural sensitivities related to negotiation, and the appropriate strategies and tactics to suit a particular situation. This research article examines the various types of negotiations and negotiation styles that may be adopted by entrepreneurs under different conditions and cultural milieus to reach an agreement while conducting business across cultures.

Negotiation defined

Negotiation is conceived as

> a process in which at least one individual tries to persuade another individual to change his or her ideas or behavior and it often involves one person attempting to get another to sign a particular contract or make a particular decision. Thus negotiation is the process in which at least two partners with different needs and viewpoints need to reach an agreement on matters of mutual interest.
>
> (5: 152)

Meanwhile, Acuff has defined negotiation as the process of communicating back and forth for the purpose of reaching a joint agreement about differing needs or ideas. Negotiation is a process in which two or more parties exchange goods or services and attempt to agree upon the exchange rate for them (1).

Arising from the foregoing definitions is the question whether the same applies to cross-cultural negotiation, an important issue that this chapter is dedicated to exploring in some detail.

Cross-cultural negotiation defined

A negotiation becomes cross-cultural when the parties involved belong to different cultures and therefore do not share the same ways of thinking, feeling and behaving (5). Thus, the meaning of the term negotiation and what it connotates can significantly vary from one culture to another. For example, Americans view negotiations as an opportunity to resolve contentious issues; Japanese, Chinese, and Mexican cultures view negotiations as a vehicle to establish a relationship – resolving problematic issues is never the first goal (25).

All global negotiations are cross-cultural. Some domestic negotiations, in spanning across two or more ethnic groups, are also cross-cultural. Global negotiations contain all of the complexity of domestic negotiations, with the added dimension of cultural diversity (2).

Cross-cultural negotiations can be very intricate, as each culture, whether it is a high or low context culture, has its own distinctive approach relating not only to the negotiating process but also to their individual and religious practices, idiosyncrasies and expectations, with each culture cohering to their own norms, values, laws and beliefs, impacting on the outcome of the agreement. Members of different cultures focus on diverse aspects of an agreement, for example, one may focus on the legal side and the other on the personal aspects. In some cultures, documenting the agreement is significant while in others the process and actual implementation is the focal point (13). For example, Americans negotiate a contract, while the Japanese negotiate a personal relationship. This is all due to the differences in cultural values and norms which stems from the dissimilarity in individualistic cultures, such as the USA, and collectivist cultures, namely Japan (23).

Cross-cultural negotiations consume much time of global managers and negotiation is often ranked as one of the most imperative skills for global managers to possess (10). From small firms, export departments and international companies to multinational corporations and politics throughout the world face-to-face negotiation or negotiation via technology is becoming increasingly widespread. Negotiations are undertaken for numerous purposes: international joint ventures, licensing agreements, seller-buyer relationships, mergers and acquisitions, just to name a few. Even domestic companies that are not multinational in their structure must encounter the challenge of globalisation (31). Global managers spend more than 50 per cent of their time negotiating, and this illustrates the importance of cross-cultural negotiation (2).

Components of negotiation

In any negotiation, we can identify three components:

- the process;
- the parties; and
- the agreement or the outcome of the negotiation.

Complications in negotiation arise as the two parties may have different objectives. These objectives may be different from what each party requires from the agreement or different in respect that one party may not even want an agreement. Another issue leading to complication could be that the intended routes of the two parties to arrive at the objectives might be quite different. The fact that these issues are often compounded in cross-cultural settings makes the process still more convoluted.

Types of negotiation

Based on cultural dimensions, there are essentially two types of negotiations: intracultural and intercultural (8).

Intracultural negotiations assume similarity in culture and fields of experience among negotiating parties. Based on this assumption, negotiating strategies are devised to influence the other party's position. Much of negotiation skills involve accomplishing three tasks:

- bringing your own perceptions in line with reality;
- ascertaining the other sides perceptions of the proposed transaction and the available alternatives; and
- finding ways to favourably alter the other side's perceptions (11).

Intercultural negotiation is about effective intercultural communication which is at the heart of successful international negotiation. Intercultural negotiation encompasses all the challenges arising from intracultural communication in addition to the difficulties relating to cultural diversity. Thus, it is worthwhile examining the influence of cultures on negotiation.

Cross-cultural influences on negotiations

Cultural differences, for example, influence the size of the team directly involved in the negotiation. According to Hofstede's cross-cultural dimensions; most Western cultures are based on individualism. In contrast, Asian, Middle Eastern and most South American cultures are predicated on the notion of collectivism. In cross-cultural negotiations, this dimension is reflected through the type of individual selected to attend negotiating sessions and to essentially make the decision. Negotiating teams from collectivist society tend to be large. For example, the Japanese as a collectivist culture prefer to use a large contingent of negotiating team. Whereas, for an individualistic culture, such as America, it is not unusual to send a single person who could represent them at the negotiating table. In addition, research (30) showed that younger negotiators are more common among American teams than in other cultures, and they are more likely to take the final decision. While a collectivist culture negotiating team, such as an Asian team that respects seniority, is likely to be led by a senior who has high status. He may play a little part in the detailed discussions but has an important 'figurehead' role (22). Further, in a collectivist culture, such as Asia, subordinates would brief superiors, who in turn use their influence to negotiate and make decisions. Everyone affected by the decision is included in the process (30).

Collectivist societies consider people very important. It is difficult for collectivists to separate people from the issues. For the same reason, collectivists are very much reluctant to express disagreement openly. Consequently, non-verbal and indirect communication cues play an important role in negotiation with collectivists. To succeed in business in Korea, for example, a person needs an extraordinary skill to read *nunchi*, which means the look in a person's eyes, the non-verbal reaction of a person to a question (7; 8).

As such, an understanding of cultural difference based on individualism/collectivism is essential for a cross-cultural negotiator who may need to incorporate these aspects as part of their overall negotiating strategies.

Based on Hofstede's analysis of cultural dimensions, negotiations between people of masculine and feminine cultures may also present challenges for them to overcome. For the negotiators from masculine societies, ego-preservation is essential. For them, to compromise may give the appearance of giving in, which could be considered a sign of weakness. On the other hand, negotiators from feminine cultures may not be aware of the importance of ego for the people of masculine cultures. Building the ego of their counterparts and focusing on the task at hand may help advance negotiations faster (8).

Negotiation is more difficult between the people of different cultures who have different value systems. Negotiators from a high-power distance culture may need more information to convince their superiors of the value of the agreement. They may also take a longer time because they have to clear most decisions with those in the position of power.

Views on the expected outcomes of the negotiation may also be culturally based. Specifically, the expected outcomes of any negotiation may be either integrative or distributive. *Integrative outcomes*, or win–win situations produce mutual benefits to both parties. Integrative negotiations result in great benefit for both parties and stable relationship (4; 8). *Distributive outcomes* are the result of competition among negotiators. Distributive negotiation is a win–lose scenario in which the negotiators believe that they have opposing interest and incompatible alternative choices (26). Americans tend to have a short-term distributive way of negotiation as they are concerned with their own interests and view negotiations competitively, often arriving at distributive outcomes.

In contrast, most Asians view negotiation as a long-term relationship and a cooperative task (20).

For example, Japanese negotiators emphasise harmonious interdependence in doing business with others, which is indicative of a distributive way of negotiating based on collectivist culture (21).

Bargaining and negotiation are a part of daily life in the Middle East. Foreigners who want to establish business relationships in the Middle East should be ready to combine personal relationships with business transactions (1).

The negotiation process

Process is the single most important factor predicting the success or failure of a negotiation. An effective process includes managing the negotiation's overall strategy or approach, its stages and the specific tactics used. As with other aspects of negotiating, process varies markedly across cultures. An effective strategy reflects the situational characteristics and personal backgrounds of the negotiators involved. It balances the position, procedure, timing and roles of the negotiating partners (2).

To successfully negotiate globally, Fisher and Ury (1981) advocate for a culturally synergistic approach, based on a principled negotiation method, which could lead to fruitful cross-cultural negotiations. This approach involves four steps:

1   separating the people from the problem;
2   focusing on interests, not on positions;
3   insisting on objective criteria (and never yielding to pressure); and
4   inventing options for mutual gain.

Principled negotiation provides participants to the negotiation with a method of focusing on the basic interests and the mutually advantageous solutions. It enables parties to reach agreement without haggling and posturing (8).

Stages of a negotiation

There are several basic steps involved in managing the negotiation process. The first phase typically begins with planning.

Planning

Planning starts with negotiators identifying those objectives they would like to attain. Next, consideration is given to areas of common ground between the parties. Other major areas include:

- the setting of limits on single point objectives;
- dividing issues between short-term and long-term considerations; and
- determining the sequence in which to discuss various issues (6).

Meanwhile, Raider advocates that successful negotiators' planning behaviour differs from less-skilled negotiators in terms of the following criteria:

- *Planning time*: successful negotiators use time in ways that are more fruitful to negotiation outcome than average negotiators and this is where successful negotiators tend to pay a lot of attention on how to use available time so as to advantage their negotiations.
- *Exploring options*: successful negotiators are inclined to come up with more wide-ranging options than average negotiators, thereby increasing their chances of success.
- *Establishing common ground*: unlike average negotiators, successful negotiators are more focused on developing common ground than paying attention to areas of conflict rather than agreement.
- *Focusing on long- versus short-term horizons*: successful negotiators are strategically focused and therefore spend more time on long-term issues than short-term issues, whereas average negotiators do not spend a substantial amount of time on strategic issues.
- *Setting limits*: unlike average negotiators, successful negotiators are focused on developing a range of objectives, thereby providing them with the flexibility necessary to succeed in their bargaining.

- *Using sequence versus issue planning*: in contrast to average negotiators, successful negotiators discuss each issue under negotiation independently with no preconceived sequence or order of priority during the negotiation process (28).

Interpersonal relationship building

The second phase of the negotiation process involves getting to know the people on the other side. This 'feeling out' period is characterised by the desire to identify those who are reasonable and those who are not. This is particularly important for collectivist cultures, as the essence of any negotiation is primarily based on how much trust is in an interpersonal relationship between partners involved in negotiation.

Exchanging task-related information

In this part of the process, each group sets forth its position on the critical issues. At this point the participants are trying to find out what the other party wants to attain and what it is ready to give up. In negotiating, cross-cultural miscommunication can give rise to numerous hurdles for the parties involved. Here is what happened as a result of the Iranians' misinterpretation of a bargaining offer in English.

> In Persian, the word *compromise* apparently lacks the positive meaning it has in English (a 'midway solution both sides can live with') and has only a negative meaning ('her virtue was compromised' or 'our integrity was compromised'). Similarly, the word *mediator* in Persian suggests 'meddler', someone who is barging in uninvited. In early 1980, United Nations Secretary General Waldheim flew to Iran to deal with the hostage question. His efforts were seriously set back when Iranian national radio and television broadcast in Persian a remark he reportedly made on his arrival in Tehran: 'I have come as a mediator to work out a compromise.' Within an hour of the broadcast, his car was being stoned by angry Iranians.
>
> Fisher and Ury (9: 33).

As can be seen from the foregoing example, a lack of proper understanding of language within its own cultural context can pose a serious hindrance to successful cross-cultural negotiations.

Persuasion

This is the most important step. The success of the persuasion often depends on:

- how well the parties understand each other's position;
- the ability of each party to identify the areas of similarity and differences;

- the ability to create new options; and
- the willingness to work towards a solution.

Goldman propounds that in negotiation what counts is not the reality but the party's perception of reality (11). There are two extreme negotiating positions of hard and soft. Those taking hard positions see every negotiation as a contest of wills. They believe that by taking extreme positions and holding out longer, they will fare better. Often, the other party responds by taking an equally hard position. This exhausts both parties and damages their long-term relationship. On the other hand, soft positions may create a one-sided deal and ill feelings. Avoiding confrontation and taking the more accommodating soft position may result in an undue advantage for the other party. Both hard and soft approaches to negotiation are not constructive. The best way would be negotiating on merits or principled negotiations (9).

With this in mind, one must also be aware of the negotiation styles across cultures which play a crucial role in persuasion.

For example, Americans push hard for direct answers and fill potential periods of silence with rhetorical embellishments. Latin Americans may simply change the topic when it becomes too pointed or uncomfortable. Chinese negotiators, on the other hand, try to avoid conceding any points until the talks near their culmination point. The Japanese seem unemotional in their persuasive techniques, whereas Koreans, Italians and Middle Eastern negotiators often rely on bravado and intimidation tactics (15).

Agreement

The final phase is the granting of concessions and hammering out of a final agreement. To negotiate effectively in international arenas, it is necessary to understand how cultural differences between the parties affect the process. For example, the way Americans negotiate is different from Russians and Asians in that Americans negotiate an issue at a time and then once that issue is resolved, they then move on to focus on the next issue. Whereas, Asians and Russians tend to negotiate a final agreement on everything and few concessions are given until the end (29).

Cross-cultural dimensions affecting negotiations

To negotiate effectively, it is important to have a sound understanding of the other side's culture. This includes consideration of areas such as communication pattern, time orientation and social behaviours (33; 34). One negotiation expert recommends the following:

- Do not identify the counterpart's home culture too quickly. Common cues (e.g. name, physical appearance, language, accent and location) may be unreliable. The counterpart probably belongs to more than one culture.
- Beware of the Western bias toward 'doing'. In Arab, Asian and Latin

groups ways of 'being', including feeling, thinking and talking, can shape relationships more powerfully than doing.

- Try to counteract the tendency to formulate simple, consistent, stable images. Not many cultures are simple, consistent or stable.
- Do not assume that all aspects of the culture are equally significant. In Japan, consulting all relevant parties to a decision is more important than presenting a gift.
- Recognise that the norm for interactions involving outsiders may differ from those for interactions between compatriots.
- Do not overestimate your familiarity with your counterpart's culture. An American studying Japanese wrote New Year wishes to Japanese contacts in basic Japanese characters but omitted one character. As a result, the message became 'dead man, congratulations' (33).

When to negotiate?

Given the enormity of global trade, it begs the question whether one would always need to negotiate in order to successfully conclude a business deal. Based on an unanimous view held by global negotiations experts, negotiation is not always the best approach to doing business. Sometimes the best strategy is to 'take it or leave it'; other times bargaining, and on some occasions negotiations involving problem solving, are most appropriate (28). Negotiation, compared with bargaining and the take-it-or-leave-it approach, demands more time. Managers should negotiate when the value of the exchange and of the relationship is important; as, for example, within the growing number of global strategic alliances.

Negotiating is generally the preferred strategy for creating win–win solutions in the global business environment. Business people should, for example, consider negotiating when any of the following conditions are apparent:

- their power position is low relative to their counterparts;
- the trust level is high;
- the available time is sufficient to explore each party's multiple needs, resources, and options; and
- commitment – not mere compliance – is important to ensure that the agreement is carried out (2).

Who should negotiate?

The other party's decisions about their representation at the negotiating table should also affect the composition of the negotiating team. Choices of representation vary. Greek and Latin American top managers may prefer to maintain personal control of all aspects of the process, and so may head the team rather than delegate to a subordinate. The identity of the other team is dealt with in terms of number of functions, gender, age and rank (23).

Number of functions

A single negotiator faces obvious difficulties if sent up against a team representing the full range of functions in the other organisation. The team from China or Japan represents a wide range of constituent groups within the organisation. An American team often includes a legal representative, which is perceived as hostile and threatening by the Japanese.

Gender

A team that includes women may be at an advantage in feminine cultures such as in Scandinavian countries, but not where women are not normally accepted in business, for instance in Arab countries.

Age

An Anglo-company may be mistaken in selecting a young high-flier to head a team negotiating with a Chinese or Japanese team. The Asian team is likely to be led by a senior and older person who has a high status as he takes a significant 'figurehead' role.

Rank

The problem of matching team leader is complicated by the far wider currency of the title 'vice president' in the US than in Japanese organisations. In the USA, the company may have twenty vice presidents whereas a Japanese company of equal size has three or four. Moreover, the ranks are not always matching across cultures (23).

Developing effective negotiation skills

According to Fisher and Ury, the essence of effective negotiation can be achieved by following these steps:

- research your opponent: acquire as much information as you can about your opponent's interests and goal for the purpose of understanding your opponent's behaviour, predicting their responses to your options and to frame solutions;
- begin with a positive overture;
- address problems not personalities;
- pay little attention to initial offers. Treat an initial offer as merely a point of departure as they tend to be extreme and idealistic;
- emphasise win–win solutions. If conditions are supportive, look for an integrative solution; and
- be open to accepting third party assistance (9).

Individual qualities of negotiators

The role that individual qualities play varies across cultures. For example, favourable outcomes are most strongly influenced by the negotiator's own characteristics in Brazil, the opponent's characteristics in the USA, the negotiator's role in Japan and a mixture of negotiator's and opponent's characteristics in Taiwan (12). Specifically, Brazilian negotiators achieve higher profits when they act more deceptively and in their own self-interest. American negotiators do better when their counterparts are honest, not self-interested and introverted. In Taiwan negotiators do better when they act deceptively and when their counterparts are neither self-interested nor have particularly attractive personalities. The key individual characteristics of negotiators for these four countries are given in the following Table 7.1.

Different approaches to negotiation

There are essentially two general approaches to negotiation, and they are *distributive bargaining* and *integrative bargaining*.

Distributive bargaining refers to the negotiations that seek to divide up a fixed amount of resources and is a win–lose solution. When engaged in distributive bargaining, the negotiator should focus on trying to get the opponent to agree to his specific target point or to get as close to it as possible (30).

This style of negotiation is most common amongst Americans.

In the same vein, Kuhn, a negotiation expert, advises American negotiators:

Table 7.1 Key individual characteristics of negotiators in different countries

American negotiator	Japanese negotiator	Chinese (Taiwan) negotiator	Brazilian negotiator
Preparation and planning skills	Dedication to job	Persistence and determination	Preparation and planning skills
Thinking under pressure	Perceive and exploit power	Win respect and confidence	Thinking under pressure
Judgement and intelligence	Win respect and confidence	Preparation and planning skills	Judgement and intelligence
Verbal expressiveness	Integrity	Product knowledge	Verbal expressiveness
Product expertise	Demonstrate listening skills	Interesting	Product expertise
Perceive and exploit power	Broad perspective	Judgement and intelligence	Perceive and exploit power
Integrity	Verbal expressiveness		Competitiveness

Source: Graham (12, as adapted by Adler (2)).

Don't worry what others get. Don't worry what others think. Just know what you want to accomplish. Keep your eye on the ball and don't allow extraneous pressures to distract you. A good deal maker is constantly enhancing his or her perceived power. The trick is track record. Everyone wants to associate with a winner.

(19: 27)

In contrast to distributive bargaining, integrative bargaining operates under the assumption that there is at least one settlement that results in a win–win situation for the parties involved in the negotiation. This is indicative of Japanese, Chinese and South Americans, which are based on collectivist culture.

In general, integrative bargaining is preferable to distributive bargaining as it builds long-term relationships and facilitates working together in the future. It bonds the negotiators and allows them to leave the bargaining table feeling that they have both achieved victory. Such an integrative strategy is recommended for cross-cultural negotiations.

Table 7.2 provides a comparison between integrative bargaining versus distributive bargaining strategies.

Negotiation strategies: some guidelines

Acuff suggests the following ten negotiation strategies that will work anywhere in the world:

- plan the negotiation;
- adopt a win–win approach;
- maintain high aspirations;
- use language that is simple and accessible;
- ask a lot of questions then listen with your eyes and ears;
- build solid relationships;
- maintain personal integrity;
- conserve concessions;
- be patient; and
- be culturally literate and adopt the negotiating strategies of the host country

Table 7.2 Distributive bargaining versus integrative bargaining

Bargaining characteristics	Distributive bargaining	Integrative bargaining
Available resources	Fixed amount of resources to be divided	Variable amount of resources to be divided
Primary motivation	'I win, you lose'	'I win, you win'
Primary interest	Opposed to each other	Compatible with each other
Focus on relationship	Short-term view	Long-term view

Source: adapted from Lewicki and Litterer (20).

environment (1).

On the other hand, Kirkbride and Tang have argued that for any negotiator to succeed in their negotiations, they need to observe the following rules:

- always set explicit limits or ranges for the negotiation process;
- always seek to establish general principles early in the negotiation;
- always focus on potential areas of agreement and seek to expand them;
- avoid taking the negotiation issues in sequence;
- avoid excessive hostility, confrontation and emotion;
- always give the other party something to take home; and
- always prepare to negotiate as a team (18).

Negotiation tactics

Negotiation includes verbal, non-verbal and situational tactics. Prevalence of these tactics is at variance across cultures. Individualist cultures representing Australians and Americans would consider verbal tactics to be most important, whereas people from collectivist cultures, such as Asians, would prefer non-verbal tactics during their cross-cultural negotiations. A brief discussion of negotiation tactics is merited here.

Verbal tactics

Negotiators use many verbal tactics. Some of the more common tactics used in negotiations include promises, threats, recommendations, warnings, rewards, punishments, normative appeals, commitments, self-disclosure, questions and commands. The use and meaning of many of these tactics varies across cultures.

Research shows that the profits of a negotiator increase when they (1) make a high initial offer; (2) ask a lot of questions; and (3) do not make any verbal commitments until the end of the negotiating process. In short, verbal behaviour is critical to the success of negotiations (14).

Non-verbal tactics

Non-verbal behaviour represents communication other than verbal. It includes how the negotiators express the words rather than the words themselves. Non-verbal behaviour subsumes tone of voice, facial expressions, body distance, dress, gestures, timings, silences and symbols. Non-verbal behaviour conveys multiple messages, many of them responded to at a subconscious level. Negotiators frequently respond more emotionally and powerfully to the non-verbal than the verbal message. As with verbal behaviour, non-verbal behaviour also differs considerably across cultures. For example, the Japanese use the most silence, Americans a moderate amount, and Brazilians almost none at all. Americans often respond to silence by assuming that the other team disagrees or has not accepted their offer.

Moreover, they tend to argue and make concessions in response to silence. This response does not cause problems in negotiating with Brazilians, but it severely disadvantages Americans when they are dealing with the Japanese. While the Japanese silently consider the Americans' offer, the Americans interpret the silence as rejection and respond by making concessions (e.g. by lowering the price) (2).

Situational tactics

Another set of tactics generally used could be classified as situational tactics, which include location, time limit and physical arrangement.

Location

Where negotiation should be held is a significant consideration in terms of a successful negotiation. Most negotiators select neutral locations for various forms of negotiations. Business entertainment has become a main feature of neutral location, used by the negotiating team primarily for becoming acquainted with members of the opposing team. Japanese business people spend almost 2 per cent of their GNP on entertaining clients – even more than they spend on national defence (1.5 per cent) (2). However, using a neutral site results in a number of benefits, such as each party having limited access to its home office for receiving a great deal of negotiating information and advice for gaining an advantage over the other. Secondly, the cost of staying at the site is often quite high, so both sides have an incentive to conclude negotiations quickly (14).

Time limit

It is an important negotiation tactic when one party is under a time constraint. The duration of a negotiation can vary markedly across cultures. Americans, being particularly impatient, often expect negotiations to take a minimum amount of time.

> During the Paris Peace Talks, designed to negotiate an end to the Vietnam War, the American team arrived in Paris and made hotel reservations for a week. Their Vietnamese counterparts leased a chateau for a year. As the negotiations proceeded, the frustrated Americans were forced to continually renew their weekly reservations to accommodate the more measured pace of the Vietnamese.
>
> Adler (2: 200)

Concessions in negotiations are usually made towards the time deadline of the party making the concession. This obviously puts time-conscious cultures, such as Americans, at a disadvantage (16).

Physical arrangements

Sitting around a boardroom table at opposite sides emphasises a confrontation situation. Sitting at right angles and facing the problem to solve rather than the other party engenders co-operation. In America the negotiating parties sit opposite each other, whereas in Japan the negotiating parties sit at right angles and face the problem together (2). For example, the physical arrangement, as shown by the Japanese is indicative of their emphasis on harmony in their approach to negotiation, which is based on their collectivist culture.

Concluding remarks

In this chapter the definition of negotiation was provided along with conceptualisations of negotiations across cultures. Further, it was argued that negotiations could be classified into intracultural and intercultural. To negotiate a business deal, international managers need to recognise the cultural differences in communication and negotiation styles. Accordingly, the skills need to be developed and appropriate strategies and tactics are to be used. Some cultures view negotiation as a competitive game, whereas some other cultures view negotiations as a relationship building exercise. Such different views call for different types of negotiations and different skills.

Finally, international managers would greatly benefit by developing high-level intercultural communication competence, a key contributing factor to successful international negotiations.

References

1   Acuff, F. L. (1993) *How to Negotiate Anything with Anyone Anywhere Around the World*. New York: American Management Association.

2   Adler, N. (1997) *International Dimensions of Organizational Behavior*. 3rd edn. Ohio, USA: South-Western College Publishing.

3   Adler, N. J. and Graham, J. L. (1989) Cross-cultural interaction: the international comparison fallacy. *Journal of International Studies* 20(3), 515–537.

4   Bazerman, M. H. and Neal, M. A. (1982) Improving negotiations effectiveness: under final offer arbitration: the role of selection and training. *Journal of Applied Psychology* 67, 543–554.

5   Casse, P. (1981) *Training for the Cross-cultural Mind*. 2nd edn. Washington DC: Society for Intercultural Education, Training and Research.

6   Chaney, L. H. and Martin, S. J. (1995) *International Business Communication*. Englewood Cliffs, NJ: Prentice Hall.

7   De Mente, B. (1991) *Japanese Etiquette and Ethics in Business*. Lincolnwood, Illinois: NTC Business Books.

8   Fatehi, K. (1996) *International Management: a cross culture and functional perspective*. Englewood Cliffs, NJ: Prentice Hall.

9   Fisher, R. and Ury, W. (1981) *Getting to Yes*. Penguin, NY.

10   George, J. M., Jones, G. R. and Gonzalez, J. A. (1998) The role of affect in cross-cultural negotiations. *Journal of International Business Studies* 29, 749–72.

11   Goldman, A. L. (1991) *Settling for More*. Washington DC: The Bureau of National Affairs.
12   Graham, J. (1983) Brazilian, Japanese and American business negotiations. *Journal of International Business Studies* 14(1), 47–56.
13   Gulbro, R. and Herbig, P. (1995) Differences in cross-cultural negotiation behavior between manufacturers and service-oriented firms. *Journal of Professional Services Marketing* 13, 23–29.
14   Hodgetts, R. M. and Luthans, F. (2000) *International Management*. New York: McGraw Hill Inc.
15   Holt D. H. and Wigginton K. W. (2002) *International Management*. 2nd edn. Orlando, USA: Harcourt, Inc.
16   Jackson, T. (1993) *Organizational Behavior in International Management*. London: Butterworth Heinemann.
17   Jackson, T. (1995) *Cross-cultural Management*. Oxford: Butterworth Heinemann.
18   Kirkbride, P. S. and Tang, S. F. Y. (1995) 'Negotiations: lessons from behind the bamboo curtain', pp. 293–304 in T. Jackson (ed.), *Cross Cultural Management*, Oxford: Butterworth Heinemann.
19   Kuhn R. L. (1988) *Dealmaker: all the negotiating skills and secrets*. New York: John Wiley and Sons.
20   Lewicki, R. J. and Litterer, J. A. (1985) *Negotiations*. Homewood, IL: Irwin.
21   Lituchy, R. (1993) 'Negotiating with Japanese: Can we reach win–win agreement?' Paper presented at the Academy of International Business conference, 21–25 October.
22   Markus, H. R., Kitayama, S. (1991) Culture and the self-implications for cognition, emotion and motivation. *Psychological Review* 98, 224–253.
23   Mead, R. (1998) *International Management: cross-cultural dimensions*. Cambridge, MA: Blackwell.
24   Menger, R. (1999) 'Japanese and American negotiators: overcoming cultural barriers to understanding', The Academy of Management Executive, 13 November, 100–101.
25   Perlmutter, H. V. and Heenan, D. A. (1974) How multinational should your top manager be? *Harvard Business Review*, November–December, 121–132.
26   Phatak, A. V. (1997) *International Management: concepts and cases*. Cincinnati, OH: South-Western College Publishing.
27   Pruitt, D. G. (1981) *Negotiation Behavior*. New York: Academic Press.
28   Raider, E. (1982) *International Negotiations: a training program for corporate executives and diplomats*. New York: Ellen Raider International Inc.
29   Reardon, K. K. and Spekman, R. E. (1994) Starting out right: Negotiating lessons for domestic and cultural business alliances. *Business Horizons*, December, 71–79.
30   Robbins, S., Bergman, R. and Stagg, I. (2000) *Management*. 2nd edn. Englewood Cliffs, NJ: Prentice Hall Publishing.
31   Samovar, L. A. and Porter, R. E. (1995) *Communication between Cultures*. Belmont, CA: Wadsworth.
32   Thompson, L. (1998) The Mind and Heart of the Negotiator. Englewood Cliffs, NJ: Prentice Hall.
33   Weiss, S. E. (1994) Negotiating with Romans: Part 1. *Sloan Management Review*, Winter, 51–61.
34   Weiss, S. E. (2006) International business negotiation in a globalizing world: reflections on the contributions and future of a (sub) field, *International Negotiation* 11, 287–316.

8 Strategies of multinational enterprises of small economies

The case of Greek multinationals in Eastern Europe 1990–2005

Ioannis-Dionysios Salavrakos and John Saee

Introduction

The aim of this chapter is to provide an analysis of the strategies that Greek entrepreneurs have used in Eastern Europe (mainly in Albania, Bulgaria, Romania, Russia and Ukraine) during the 1990s. Here we refer to the strategies that have been used in local markets by international joint ventures (JVs) that Greek companies have established in the region in various industrial sectors. The structure of this chapter is as follows.

In the first section we provide an overall description of the evolution of Greek international business in these particular countries and in the broader Eastern Europe Black Sea region. This is essential for the reader who is not familiar with the development of ethnic international business (in this case that of the Greek entrepreneurs).

The second section provides a theoretical framework which includes important issues such as: the motives that Greek entrepreneurs had in order to enter the region and also the motives of penetrating the local market with different entry modes (wholly owned subsidiary versus international JV). We also consider various internal and external destabilising forces that Greek entrepreneurs faced when they conducted business in the region.

The third section attempts to assess the performance of the Greek multinationals in Eastern Europe and to evaluate the future prospects, taking into consideration the globalisation versus localisation element, which also provides opportunities and threats to Greek business in the region.

The final fourth section attempts to provide an assessment, taking into consideration the EU enlargement in Eastern Europe. Then it produces some expectations for the future development of Greek business in the region.

At this point we stress that we did not follow an empirical evidence modelling approach. Rather, we followed an economic/business strategy approach. In our research we follow the methodology of Kinnear and Taylor (1979). Three types of research have been identified: exploratory, conclusive and performance-monitoring. Exploratory research is used for identifying problems or opportunities and is characterised by its flexibility. Conclusive research is designed to provide information for the evaluation of alternative courses of action and is subdivided into descriptive and causal research. Descriptive research is used for describing the characteristics of marketing phenomena and determining the frequency of occurrence, for establishing degree of association among variables and for predicting the occurrence of marketing phenomena. However, it does not show cause-and-effect relationships among variables. For exploring which variables are the cause of what is being predicted, causal research is performed. The main data collection tools for causal research are surveys and experiments. We use the principle of 'informational saturation' that is the point in which the researcher does not learn anything new about his research. In other words, after a certain point we can generalise our conclusions since the additional information does not provide anything substantive. By repeating interviews several times we established a 'validity check' and thus our results satisfy the scientific criterion of replicability.

The development of Greek international business in Eastern Europe – Black Sea Economic Cooperation Area (1989–2005)

Historically, the presence of Greek entrepreneurial activity in the region of the Black Sea Economic Cooperation Area (BSECA) is dated from the seventeenth century. To illustrate, Babanasis (1997) points out that until the end of the nineteenth century the major trading partners of Greece were the countries of Central and Eastern Europe. In 1887, 58.3 per cent of Greek imports and 12.3 per cent of Greek exports were with those countries, while in 1912 the figures were 40.2 per cent and 17.8 per cent respectively. The Greeks in Russia and Ukraine, despite their small number (around 10,000), had established approximately 160 trading companies, which controlled trade and shipping activities in the Black Sea region. The British and the Russians called them the 'Kings of Wheat'. Furthermore, Katseli (1994) points out that

> from the seventeenth century Salonika was the biggest commercial centre of the Balkans . . . and . . . Greek commercial networks united the markets of the Balkans, with those of Constantinople, and the Black Sea basin with . . . Italy and the South of France. Almost all the transactions in Balkan trade during the eighteenth and nineteenth centuries were made in Greek language.

She adds that 'in 1815 three-quarters of the French trade in the Eastern Mediterranean was made by the Greeks'. Karafotakis (1994) shares similar views, pointing out that

> at the end of the nineteenth century, a partial retreat of Greek positions in the trans-Balkan trade is observed as an outcome of the initial nationalistic targets from all Balkan countries. The situation worsened after the Balkan wars; however, it showed some stability in the inter-war period. During the same period the development of German positions in the area . . . became dominant . . . [but] . . . with the Second World War trade relations ceased to exist, and they restarted in 1990 and afterwards.

Following the collapse of the Iron Curtain in 1989 Greek entrepreneurs have invested, until the end of 2000, approximately US$4 billion in the Balkans and the countries of the Black Sea Economic Cooperation Area (BSECA). Additionally, they have invested around US$2 billion in Central and Western Europe, USA and the rest of the world, so the book value of their total investment, excluding those in shipping, exceeds US$6 billion (McDonald, 2000). During the first four months of 2000 there was also a net outflow of direct investment of US$217 million from Greece, making Greece a net direct investor for the first time in its history (McDonald, 2000). The data for the 2000–2004 period confirms that this process has developed further, in spite of the fact that it is incomplete. To illustrate, current reports from the Hellenic Industry Association (2002) and other economic authorities suggest that the total sum invested in the Balkan region alone (Albania, Former Yugoslav Republic of Macedonia (FYROM), Bulgaria, Romania, Serbia, Montenegro and Turkey) is now US$6 billion.[1]

According to the Bulgarian Service for Foreign Investments the total Greek investments in Bulgaria are provisionally calculated as US$634.3 million in the period 1992–2003 (this figure excludes some investment projects). This places Greece as the second largest foreign investor in Bulgaria, just behind Germany (with a total of US$637.6 million in the same period). According to the same source, around US$210 million was invested by Greek companies in the local economy during 2001. The aggregate volume of Greek investments in the country exceeds US$1 billion. By 2005 the Greek FDI in Bulgaria was €1.65 billion.

In Romania during 2002 there were 2351 registered Greek companies with a total capital of US$291.5 million, according to the data of the Romanian authorities. However, this figure does not take into consideration reinvested profits or investments which Greek companies made through other countries for tax reasons. Taking these into account, Greek sources provide an overall estimate for the 1989–2002 period of US$2 billion. By 2005 total Greek FDI in Romania exceeded €3 billion.

In the Former Yugoslav Republic of Macedonia (FYROM) Greece is the largest foreign investor with investments that exceeded US$570 million by 2002. In that country aggregate estimates for 2004 point out that the Greek investments are in excess of €1.1 billion. In that country the presence of Greek banks and enterprises is very dominant. To illustrate, the National Bank of Greece via its subsidiary Stopanska Banka controls 30 per cent of retail banking business. The total assets of Stopanska Banka are estimated at €500 million, and the total investment of the National Bank of Greece is €140 million. By 2004 the investments of Hellenic Petroleum in the country are estimated at €200 million. Furthermore, Hellenic Telecommunications have invested more than €135 million. The investments of 3E, one of the biggest Greek producers in the food and beverages industry, are estimated at €60 million. The investments of Titan cement industry are estimated at €7 million, whereas the Greek supermarket chain Veropoulos has invested €30 million. Smaller investments have been made by other Greek companies (e.g. Alpha Bank, €7 million; Kri-Kri, €3 million; Aloumil, €1 million).[2]

Greek investments in Turkey increased during 1997–2000, however, because of Turkey's domestic economic crisis that occurred in 2001, this trend has been reversed and only 49 to 50 Greek investment projects were in progress during 2003. This was changed in 2006, after the decision of the National Bank of Greece to acquire Turkey's Finanz Bank for the sum of €5 billion.

In the Ukraine Greek investments increased in spite of domestic economic difficulties. According to the Ukrainian Ministry of Economics, there were thirty-seven Greek firms with a total capital of US$12.5 million in 1996. By 2002 there were sixty-two Greek firm investments with a total capital exceeding US$300 million (this figure takes into account investments of US$270 million made by the Greek firm 3E in the beverages sector, even if these funds come from other countries for tax reasons). In Moldova Greek firms had invested US$13 million by the end of 2001.

Furthermore, by early 2003 Greek banks had invested US$5.5 billion, by acquiring fourteen banking institutions throughout Eastern Europe. By 2004 aggregate estimates of the FDI figures are US$7–8 billion. The overall investment activity of Greek entrepreneurs in the region is expanding rapidly. Although the exact level of investment capital is debatable, since different sources provide different data, we observe increasing investments every year. By 2005 more than €12 billion were invested in the foreign countries from Greek enterprises. The bulk of the above investments (more than 70 per cent) was invested in Bulgaria, Romania, Albania, and FYROM. The banks alone have invested more than €2.5 billion in the region, creating more than 14,000 new jobs. Trade relations have also expanded. Greek exports to Bulgaria and Romania increased from US$112 million in 1990 to US$1524 million in 2005.[3]

This indicates that Greek foreign investment activity has concentrated in south-eastern Europe and the Black Sea. These are areas with which the Greeks have historically had extensive political, cultural and economic links (Salavrakos, 2006). When one considers that until recently Greece was a net recipient of FDI this phenomenon is remarkable. In the BSECA countries Greek entrepreneurial activity has taken the form of both FDI and of setting up trading companies. Elsewhere, it has been mostly direct investment.

This region had been out of reach since 1945, however, with the collapse of the Iron Curtain in 1989 and subsequent break-up of the USSR the Greeks resumed their old economic links. This resumption was slow initially (in the period 1989–1991) but accelerated after 1992 (particularly after 1995, when the bulk of investment occurred). The present chapter provides further insight on Hellenic FDI activity by focusing on the functions of the international JVs between Greek firms and firms from Eastern European countries (Albania,bulgaria, Romania, Russia and Ukraine).

The main sectors that attract Greek FDI are banking and insurance institutions, beverages, telecommunications, oil, petrol and lubricants, textiles, food, construction, mining, glassware, steel, tourism, plastics, energy, computers and IT equipment, metallurgy, tobacco, flour mills, paper and wood products.

The kind of enterprises which invest in the region can be categorised in three different types: the first consists of large firms which invest in projects with value in excess of US$100 million. In this category we can identify more than 50 large Greek firms (OTE-Telecommunications, DELTA-Food industry, INTRACOM-High technology, IT, Computers, 3E-Beverages, Yula Group-Steel, Metallurgy, Glassware, etc). These companies are engaged in multiple investments in the region and they establish multiple JVs or wholly owned subsidiaries in these countries. They engage mainly in FDI and they also marginally conduct some intrafirm trade.

The second type of company consists of small and medium size enterprises (SMEs) which invest less than US$500,000 in the countries of the region. These are mainly in the sectors of textiles, general trade, paper and wood. These firms are engaged in both FDI and trade. The latter can be intrafirm or across countries (i.e. Greek exports to Bulgaria).

The third type consists of very small firms with very limited capital (a few hundreds or thousands of US$) and they have as a primary orientation regional or cross-border trade. Thus, they are not engaged in any FDI activity.

Finally, the activities of banking and insurance institutions are different. They provide insurance to local and foreign entrepreneurs and they also finance imports and exports across countries.

The Hellenic FDI in Eastern Europe: historical dimension and methodological issues

Greek entrepreneurs could choose to enter markets by means of wholly owned subsidiaries (WOSs), whether through greenfield investment or the takeover of existing local firms, or through the formation of international joint ventures (IJVs), with local interests. By and large, in the BSECA region the latter route was chosen. In most instances, it was the only way to enter such markets as, for example, in the case of Hellenic Telecommunications Organisation (OTE) where the local partner already enjoyed monopoly status. However, this route was mainly chosen for a number of financial, strategic and country-specific reasons, virtually all of which were motivated by risk reduction. To investors in foreign markets operations some of the Balkan countries carry risks beyond the normal currency, economic and political risks. This is because of both the extreme political volatility (Albania in 1997 and the former Yugoslavia) and the opaque nature of the legal environment. Foreign investors may consider the establishment of a JV with local interests as the only practical way to enter such markets as it minimises such risks.

While Greece has important historical, political, cultural and economic links with the countries of the BSECA region they are not, in our opinion, sufficient to explain the extent of Greek FDI and trade in this area. It should also be remembered that the earlier Greek entrepreneurial presence in that region was confined to commercial and shipping activities, while now it has also taken the form of international production. For a better understanding of Greek outward FDI, the aim of this chapter is to provide an assessment of the correlation between a firm's performance and eleven control mechanism variables in Hellenic JVs with firms from the BSECA region, using ordered dependent variable models. The remainder of the chapter is organised as follows. The next section discusses the theoretical background that associates control mechanisms with a firm's performance. Section 3 presents the empirical modelling and the final section draws conclusions and provides a tentative evaluation of the future prospects of Greek entrepreneurial activity. The above introductory paragraphs were necessary for the reader who is not familiar with the foreign investments from a small, open, relatively backward economy.

Theoretical framework

The theoretical framework consists of various issues that have to do with the motives for engaging in international production, the motives for selecting a specific mode of entry, and internal and external forces which may jeopardise the activities of the local firm. These will be analysed in the following sections.

Motives to expand abroad

The motives that firms have in order to expand abroad (i.e. become multinationals), is an issue that has been analysed extensively by various authors, directly or indirectly in the international bibliography. The various authors apply strategic motivation rationales, or transaction costs, or industrial organisation theories and even Marxist views in order to analyse the phenomenon of international production.[4] In the case of Greek firms which have expanded in Eastern Europe/Black Sea Economic Cooperation Area (BSECA) the above rationales can be applied as well. Therefore, potential motives can be grouped in three categories:

(1) firm-specific motives. These include access to cheaper financial capital, better technology compared to local firms, and superior entrepreneurial and managerial capabilities compared to local firms;

(2) firm-strategic motives. These include first-mover advantage, cost-leadership and cost-focus strategy, product differentiation and differentiation-focus strategies, geographical diversification strategy and competitive international industry approaches;

(3) home and host country-specific motives. These include exploitation of host country's land and/or natural resources, demand conditions in the host country, bypass of trade barriers, exploitation of host country's infrastructure, high interest rates in Greece which render investments unprofitable thus FDI in these countries enhance competitiveness in Western markets.

The motives that Greek entrepreneurs have reflect both financial and strategic considerations.[5] To illustrate, investments in the region reflect the cost minimisation strategy of the firms (i.e. the ability to produce their products at lower cost), which provides a motive for FDI in these countries. This is directly related to the concept of cost-minimisation strategy (cost-leadership and cost-focus) which is used by Porter (1985). Additional motives (during the 1990s and before the Greek entry in the EMU) were the high interest rates in Greece which made any investments inside the Greek market unprofitable. Thus investments in the BSECA enhanced competitiveness in Western markets. It is interesting to point out that various Greek managers have expressed the view that due to high degree of economic volatility and uncertainty in transition economies throughout the 1990s the comparative advantage of higher managerial capabilities possessed by Western managers may be of very little use. Thus, in the Greek case, elements of the OLI Paradigm cannot explain the shift of production from Greece to these countries. (In this case the possession of superior entrepreneurial managerial capabilities compared to local firms.)

Choice of entry mode

The other important issue is the entry mode that the Greek entrepreneurs will choose in order to penetrate the local markets. Their options are between (a) exporting; (b) licensing; (c) franchising; (d) mergers and acquisitions; (e) WOSs; and (f) IJVs. The majority of them choose the IJV option. This is the outcome of various reasons. Theoretically the motives for JV formation can be grouped also in three categories. These have been identified by various authors in the international bibliography.[6]

(1) financial motives. These include portfolio diversification, risk minimisation and shorter payback period;
(2) strategic motives. These include access to raw materials, access to cheap labour, access to distribution channels, exploitation of economies of scale and scope, risk reduction in a socially, legally and politically unstable environment, overcoming cultural differences and absorbing local know-how, and low-cost strategic benefits due to advantages that the local partner may have; and
(3) country-specific motives. These include bypass of government barriers, increased bargaining power with local authorities, legal barriers which make the decision for JV formation compulsory.

In the Greek case, the most important are two strategic determinants: access to distribution networks and exploitation of economies of scale and scope.

In the case of the former the relatively high transaction costs involved would favour the ownership structure of the JV. While the Greek partner had to upgrade and rebuild the existing distribution networks, in most of the cases he did not have to start from the beginning, which created adequate savings in terms of time and finance. In the Balkan countries before 1989 the structure of the distribution networks and the sale points was vertical. This means that every enterprise (factory) possessed its own distribution network and points of sale. Since the collapse of the Iron Curtain, a horizontal structure has emerged of the following form:

production-wholesale, trade-retail and trade-consumption, the latter at the small level of firms. The majority of these networks have a domestic, local and peripheral character, although some international networks still exist. Most sale points, however, tend to be small and inadequate due to their local profile. In certain cases (like that of the food and beverages industry) essential infrastructure, like refrigerators, had to be replaced because of their low quality or they were totally missing. In the case of big firms a national distribution system also had to be created in order to replace the local ones which served only isolated geographical regions.

For the exploitation of economies of scale and scope we observe that there are considerable synergies with the former point of the distribution networks. In order to have economies of scale you have to resolve technical production problems and increase output while reducing the unit costs. However, this output has to reach the final consumer in order to create the revenues. Therefore it follows that distribution networks as well as marketing and advertising techniques which will make the product appealing to the local customer are essential preconditions.

Internal and external destabilising forces

When the Greek entrepreneurs enter the local markets they face a number of difficulties. These can be grouped into two broad categories.

The first is the difficulties which arise inside the JV (internal pressures) due to different and conflicting managerial/entrepreneurial culture. These pressures create problems in the decision-making inside the local firms. As a result, firm performance in many cases is poor (low level of profits or even losses, low market share, low productivity levels, etc.). Under this broad category we can include the following internal destabilising venture-specific forces, which the international bibliography identifies:

- partners attempt to pursue personal goals;
- different cultural backgrounds;
- different strategic goals of the partners;
- different time horizon in the strategy of the partners;
- competition between parent firms;
- transfer of knowledge;
- use of the same trademark;
- disagreement between partners for the distribution of profits;
- different management style;
- bad personal relations inside the JV; and
- conflict between the JV's general manager (GM) and the parent firms.[7]

The second category refers to external problems that may be harmful to the activities of the local enterprise. These problems occurred throughout the 1990s due to the political, economic and social instability in the countries of transition. These include host country-specific pressures. Here we can identify:

- corruption (opportunism);
- bureaucracy;
- foreign exchange problem;
- poor telecommunications;
- lack of appropriate banking support; and
- volatile legal framework.

The above will be analysed in the following paragraphs.

Internal destabilising forces and strategies to face them

The relationships between the Greeks and the local managers were (and still are) in many cases problematic. According to Radaev (1993)[8], three groups of entrepreneurs can be found in the countries of transition. The first is the largest. It comes from the 'state run institutions, including officials from state ministries . . . and from state run-enterprises'. The economic resources of this group comes from the 'transformation of state owned property' (privatisation). The second group consists of the 'independents' – as Radaev calls them – true entrepreneurs. Their activity is small business oriented, and their capital comes either from bank loans or personal savings. The third group consists of 'shadow dealers'; their capital comes from illegal activity and is 'transferred into legal activities'.

These entrepreneurs function in an economy with a short-term business horizon. Nowadays, in many Eastern European countries a shift is occurring from production-oriented activities to trading activities and services. This is the outcome of the transformation of the economy, with services and trading activities apparently providing quick returns on low capital cost. That is how these entrepreneurial groups currently function since the environment 'creates a situation for speculative and short sighted activities'. The issue of trust and personal links is still essential in the new Russian enterprise, as it was in the previous Soviet construction. The principal of 'one man's decision making' still exists, but what has changed is the employment system. Nowadays, it is based on 'a contractual rather than permanent basis'. A short-term contract is the most common contractual arrangement between employers and employees. However, personal links exist, since employers 'look to relatives and personal acquaintances first and also follow recommendation they believe to be reliable'. The attempt to hire an unknown worker is the last option the employer will exercise.

Another essential feature of the emerging economic order is the lack of any entrepreneurial ethics. This aspect is very well described by Radaev (1993), who also points out that 'business ethics are emerging in some market segments, but they are still rather fragmented'. The diverse (and often inexperienced, and even illegal) entrepreneurial culture is best captured by Lambropoulos (1995), who describes the new local entrepreneurs of Albania, Bulgaria and Romania. He writes:

> The local private entrepreneurial activity comes from different types of bodies, which have created three types of business-people: those who come from

the legal, semi-legal and illegal market of the former economic system, those who become entrepreneurs from the administrative positions which had been, or still were, in the state enterprises . . . and those who developed their entrepreneurial activity (scientists, technicians and others) in the framework of the new economic institutions . . . the first category is inclined to opaque and illegal entrepreneurial conduct . . . Trade and the provision of certain services are, until now, the most desirable grounds for them to exercise their entrepreneurial abilities . . . The second category is inclined to consider as a primary source of its revenues . . . the state funding of any entrepreneurial activity. This group is the preferential local partner of western industrial joint venture enterprises. The third category has no entrepreneurial past. This group consists of smart people, usually educated, who speak foreign languages, and start their own initiative with almost no financial capital . . . They are active in low volume domestic and international trade, in the provision of certain services and in handicraft production.[9]

Three essential points have to be made: the first is that the manager of the former socialist state enterprise was a bureaucrat. His entrepreneurial and managerial capabilities were extremely limited, and he can be characterised as an inflexible decision-maker. The second point is that, nowadays, the majority of individuals in these societies are characterised by very narrowly self-motivated behaviour, which is a new characteristic of almost every aspect of their social life. This leads to a lack of any entrepreneurial ethics, as these are perceived in the West. The combination of the above two characteristics is the most essential barrier to entry by Western enterprise, and can jeopardise any East-West JV. The third point is that the evolution of domestic entrepreneurship in these countries has been very similar in the last fifty years (1945–1995). During the era of central planning the centralised economic model prevailed in all of them, and entrepreneurship was similarly stilled in all of them. After the collapse of the old regime, the forms of entrepreneurship, which developed in the Balkan countries and Russia, were almost identical. The different cultural backgrounds is one of the most essential internal problems that Greek managers have to face.

In order to avoid the problem the Greek firms had to establish majority ownership JVs in most of the cases. The majority ownership, which in some cases is up to 95 per cent of the shares, practically create JVs which are very similar to WOSs. Furthermore, the Greek parent firms exercise dominant control on the ventures with a variety of formal and informal mechanisms. This policy of dominant control will continue for as much time as is needed in order to transform the Eastern Europeans from bureaucrats to 'real managers' (i.e. managers who understand market forces and mechanisms) and, thus, they are able to make decisions by themselves.

External destabilising forces and strategies to face them

Any multinational operating in a foreign country will face certain kinds of political and/or economic pressure from the local environment. In the case of Greek

JVs in Eastern Europe, during the 1990s the Greek managers had to face a variety of problems, such as (1) corruption; (2) bureaucracy; (3) foreign exchange problem; (4) telecommunications; (5) lack of appropriate banking support; and (6) volatile legal framework.

Corruption is an essential issue in the countries of transition. For many experts corruption is a phenomenon associated with private gain, through illegal or opaque activities, bribery, embezzlement and fraud. It is associated with the public sector and specific activities like contractual arrangements, public revenues, regulation etc. In our case, the concept can be captured by the term 'opportunism', as this has been introduced by Williamson (1993). It has been proved that this is not an essential barrier for the Greek entrepreneurs for conducting business in the region.

Bureaucracy is regarded as an additional external barrier for foreign business. This has been identified as a major obstacle for doing business in the transition economies. One way to face it was the use of the local partner's ability to establish links with the local authorities.

The foreign currency/foreign exchange problem has been a major obstacle in the case of Hellenic enterprises in Eastern Europe. Throughout the 1990s foreign exchange was in short supply in all the countries of the region. Furthermore, hyperinflation and huge trade deficits created a constant depreciation of the local currencies values, which had a harmful outcome on FDI activities. One way to face it was through barter exchange. Many companies used to accumulate various stocks of goods or raw materials or semi-finished items that they were ready to sell in the market in higher prices when a foreign exchange (FX) shortage was taking place. Volatile legal framework has also been identified as a major obstacle to international business.

Incomplete regulation about private property, property rights, taxes and profits repatriation etc. affects FDI decision making. The volatile legal framework creates additional transaction costs associated with the constant monitoring of often complex and time-consuming legal activities and processes.

On the other hand, the lack of banking support and the poor level of telecommunications did not play a major inverse role on Hellenic FDI. This is partially explained by the involvement of major Greek telecommunication companies, as well as financial institutions in the region.

The strategies of Hellenic multinationals under the scope of the globalisation versus localisation approach

As Porter and Solvell (1998) point out,

> Early observers . . . began to emphasize that globalisation has neutralized many traditional competitive advantages and that the new methods of production in the 'post-Fordist' era and new modes of transaction based competition are a rejuvenating force for localization . . . With the basis of competitive advantage rapidly shifting from static advantages of scale and low input prices to relentless innovation and upgrading of competitive advantage, the

role of location is enhanced . . . Where the leading MNCs are actually head-ing – global integration or multilocal specialization – is an empirical question and there is some evidence for both cases . . . If . . . MNCs face inefficiencies resulting from internationally coordinated innovation processes they would probably retain their character of local innovators and remain global com-mercializers. In the case of the diversified MNC, one might expect that each business segment would concentrate its core resources in the most dynamic regions or nations . . . Strategists are now turning to the role of regions and nations in shaping the competitive advantage of firms in general and multina-tional corporations in particular.[10]

(At this point we stress that with the term 'Fordist-era' we mean the policy of the US car-making company which tried to follow the Levitt's concept of 'we sell the same things in the same way everywhere'.) This entrepreneurial philosophy tried to create the 'world' or 'universal' car, that is, a car that would be accepted by all consumers in spite of their preferences and needs around the world. The first attempt occurred during the 1970s and failed. In the 1990s a new attempt was made with the introduction of the Mondeo model. It has been noted that Ford tried to became a global player based on its product line and not on spatial, geographical plants.

In general, the authors describe both paths as possible. The first is Centre–Innovation, Region–Commercialisation. The second scenario is the opposite. The third is a mixture. That is, the centre is associated with both innovation and commercialisation and the same applies in the region. This scenario is the most realistic if we take into consideration the empirical evidence. These concepts, however, have limited value in the case of Greek firms in Eastern Europe, since most of them produce or trade goods with low technological inputs.

The other dimension of the globalisation versus localisation debate is the is-sue of how firms operate in foreign markets and be sensitive to the cultural and specific needs of that market but simultaneously remain profitable and loyal to the values of the parent firm. Following the work of Kotabe and Helsen (2004) we can identify the following marketing strategies.

- Domestic marketing. This mainly represents activities that companies follow when they operate in domestic national markets. In this case all products and services produced are meant solely for the domestic consumer.
- Export marketing. This consists of direct and indirect modes. Export marketing is also ethnocentric since the products are designed with the local market in mind. The exporter is a reluctant player in foreign markets and usually simply satisfy specific orders from a small number of foreign customers.
- International marketing. In this case the company terminates the rationale of the single product that is sold in the domestic market and begins to accept the notion that the different needs that customers have in other regions beyond the national boundaries must be incorporated in the company's strategy. This is a 'country-by-country' strategy.

- Multinational marketing. This is a 'region-by-region' strategy. In this case, the company attempts to achieve maximum benefits in one particular geographical region.
- Global marketing. This combines all of the above strategies (ethnocentric, polycentric and region-centric) in a smooth and balanced way.

Obviously, the Greek firms are not engaged in global strategies (with the exception of 3E). However, all the regional activities of the Greek firms take into consideration the local culture, as well as special domestic needs. However, due to cultural similarities, in most cases the Greek firms can offer standardised products to the local consumers. These, in the majority of cases, are of superior quality compared to those which local firms produce. Thus, the Greek firms, although they are aware of the strategy of multiple products for every different market, in practice and in most cases provide a standardised good in these markets.

Another issue of importance for them is the creation of entry barriers for other potential competitors who may have the same aspiration of conducting business in these regions. Thus, large Greek companies who are engaged in manufacturing and services have tried to raise entry barriers by acquiring direct access to final consumers. For example, in the food industry, a number of firms have established their own distribution networks and are cooperating with other Greek food manufacturers to derive the benefits of synergies.

In other cases, when it was obvious that the Greek firms would not be able to stop the entry of other dominant Western multinationals, they attempted to form strategic alliances with these firms, thus transforming the potential competitor to a partner. The case of the Greek firm DELTA with the French firm Danone is a typical example in the milk industry in Bulgaria and Romania.

Concluding remarks

The Greek firms have regained a dominant presence in the emerging markets of Eastern Europe and the BSECA after the collapse of the Iron Curtain. They are active in various industries, such as banking and insurance, telecommunications, IT, textiles, cement, etc. Their main motives were the achievement of cost minimisation and their desire to enhance their competitiveness in the international markets. Their most desired entry mode is that of the IJV due to the access to distribution systems and exploitation of economies of scale and scope.

During the 1990s the Greek firms that operated in these countries had to face certain internal as well as external pressures. The former were associated with cultural differences between the Western (Greek) and the Eastern European partner. In order to face these pressures the Greek firms exercised dominant control on the venture with a variety of mechanisms as long as this was needed in order to transform the East European to a manager who is able to understand market forces and take decisions. They also had to face external destabilising forces, mainly FX shortage, volatile legal framework and bureaucracy. In order to face all these pressures the Greek partner had to engage in barter exchange, monitor legal evolution carefully and bypass bureaucracy with various strategies (use of the local partner, establishment of contacts with local authorities, etc.). These strategies increased transaction costs but they were needed in order to face these external pressures.

Finally, Greek firms, although they are aware of the cultural sensitivities and the specific needs of the local markets, in most cases tend to provide standardised products, similar to those produced for the Greek market. This is happening since there is some similarity between these countries and Greece and since in most cases the Greek products are of superior quality compared to those that the local consumers previously had.

In order to assess the future of Hellenic business in the region two issues must be stressed. The former has to do with the large Greek companies who possess competitive advantages and an already dominant position in these markets. These companies can face the future from a position of strength and provided that they retain their advantages, they certainly have a positive future. On the other hand, firms which simply followed short-term 'hit and run' strategies will have very limited chances of success.

The latter has to do with the fact that already eight Eastern European countries are EU members and Bulgaria and Romania are expected to join in 2007. Clearly FDI has assisted the regional integration and, thus, although the motives of Greek entrepreneurs were of microeconomic nature (cost reduction etc.), their activities had broader economic ramifications. To summarise, FDI has assisted the process of globalisation in the region. In this the role of Greek entrepreneurs has been pioneering. They entered a volatile region in the beginning of the 1990s with very limited protection against various types of risks but they managed to create successful strategies and establish a dominant presence there. As the countries of the region started to enter the EU the benefits that Greek firms will have over others from Western countries in the new EU market will be seen in the next decade.

Notes

1 See www.bulgarianeconomy.gr/gr_ependisis_2001.htm. Data was provided to the authors from the Institute of International Economic Relations, Athens, Greece.
2 See Papaioanou 2004.
3 See *Economic Kathimerini* , 29 June 2006, p. 27.
4 See Hood and Young 1979; Michael Porter 1985; Dunning 1981, 1993; and Caves 1996. Finally, for a selection of different perspectives on the issue of the multinational enterprise see C. Pitelis and R. Sudgen (eds.) 1991.
5 See Salavrakos 1999, pp. 161–172; Salavrakos and George A. Petrochilos 2003. For the motives of Greek banks see Aristidis Bitzenis 2004.
6 See Gullander 1976; Raveed and Renforth 1983; Contractor and Lorange 1988, pp. 3–28; Dunning 1993.
7 See Lane and Beamish 1990; Ganitsky and Watzke 1990; Geringer and Frayne 1990; Anderson 1990, pp. 19–30; Kogut 1989, pp. 183–198; Casseres 1987, pp. 97–102; Killing 1982.
8 Radaev 1993. Although Radaev refers exclusively to Russian entrepreneurs, his pattern can be generalised across Eastern Europe.
9 See Lambropoulos 1995, pp. 273–284 (in Greek).
10 See Chandler, Hagstrom and Solvell 1998, pp. 263–457.

Bibliography

Anderson, E. (1990) Two firms one frontier: on assessing joint venture performance, *Sloan Management Review* 21(2), 19–30.

Babanasis, S. (1997) *Changes and Entrepreneurial Opportunities in Central and Eastern Europe*. Athens: Papazisis editions (published in Greek).

Bitzenis, A. (2006) Determinants of Greek FDI outflows in the Balkan region. The case of Greek entrepreneurs in Bulgaria. *Eastern European Economics* 44(3), 79–96.

Bitzenis, A. (2004) Why Foreign Banks are Entering Transition Economies: The case of Bulgaria. *Global Business and Economics Review* 6(1), 107–133.

Buckley, P. J. and Casson, M. (1976) *The Future of the Multinational Enterprise*. New York: Macmillan.

Cantwell, J. (1989) *Technological Innovation and Multinational Corporations*. Oxford: Blackwell Scientific Publications.

Cantwell, J. (1991) 'A Survey of theories of international production', in Ch. Pitelis and R. Sudgen (eds) *The Nature of the Transnational Firm*. Routledge.

Casseres, G. (1987) Joint venture instability: is it a problem?. *Columbia Journal of World Business* 22(2), 97–102.

Casson, M. C. (1987) *The Firm and the Market*. Oxford: Blackwell.

Caves, R. E. (1996) *Multinational Enterprise and Economic Analysis*. 2nd edn. Cambridge: Cambridge University Press.

Chandler, A., Hagstrom P. and Solvell O. (eds) (1998) *The Dynamic Firm*. Oxford: Oxford University Press.

Coase, R. (1937) The nature of the firm. *Economica* 4, 386–405.

Contractor, F. and Lorange, P. (1988) 'Why should firms co-operate? The strategy and economic basis for cooperative ventures', pp. 3–28 in F. Contractor and P. Lorange (eds) *Co-operative Strategies in International Business*, Lexington Books.

Dunning, J. H. (1981) *International Production and the Multinational Enterprise*. London: Allen & Unwin.

Dunning, J. H. (1993) *The Multinational Enterprise and the Global Economy*. Reading: Addison-Wesley.

Ganitsky, J. and Watzke, G. (1990) Implications of different time perspectives for human resource management in international joint ventures. *Management International Review* 30, 37–51.

Gedeshi, I. and Mara, H. (2001) 'Economic transition in Albania: possibilities for co-operation with Balkan countries', in G. Petrakos and S. Totev (eds), *The Development of the Balkan Region*. Ashgate.

Geringer, M. J. K. and Frayne, C. (1990) Human resource management and international joint venture control: a parent company perspective. *Management International Review* 30, 103–120.

Gullander, S. (1976) Joint ventures and corporate strategy. *Columbia Journal of World Business* 11(1), 104–114.

Hios, N. (1999) Investing in the Balkans: facts and figures focusing on the economies in a sensitive area, *Hermes*, issue 35, June.

Hood, N. and Young, S. (1979) *The Economics of the Multinational Enterprise*. New York: Longman.

Karafotakis, E. (1994) 'Transbalkan distribution networks', in proceedings of the papers presented at the International Forum for the Black Sea Cooperation Conference, Hellenic Centre for European Studies, Thessaloniki, 24–26 November (published in Greek).

Katseli, L. (1994) 'Strategy for the establishment of a Balkan regional market', in proceedings of the papers presented at the Conference, 'Northern Greece and the Balkans: the time of entrepreneurial drive', Thessaloniki, 4–5 April (in Greek).

Killing, J. P. (1982) How to make a global joint venture work. *Harvard Business Review* 60(3), 120–127.

Kinnear, Th. and Taylor, J. (1979) *Marketing Research: an applied approach*. New York: McGraw Hill.

Kogut, B. (1989) The stability of joint ventures: reciprocity and competitive rivalry, *Journal of Industrial Economics* 38(2), 183–198.

Kotabe, M. and Helsen, K. (2004) *Global Marketing Management*. 3rd edn. John Wiley & Sons.

Lambropoulos, K. (1995) 'The strategy of Greek entrepreneurial activity in the Balkans', pp. 273–284 in L. Maroudas and Ch. Tsardanidis (eds), *The Greek-Bulgarian Relations: modern economic and political dimensions*, Athens: Papazisis (published in Greek).

Lane, W. H. and Beamish, P. (1990) Cross-cultural co-operative behaviour in joint ventures in less-developed countries. *Management International Review* 30, 87–102.

McDonald, R. (1995) California here I come: a survey of Greek investments in post-Soviet Europe. *Business File, Greek Special Survey Series 17, of Industrial Review* (Oikonomikoi Viomichaniki Epitheorisi), October (in English).

McDonald, R. (1998) Mini multinationals. Greek outward investments. *Business File, Greek Special Survey Series 29, of Industrial Review* (Oikonomikoi Viomichaniki Epitheorisi), September–October (in English).

McDonald, R. (2000) Breaking out: a survey of the Greek foreign investment. *Business File, Greek Special Survey Series 37, of Industrial Review* (Oikonomikoi Viomichaniki Epitheorisi), September–October (in English).

Papaioanou, G. (2004) Essential Hellenic Presence in Skopjie. *To Vima*, 14 November.

Petrochilos, G. A. and Salavrakos, I. D. (2001) 'An analysis of the mode of entry of Greek outward foreign direct investment in the Balkans and the Black Sea Economic Co-operation Area (BSECA)', pp. 594–606 in D. Kantarelis (ed.), *Global Business and Economics Review-Anthology 2001*. Worcester, MA: Business & Economics Society International.

Pitelis, C. and Sugden, R. (eds) (1991) *The Nature of the Transnational Firm*. Routledge.

Porter, M. (1990) *The Competitive Advantage of Nations*. New York: Free Press.

Porter, M. and Solvell, O. (1998) 'The role of geography in the process of innovation and sustainable competitive advantage of firms', pp. 440–457 in A. D. Chandler Jr. P. Hagstrom and O. Solvell (eds), *The Dynamic Firm: the role of technology, strategy, organisations and regions*. Oxford University Press.

Radaev, V. (1993) Emerging Russian entrepreneurship: as viewed by the experts. *Economic and Industrial Democracy* 14, 55–77.

Raveed, S. and Renforth, W. (1983) State Enterprise–Multinational corporation–Joint Ventures: how well do they meet both partners' needs?. *Management International Review* 5, 47–57.

Salavrakos I. D. (1999) 'The Black Sea Economic Co-operation: Macro and Microeconomic Dimensions of Integration with the Global Economy', Scientific Library, Kritiki, Athens (in English).

Salavrakos, I. D. (2000) 'The Conflicting Entrepreneurial Mentality, Between Western and Eastern European Managers', Occasional Paper, OP No. 17, June, Institute of International Economic Relations, Athens, Greece [ISBN: 960–7853–06–7]

Salavrakos, I. D. (2006) Explaining different FDI inflows in Eastern European countries with reference to economic history. *Global Business & Economics Review* 8(1/2), 60–87.

Salavrakos, I. D. and Petrochilos, G. A. (2003a) An assessment of the Greek entrepreneurial activity in the Black Sea area (1989–2000) causes and prospects. *Journal of Socio-Economics* 32, 331–349.

Salavrakos, I. D. and Petrochilos, G. A. (2003b) 'The stability of international joint ventures: evidence from Greek joint ventures in Eastern Europe', pp. 179–195 in C. Veloutsou (ed.), *Communicating with Customers: trends and developments*, ATINER (Athens Institute for Education and Research).

Salavrakos, I. D. and Petrochilos, G. A. (2004) Control and conflict in international joint ventures: evidence from Greek joint ventures in Eastern Europe. *Global Business & Economics Review – Anthology 2004*, 371–382.

Salavrakos, I. D. and Stewart, C. (2006) Partner selection criteria as determinants of firm performance in joint ventures. Evidence from Greek joint ventures in Eastern Europe. *Eastern European Economics* 44(3), 60–78.

Williamson, O. E (1993) 'The Economic Analysis of Institutions and Organisations – In General and with Respect to Country Studies', Working Paper No. 133, OECD, Paris.

9 The merger phenomenon in higher education

Jennifer Lawlor and Emily Boyle

Introduction

Interfirm collaboration and cooperation has become an integral part of the world's economic and business arena,bringing with it a wealth of benefits and opportunities to organisations, operating in both the public and private sectors. Saffu and Mamman (2000) postulate that in an era of globalisation with its concomitant competition, cooperative strategies are becoming an increasingly essential ingredient in the success of businesses. The wide range of interfirm collaborative arrangements can perhaps best be embodied by the gamut of recent mergers and acquisitions, strategic alliances, joint ventures, cross-border intraorganisational partnerships, consortia and other interfirm cooperative and collaborative arrangements. Public and private sector organisations are recognising the limitations of pursuing a 'go-it-alone' strategy and are forming collaborative relationships in a bid to consolidate their strategic position and improve their overall economic health.

Specifically referring to the public sector, Huxham and Vangen (2000) state that there seems little doubt that public sector management in the twenty-first century will need to be sophisticated in its understanding of the skills, processes, structures, tools and technology needed for working across organisational boundaries. It would certainly appear that various forms of collaborative arrangements now form a distinct part of institutional life in the public sector, for example within health care and education.

This chapter aims to focus on one aspect of the aforementioned collaborative relationships – that of merger activity in the public sector, specifically within the higher education sector. It is interesting to note that a significant amount of merger activity has been undertaken in the private sector to date, culminating in the acknowledgement by the business community that 1998 was 'the year of the mega-merger'. This was particularly evident in a wide variety of industrial sectors, including the pharmaceutical, retail, airline, financial services, telecommunications and media sectors.

For many decades, mergers have been viewed by the private sector as a very attractive and popular organisational strategy. The literature relating to merger activity in the private sector reflects this viewpoint (see Child, Pitkethly and Faulkner, 1999; Shrivastava, 1986; Kitching, 1967).

It may be argued that a significant amount of attention regarding such activity appears to have emanated within the private sector. However, the use of mergers in the public sector should not be ignored and are worthy of discussion and research.

This chapter seeks to understand the rationale underlying mergers within this sector and briefly address the gaps in the literature relating to the 'post-merger' or 'post-integration' stage. It is interesting to note that as commentators refer to the 'greatest wave of mergers' ever recorded, Bower (2001: 93) contends that 'we know surprisingly little about [them]'.

The merger phenomenon in higher education

Harman and Meek (2002) acknowledge that merger activity in higher education has attracted much attention worldwide over the past two or three decades, particularly as a result of governments using mergers and other forms of consolidation to initiate systematic restructuring of higher education. The use of mergers as a tool of significant organisational change within the higher education sector worldwide has been widely documented in the literature (see Norgard and Skodvin, 2002; Hay and Fourie, 2002; Wyatt, 1998).

According to Clarke and Hermens (2001), education is poised to become one of the largest sectors in the world economy and as such it is increasingly subject to pressures to change. The key challenges facing the higher education sector are numerous and varied and are forcing institutions to rethink their strategic positions and strategies. The key drivers of change within the sector include the need to increase efficiency and effectiveness (Harman and Meek, 2002); the introduction of a sharper business focus and a customer-led approach (Mavin and Bryans, 2000); the decline in government funding and the massification of higher education (Bayenet, Feola and Tavernier, 2000); the social and economic use of the results of university research and the more active role of the university in economic, social, political and cultural development at both regional and national level (Gueissaz and Hayrinen-Alestalo, 1999) and a move towards the reduction in the number of many small, specialised, single-purpose colleges to the creation of larger multipurpose, multidisciplinary institutions (Goedegebuure and Meek, 1997).

Cunningham *et al.* (2000) cited in Clarke and Hermens (2001) further highlight the following factors which are fuelling the transformation of higher education:

- advance of globalisation with a demand for world-class products, services and technical infrastructures;
- emergence of post-industrial information age, with sophisticated communications systems, and the explosive growth and distributed nature of new knowledge;

- demand for greater access to tertiary education and the need for lifelong learning created by rapid changes in the economy; and
- dissatisfaction of industry with the responsiveness of traditional providers.

Definition of a merger in higher education

As in the private sector literature on mergers, there is a plethora of definitions surrounding exactly what constitutes a merger in the public sector. Within the private sector literature, Haberberg and Rieple (2001) characterise a merger as the creation of a new legal firm by the bringing together of two or more previously independent companies. They further suggest that a merger may imply a consensual element to the deal, where both firms agree to combine. A merger may also imply a relative equality in the size and strength of the combining firms (Haberberg and Rieple, 2001). This definition is broadly supported by Gill and Foulder (1978: 15), who characterise a merger as 'organisational change wherein the object of the change is to create one organisational system from two previously distinct entities'.

There does not appear to be any universally accepted definition of a merger due to the variety of activities and structures in the higher education system worldwide. Rather, according to Wyatt (1998), higher institutions should concentrate specifically on 'what works' for them. However, a widely cited definition of a merger is that proposed by Goedegebuure (1992):

> A merger in higher education is the combination of two or more separate institutions into a single new organisational entity, in which control rests with a single governing body and a single chief executive body, and whereby all assets, liabilities and responsibilities of the former institutions are transferred to the single new institution.

Goedegebuure (1992) further classifies mergers as being *vertical* or *horizontal*. Vertical mergers may occur between university and non-university institutions and horizontal mergers may occur between 'mission-complementary institutions' (Goedegebuure, 1992).

Harman (2000) distinguishes between different forms of mergers. The first key distinction he makes is between voluntary and involuntary mergers. A *voluntary* merger is where two or more institutions initiate a merger themselves, rather than as a result of being forced or strongly encouraged to by government (Harman, 2000). His second distinction may be made between consolidations and acquisitions. *Consolidations* occur where one participating institution continues largely unaffected, with other institutions being absorbed, whereas *acquisitions* involve all participating institutions coming together to establish a new organisation (Harman, 2000). He identifies a third distinction between the combination of two or more institutions from the *one sector* and *cross-sectoral* mergers. A fourth distinction may be made on the basis of the number of institutions involved in a merger, from *two* or more institutions to *multi-institution* mergers. A fifth distinction is made between *horizontal* and *vertical* mergers (Harman, 2000).

Lang (2002) proposes an alternative merger classification based on organisational outcomes, that is, how the former institutions fit together to form a new institution. He identifies several outcomes – consolidation, transformation, pure acquisition and semi-autonomous acquisition. *Consolidation* is the combination of two or more institutions to form a new institution. *Transformation* occurs where one partner absorbs the other but changes substantially as a result. *Pure acquisition* occurs when one institution absorbs another without being substantially affected in the process. *Semi-autonomous acquisition* involves a loss of autonomy for at least one of the participating institutions (Lang, 2002). Lang's (2002) classification is broadly supportive of that proposed by Harman (2000).

By their nature, academic mergers denote significant, and indeed, radical change. It would appear from the above definitions that a merger occurs between two or more institutions, not necessarily of similar size or scope, resulting in the evolution of a new organisational entity. However, one of the striking differences between the decision-making processes of a commercial organisation and a public sector academic institution to merge, is the extent to which a merger is voluntary and consensual or involuntary and forced (by government). Table 9.1 details an overview of forced and voluntary mergers in a number of countries.

Table 9.1 An overview of forced and voluntary mergers

Country	Forced	Voluntary
Australia (1960s, 'the binary system'; 1987–90, 'the unified system')	X	
USA (1960–1997)	X	X
Canada (the reform of college education; the creation of Cegeps in the 1960s; the establishment of a new regional network university in the 1990s)	X	X
Norway (the state college reform in 1994)	X	
Sweden (the university and college reform in 1977, and the establishment of Mid-Sweden University in 1993)	X	X
The Netherlands (HBO reform 1983–87, and the new voluntary mergers from 1988)	X	X
Belgium (Flemish college reform 1994)	X	
Germany (*Gesamthochschulen* during the 1970s, *Fachhochschulen* during the 1980s)	X	X
Great Britain (the polytechnic reform during the 1960s and 1970s, and new voluntary mergers in 1980–1990s)	X	X
Finland (the polytechnic reform, 1991–95)	X	

Source: Skodvin, O.-J., 1999.

Rationale for merger activity in higher education

The literature recognises that while merger activity in higher education may be traced back to the late nineteenth century (Harman, 2000), it is only within the last twenty or thirty years that it has attracted significant scholarly activity (Harman, 2002; Harman and Meek, 2002). So what are the driving forces behind merger activity within higher education?

The underlying reasons for pursuing such a strategy within the education sector stem from availing of economies of scale. Norgard and Skodvin (2002) contend that the main intention of merging higher educational institutions has often been that the establishment of larger units should result in academic and administrative economies of scale. This view that mergers in higher education are commonly driven on an expectation of increased financial and economic health is widely held (see Curri, 2002; Kyvik, 2002; Wang, 2001).

Specifically referring to the merging of the education system in Norway, Kyvik (2002: 53) states that

> the purpose of the reorganisation was to enhance the quality of administrative functions and academic work through the creation of larger administrative and academic units, to break down barriers between the former colleges, and to develop new and broader study programmes.

In a continuation of the theme that financial considerations drive many mergers in higher education, Lang (2002) suggests that institutions merge in order to benefit from government incentives that encourage such merger activity.

The literature also suggests strategic reasons for pursuing a merger strategy, the most frequently cited reason being the need to improve or enhance their strategic position in their national higher education market. Where mergers are forced and involuntary, the key driving factor may be the need to restructure and reorganise part or the entire national higher education system, such as that which occurred in Norway and Australia (Skodvin, 1999).

The literature concludes that the main driving force behind merger activity in higher education is some kind of financial gain. Skodvin (1999: 68) asserts that

> the most frequent motive is the wish to achieve administrative, economic and academic benefits, by merging several (small) institutions into a larger unit. The thought is that larger units would yield qualitatively stronger academic institutions, better management and use of administrative resources and they would improve the use of physical facilities.

He further contends that 'administratively, the intention is to achieve economies of scale with regard to the number of administrators, and to get a more professional and efficient administration' (Skodvin, 1999: 68). Academically, the intention is to eliminate duplicative programmes, increase academic integration and collaboration and diversify academic profiles (Skodvin, 1999).

It is interesting to compare and contrast the motives for pursing a merger strategy with organisations operating within the private sector. The more commonly cited drivers of mergers in the private sector include risk sharing and market dominance; cost reduction; improving overall performance by achieving synergy, and availing of economies of scale (for example, Saffu and Mamman, 2000; Appelbaum, Gandell, Yortis, Proper and Jobin, 2000; Bastien, 1987).

The post-merger integration stage

The literature suggests that any organisation that is in contemplation of entering into a merger with another friendly soulmate goes through a logical and structured process, one that has been likened to that of a marriage. Indeed, the literature is peppered with references to the marriage metaphor, where two interested parties meet, get to know one another via a courtship, announce their engagement, celebrate their marriage and 'live happily ever after', that is, the 'pre-merger' stage, 'during-the-merger' and 'post-merger' or 'post-integration' stages. However, in numerous cases, seemingly eternal partners who have expressed their undying love for one another still end up in the 'divorce courts'.

This chapter is particularly interested in the post-integration stage of the merger process. An observation arising from a review of the private sector literature is that an emphasis appears to be placed on the 'courtship' (pre-merger state) and the 'marriage' (the merger process). There is support within the literature for more research to be conducted into the aftermath of a merger, in other words, how the organisation fares 'post-integration' (for example, Vaara, 2002; Kitching, 1967).

Shrivastava (1986: 65) contends that 'few analysts have examined the problems of integrating firms after the merger has been consummated and the impact of this lack of integration on performance'. This is supported by Child, Pitkethly and Faulkner (1999: 186) who agree that 'there have been relatively few studies examining the post-acquisition performance of acquired companies'.

Walsh (1989: 320) argues that 'a complete understanding of the post-acquisition processes' is necessary and believes that 'we know very little about the effects of such upheaval on the individuals within these organisations, and on the organisations themselves'. This is supported by Napier (1989), who concludes that mergers are generally poorly understood and managed, especially regarding human resource issues.

Furthermore, Marks (1997: 267) suggests that newly merged entities are 'underestimating the multitude of integration issues and problems that arise as organizations come together' and are 'underestimating the pervasiveness and depth of the human issues triggered in a merger'.

Indeed, in a seminal article published by the *Harvard Business Review* in 1967, entitled 'Why Do Mergers Miscarry?', John Kitching concluded that a review of the literature 'revealed that research to date has concentrated only on the events leading up to and immediately following acquisition'. Thirty-seven years later, the situation remains somewhat similar.

This dearth of research regarding the post-merger integration stage is reflected in the public sector. To this end, this chapter presents a research agenda pertaining to the merger of a third-level educational institution in the Republic of Ireland, and specifically addresses the issues arising in the 'post-merger' or 'post-integration' stage.

Conclusion

There is widespread agreement that any form of merger activity results in organisational change – economic, academic, administrative, structural, organisational, social and cultural change.

Higher education institutions are facing a period of intense challenge and change resulting from a variety of demographic, technological, social, economic, environmental and cultural factors. So much so that a higher education institution 'is no longer a quiet place to teach and do scholarly work at a measured pace and contemplate the universe as in centuries past. It is a big, complex, demanding, competitive, business requiring largescale ongoing investment' (Downer and Thornhill, 2001: 7).

References

Appelbaum, S. H., Gandell, J., Yortis, H., Proper, S. and Jobin, F. (2000) Anatomy of a merger: behaviour of organisational factors and processes throughout the pre-during-post stages (Part 1). *Management Decision* 38(9), 649–661.

Bastien, D. T. (1987) Common patterns of behaviour and communication in corporate merger and acquisitions. *Human Resource Management* 26(1), Spring, 17–33.

Bayenet, B., Feola, C. and Tavernier, M. (2000) Strategic management of universities: evaluation policy and policy evaluation. *Higher Education Management* 12(2), 65–80.

Bower, J. L. (2001) Not all M&As are alike-and that matters. *Harvard Business Review*, March, 92–101.

Child, J., Pitkethly, R. and Faulkner, D. (1999) Changes in management practice and the post-acquisition performance achieved by direct investors in the UK. *British Journal of Management* 10, 185–198.

Clarke, T. and Hermens, A. (2001) Corporate developments and strategic alliances in e-learning. *Education and Training* 43(4), 256–267.

Curri, G. (2002) Reality versus perception: restructuring tertiary education and institutional organisational change – a case study. *Higher Education* 44, 133–151.

Downer, R. and Thornhill, D. (2001) Foreword in M. Skilbeck, (2001) *The University Challenged, A Review of International Trends and Issues with Particular Reference to Ireland*. Dublin: The Higher Education Authority.

Gill, J. and Foulder, I. (1978) Managing a merger: the acquisition and the aftermath. *Personnel Management* 10, 14–17.

Goedegebuure, L. (1992) *Mergers in Higher Education, A Comparative Perspective*. Utrecht: Lemma.

Goedegebuure, L. and Meek, V. L. (1997) On change and diversity: the role of governmental policy and environmental influences. *Higher Education in Europe* 22(3), 309–319.

Gueissaz, A. and Hayrinen-Alestalo, M. (1999) How to integrate contradictory aims: the configuration of actors in the evaluation of universities. *European Journal of Education* 34(3), 283–297.

Haberberg and Rieple, A. (2001) *The Strategic Management of Organisations*. Englewood Cliffs, NJ: Prentice-Hall.

Harman, G. (2000) Institutional mergers in Australian higher education since 1960. *Higher Education Quarterly* 54(4), 343–366.

Harman, K. (2002) Merging divergent campus cultures into coherent educational communities: challenges for higher education leaders. *Higher Education* 44(1), 91–114.

Harman, K. and Meek, V. L. (2002) Introduction to special issue: Merger revisited: international perspectives on mergers in higher education. *Higher Education* 44(1), 1–4.

Hay, I. and Fourie, M. (2002) Preparing the way for mergers in South African higher and further education institutions: an investigation into staff perceptions. *Higher Education* 44(1), 115–131.

Huxham, C. and Vangen, S. (2000) Leadership in the shaping and implementation of collaboration agendas: how things happen in a (not quite) joined-up world. *Academy of Management Journal* 43(6), 1159–1175.

Kitching, J. (1967) Why do mergers miscarry?. *Harvard Business Review* 45, November–December, 84–101.

Kyvik, S. (2002) The merger of non-university colleges in Norway. *Higher Education* 44(1), 53–72.

Lang, D. W. (2002) There are mergers, and there are mergers: the forms of inter-institutional combination. *Higher Education Management and Policy* 14(1), 11–50.

Marks, M. L (1997) Consulting in mergers and acquisitions, interventions spawned by recent trends. *Journal of Organisational Change Management* 10(3), 267–279.

Marvin, S. and Bryans, P. (2000) Management development in the public sector – what roles can universities play?. *The International Journal of Public Sector Management* 13(2), 142–152.

Napier, N. (1989) Mergers and acquisitions, human resource issues and outcomes: a review and suggested typology. *Journal of Management Studies* 26(3), 271–290.

Norgard, J. D. and Skodvin, O-J. (2002) The importance of geography and culture in mergers: a Norwegian institutional case study. *Higher Education* 44(1), 73–90.

Saffu, K. and Mamman, A. (2000) Contradictions in international tertiary strategic alliances: the case from Down Under. *The International Journal of Public Sector Management* 13(6), 508–518.

Shrivastava, P. (1986) Postmerger integration. *Journal of Business Strategy* 7, 65–76.

Skodvin, O-J. (1999) Mergers in higher education – success or failure?. *Tertiary Education and Management* 5(1), 65–80.

Vaara, E. (2002) On the discursive construction of success/failure in narratives of post-merger integration. *Organisation Studies* 23(2), 211–248.

Walsh, J. P. (1989) Doing a deal: merger and acquisition negotiations and their impact upon target company top management turnover. *Strategic Management Journal* 10, 307–322.

Wang, X. (2001) A policy analysis of the financing of higher education in China: two decades reviewed. *Journal of Higher Education Policy and Management* 23, November, 205–217.

Wyatt, J. (1998) A rapid result: the achievement of a merger in higher education. *Higher Education Review* 31(1), 15–35.

10 Effective corporate strategies for implementation of quality management in service organisations

An empirical research study

John Saee and Zahid Mahmood

Growing interest in QM

QM is a holistic management philosophy that emphasises the involvement of every employee at different levels of an organisation to achieve customer satisfaction and improve the organisation's effectiveness through continuous process improvement. QM principles and techniques have gained, and are gaining, both the attention and acceptance of practitioners as well as a growing number of academics. Advocates of this approach argue that a dynamic movement towards quality is critically needed, and the issues addressed by the 'quality movement' are both extensive and interrelated (Dow *et al.*, 1997).

Some QM critics report that the principles of QM are either too theoretical or too broad to be practical. The review of the literature shows that while these factors appear obvious, many organisations have in fact found them very difficult to execute. It is noteworthy that no single approach contains all of the keys to quality, and no cookbook approach can be applied to any company's situation and cultures. In short, a combination of many different factors, such as an organisational culture conducive to QM, the proper QM infrastructure and system readiness contribute to the success or failure of QM programmes.

It is not the aim of this chapter to discuss all the factors which may constrain an organisation's ability to nurture the implementation of QM; rather the intention is to examine corporate cultural change (CCC), internal organisational communication (IOC) and internal marketing (IM) in regard to the development of QM implementation initiatives. The contention is that the role of these factors in facilitating the articulation of a QM ethos is fundamentally undervalued and misunderstood in organisational settings. Here we argue that CCC, IOC and IM influence the extent to which organisations are successful in effecting a chosen strategic direction. Hence, if such strategic actions encompass a QM implementation, it can be argued that the proposed factors contribute to the success of QM implementation. These factors are briefly discussed in the next section.

The notion of internal marketing

IM is a tool that can be used to develop and motivate customer consciousness among employees. The concept of IM has been examined by a number of authors in the literature, yet no single unified definition exists (Rafiq and Ahmad, 1993). However, a review of the concept suggests that it can be related to a number of constructs, including market orientation, service culture or even empowerment of service providers (Spitzer, 1995; Hartline, 1994). IM as a philosophy described a customer-oriented culture in which everyone understands strategic intent or purpose and is motivated to participate in implementing the strategy. Integrating front and backstage activities requires a shared understanding of objectives and desired outcomes, as well as the role of these activities in the delivery process (McGuire 1999: 338).

This study proposes IM as a central component of QM initiatives, with the objective of getting everyone in the organisation oriented towards the same direction, and to developing awareness of the implementation of QM programmes and fostering a team spirit within the organisation. The specific objectives of IM from the perspective of the current study are described as follows:

- marketing activities are directed at employees, with the intention of motivating employees to better performance and improving relationships with each other; and
- marketing as an internal function with departments marketing their roles with each other and encouraging other functional areas to market themselves within the organisation.

Corporate cultural change

Accordingly, corporate culture is defined as 'the pattern of beliefs, values, rituals, myths, and sentiments shared by members of an organisation' (Harrison and Stokes 1992: 1). It is

> made up of those aspects of the organisation that give it a particular climate or feel. Culture is to an organisation what personality is to an individual. It is that distinctive constellation of beliefs, values, work styles, and relationships that distinguish one organisation from another.
>
> (Harrison and Stokes 1992: 13)

Ott (1989) indicates that corporate culture:

> is helpful for understanding and predicting a host of holistic organisational phenomena and behaviours involving, for example, employees' commitment and loyalty, leadership effectiveness, leadership succession, creativity, and innovation and organisational survival strategies.
>
> (p. 5).

The role of corporate culture in today's management is significant, as Shafritz and Ott (1992) point out:

a strong corporate culture literally controls organisational behaviour. For example, a corporate culture can block an organisation from making changes that are needed to adapt to a changing environment.

(p. 482)

The review of the literature implies that CCC is a potentially powerful explanatory variable in the implementation of a QM programme. Corporate culture in this study can be conceptually defined as the patterns of shared values, beliefs and organisationally relevant policies, plans and structures which shape how people should behave at work and which determine what tasks and goals are important.

Internal organisational communication

There is no commonly accepted definition of IOC; the concept seems to incorporate the message-sending and message-receiving behaviours of superiors, subordinates and peers with regard to task, personal and innovative topics. In the organisational communication literature IOC has been defined as face-to-face, meaning-centred interaction conducted as part of the managing role by managers in their organisations (Ticehurst *et al.*, 1991). Mastenbroek (1991: 27) argues that communication within the organisation aims 'to establish mutual understanding and trust between employees and functional departments. Cooperation is a critical success factor in building the necessary organisational culture and capability'. Further, he says it develops a clear conceptual framework that combines thinking on integrated internal and external communications and relationships among organisational members. Ticehurst *et al.* (1991) defined

> internal corporate communication as being broadly concerned with managing and administering communication resources and processes to facilitate communication within the organisations and between organisations and their communities.

(p. 81)

In the light of the literature review internal organisational communication in this study can be defined as the probability that an individual will attempt to share accurately his or her views, feelings and intentions with another, on matters pertinent to organisational objectives. IOC is a vehicle for achieving and maintaining a level of cooperation among organisational members by providing them with knowledge, skills and attitudes that create and maintain a corporate culture in which all members are enthusiastic for and committed to the implementation of new ideas. This is especially pertinent for present purposes since QM can be regarded as a new idea in contemporary organisations.

A conceptual model

To draw the existing knowledge and relevant factors into sharp focus, a conceptual model for the implementation of QM is proposed. This model aids in the formulation and empirical analysis of QM issues. One of the desired outcomes of this study is the identification of means for predicting, at an acceptable level of confidence, the likelihood of the successful implementation of QM programmes in service organisations. The proposed conceptual model of QM implementation specifically focuses on the role of IM in the creation of CCC; and also on internal organisational communication, which is conducive to the successful implementation of a QM programme.

The review of the literature reveals three higher-order concepts (IM, CCC and IOC) that are central to QM programmes and appear to be critical to their successful implementation. Although several studies have discussed the individual importance of these factors, none has integrated them into a conceptual framework and empirically examined the effects of these factors on QM implementation. Based on the conceptual framework of the study and the review of the literature, the general null hypotheses are:

H1 The level of perceived understanding of the common concepts of QM programmes is unrelated to the success of implementation of QM.
H2 There is a strong positive relationship between the level of internal marketing and effectiveness of internal organisational communication.
H3 The more importance that an organisation places on effective internal organisational communications, the more likely it is that QM implementation will be successful.
H4 There is a strong positive association between 'managed cultural change' and the level of internal marketing.
H5 Organisations that devote more effort to internal marketing are characterised by a corporate culture that supports change.
H6 Organisations in which the corporate culture supports change are more likely to be successful in QM implementation.

From both conceptual and practical standpoints it is both highly plausible and of considerable importance to recognise that the successful implementation of QM programmes is conditioned by the simultaneous effects of IM, IOC and CCC. At this point it is appropriate to integrate the foregoing discussion into the conceptual model, as shown in Figure 10.1.

Brief overview of research objectives

The emphasis in this investigation is on these factors (IM, IOC and CCC) and their interaction in the context of the implementation of QM programmes, rather than on more general QM issues that have been the subject of more 'popular' writing and investigation. In summary terms, the objectives are stated below:

1 The first objective of this research includes the examination of the current status of the implementation of QM programmes in the service sector.
2 The second goal of this study is to investigate and analyse the role of specific organisational and behavioural factors in promoting the successful

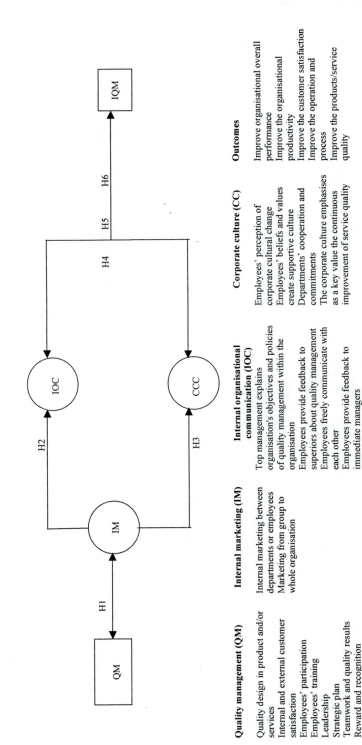

Quality management (QM)

Quality design in product and/or services
Internal and external customer satisfaction
Employees' participation
Employees' training
Leadership
Strategic plan
Teamwork and quality results
Reward and recognition

Internal marketing (IM)

Internal marketing between departments or employees
Marketing from group to whole organisation

Internal organisational communication (IOC)

Top management explains organisation's objectives and policies of quality management within the organisation
Employees provide feedback to superiors about quality management
Employees freely communicate with each other
Employees provide feedback to immediate managers
Employees provide feedback to top managers

Corporate culture (CC)

Employees' perception of corporate cultural change
Employees' beliefs and values create supportive culture
Departments' cooperation and commitments
The corporate culture emphasises as a key value the continuous improvement of service quality

Outcomes

Improve organisational overall performance
Improve the organisational productivity
Improve the customer satisfaction
Improve the operation and process
Improve the products/service quality

Figure 10.1 A conceptual model of the process of implementation of quality management (QM).

implementation of QM programmes in the service sector. Specifically, this study focuses on factors set forth in the literature that are believed to determine the fate of the implementation of QM programs.

3   The third aim of this research is to develop a conceptual model by making explicit the nature of the interaction between the proposed constructs (IM, IOC and CCC).

4   The fourth is based on the results of the study, and will be concerned with developing practical guidelines for the successful implementation of QM programmes, and the identification of practical guidelines for QM implementation.

The research question

The extensive review of the literature provides numerous instances of organisations that have implemented QM programmes and have achieved negative outcomes. While the issue defies meaningful quantification post facto, positive results from QM programmes would appear to be the exception rather than the rule. In fact, it has been suggested that the number of successful implementations of QM programmes may be insignificant when compared with the number of futile implementations (Parry and Song, 1993). Beyond the hyperbole, later surveys have suggested that over 80 per cent of organisations implementing QM programmes have failed to achieve measurable let alone positive results (Schaffer and Thomson, 1992).

The available evidence, while not unequivocal, would strongly suggest that there are some significant defects in or problems with what can generally be labelled as 'QM'. It is this domain that underlies this research. However, 'what exactly is the problem' is the question that must first be addressed. The specific research question that relates to the goal stated may be broken into three distinct but related parts, expressed here as questions:

1   Are QM practitioners (the individuals who are given the specific responsibility for the implementation of QM activities) conversant in any meaningful way, with the details QM (implementation components of QM programmes) and if so, how do they go about implementing a QM programme in the service sector?

2   What is the nature of the interaction, if any, between IOC, CCC and IM as determinants of the successful implementation of a QM programme?

3   What roles are played by IOC, CCC and IM settings adopted by the service organisations in the successful implementation of a QM programme?

Research methodology and data collection

This part of the study describes the research methodology and the process of data collection needed in order to empirically test the model developed in the previous section. For this purpose it is clear that both an appropriate research methodology and a substantial body of data are necessary. In constructing a research design this study addresses a number of critical questions including the unit of analysis, the time frame of the investigation, the sampling unit, anticipated challenges to the research and the method of data collection. The following sections discuss the critical components that comprise the design of this study under these headings.

The unit of analysis

The unit of analysis in this study is a *service organisation*. Conceptually, a service organisation is any organisation that is engaged in the delivery of one or more offerings that are not simply, or even predominantly, tangible products. Clearly, the overwhelming majority of organisations would qualify as service organisations if this were taken to its limits. The intention here is to make a distinction, albeit somewhat arbitrarily, between organisations for which the intangible or service component of their activities is a substantial part of the total offering.

Therefore, operationally in this research, a service organisation is any organisation in the public sector service, not-for-profit sector as well as private for-profit or industrial organisations which have implemented QM programmes (with a population of at least 50 employees) who are given the specific responsibility for QM activities within the organisation.

This study examines a set of service organisations that have been engaged in a QM programme. The informants in this investigation were individuals within chosen service organisations who have had some level of involvement in the creation and implementation of a QM programme. These informants were surveyed and the data gathered using a structured research instrument and the information derived was used to answer the research questions.

The time frame

The second issue was the time frame of the study. However, the time constraints and the indeterminate duration of QM projects make this virtually impossible to do, at least within the scope of this research. The approach adopted aims to maximise the informative power of the data gathered and to gain insights about the organisations through time by means of informant opinion and recollection.

The sampling unit

The researchers personally approached selected major service organisations, which were known from published sources to have implemented a QM programme in the recent past within their operations in Australia. The number of informants from each organisation was not predetermined, but a process of judgement sampling of informants was adopted. A questionnaire was distributed to respondents by hand after they had been nominated by a key informant in each organisation. Respondents were given detailed instructions for completing the survey in a covering letter accompanying the questionnaire under the aegis of the University of Western Sydney.

Anticipated challenges to the research

Though the theoretical foundations of QM have been long established, the practical implementation of the various QM methodologies is still in its early stages. As a consequence, and moreover because of the nature of this form of managerial process being largely unobservable and confidential, it is challenging to even identify organisations that have been involved in such practices. Consequently, gaining access to the field has been one of the greater challenges to this research.

Data collection

Prior to distributing the questionnaire, a selected number of service organisations were asked by the researcher whether they were willing to participate in this study. Then the method of data collection which can best be described as 'personal delivery, explanation and personal collection' was adopted. The researcher contacted each selected organisation and established the identity of a key contact who would be the primary source of contact with that organisation. The author explained to this contact the purpose of the study, the length of the questionnaire, the method of its completion and the procedure for distributing the questionnaire to those employees who are involved in the implementation of QM programmes, and was also assured of the confidentiality of the results. The contact was asked to coordinate the distribution and return the completed questionnaires.

Data analysis and findings

The purpose of this section is to examine the relationship between the independent variables (IOC, CCC and IM) and the dependent variable (implementation of QM programmes) and to test the hypotheses pertaining to these relationships. These examinations are performed by the following steps:

1   an examination of the respondents' perception of QM's implementation components[1] and the implementation of a QM programme; and
2   an assessment of the role of IOC, CCC and IM in facilitating and promoting the implementation of QM programmes.

The roles of these factors, both combined and individually, are examined based on two separate but related measures: extent and importance. The main purpose of these two measures is to provide an exploration of the ways in which the major issues (IM, IOC and CCC) relate to the successful implementation of QM programmes. *Extent* refers to the incidence with which specific components of QM implementation occurred, and *importance* reflects the evaluation by the observer of the importance of each component of the implementation process. The comparison of these two measures was undertaken in order to allow the researcher to draw conclusions in the light of the study model. First, however, a brief overview of the types and characteristics of respondents to the survey is provided.

Characteristics of the study respondents

The respondents in each of the subject service organisations consisted of quality managers, chief executive officeers/top management, customer service managers, account/financial managers and operation managers. Table 10.1 presents the distribution of respondents according to their title, the nature of their organisation and related descriptors.

Hence, the achieved sample can be characterised as comprising mostly males, who have mostly been in their current position for a short time, and in roles that, judging from the terminology used in describing their position, are largely service-quality connected. The organisations studied can be typified as being predominantly less service-oriented (e.g. wholesalers and others), as relatively recent 'converts' to QM and as organisations that were judged by respondents to be spending about the right amount of resources on QM.

Basic description of the achieved data set

The purpose of this section is to provide a broad description and appreciation of the nature and scope of the data collected. This section is divided into three parts, each dealing with an aspect of responses achieved, namely:

Table 10.1 Distribution of position titles of respondents

Category	Classification	Frequency	Percentage
Nature of organisation	Highly service-oriented	46	22
	Largely service-oriented	17	8
	Partly service-oriented	33	17
	Less service-oriented	108	51
Period of QM implementation	1984–1990	5	3
	1990–1995	20	10
	1996–2000	50	87
Total spending on QM implementation programme	Far too little	32	15.2
	About right	142	67.3
	Much too much	9	4.3
Title of respondents	CEO/Top management	26	12
	Quality managers	90	43
	Service managers	26	12
	Finance managers	6	3
	Operation managers	37	16
	Other	1	0.5
Length in position	1 year	194	91.9
	2 years	16	7.6
	3 years	1	0.5
Gender	Male	124	59
	Female	73	35
Total organisations		124	59

1 respondents' overall rating of the degree of success achieved in the implementation of QM programmes;
2 ratings of the incidence and importance of each of the implementation components that typically comprise a QM programme; and
3 summary results in respect of CCC, IOC and IM.

Respondent evaluation of QM success

The first section of the survey assesses the respondent's overall impression of the level of success of the implementation of QM programmes in their organisation, for which a four-point scale was used.[2] The achieved distribution of cases across this critical dependent variable was as follows (Table 10.2).

These results led the analyst to review the differences between the scale positions for this critical dependent variable, noting the quite unequal distribution between successful and unsuccessful organisations. Taking account of the fine semantic distinction that respondents were expected to make between the positions of 'completely' and 'largely' at both ends of the scale, it was judged that a more parsimonious account of the variation would be desirable, with minimal loss of information. Moreover, the focus of the research was on the determinants of success and failure, and the issue of *degree* of success as implied by the original scale was not of central concern at this stage of the analysis. In addition, considering the alternative analytical approaches to the data that could be taken, the fact was that the scale as originally devised was categorical in character with no pretence to metric properties, and hence a classificatory technique would have been, and indeed was still, most appropriate.

As a consequence, it was resolved to collapse the scale to a simple dichotomy, reflecting a clearer delineation between organisations judged to be successful and those judged to be less than successful. Thus, the analysis was undertaken on this recoded dichotomy for the dependent variable (Table 10.3).

The second section of the questionnaire dealt with the respondent's understanding of the components of QM and how they had been addressed in the process of QM implementation. Questions 1 to 16 of this section contained measures of the usage of these components. These measures provide an answer to the first part of the research question, namely 'Are individuals who are given specific responsibility for the implementation of QM activities conversant with the details of QM programmes and if so, how do they go about implementing a QM programme?'.

Table 10.2 Respondent's overall impression of success

Scale position	Number of cases	% achieved
1 Completely successful	40	19.0
2 Largely successful	130	61.6
3 Largely unsuccessful	36	17.1
4 Completely unsuccessful	5	2.4
Total	211	100.0

Table 10.3 Successful and less than successful companies

Recoded scale position	Number of cases	% achieved
1 Mostly successful	40	19.0
2 Mostly unsuccessful	171	81.0
Total	211	100.0

Respondents were asked to rate each issue on a six-point Likert-style scale, drawn from Tagliaferri's total quality management survey (Tagliaferri, 1991).

The third part of the questionnaire considered the respondent's perception of the specific contextual issues pertinent to the implementation of QM. In this section of the questionnaire, respondents were asked to rate two dimensions of each of the sixteen contextual issues. Ratings were obtained of both (a) 'the extent to which the issue is evident or happens in your part of this organisation' and (b) 'how important you believe each issue is to your part of this organisation', as discussed earlier in this chapter. This 'dual' measure was adopted based upon established procedures in survey research in which both the presence or absence of some phenomenon, and the importance of that phenomenon, are measured in order to give a richer appreciation of the issue being investigated.

Hence, respondents were asked to rate, using a four-point scale[3], the degree to which they perceived that each of the predictors of success in QM implementation was evident in their organisation. This part of the study provides an answer to the second part of the research question concerned with being able 'to determine the interaction of IOC, organisational culture and IM for the successful implementation of QM programmes'.

The last part of Section 3 of the questionnaire asked respondents to rate on a five-point scale[4] (Yusof *et al.*, 1999) the degree of importance of each of the factors identified as being relevant to the successful implementation of QM in their organisation. The findings of this part of the study provide an answer to the third part of the research question, namely 'What is the relative importance of IOC, corporate cultural issues, and IM settings adopted by the organisation for the successful implementation of a QM programme?'. The final part of the survey addressed aspects of the respondent's background and general questions relating to the organisation for which each worked. The measures included here were Table 10.4.

Overall evaluation of the successful implementation of QM programmes

The status of the implementation of QM was evaluated based on respondents' overall perception of the QM programme in their organisation. Only 19 per cent of organisations were judged to have been completely successful, whereas 81 per cent were in the other categories, suggesting less than complete success. Clearly, in this study the ratio of successful to unsuccessful is considerably less than one might expect in the light of the level of attention devoted to QM in the literature

Table 10.4 Organisational and respondent measures taken

Organisational measures	Respondent measures
Name of organisation	Formal title of the person completing the survey
Type of organisation	
Length of time for QM programme implementation	Length of tenure in his or her current position
Budget allocation for the implementation of QM programmes	
Annual revenue of the organisation	Respondent gender
Total spending on the implementation of QM programmes	

and the strong advocacy in contemporary business practice of the virtues of QM. When employees and managers, such as those studied here, rate the success of QM, one gets the strong indication from this sample that the majority of instances in which firms have attempted to implement QM could in fact be described as unsuccessful. Certainly, one has to question the objectivity of observers who are themselves part of the system that they are evaluating, but one might under these conditions expect an upward bias in estimates of the incidence of success, rather than the apparent negativity evident in these findings.

The above results show that organisations that have successfully implemented QM programmes and achieved positive results are in the minority. In fact, based on anecdotal accounts in addition to the results such as were obtained in the present study, one could be excused for assuming that the incidence of successful implementation of QM is insignificant when compared with the number of unsuccessful implementations. One is unlikely in any case to be able to assess this question in any rigorous fashion, for the foregoing reasons.

A more concrete, alternative measure of success is to adopt a 'self-designated' measure, derivable by simply asking informants in organisations to rank, in a non-comparative way, their success using a questionnaire, and this alternative was adopted with arguably good effect in the present study. No evidence was found of this approach having been adopted in any of the literature on QM.

QM programmes implementation process

The process of QM implementation in an organisation is dependent on the institution of a number of steps or activities. These activities are typically adopted in practice and are commonly specified in the literature as being necessarily undertaken by organisations that are committed to QM (Deming, 1986; Eklof *et al.*, 1999; Guilhon, 1998). Hence, the results of the ratings of these 'critical elements' of QM are considered next. The mean and standard deviation of the ratings of each of the implementation components of QM programmes are shown in Table 10.5.

Table 10.5 Incidence of presence of QM implementation components

Implementation components of QM programmes	Mean	Standard deviation
(1) Quality design in products and services		
There is a programme to build quality into the design and development of all our services	2.14*	1.09
(2) Internal and external customers satisfaction		
The service requirements of external customers are understood by staff who should understand their needs	2.20*	1.11
The service requirements of internal customers are understood by staff who should understand their needs	2.24*	0.97
Customer satisfaction research is conducted in this organisation	2.06*	1.32
(3) Employee participation		
Employees in this organisation are supportive of our QM implementation	2.36*	1.02
(4) Employee training		
Employees at all levels are provided with training about their role in our QM programme	2.18*	1.17
(5) Leadership		
Our top management is committed to the implementation of QM	1.72*	1.02
Our top management provides effective leadership in QM	2.10*	1.09
(6) Strategic plan		
QM principles are an explicit part of this organisationís overall strategic plan	1.90*	1.09
This organisation has specific goals and objectives to improve service quality	1.97*	1.16
This organisation uses strategic planning processes to decide where it will be in the next five to ten years	1.43*	1.99
Our formal strategic planning guides the implementation of QM programme	2.37*	1.35
(7) Teamwork and quality results		
The focus in this organisation is on developing effective QM work teams to achieve common goals	2.34*	1.16
There have been improvements to performance as a direct result of QM	2.05*	1.18
(8) Reward and recognition		
QM teams are formally recognised for their QM implementation efforts	2.51*	1.28
QM teams are formally rewarded for their QM implementation	2.92*	1.33

Notes
* indicates significant differences beyond $P < 0.001$ in the mean.
A higher mean score on the scale indicates that a component was perceived to be done less often.

Descriptive results for implementation factors (IM, IOC and CCC)

The conceptual model developed in the above section prescribed three broad classes of organisational factors (IM, IOC and CCC), which combine to promote the successful implementation of QM programmes. A comparison of respondents' ratings of the extent to which each was utilised and of the importance of each class in determining the success of QM implementation was the initial focus of analysis.

A composite measure (extent and importance) was formed from the implementation issues of QM programmes. The composite scale was computed by multiplying the value of each item (extent and importance) on a scale of one to five, which give a richer appreciation to the analyst of both what was done and how important it was that each element was done. In Table 10.6 the mean and standard deviation of composite measure of each item is presented.

Multiple determination of group membership

The analytical objective at this stage was to be able to optimally discriminate between the categories of the dependent variable, and hence to be able to predict success on the basis of the scores achieved on the large number of independent variables. The procedure most suited to this purpose was judged to be multiple discriminant analysis (MDA) (Hair *et al.*, 1992). The following section describes the MDA approach to determining whether statistically significant differences exist between the average score profiles of the groups of the dependent variable, which in this case was a measure of perceived success in implementation of QM. Further, the objective was to determine which of the independent variables accounted most for the differences in the average score profiles of the two groups of 'success'. The dependent variable was measured by the question, 'All things considered, in my view the QM programme was or has been (circle one number)', and this was scaled as: 1, completely successful; 2, largely successful; 3, largely unsuccessful; and 4, completely unsuccessful.

In order to more realistically represent the summary judgements of respondents this scale was collapsed and dichotomised into: 1, mostly successful; and 2, most unsuccessful. The use of MDA was deemed most appropriate in this study because of the foregoing objective and because there was a single, non-metric or categorical dependent variable and a large set of metrically scaled independent variables (Hair *et al.*, 1992: 94).

The specification of independent variables

The discriminant function is represented by

$$Y = v_1 X_1 + v_2 X_2 + \ldots v_n X_n$$

where Y is the discriminant score for a given case and v_n represents the standardised discriminant coefficient for each of the n independent variables.

Table 10.6 Implementation issues in QM programmes

Implementation issues in QM programmes	Extent of usage		Importance		Composite measure	
	Mean[a]	Standard deviation	Mean[b]	Standard deviation	Mean	Standard deviation
Internal marketing						
Departments practise internal marketing in dealing with other departments	2.85	1.02	3.60	1.11	10.46	5.20
A key aspect of our internal marketing programme is effective communication within the organisation	3.06	0.94	4.06	1.00	12.75	5.54
A key component of our internal marketing programme is the creation of a pleasant working environment	3.20	0.94	3.99	0.92	12.96	5.14
A key component of our internal marketing programme is QM training for all employees	3.07	0.98	4.09	0.94	12.86	5.50
This organisation gives equal attention to internal and external marketing	2.88	1.07	3.69	1.07	10.98	5.75
Group means	3.01		3.89			
Internal organisational communication						
Top management openly communicates with their subordinates about the objectives, policies and plans for QM	3.27	0.77	4.27	0.86	14.10	4.74
Employees are encouraged to provide feedback to superiors about QM issues	3.26	0.80	4.09	0.88	13.59	4.88
Employees are encouraged to freely communicate with each other about QM issues	3.36	0.85	4.09	0.94	14.01	5.24
Employees provide feedback to their immediate managers about QM issues	3.12	0.76	4.12	0.85	13.10	4.68
Employees provide feedback to top managers about QM issues	2.73	0.84	3.86	0.91	10.87	4.90
Group means	3.15		4.09			
Corporate Cultural Change						

Implementation issues in QM programmes	Extent of usage		Importance		Composite measure	
	Mean[a]	Standard deviation	Mean[b]	Standard deviation	Mean	Standard deviation
Our corporate culture has changed in order to support QM implementation	3.30	0.87	4.20	0.83	14.05	4.98
Our corporate culture encourages QM implementation	3.36	0.82	4.22	0.86	14.38	4.85
Top management express their strong beliefs and values, which helps to create a QM culture	3.22	0.87	4.24	0.83	13.82	4.98
The corporate culture emphasises as a key or core value, the continuous improvement of service quality	3.46	0.78	4.34	0.75	15.15	4.57
Departments cooperate in implementing our QM programme	3.10	0.71	4.25	0.78	13.34	4.28
Management encourages departments to cooperate in implementing our QM programme	3.31	0.78	4.11	0.79	13.69	4.51
Group means	3.29		4.23			

Notes
a A low mean score suggests less commonly done.
b A high mean score suggests less importance attached to an item.

The discriminant coefficients measure the contribution that each independent variable makes to the discrimination function. Discriminant analysis was used to determine which of the independent variables best distinguish between the two groups of the dependent variable in a general test of Hypothesis 1, namely that 'the level of perceived understanding of the common concepts of QM programmes is unrelated to the success of implementation of QM'.

Sample division for validation purposes

In accordance with the established cross-validation approach (Frank et al., 1965; Green and Carroll, 1978; Perreault et al., 1979), the sample was divided equally into analysis and holdout subsamples. Thus, the analysis sample was used to derive the discriminant function and the results were applied to the latter. The results of this process are reported later, following the derivation of the functions.

MDA function derivation

The MDA was conducted using the SPSSPC for Windows Version 10.0 package, adopting stepwise analysis, with prior probabilities set equal to group size. In the following tables the detailed results of the discriminant analysis are shown in standard format as produced directly from the SPSSPC results file. These outputs of the discriminant analysis are the standardised discriminant function coefficients, the structure matrix of the discriminant functions evaluated at the centroids of the two groups and the classification of results. The results are reported in Tables 10.7 and 10.8.

As is customary, the first step in MDA is concerned with derivation of a discriminant function (Hair *et al.*, 1992: 111) and in this context the derived MDA functions can be summarised as follows.

Thus, the first function accounted for the majority of the variance and was shown to be significant beyond the .000 level, and was thus retained for the second stage of validation.

Validation of discriminant functions

Next, with respect to validation of the discriminant function, one generally has regard to the classification matrix, which shows the predictive accuracy of the derived functions.

Considering the foregoing results, it is clear that the derived discriminant function 1 provides improved predictive power over chance allocation. The maximum chance criterion is the hit-ratio (correct classification) if all cases were simply assumed to be in the largest class. For this discriminant function the maximum chance criterion for the total sample was 76.9 per cent (based on the majority of respondents who were in group 2). On this basis, the derived function that correctly classified 80.0 per cent improved marginally on the maximum likelihood criterion, providing some reassurance as to function validity.

An alternative basis for establishing validity is to consider the proportional chance criterion, or C_{pro}. The proportional chance criterion is calculated by squaring the proportions in each group, $C_{pro} = p_1^2 + \ldots p_n^2$, which gives the results in Table 10.9.

Hence, the proportional chance criterion was 57 per cent for the analysis sample, and 53 per cent for the holdout sample, providing further evidence of the validity of the derived discriminant function. The maximum chance criterion suggests that 76.9 per cent of cases would be correctly classified for the analysis

Table 10.7. Summary of canonical discriminant functions

Function	Eigenvalue	% of variance	Cumulative %	Canonical correlation
1	0.410[a]	100	100	0.539

Note
a First 1 canonical functions were used in the analysis.

Table 10.8. Wilks' lambda

Test of function(s)	Wilks' lambda	Chi-square	df	Sig.
1	0.709	34.726	2	0.000

sample and 82.2 per cent for the holdout sample. These findings suggest that the validity of the derived function is acceptable in a study of this kind (Hair et al., 1992).

As a further test of the discriminating power of the classification matrix when compared to chance, Press' Q was calculated using the following formula:

$$\text{Press' } Q = \frac{\left[N - \left(n \times K\right)\right]^2}{N\left(K - 1\right)}$$

where N is the total sample size, n = number of observations correctly classified and K = number of groups.

For the analysis sample this provides the following result:

$$Q = \frac{\left[110 - \left(88 \times 2\right)\right]^2}{110\left(2 - 1\right)}$$

$$= 39.2$$

For the holdout sample the results were:

$$Q = \frac{\left[101 - \left(86 \times 2\right)\right]^2}{101\left(2 - 1\right)}$$

$$= 49.6$$

The above measures consider the numbers of correct classifications in light of the total sample sizes and the number of groups. The calculated value is then compared with a critical value (which for this instance is the chi-square value for one degree of freedom at the desired confidence level), and if it exceeds this critical value, then the classification matrix can be deemed statistically better than chance allocation (Hair et al., 1992: 106). The critical value at a significance level of 0.01 is 6.63. Hence with calculated Q at 39.2 and 49.6, the derived discriminant

Table 10.9 Classification of result

Proportional chance criterion calculation for the analysis sample, $n = 110$	Proportional chance criterion calculation for the holdout sample, $n = 101$
$C_{pro} = (24/110)^2 + (80/110)^2$	$C_{pro} = (15/101)^2 + (72/101)^2$
$C_{pro} = 0.57$	$C_{pro} = 0.53$

analysis can be described as predicting group membership better than chance, albeit with due attention to the caveat about the effect of large sample size on the stability of Press' *Q*. (Hair *et al.*, 1992: 106).

Discriminant analysis of independent variables

In the following section, the results of the MDA analysis for all the independent variables are presented. The interpretation of the derived discriminant function for each component constitutes the focus of the following discussion. The standardised discriminant function coefficients for a given independent variable reflect the discriminatory power of each independent variable, and are sometimes referred to simply as discriminant weights. The following Table 10.10 shows that two of the independent variables had large discriminant coefficients.

These results identify the most significant discriminating variables as being concerned with 'employees support the implementation of QM programmes' and 'management encourages departments for the implementation of QM programmes'. However, while these variables are identified as being the best discriminators, a range of additional factors are suggested as being of relevance. In fact, from the structure matrix it is possible to suggest that a number of additional factors are relevant in this context, despite the lack of strict statistical significance, and these variables are listed in the following Table 10.11.

As is shown, the derived discriminant function is highly significant, indicated by the chi-square value of 34.726 and the associated significance level of 0.000. The canonical correlation of 0.539 shows the degree of association between the discriminant scores and the two groups. Collectively, these results suggest that the discrimination is both statistically significant and quite robust.

The structure matrix indicates the relative contributions of each of the independent variables to the discriminant function. 'Employees support the implementation of QM programmes' and 'management encourages departments for the implementation of QM programmes' were shown to be the best discriminators between the two groups of the dependent variable, and hence are indicated as the most critical factor in the success of QM. The magnitude of the coefficients can be interpreted as indicating the relative importance of 'employee support' and 'management encouragement' for the successful implementation of QM programmes.

Although all other independent variables (implementation components and issues of QM programmes) are statistically significant ($P<0.001$), employee support and management encouragement evaluated value for the discriminant function at

Table 10.10 Standardised canonical discriminant function coefficients

Variables	Function 1
The role of employee support for the implementation of QM programmes	0.670
Management encourage departments to cooperate for the implementation of QM programmes	−0.664

Table 10.11 The role of each independent variable

	Function
	1
Employees support for QM implementation Q4	0.752
Management encourage departments for QM implementation (issue) Q11	−0.747
Employees are encouraged to freely communicate with each other about QM issues Q3[a]	−0.581
Internal customer needs Q3[a]	0.579
Top management leadership Q8[a]	−0.569
Employees feedback to superior (issue) Q2[a]	−0.567
Employees feedback to managers (issue) Q4[a]	0.561
Corporate culture encourages QM (issue) Q7[a]	−0.554
Departments cooperate in QM implementation (issue) Q1[a]	−0.552
Corporate culture emphasises QM (issue) Q9[a]	−0.543
IM is QM training for employees (issue) Q15[a]	−0.529
Top management communicate with employees (issue) Q1[a]	−0.527
Developing QM team Q10[a]	0.523
Corporate culture supports QM implementation (issue) Q6[a]	−0.516
Employees feedback to top management (issue) 5[a]	−0.509
Direct result of QM implementation Q16[a]	0.501
Customer satisfaction research Q6[a]	0.500
Employees training for QM programmes Q5[a]	0.495
Top management strong belief (issue) Q8[a]	0.492
IM create pleasant environment (issue) Q14[a]	−0.491
Top management commitment Q7[a]	0.473
QM team recognised Q11[a]	0.458
QM principles are explicit Q9[a]	0.436
External customer needs Q2[a]	0.433
QM teams rewarded Q12[a]	0.430
Formal strategic planning Q15[a]	0.402
Quality deisgn in service and product Q1[a]	0.391
Department practice IM (issue) Q12[a]	−0.382
IM effective communication (issue) Q13[a]	−0.371
Equal attention internal and external marketing (issue) Q16[a]	−0.367
Specific goals and objectives Q13[a]	0.306
Strategic planning for next 5 to 10 years Q14[a]	0.286
Respondent title[a]	0.105
Type of industry[a]	0.066

Notes
Pooled within-groups correlations between discriminating variables and standardised canonical discriminant functions.
Variables ordered by absloute size of correlation within function
a   This variable not used in the analysis.

the group centroids show good separation between the groups. Further, the computed values show that the 'mostly successful' group means of these factors are 1.54 and 17.25, and 'mostly unsuccessful' group means are 2.6 and 13.62.

Summary

The reported results emphasise the need to closely integrate employee support and management encouragement of departments in the overall QM process in the pursuit of quality objectives. The findings derived are important in that the managers questioned generally place less emphasis on standards and specific procedures in effecting quality; instead they stress the importance of human aspects of QM implementation. Thus, the findings hold practical relevance for management in service organisations concerned with implementing QM programmes.

Indeed, the results offer support to the growing emphasis that is being placed on the 'soft' aspects of QM and fit well with the evolving literature which emphasises the importance of the issues of employee support and management encouragement of departments in QM implementation. Hill (1995), for example, has argued that the major exponents of QM have not articulated a comprehensive stance on issues relating to the support for QM by employees or adequately conceptualised the role of departmental management. They added that this is an important consideration, especially since the success or failure of QM depends on the way it is made to work by employees, from the frontline through all levels of management (p. 12). However, it would be unwise to assume that just because managers subscribe to the notion that the human-related dimension underpins the QM implementation process that this dimension is necessarily practised in their organisations.

While recognising the necessity for employee support and management encouragement of departments, most QM writers have suggested that effective QM implementation requires a formally organised QM function within the organisation (Deming, 1986). The role of employee support and departmental encouragement is to facilitate the development and execution of QM-related issues (Oakland and Oakland, 1997). This facilitative role is in contrast to the task-based role that QM functions have traditionally played in organisations where the primary activity was, figuratively speaking, to 'inspect quality in' by undertaking rigorous inspection of incoming materials and outgoing products/services (Garvin, 1988).

The results of the present study suggest the possibility that these assumptions may be flawed. One plausible explanation of these results is the widely held view that QM programmes failures are caused by implementation-related deficiencies. This study has identified the fact that informed individuals in organisations emphasise employee support and management encouragement of departments as being the primary issues underlying the successful implementation of QM programmes. However, it is possible that many organisations may not be pursuing QM with a balanced view towards internal organisation and human-related dimensions of the organisations functioning. These findings are consistent with Menon *et al.* (1997), who suggested the possibility that interactions between functional areas and employee involvement may be more important drivers of the successful implementation of QM programmes.

Limitations of study

It is readily acknowledged that this study has some shortcomings and limitations in the area of the specifics of 'how to' regarding the successful implementation of QM in the service sector. Although this study did determine, within the limitations of the method, the determinants of 'successful implementation', there still exists a deficiency of understanding of the measures (the role of employee support and management encouragement of department) of QM implementation programmes.

The insights into the implementation of QM programmes were gained through quantitative research (survey method). Due to the comfort level, or lack thereof, of the frontline employees in verbalising their perceptions of QM programmes, the researcher would suggest that future research should incorporate a component of qualitative research (focus group interview) to gain greater insight into the nature and context of QM implementation.

Notwithstanding the methodology aspects of the study, there are still limitations to the database and analyses that must be highlighted. This survey is a cross-sectional sample at one specific point in time. As a result, while causal relationships can be inferred, they cannot be strictly proven. A longitudinal research design with requisite controls and before–after measures would be necessary to properly test causality. This, unfortunately, is difficult to achieve with subjects such as the organisations and their employees. Such investigation would almost certainly represent a major imposition on respondents and an intrusion into the daily operation of service organisations.

Further research

The review of the literature leads to three research questions regarding the overall implementation of QM programmes: are QM practitioners conversant with the details and how do they implement programmes; what is the interaction of critical factors; and what is the role of these factors for the successful implementation of QM programmes? The first research question is confirmatory in nature and can be broken into a specific hypothesis. In this study discriminant analysis was used to determine which of the independent variables best distinguishes between the two groups of dependent variable in a general test of the first hypothesis.

The second and third research questions are largely exploratory and, thus, are not amenable to developing a set of testable hypotheses. For this reason, the survey data has been split into analysis and holdout subsamples. The results of these investigations indicate that a significant relationship does exist between the factors that contribute the successful implementation of QM programmes in the service sector. This can be explored with minor modifications to the conceptual model, which arrived different to the model in Figure 10.1. The model did not test for the existence of reciprocal effects (e.g., between QM and IM, IOC, CCC) and the research hypotheses (e.g., level of perceived understanding, level of IM, effectiveness of internal organisational communication, managed cultural change, effort devoted to IM, and corporate culture that support change).

It is difficult to attain a correctly identified model that contains bidirectional parameters. However, results from estimation of models with alternative causal orderings suggest that if technical difficulties can be overcome, future tests of bidirectional effects are likely to strengthen the model (Heskett, Sasser and Schlesinger, 1997). The successful implementation of QM programmes explained by the model is substantial, further elaboration of the model through incorporation of additional theoretically important variables is likely to enhance its explanatory power. These include the perceived understanding of QM, and supportive corporate culture. To determine the generalisability of the model and identify the boundary conditions, the model should be tested in a range of service delivery environments.

In all investigations of this type the choice of analytical approach to the data is guided as much by the data as by the research objectives and the proclivities of the researcher. In the present study there were obstacles to pursuit of classification using factor analytic methods, and this would certainly be an area worthy of further investigation. This study has employed the MDA technique in assessing the interaction of variables and the classification of organisations.

The major conclusion of this study is that QM should be perceived as a major cultural change issue for any organisation. QM logic is a different way of thinking, and it represents a paradigm shift in terms of management style and organisational restructuring. QM requires collaboration and involvement of all the group members, and that calls for a team spirit in order to achieve the desired goals. The challenge for service organisations, public or privately owned, is to re-educate the employees to recognise the group rather than the individual player as the centre of organisational activity.

Notes

1 These are quality design in products or services; internal and external customer's satisfaction; employee's participation; employee's training; leadership; strategic planning; teamwork; quality results; and reward and recognition.
2 1, completely successful; 2, largely successful; 3, largely unsuccessful; and 4, completely unsuccessful. Hereafter referred to as Scale A.
3 1, not at all; 2, rarely to a minor extent; 3, mostly to a limited extent; 4, always to the fullest extent; and X, I am not sure about this issue. Hereafter referred to as Scale C.
4 1, not at all important; 2, below average importance; 3, average importance; 4, above average importance; and 5, extremely important. Hereafter referred to as Scale D.

Bibliography

Becker, S. W. *et al.* (1994) TQM and organisation of the firm: theoretical and empirical perspectives. *Quality Management Journal* 1, 18–24.

Berry, L. L. (1984) The Employees as Customer. *Journal of Retail Banking* 3, 33–44.

Bounds, G. *et al.* (1994) *Beyond Total Quality Management: toward the emerging.* New York: McGraw-Hill.

Carman, J. M. (1993) Continuous quality improvement as a survival strategy: the Southern Pacific experience. *California Management Review* 35, 118–132.

Deming, W. E. (1986) *Out of the Crisis.* Cambridge, MA: MIT Centre for Advanced Engineering.

Dow, D. *et al*. (1997) 'Exploding the myth: do all quality management practices contribute to superior quality performance?', working paper, Melbourne Business School, University of Melbourne, Melbourne.

Easton, George S. (1993) The 1993 state of US total quality management: a Baldrige Award examiner's perspective. *California Management Review* 35(33), 32–54.

Eklof, J. A. *et al*. (1999) On measuring interaction between customer satisfaction and financial results. *Total Quality Management Journal* 10(4/5), 514–22.

Fisher, T. J. (1993) The view from the top: chief executive's perceptions of total quality management. *Australian Journal of Quality Management* 18, 181–195.

Frank, R. E. *et al*. (1965) Bias in multiple discriminant analysis. *Journal of Marketing Research* 2(3), 250–58.

Garvin, D. (1988) *Managing Quality*. New York: Free Press.

Green, P. E. and Carroll, J. D. (1978) *Mathmetical Tools for Applied Multivariate Analysis*. New York: Academic Press.

Greising, David (1994) Quality: how to make it pay. *Business Week* 8, August, 54–59.

Guilhon, A. (1998) 'Quality approaches in small or medium-sized enterprises: methodology and survey results. *Total Quality Management* 9(8), 689.

Hair, J. R. *et al*. (1992) *Multivariate Data Analysis with Readings*. 3rd edn. New York: Macmillan Publishing Company.

Harrington, D. and Akehurst, G. (2000) An empirical study of service quality implementation. *The Service Industries Journal* 2, 133–156.

Harrington, D. and Akehurst, G. (1996) An exploratory investigation into managerial perception of service quality in UK hotels. *Progress in Tourism and Hospitality Research* 2(3), 135–50.

Harrison, R. and Stokes, H. (1992) *Diagnosing Organisational Culture*. San Diego, CA: Pfeiffer and Company.

Hartline, M. D. (1994) Managerial determinants of service quality implementation: a test of normative principles. *Marketing Theory and Application* 5.

Helmi, A. M. (1998) Measuring the effect of customer satisfaction on profitability: a challenging role for management accountants. *The National Public Accountant* 43(10), 1–8.

Heskett, James L., Sasser, W. Earl Jr. and Schlesinger, Leonard A. (1997) *The Service Profit Chain*. New York: Free Press.

Hill, S. (1995) 'From Quality Circles to Total Quality Management', pp. 33–53 in Adrian Wilkinson and Hugh Willmott (eds) *Making Quality Critical: new perspectives on organizational change*. London: Routledge.

Ittner, C. D. (1994) An examination of the indirect productivity gains from quality improvement. *Production and Operations Management* 3, 153–170.

Kerlinger, F. N. (1986) *Foundations of Behavioural Research*. 3rd edn. Orlando, FL: Holt, Rinehart and Winston, Inc.

Kordupleski, R. E. *et al*. (1993) Why improving quality doesn't improve quality (or whatever happened to marketing?). *California Management Review* 35 (Spring), 82–95.

Kotler, P. (1996) *Marketing Management: Analysis, Planning, Implementation, and Control*. 8th edn. Englewood Cliffs, NJ: Prentice Hall.

Mastenbroek, W. F. G. (1991) 'Co-operation as a critical success factor: functional quality and corporate culture' in editor? *Managing for Quality in the Service Sector*. Oxford: Blackwell.

McGuire, L. (1999) *Australian Services: Marketing and Management*. South Yarra: Macmillan Education Australia Pty Ltd.

Menon, A. *et al*. (1997) Product Quality: Impact of Interdepartmental Interactions. *Journal of the Academy of Marketing Science* 25(23), 187–200.

Mohram, S. A. *et al.* (1995) Total quality management: practice and outcomes in the largest US firms. *Employee Relations* 17(5), 25–40.

Monica, S. (2000) The development and application of an instrument from measurement of quality institutionalisation. *Proceedings of the Human Factors and Ergonomics Society:* Annual Meeting.

Oakland, J. S. (1993) *Total Quality Management, Britain.* London: Betterworth & Heineman.

Oakland, J. S. and Oakland, Susan (1997) The links between people management, customer satisfaction and business results. *Total Quality Management* 9(4/5), 185–190.

Ott, J. S. (1989) *The Organisational Culture Perspective.* Pacific Grove, CA: Books/Cole Publishing Company, USA.

Parry, Mark E. and Song, X. Michael (1993) Determinants of R&D–marketing integration in high-tech Japanese firms. *Journal of Product Innovation Management* 10(1), 4–22.

Perreault, W. D. *et al.* (1979) Alternative approaches for interpretation of multiple discriminanat analysis in marketing research. *Journal of Business Research* 7, 151–73.

Rafiq, M. and Ahmad, P. K. (1993) The scope of internal marketing: defining the boundary between marketing and human resource management. *Journal of Marketing Management* 9(3), 219–32.

Reger, R. K. *et al.* (1994) Reframing the organisation: why implementing total quality is easier said than done. *Academy of Management Review* 19(3), 565–584.

Rubin, A. and Babbie, E. (1989) *Research Methods for Social Work.* Belmont, CA: Wadsworth Publishing Company.

Rubin, A. *et al.* (1995) *Bayesian Data Analysis.* London: Chapman Hall.

Rust, T. R., Zahorik, A. J. and Keiningham, K. T. (1996) *Service Marketing.* New York: Harper Collins.

Saraph, J. V., Benson, P. G. and Schroeder, R. G. (1989) An instrument for measuring the critical factors of quality management. *Journal Decision Science* 20(4), 810–29.

Sasser, W. E. and Arbeit, S. (1976) Selling job in the service sector. *Business Horizons* 19 (June), 61–65.

Schaffer, R. and Thomson, H. (1992) Successful change programs begin with results. *Harvard Business Review* 70(1), 80–92.

Schein, E. H. (1984) Coming to new awareness of organisational culture. *Sloan Management Review* 25, 3–16.

Schein, E. H. (1985) *Organizational Culture and Leadership.* San Francisco, CA: Jossey-Bass Publishers.

Schein, E. H. (1990) Organisational culture. *American Psychologist* 45, 109–119.

Schein, E. H. (1992) *Organisational Culture and Leadership.* 2nd edn. San Francisco, CA: Jossey-Bass Publishers.

Shafritz, J. M. and Ott, J. S. (1992) *Classics of Organisation Theory.* 3rd edn. California: Pacific Grove Brooks/Cole Publishing Company.

Spitzer, R. D. (1995) TQM: the only source of sustainable competitive advantage. *Quality Progress* 26, 59–64.

Tagliaferri, L. E. (1991) *Total Quality Management Survey.* San Diego: Pfeiffer and Company.

Ticehurst, B., Walker, G. and Johnston, R. (1991) Issues in communication management in Australian organisations. *Australian Journal of Communication* 18(3), 126–140.

Weisendanger, Betsy (1993) Deming's Light Dims at Florida Power & Light. *Journal of Business Strategy* 14, September–October.

Yusof., S. M. *et al.* (1999) Critical success factors in small medium enterprises: survey results. *Total Quality Management* 11, 4–6.

11 Adaptation of Polish hospitals to radical environmental change

Mariola Ciszewska, Andrzej Kuśmierz and Krzysztof Obloj

Introduction

This chapter examines organisational adaptations to a revolutionary change of an environment – a redesigning of a Polish healthcare sector by introducing a new system of payment and a new form of ownership (from state-owned to locally owned), what has put on hospital managers different pressures to improve performance and use of public money.

The Polish hospitals' adaptation to healthcare sector reforms has practically not been researched. The institutional and economic context has dramatically changed between 1998 and 2002, but still little is known about the processes and mechanisms of hospitals' responses to the changes. The aim is to discover conditions underlying the process of formulating and implementing different strategies in hospitals and to identify general patterns of the best and worst strategies.

Keywords: adaptation, strategic change, industry revolutions, managerial governance.

Institutional context – changing environment

In the Polish economy it is difficult to find a sector as socially important and politically sensitive important as healthcare. In 1999 an act on common health insurance was accepted. Through determining a direct compulsory insurance premium in height of 7.75 per cent extracted of workers' income and it created financial bases for healthcare functioning as well as an institutional base for redistribution of these means through the foundation of 16 regional patients' funds (*Kasy Chorych,* similar to health management organisations). Patients' funds were designed as autonomous, professional organisations supervised by the Health Insurance Supervisory Office, with the objective of financing services of medicare. The functioning of the patients' funds has met a massive critique from healthcare organisations, patients, media and politicians. Limited number of actors indicated, however, that patients' funds play a very positive role forcing hospitals to adapt, change the operating methods, reduce and rationalise costs.

The healthcare reform created new demands and conditions for both basic care and doctors' and hospitals' activities, but evidently it has not met social expectations because there are errors in the reform's concept per se on one hand, while the adaptative behaviour of healthcare units have not occurred at an expected pace on the other.

Typical analyses and discussions concentrate on the reform's errors, but equally important or even more important is what the analyses and discussions do not encompass because of the lack of research: the velocity and way of hospitals' adaptation to the new context.

Adaptation strategies – organisational response

As Rajagopalan and Spreitzer (1996) have noted, after a few decades of research two perspectives of organisational change thought emerged – the *process school*, in which the role of managers in the change process is highlighted (Barr *et al.*, 1992) and the *content school*, which focused on reasons and consequences. Research conducted in both tracks not only not complement each other but are also frequently internally contradictory, leaving questions without good answers (Mintzberg and Westley, 1992; Van de Ven and Poole, 1995; March, 1996).

Concentration on just one perspective offers only partial explanations of a complex phenomenon such as organisational change process. Because of that, the identification of the interdependencies between the existent theories contributes to a complex understanding of an organisation's functioning (Meyer, Brooks and Goes, 1990; Van de Ven and Poole, 1995).

Addressing this problem, Rajagopalan and Spreitzer (1996) distinguished three different change perspectives (rational, learning and cognitive), which they integrated into one model. Mintzberg and Westley (1992) have also adopted a complex approach to the problems of change process, distinguishing mechanisms of change, the phases of change in organisations and process patterns.

Organisational change theory and problems of adaptation in the context of the healthcare sector

Hrebiniak and Joyce (1985) presented the most classic framework relating the influence of environmental determinism and the managerial strategic choice on organisational change and adaptation. Polish hospitals have been operating in a strongly regulated (determined) environment and at the same time maintained a high degree of freedom of strategic choices. According to the suggestion of Hrebiniak and Joyce, such a situation allows organisations to define their objectives in a limited way (because they are to a high degree determined by the environment), but they can try to reach them in potentially many ways. This gives way to a broad spectrum of possible strategies, and the more dynamic organisations will actively try to decrease the role of limitations – for example, through a tentative to gain autonomy (freedom) within the limits.

In the healthcare system determinism is caused by a high degree of legal and financial regulation as well as by impacts of the regulating bodies. Hospitals can, within frames of these limitations, pursue many options – among others they can actively change the structure (after having reached an agreement with the foundation body), they can configure the activity of wards and departments according to the expectations of the market, and they can cooperate in various ways with local authorities as well as with each other or reduce costs in diverse manners.

Research revealed several tendencies of adaptation to the high determinism–high strategic choice situation. Alexander *et al.* (1986) pointed to the fact that in a turbulent environment a bigger chance of success belongs to the universal hospitals, whereas in a stable environment a higher rentability is enjoyed by specialised hospitals. Hence, in the first case hospitals will naturally try to enlarge its range of operations, for example, through opening new departments, alliances or mergers with other hospitals. In a stable environment a trend to open specialised hospitals and clinics, as well as to narrow the range and to orientate towards specialisation, will be observed.

In such a situation politics and conflicts start to play an important role. If institutions determining the environment have been established, different hospital stakeholders including local politicians, main suppliers or professional corporations can be tempted to influence these institutions or control the communication channels between the organisation and the environment. In turn, at the organisational level and the level of choice of a performance option, 'temptations' to influence the process of an option's choice emerge, in a way to fulfil the interest of a given group of stakeholders. The effect of such a perspective on hospital changes will be, therefore, 'politics making' in both dimensions of the model by Hrebiniak and Joyce (1985).

Meyer's (1982) research on hospitals' adaptation strategies to environmental changes showed they react differently to a similar environmental factor, for example, a doctors' strike. The differences in the effects of hospitals' operations were so significant (from bankruptcy to income growth) that it could not be explained with 'deep pockets', meaning the difference in units' resources. The organisations that were prepared for a potential strike adapted better, reacting rapidly (not necessarily dismissing people, but repositioning them in a sensible way), leaving the service range unchanged and did not demonstrate its troubles to the patients 'outside'. An additional conclusion was that poorer hospitals performed better in crisis, probably because of lack of typical mindset of 'we are rich – we can wait' and lack of organisational slack.

Also, an additional factor – time of presence of pressure in the environment should have a similar (positively correlated) influence on the amount of changes occurring in the sector. Young, Charns and Shortell (2001) proved that the amount of changes launched in a concrete, homogenous sample has a distribution similar to Gauss's curve. It stems especially from the popularisation of the best solutions in the sector that occur through a natural flow of educated staff, publications (knowledge diffusion), trainings and benchmarking. So if any adaptation is relatively more effective, it will be ever more imitated by the whole population (until its exhaustion).

This creates a rich ground for discussion, because on one hand the population ecology claims the effectiveness of a quick adaptation (Hannan and Freeman, 1977), the augmentation through it of the chances for the organisation to survive and/or the improvement of coefficients, and on the other hand Quinn (1978: 80) stresses the dangers of a too-fast reaction. It can be disastrous if changes in response to not entirely defined pressures are implemented too rapidly. Additionally, Young *et al.* (2001) highlighted the manager's role – as a leader and organisational factor initiating and implementing changes. They stated that for an effective adaptation it has always been important that the initiative and implementation come form the 'leading factor' and that, if it was strong enough, it used to be overtaken by the 'organisational factor', which brought the change to an end.

Cook *et al.* (1983) studied hospitals' adaptations and they proposed the sequence of adaptation process to the regulatory (deterministic) changes in a given organisation and in its relationships with other subjects from the sector. They showed a keen interest in hospitals' behaviours leading to the adaptation of these changes in regulations. It is important that the analysis of the change process has been generally referred to just one stimulus – change in the environment's deterministic dimension. This article is interesting also because of isolating a common ground of changes in a hospital, which can be compared to the domain of solutions. It is an important complementation of Hrebiniak's model by proposing three different levels (institutional, managerial and technical) of possible behaviours (examples of reactions to stimuli), which can be identified with the strategic choice options. If an organisation has more possibilities of reaction on a given level, the bigger is its degree of strategic choice. The authors take a step further and display a full process, which according to them should take place while changes in hospitals are implemented. Its most important feature is the concretisation of the sequence in which changes should occur on various levels. They remark that the most important feature of the change process in a hospital is its hierarchy, that is, it starts on the institutional level and successively descends on lower organisational levels (Figure 11.1).

As far as hospitals are concerned, an interesting research question is how high- and low-performing hospitals define degrees of freedom in the changing environment and what consequence this has on the undertaken activities (how perception of freedom in the field of strategic choice influences the undertaken activities).

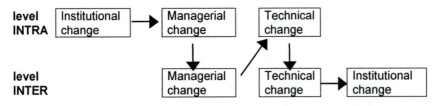

Figure 11.1 Sequence of changes. Source: Cook, K., Shortell, S. M., Conrad, D. A. and Morrisey, M. A. (1983) A theory of organizational response to regulation: the case of hospitals. Academy of Management Review 8, p. 199.

Besides, a big role in the explanation of organisational change process in response to environmental changes can be ascribed to the perspective of dependence on resources and the net of mutual links, which – depending on situational conditioning – have for the organisation inertial and adaptative consequences (Tushman *et al.*, 1986; D'Anuno and Zuckerman, 1987). Meyer, Brooks and Goes (1990) think that a revolutionary change in the environment stimulates the appearance of interorganisational links and influences the experimenting with new organisational forms in order to acquire resources beyond the organisation or to diminish the dependence on the dominant player. When it comes to hospitals, an interesting question becomes in that context to which degree the ability to use and control resources (including relational resources) differentiates the abilities of high- and low-performing hospitals to adapt, in response to revolutionary environmental changes.

Research model

The aim of our research was to identify conditions and mechanisms underlying the process of Polish hospitals' adaptation to changes resulting from the healthcare system reform. Our research model incorporates the results of discussed organisational change theory and research. The model assumes three phases of adaptation process: (1) interpretation of environmental pressures; (2) organisational response; and (3) evaluation and learning. It integrates both adaptive and evolutionary approaches by assuming that in the second phase (response), hospitals can either implement adaptive changes or stay inertial. However, the choice of the strategy can have many aspects that have been examined, for example, hospitals' prior model of actions; structures and procedures; size; resources diversity (financial, technical, human); and relations with the environment.

To narrow the research focus we chose the following research questions: how the response of high and low performers differ? What conditions influence the choice of specific adaptation strategy? Whether and why managers of two groups of hospitals perceived environmental determinism differently? Whether there exists a link between the way of this perception and strategic actions taken by them?

The results of a chosen strategy are evaluated by crucial institutions in environment (healthcare department, funding organisations, social institutions, etc.) and hospital management itself. This evaluation can be both positive and negative; what in turn can lead to reinforcement of the change process or to weakening and restraining it. New strategic priorities will create positive feedback in a change process (when organisational response leads to success, and then to further changes in a model of behaviour, for example, through intensifying actions) or negative feedback (when effects lead to corrections extinguishing the adjustment change process). Understanding the logic of this few phases loop, environmental pressures–adaptation strategy–effects–correction and new strategic priorities, has fundamental meaning for evaluation of the effectiveness of the adaptation process of hospitals.

Research design

Research was conducted by using outliers method, that is, we focus on extremes instead of central tendencies. Two cases of hospitals with exceptionally high performance and two low performers were examined. The set of four examined hospitals has been indicated by experts' panels consisting of academics specialising in healthcare, directors of hospitals and members of healthcare regulatory institutions. In order to study what kind of organisational response characterises high and low performers in turbulent environments we decided to study hospitals that are located in the same *vojevodship* in order to avoid the problem of different local conditions and payment procedures.

The outliers method requires defining the objective criteria differentiating the examined organisations. Prior research showed two basic criteria: the first is connected with economic effectiveness of organisational behaviour, the second with quality of medical services and standards. Hospitals whose strategies of action and change allow for best adaptation should achieve high economic performance together with high quality and ethical standards.

Contrasting the cases allowed for drawing more reliable conclusions concerning sources of effective adaptation activities and practical recommendation for both macro level (institutional and economic context of healthcare system in Poland) and micro level (building the model of effective adaptation strategy for an organisational unit such as a hospital).

After securing permission from the chief executive officers, we conducted a series of extensively structured interviews, ranging from one to two hours in each hospital, with top managers and other key employees. Interviews were enriched by quantitative part comprising basic organisational and financial parameters (e.g. number of employees, average time of hospitalisation, cost/revenues structure). A total number of thirty-four interviews were performed – ten at most and seven at least in each (Table 11.1).

For analysing collected data we used a qualitative data analysis software program called Atlas.ti. It simplified the process of coding and systemising data for further theory building. At the beginning of data analysis we proposed over forty detailed codes. Those codes reflected three hypothesised stages of hospitals' adaptation (i.e., environmental pressures interpretation phase, reaction phase and evaluation phase), and they covered all important adaptation activities in examined hospitals.

After initial analysis we grouped all codes into more general categories. Three meta-codes explaining the success of adaptation were identified. These were rich

Table 11.1 Data collection methods in each hospital's case study

	Hospital A	*Hospital B*	*Hospital C*	*Hospital D*
Number of interviews	10	8	7	9
Access to financial reports	Yes	Yes	Refusal	Refusal

perception of an environment, leadership and change sequence. The change sequence consisted of three basic types of change (technocratic, development and organisational), whose timing influence the final effectiveness.

Although the access to financial reports was limited, in some cases we were able to verify actions aimed at revenue growth and those that focused on cost restructuring or productivity growth against their financial consequences. We used this as an additional filter of effects.

Effective adaptation

The basic focus of the research was effective adaptation of hospitals to dramatic change of rules caused by the complex healthcare system reform. Some other researchers in this field in Poland (Kautsch, Klich and Stylo, 2001; Golinowska *et al.* 2002; Trocki, 2002) suggested that:

- hospitals modify their behaviour in response to environment stimuli. In their response simple restructuring changes dominate (cost reduction, wards joining, services profiling);
- hospitals characterised by a higher level of management professionalism are quicker in leaving behind inertial behaviours and simple restructuring – instead they adopt proactive behaviour focusing on the exploitation of opportunities created by actions of main reimbursement institution (National Health Fund) and finding new sources of financing;
- small hospitals adapt most quickly as market and institutional pressures influence them much stronger; and
- institutional healthcare reform and formation of the National Health Fund (NHF) did not result in hospitals' selection, however, they are catalyst for some managerial changes in hospitals.

These conclusions are congruent with broader organisational change theory and research of adaptation in the hospitals sector. It is agreed that, apart from a few exceptions, the source of change in hospitals' strategies is the need to adapt to environment. Environmental stimuli, both durable and situational, create threats and opportunities, to which organisations try to react. However, organisations are fundamentally conservative (March, 1996). In a complex and dynamic environment such behaviour is rational as it is quite easy to evaluate effectiveness and efficiency of traditional solutions, but it is hard to foresee effectiveness and efficiency of new ones. Organisations adjust their adaptation to range, scope and strength of pressures, but this process is not continuous, fully rational and predictable. Whether the organisation will achieve the state of effective adaptation or will respond in a more or less chaotic way to selected environmental pressures depends on the strength of inertia forces, effectiveness of leadership, environment perception, choice of mechanisms and content of changes.

The results of our research (see Table 11.2) support theoretical and practical implications of previous works on hospitals' adaptation and organisational change.

Table 11.2 Main aspects of adaptation strategies in studied hospitals

	Hospital A	Hospital B	Hospital C	Hospital D
Environment perception	Pressures: economic (NHF, competitors) and social (patients)	Pressures: economic (NHF, competitors) and social (patients)	Pressures: economic (NHF) and political	Pressures: economic (NHF, competitors) and political
	Actors: NHZ, owner (local authority), healthcare department, hospitals and medical units, media, patients, pharmaceutical companies, others	Actors: NHZ, owner (local authority), healthcare department, hospitals and medical units, media, patients, pharmaceutical companies, others	Actors: NHZ, owner (local authority), hospitals	Actors: NHZ, owner (local authority), hospitals and medical units, media, patients, pharmaceutical companies, tax authorities, others
	Environment scanning and external relations management to reinforce own bargaining power	Environment scanning and external relations management to reinforce own bargaining power	Less pressures are perceived, social (patient) pressures are very weak, but political one is strong	Less pressures are perceived, social (patient) pressures are very weak, but political one is strong
	Spotting opportunities	Spotting opportunities	Not many actors and linkages between them are not perceived	Less actors, but linkages between them are perceived
	Activity on institutional level of change	Activity on institutional level of change	Response has one direction – adjustment changes comprise interior of organisation	Cooperation with actors that influence the market
	Cooperation with other hospitals and medical units (interlevel change)	Cooperation with other hospitals and medical units (interlevel change)	Limited attempts to influence environmental actors (only the owner)	Response has two directions – internal and external

Continued overleaf.

Table 11.2 Continued.

	Hospital A	Hospital B	Hospital C	Hospital D
	Promptness, plasticity and pragmatism of response to system stimulus and pressures (prediction of NHF behaviours and adjustments to it) Response has two directions – internal and external	Promptness, plasticity and pragmatism of response to system stimulus and pressures (prediction of NHF behaviours and adjustments to it) Response has two directions – internal and external		
Changes	Motive: economic, but maintaining quality Initiative: top and middle level management (decentralisation) Balance between economic and quality aims Employees' acception and involvement Middle management initiatives Focus on clear communication	Motive: economic, but maintaining quality Initiative: top and middle level management (decentralisation) Balance between economic and quality aims Employees' acception and involvement Middle management initiatives Focus on clear communication	Motive: economic, regardless of quality Initiative: top management (centralisation) Economic aims dominate quality aims Internal conflict Lack of clear communication and information transparency	Motive: economic, but maintaining quality Initiative: top and middle level management (decentralisation) Balance between economic and quality aims Employees' acception and involvement Middle management initiatives Focus on clear communication
Results	Economic: financial balance, investment Improved contract Quality: improved	Economic: financial balance; patient satisfaction, brand, better contracts with NHF	Economic: financial balance; worsening of the contract with NHF	Economic: financial balance; investment Improved contract with NHF Quality: improving

First, Polish hospitals adapted efficiently to environmental changes in a way well described and foreseen by theory. Strong environmental pressures – institutional, competitive and market – resulted in a rapid response in the hospitals. Some of their reactions were hysteric or regressive, yet the model of incremental adaptation consistent with evolutionary motor of change (Van de Ven and Poole, 1995) predominates. The hospitals with high performance act in a way shown in Figure 11.2. There are two levels of organisational response to environmental pressures. On the first level a change in cognitive perspective is observed (and that should be added to the proposed model); on the second level there are reactions postulated by the research model – organisational improvements predominate, but also some innovative behaviours occur. The hospitals that have lower performance (i.e. hospitals C and D) lack both elements.

The second general conclusion is that effective adaptation process results from three mutually interconnected factors: environment perception, leadership and change sequence.

Environment perception

Environment perception clearly differentiates two groups of researched hospitals in three dimensions: number of perceived stakeholders, their potential importance, and character of the pressure. We can specifically say that hospital adaptation process is proceeding more smoothly when the organisation: (1) perceives a bigger number of stakeholders in its environment; (2) is able to make them act in its own adaptation process; and (3) is able to exploit opportunities created by the stakeholders/actors. In other words, hospitals that have effective adaptation strategies see more actors in their environment, try to actively influence stakeholders' behaviour treating them as a resource–network, that has to be used in the adaptation process, and they see more opportunities than threats. It can be easily noticed on the environment perception model in hospital A, shown in Figure 11.3.

Such a consciously built broad environment model, which portrays numerous players with a different influence of power on the hospital, appears to be, in the light of our research, a critical factor for effective adaptation since it simultaneously allows for:

*   spotting mutual dependence between players at the level of local environment, and observing influence that some players have on others (e.g. local media influence on the owner or pharmaceutical wholesalers' influence on pharmaceutical producers);
*   setting up cooperation with local healthcare units – establishing consortiums, alliances and gathering information concerning opportunities in environment (additional financing) or practices used by other hospitals;
*   managing relations with NHF and owner (local authority), that are crucial for reinforcing hospital position in negotiating contracts and gaining autonomy for the organisation (decision-making autonomy was achieved through establishing relations based on trust and full information between organisation

Environmental pressures	Organizational response
• Formulation of NHF and hospitals' owners (local authorities) ⇒ pressure to achieve financial balance. • Establishing competition between hospitals . • Increase in patients' expectations and demands. • Media actions .	• Change in employees' attitude: 'a hospital is a company', 'we have to actively look for money, costs have to be reduced'. • A hospital is perceived as any other organization that has to respect market rules. • Change in medical staff' attitude towards patients – seen in market terms of customers. • Implementation of numerous changes in 2001–2003 with the aim of cost reduction, quality improvement, assortment broadening . • Innovative exploitation of NHF actions in order to strengthen own bargaining power; product and organizational innovations (e.g. strategic alliances).

Figure 11.2 Hospital's response to environmental pressures

and the owner, resulted in change in statutory regulations increasing autonomy of hospital management);

- shaping patients' opinions through numerous actions that make the hospital well visible in local environment and against competitive background (e.g. 'white Sundays'); through media that convey information about the hospital and offered services; through other institutions that are bringing patients together (e.g. church, other social/religious associations);
- building relations with local companies in order to gain additional sources of financing (through contracts and sponsoring), building local linkages, accumulation of knowledge, experiences and influence; and

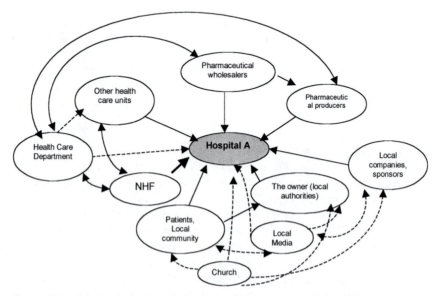

Figure 11.3 Main institutions in environment that are analysed by Hospital A decision-makers

- creating a company mindset (cognitive map) inside the hospital, which has its competitors and has to formulate strategy taking into account both cost reduction and differentiating its services against competitors through innovations, high quality, reputation, etc.

Rich environment map and consistently built relations with numerous actors become the major resource and adaptive capability that differentiates two groups of hospitals in terms of 'multitude responses' to pressures. Hospitals that adapt to environment efficiently cooperate with many external institutions. They also establish cooperation with other hospitals, search for additional sources of financing, build alliances to increase their own bargaining power towards suppliers, etc. Cooperation between different hospitals' wards begin, as well as with clinics, and quality of services is increased through contacts with national specialists.

Hospitals with lower performance are mostly initiating actions that aim at extracting some help from main institutions in the environment (NHF, owners, government agencies, sponsors). Their actions are less varied and diverse, as they are focused on exerting political influences in the hope that because they are 'most important' it will secure them extra benefits (mainly it is the case of hospital C). Hospital D, in which the management has changed during the time of research, started slowly to move away from this model, and established more serious relations with other institutions, but was still a long way ahead to build such a network of relations that hospital A or B have. Therefore, we can conclude that high performers behave consistently with Cook *et al.*'s (1983) predictions. They respond with a series of actions on each level, while low performers do not enter institutional and interlevel response and focus on introducing changes on a managerial level.

This conclusion has important theoretical and practical implications. On one hand it supports modern resource and organisational linkages theories, according to which building a network in an environment is a critical organisational resource in the adaptation process. On the other hand, it offers a clear and practical managerial directive for how to increase the effectiveness of the adaptation process when internal resources are scarce.

Leadership

Leadership is an essential part of each change model – from teleological to life cycle framework (Van de Ven and Poole, 1995). In our research the role and significance of leaders in agreed adaptation strategies are also clearly visible.

Continuity of leadership is the first important factor. In hospitals A and B leaders did not change and are able to develop a long-term sequence of adaptive changes. In hospitals C and D managements changed several times during the last seven years. This rotation of managers proved to be according to respondents in each hospital a crucial threat to organisation as it destroys the logic and continuity of changes, creates conflicts and blocks the acception of clear concept of actions.

The crucial aspect of managerial actions in the first phase of adaptation is continuous multilevel and multidimensional communication with employees and representatives of external institutions. It seems to be even more important than the content of changes, because any change strategy can be blocked by different professional groups (doctors, nurses, administrative staff), trade unions, local authorities or others. A fundamental function of the manager shaping the adaptation process of the hospital is the efficient communication with and motivation of employees. The content of the vision of the changes then plays a second-rate role.

Efficient leaders in hospitals A and B decentralised initiatives and centralised decisions because of communication priority and internal structure of a hospital (where managerial orders can be easily blocked by not a trivial argument concerning human life). In every case of successful adaptation, major decisions are centralised while the key to success seems to be a decentralisation of incremental adaptive changes mainly because of many environments in which the hospital operates. Each ward has its own specific technological, social, political and economic (different costs) environment and, therefore, formulation of effective adaptation programmes at only the top management level is almost impossible. In the case of the most exemplary adaptation (hospital A) task division is clearly visible. The leader controls the formulation and implementation of the institutional changes in the hospital. He influences the institutional environment, participates in the creation of managerial changes both in the hospital and in the environment (alliances, joint training programmes, principles of cooperation with pharmaceutical companies), leaving the medical staff the right and the obligation to implement necessary technical changes. Therefore, a good leader creates a cascade of responsibilities, decentralising the adaptation process. In this way middle management became strongly involved in the search for additional sources of financing (such as special programmes, for example, on heart disease financed by specialist health-promoting associations, sponsors etc.). In such a way they gain sources to finance partly operational activities. On the other hand, the medical middle management in hospitals with lower performance play only the traditional clinical roles of physicians responsible for a ward and patients' well-being, but concerns about development of new offerings, initiatives to cut costs, willingness to create alliances or even to participate in joint managing of adaptive changes were not observed.

However, we must stress that prior to decentralisation of change implementation in effective hospitals, the middle level management has been generally changed or replaced. In hospitals with higher performance this phase comprised a significant part of elderly medical staff, who could not or did not want to take increased responsibility. This pattern is also confirmed in hospital D, where the most involved employees in adaptation processes were newly employed heads of hospital wards, and the most ferocious opponents were employees with the highest job seniority.

Change sequence

The results of this research support previous works, indicating significant possibilities for cost reductions. In general, at the moment of introducing the healthcare system reform, hospitals had a surplus of employees, did not care for costs (which nobody was able to control and count), and were highly centralised. Therefore, hospitals started the adaptation process from technocratic changes, focused on improvements in financial aspects of performance. They implemented cost reduction programmes. Such programmes can lead to cost reduction despite the unfavourable circumstances (such as isolation of the programme, absence of a leader, neglecting resources outside organisational borders), but at the same time they can result in conflicts. Fear, lack of motivation and searching the possible ways of removing CEOs by all involved actors – employees who believe that the next CEO will not fire them or the owner (local authority) that looks for social peace in its region. For these reasons the cost reduction programme has to have its mirror reflection in a programme focused on development and broadening the assortment (development changes), which allow for increasing revenues and 'buy' legitimisation among employees for cost cutting. Both programmes are enriched by social changes (e.g. establishing clear communication or building a motivation system), and by managerial changes (e.g. decentralisation of decisions and changes in a hospital's structure, professional negotiations with NHF, training). Thus, the results of our research show that an effective and efficient adaptation process is not a simple intuitive change sequence of technological, economic and organisational changes (see Figure 11.4), during which positive (negative) evaluation of each phase will reinforce (weaken) further stages of adaptative process. One of the main reasons is that the focus on the first stage causes such problems and threats that a hospital has huge difficulties of entering into the next phase in the sequence.

The effective adaptation process (hospitals A and B) is more complex and sophisticated. It has begun with a set of technocratic changes connected with cost reduction, but soon it has been broadened by development changes and changes

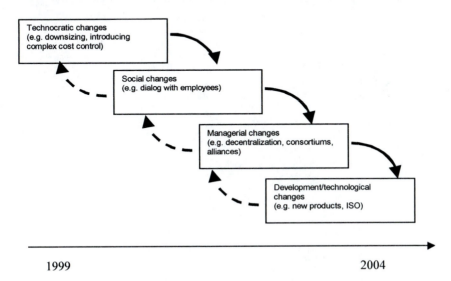

Figure 11.4 Hypothesised change sequence of effective adaptation process

allowing for more efficient play with the main actor (NHF) during contract negotiations and a programme of quality improvement. The process is reinforced by a
leadership based on vision, continuous communication, mitigating conflicts and
creating the atmosphere for initiatives bottom-up, and rich perception of actors in
an environment that allows for spotting distant opportunities and resources. The
adaptation process of exemplary hospitals in the research is thus less sequential
and has more loops – as was suggested by J. G. March (1996), who wrote about
the essence of the change. It is therefore well modelled by a mix of teleological
and evolutionary models of organisational change (Van de Ven and Poole, 1995).
Figure 11.5 depicts the process in practice.

Conclusions

Our research of Polish hospitals' adaptive strategies indicate that the critical performance differences between high- and low-performing hospitals are explained
by leadership, environment perception and change sequence factors. These three
factors are mutually supportive and they form consistent feedback loops, which
explain the level of effectiveness of the hospital adaptation. High performers have
a complex and diverse picture of environment that allows for optimism, spotting
opportunities among many threats and problems, and finding allies for a hospital success. Such a rich environment picture, built on relations with key actors
and interorganisational cooperation, facilitates exchanging information between
an organisation and its environment, which results in turn in perceiving more
freedom by an organisation in the field of strategic choice. Leadership is based on
efficient communication, appointing clear aims and task decentralisation permits
to exploit these opportunities and builds motivation to experiment. A sequential
process of adaptive changes forms effective strategy as each consecutive phase of
changes (technocratic, managerial, developmental) triggers and allows for incremental changes in other fields. That in turn activates the next change loop.

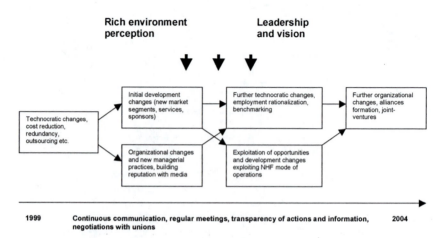

Figure 11.5 Effective change sequence in hospitals A and B

The main reasons for ineffective adaptation strategies of low performers are lack of at least one of the factors (narrow environment perception, weak leadership, rigidly holding to change sequence), or destruction of the linkages between the factors. Such results support the complex view of organisational adaptation and have several practical implications.

Effective adaptation process requires a high level of managerial professionalism. Therefore, a typical adaptive change programme led by physicians elevated to leader positions typically fails, as in the cases of hospitals C and D. Leaders with professional management training (but formerly physicians, in the cases of hospitals A and B) have a much better chance of success. Therefore, any radical overhaul of national medical systems should be accompanied by high quality, professional training programmes for hospital managers. Despite the fact that management programmes for hospital managers recently became abundant in Poland, they are still poorly equipped with good research, tools and case studies, and typically they are not well adapted to specific problems and challenges in the sector of healthcare. Effective adaptation strategy also requires participation and building involvement in different groups in an organisation (trade unions and professional groups). So there is a need for training for these groups and providing the system of exchanging experiences and information between involved parts. This is a necessity in order to break down inertia and resistance that will only escalate, together with pressure on cost reduction, in hospitals that did not manage to enter a higher adaptation level.

Effective adaptation strategy requires not only a simple sequential programme of actions, but also a concept of 'strategic stairs' that allows for permitting different stages of restructuring. The model illustrated in Figure 11.6 seems to be a good approximation of such a process and can be a useful teaching tool. Because of the specificity of hospitals as professional bureaucracies, a sequential scheme that works in classical business organisations in which resistance to change can be broken because product assortment, prices and offered quality are the areas of decision-making process and not moral debate, would be rather inefficient and could destroy involvement and motivation, and arise concern and fear. An effective adaptation model is incremental, not revolutionary.

Bibliography

Alexander, J. A., Kaluzny A. D. and Middleton, S. C. (1986) Organizational growth, survival and death in the US hospital industry: A population ecology perspective. *Social Science & Medicine*, 22(3), 303–308.

Barr, P. S., Stimpert, J. L. and Huff, A. S. (1992) Cognitive change, strategic action and organizational renewal. *Strategic Management Journal* 13.

Cook, K., Shortell, S. M., Conrad, D. A. and Morrisey, M. A. (1983) A theory of organizational response to regulation: the case of hospitals. *Academy of Management Review* 8.

D'Aunno, T. A. and Zuckerman, H. S. (1987) A life-cycle model of organizational federations: the case of hospitals. *Academy of Management Review* 12(3).

Golinowska, S., Czepulis-Rutkowska, Z., Sitek, M., Sowa, A., Sowada, C. and Włodarczyk,

C. (2002) Opieka zdrowotna w Polsce po reformie, *Raporty* case no. 53/2002, Warsaw.

Hannan, M. T. and Freeman, J. (1977) The population ecology of organizations. *American Journal of Sociology* 82(5).

Hrebiniak, L. G. and Joyce, W. (1985) Organizational adaptation: strategic choice and environmental determinism. *Administrative Science Quarterly* 30(4).

Kautsch, M., Klich, J. and Stylo, W. (2001) Funkcjonowanie zakładów opieki zdrowotnej w reformowanym systemie. Raport z badań. Ministry of Health, *Biblioteka Zdrowia Publicznego* 7.

Trocki, M. (ed.) (2002) *Warunki systemowe zarządzania opieką zdrowotną.* praca zbiorowa, Instytut Przedsiębiorczości i Samorządności, Warsaw.

Krupski, R. (1999) Zarządzanie strategiczne, Wrocław, 1999 (praca zbiorowa).

March, J. G. (1996) Continuity and change in theories of organinzational action. *Administrative Science Quarterly* 41.

Meyer, A. D. (1982) Adapting to environmental jolts. *Administrative Science Quarterly* 27.

Meyer, A. D., Brooks, G. R. and Goes, J. B. (1990) Environmental jolts and industry revolutions: organizational responses to discontinuous change. *Strategic Management Journal* 11.

Mintzberg, H. and Westley, F. (1992) Cycles of organizational change. *Strategic Management Journal* 13.

Quinn, J. B. (1978) Strategic change: 'logical incrementalism'. *Sloan Management Review* 20(1).

Quinn, J. B. (1980) Managing strategic change. *Sloan Management Review* 21(4).

Rajagopalan, N. and Spreitzer, G. M. (1996) Toward a theory of strategic change: a multilens perspective and integrative framework. *Academy of Management Review* 22(1).

Tushman, M., Newman, W. and Romanelli, E. (1986) Convergence and upheaval: managing the unsteady pace of organizational evolution. *California Management Review* 29(1).

Van de Ven, A. H. and Poole, S. M. (1995) Explaining development and change in organization. *Academy of Management Review* 20(3).

Young, G. J., Charns, M. P. and Shortell, S. M. (2001) Top manager and network effects on the adoption of innovative management practices: a study of TQM in a public hospital system. *Strategic Management Journal* 22.

12 Evolution of structure and strategy of the Turkish automobile industry

I. Hakki Eraslan and Melih Bulu

World automobile industry

The automobile industry can be defined as a sector that produces passenger cars and other gasoline-powered vehicles, such as buses, minibuses, midibuses, trucks and farm tractors, which can be traced back to the end of the nineteenth century, meaning that the automobile industry is more than one hundred years old.

The sector is often regarded as the main engine of industrial growth of the twentieth century, and now is one of the most important industries in the world. It affects not only the economy but also the cultures, urban life and environments of the world. Due to its huge requirements and dependencies, the other sectors have also flourished remarkably from mining, natural rubber, leather, petrochemical engineering and electronics sectors to related service and support industries since its existence.

The industry has made profound effect to production techniques, particularly in assembly lines; of course, Henry Ford revolutionised manufacturing with his Highland Park, using innovative production techniques, a constantly moving assembly line, subdivision of labour and careful coordination of operations, consequently realising huge gains in productivity. In that time, this was a stunning improvement over the earlier production time of 728 minutes to make one car. These manufacturing techniques also gave a new horizon to organisation and technology of other industries and services.

As Table 12.1 shows, automobile firms have great economic power, that is, they are among the largest companies in the world – Toyota's turnover last year, for example, was US$125 billion. These corporations are often multinational. These companies often share parts, or use parts made in foreign factories through getting strategic alliances.

Strategic alliances can have a variety of organisational arrangements, such as joint ventures (JVs), licensing agreements, distribution and supply agreements, research and development partnerships, and technical exchanges. The most eminent form is, of course, international JVs. As shown in Figure 12.1, the automobile giants have almost all of these kinds of characteristics. Strategic alliances have many competitive advantages. Kolasky (1997), advocating the management

Table 12.1 The largest automobile companies within global 500 companies (2000) (US$ million)

Company	Country	Profit 2000	Rank	Profit 1999	Rank	Profit 2000	Rank	Profit 1999	Rank
General Motors	US	184,632	1	176,558	1	4452	2	6002	3
Ford Motor	US	180,598	2	162,558	2	3467	4	7237	1
DaimlerChrysler	Germany	150,070	3	159,986	3	7295	1	6129	2
Toyota Motor	Japan	121,416	4	115,671	4	4263	3	3653	5
Volkswagen	Germany	78,852	5	80,073	5	1896	7	875	7
Honda Motor	Japan	58,462	6	54,773	6	2100	6	2357	6
Nissan Motor	Japan	55,077	7	53,680	7	2994	5	(6146)	25
Fiat	Italy	53,190	8	51,332	8	614	13	377	17
Peugeot	France	40,831	9	40,328	9	1213	9	778	8
Renault	France	37,128	10	40,099	10	998	11	570	9
BMW	Germany	32,675	11	36,696	11	948	12	(2653)	24
Mitsubishi Motors	Japan	29,636	12	29,951	12	(2516)	27	(260)	22
Delphi Automotive[a]	US	29,139	13	–	–	1062	10	–	–

Robert Bosch[a]	Germany	29,083	14	29,727	13	1224	8	428	14
Hyundai Motor	S. Korea	28,755	15	20,566	14	534	16	462	13
Mazda Motor	Japan	18,232	16	19,413	15	(1404)	26	235	21
Denso[a]	Japan	18,224	17	16,915	17	550	15	556	10
TRW[a]	US	17,231	18	16,969	16	438	19	469	12
Johnson Controls[a]	US	17,155	19	16,139	18	472	18	420	15
Man Group[a]	Germany	14,611	20	15,007	20	390	20	389	16
Suzuki Motor	Japan	14,473	21	13,662	21	183	24	241	20
Isuzu Motors	Japan	14,193	22	13,531	22	(604)	25	(936)	23
Volvo	Sweden	14,189	23	15,121	19	514	17	3897	4
Lear[a]	US	14,073	24	12,428	24	275	22	257	19
Dana[a]	US	12,691	25	13,353	23	334	21	513	11
Fuji Heavy Industries	Japan	11,865	26	11,946	25	205	23	282	18
Magna International[a]	Canada	10,513	27	–	–	598	14	–	–
Total number of firms			27		25		25		14
Total sales		1,286,994		1,216,482		32,495		26,132	

Note

a   Automotive parts companies   Source: *Fortune Global*, The World's Largest Corporations

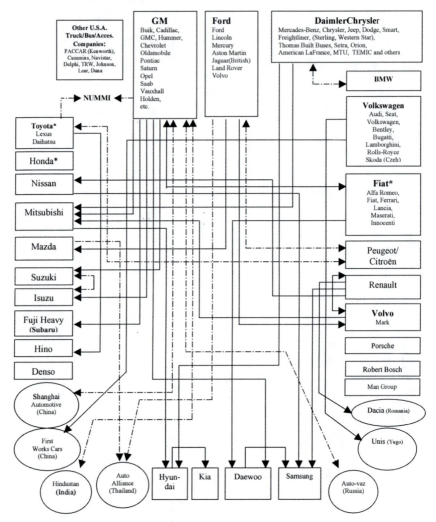

Figure 12.1 Strategic Alliance and M&A in the world automobile industry in 2001 Note:
Whole or partial stakeholder. *GM has technology collaboration and/or vehicle venture.
Strategic Alliance/Joint Venture. Source: Adapted from Elaboration by Lee, Hyun-Sook
(2003).

literature, explains that the growing popularity of strategic alliances as a response
to the greater need for cooperation to keep pace with increasingly complex technologies and global markets. Arms-length dealings and open market transactions
are often insufficient to serve the needs of firms trying to stay competitive. Several
factors in particular have contributed to this greater need for cooperation.

Globalisation

Competing in a global economy requires a much larger scale and scope of operations. In addition, in many national markets the presence of well-entrenched local firms, different cost structures, local customs and preferences, and restrictive national laws make it difficult for foreign firms to compete successfully. Strategic alliances provide a way to achieve the scale and scope necessary to compete globally and to overcome the many obstacles to global expansion.

Increasing economies of scale and scope

More generally, in more and more industries, the scale and scope of the optimal-sized firm seems to be expanding dramatically due to technological change. Again, strategic alliances provide a means of competing on a much larger scale through a network of firms.

Specialisation

At the same time as the economies of scale and scope in individual markets increase, there is increased consciousness of the diseconomies of a large firm trying to do everything itself. The current business school mantra (tune) is to concentrate on your core competencies. This imperative drives firms to outsource everything else and to form strategic alliances with the firms on whom they then become dependent for strategically important functions.

Complexity

Many key technologies have grown so complex that few if any companies can master them all, especially considering the risk involved. This drives firms to look for partners who can provide the expertise they themselves lack.

Pace of technological change

R&D alliances are frequently a response to the need to move quickly in rapidly changing markets. Alliances are flexible enough to adapt to changing market conditions, have comparatively low entry and exit costs, and can be abandoned if the market, or the technology, takes a different course.

Network effects

In technology-driven markets, network effects make it critical that a firm capture the first-mover advantage so that its technology becomes the industry standard. Alliances between new technology firms and established manufacturers are often used as a way to get off the starting block more quickly in order to capture these network effects.

Especially after 1990, along with globalisation progress, the automobile giants focused on joint international ventures. The reasons offered for an increase in strategic alliances are varied in automobile industry, such as the need for technical cooperation, market power, transaction costs, innovation and global competition. In other words, the alliances strategy is of immense importance as it contributes to gaining competitive advantage and sustaining growth, and improving productive performance of automobile firms. On the other side, globalisation has made it increasingly difficult to identify an automobile as the product of one company or country. As shown in Figure 12.1, there is an immense interrelationship among automobile firms through strategic alliances and/or partial acquisition of mutual stakes as control of a competitor, market access, extension of models, to learn others' know-how, etc. (Lee, 2003). This can be directly attributed to the progress of the world's globalisation in this industry. Therefore, a strategic alliance is an ongoing learning institution linking enterprises through situationally appropriate organisational and managerial arrangements, which build on and synergise core competencies of the participants for gaining or sustaining competitive advantage and growth in existing and new markets in a globalising economy (Syeda and Ganeshe, 1992). From this point of view, the Turkish automobile industry also imitated this globalisation trend, and, along with the liberalisation progress, especially after the 1990s, the Turkish automobile industry opened its door to foreign partners through strategic alliances.

Geo-strategic position of Turkey

Turkey is a middle-income country with a GNP per capita of $2649 and a population of 70 million (SIS, 2002). The Turkish Republic is a social, democratic and secular state, and is one of the most developed Eastern European countries, and is industrialising at a rapid rate. Trade has been increasing and Turkey has become more open to the Western world. Turkey is bordered by six countries and is at the crossroads between Asia and Europe, and serves as a link and a strategic barrier between the Southern Caucasus and the northern Middle East. Its area is 779,452 sq km, and is surrounded by three different seas, the Black Sea to the north, the Mediterranean Sea to the south and the Aegean Sea to the west, which provide good sea transportation opportunities for international trade.

The Western part of Turkey in particular is identified more with Europe than the Middle East. Turkey's strategic position provides access not only to her traditional trade partners such as the Middle East countries, but also to the newly emerging countries of Eastern Europe and the Central Asian Republics with whom she has intensive reciprocal commercial and investment activities. The end of the Cold War, the dissolving of the USSR, the transition period of Eastern European countries to market economies and peace settlements in the Middle East have created new economical and political chances for Turkey.

On the other hand, economic and cultural cooperation with the newly established Turkic republics in Central Asia have given new opportunities for Turkish economic and political development. The political, strategic and economic importance of Turkey has especially improved after the collapse of the former USSR. One of the most important reasons for this is that Turkey now acts as a sister state to the new Central Asian Turkic Republics (Winrow, 1995: vii). Trade between Turkey and the Turkic Republics, namely Azerbaijan, Kazakhstan, Uzbekistan, Turkmenistan, Tajikistan and Kyrgyzstan, has increased dramatically in recent times.

On the other side, Turkey is a member of various international political, social, economic, cultural and military organisations, which include the Council of Europe, the UN, the World Bank, the IMF, the OECD, the WTO, the Multilateral Investment Guarantee Agency (MIGA) and NATO.

Turkey's accession process to the European Union

Turkey has had a history of cooperation with the European integration movement since the movement's early beginnings. In 1963 Turkey and the European Community (EC) signed the Turkey-EC Association Agreement. This agreement outlined ways in which the EC and Turkey could promote trade within Europe and also achieve the necessary political and human rights standards to eventually allow Turkey to enter the EC. In 1987 Turkey formally applied for accession to the EC. Nevertheless, the Commission recommended continuing cooperation with Turkey, and this cooperation eventually led to the formation of an EU customs union with Turkey in 1995. In April 1997, at the EU Intergovernmental Conference, the EU announced that Turkey would remain eligible for accession on the same political criteria as other applicant countries (Banani, 2003: 113–128).

The Helsinki European Council formally recognised Turkey as a candidate for accession to the European Union in December 1999. In December 2002, the Copenhagen European Council resolved to decide on the launching of accession negotiations with Turkey at the end of 2004 based on a progress report and recommendation by the European Commission. Provided that the political criteria are fulfilled, accession negotiations could then begin without delay. The decision by the Copenhagen European Council is flanked by a package of steps to further enhance the pre-accession strategy. These steps include more intensive alignment of Turkish law and the *acquis communautaire*, the extension of the custom's union as well as a bolstering of financial pre-accession assistance. With a view to supporting the pre-accession process and the necessary reform measures, the European Union has, since 2000, been providing pre-accession assistance for Turkey to help deepen the custom's union with the EU and to promote the country's economic and social development. A total of €1.050 billion is planned by 2006. Furthermore, Turkey is eligible to receive loans from the European Investment Bank. In its 2003 progress report, the Commission commends the considerable progress made on fulfilling the Copenhagen criteria yet concludes that Turkey has not yet entirely met the political criteria. Nowadays, Turkey is trying to fulfill all criteria.

During Turkey's long journey to the EU, various strategic movements have occurred among Turkish and EU country companies. After the custom union in

1995, the volume of cooperation started to increase especially. Membership talks began in 2005. Serious FDI is expected to pour into Turkey and this will open a new and interested area for strategic movements in Turkey.

The structure of the Turkish automobile industry

The automobile industry has been one of Turkey's fastest growing manufacturing industries, with an average annual growth rate of 12 per cent between 1993 and 2002 (AMA, 1999, 2001, 2002, 2003). The Turkish automobile industry has continued expanding in both quality and quantity and in the development process since the 1950s. The industry has been protected through high customs barriers and developed through establishing JVs and licence agreements with MNEs, and through the implementation of an Import Substitution Strategy (ISI) plan until 1980. Under the liberalisation policy and decision of the export-led growth (ELG) strategy a new horizon was given to Turkish industry and international trade. Therefore, the production units of automobiles have increased continuously except during the two economic crises and following recessions.

Along with the wind of financial liberalisation and globalisation process, custom union (CU) treaty, and foreign investment, the sector has made a great step, and gone through fundamental changes and significant initiatives in 1990s. Facing a boom in domestic demand in 1992 and 1993, the automotive industry initiated rapid expansion plans and engaged in various investments (DEIK, 2002). As is seen in Table 12.2, a number of automobile giants such as Toyota, Honda and Hyundai have introduced initiatives for new investments through strategic alliances; producing passenger cars and minibuses with a 100,000-production unit capacity in Turkey from last decade.

From the seventeen automotive companies in the sector, nine have business relations with foreign firms and two are subsidiaries with 100 per cent foreign capital. EU firms that have invested in the Turkish market are Fiat (JV), Ford (JV), Rover (L), Man (JV), Mercedes Benz (JV), Peugeot (L) and Renault (JV). Three Asian firms – Toyota, Hyundai and Honda – have acquired investment incentives from the Turkish government and have established JVs with Turkish firms. Six firms (Fiat-Tofas-Fiat, Oyak-Renault, Toyota, Hyundai Assan, Honda and Ford-Otosan) manufacture passenger cars. The passenger car market is dominated by two producers with a total market share of 92 per cent (DEIK, 2002: 6–7).

However, being one of the most affected sectors in the 1994 crisis, recession, which continued until 1996, has badly affected the sector. It recovered in 1997 and revealed an upswing in 1997 and in the first half of 1998. It again has begun to decline in 1999 as a result of the effect of both the Far Eastern and Asian crises. 2000 was a good year for almost all the sectors of the economy. The delayed demand of 1998 and 1999 and also the future demand due to consumer expectations were realised in 2000. The 2001 crisis depressed the production down to the 1990 level. The sector recorded a recognisable increase in exports in an effort to manage the twin crises in late 2000 and 2001 (DEIK, 2002: 3).

Table 12.2 Automobile manufacturers in Turkey

Firms	Established	Local partner	Strategic alliances	Total foreign capital (%)	Alliance types
Anadolu Isuzu	1965	Anadolu Group	Isuzu/Itochu	29.75	Licence
Askam	1962	Ciftciler Group	Chrysler/Hino	–	Licence
BMC	1964	Cukurova Group	–	–	–
Ford Otosan	1959	Koc Group	Ford	41	Joint venture
Honda Türkiye	1997	–	Honda	100	Wholly owned
Hyundai Assan	1997	Kibar Group	Hyundai	50	Joint venture
Karsan	1997	Kiraca Group	Peugeot	–	Licence
MAN Türkiye	1966	MAN	MAN	99	Wholly owned
M. Benz Türk	1968	Mengerler	Mercedes-Benz	66.91	Joint venture
Otokar	1963	Koc Group	Land Rover	–	Licence
Otoyol		Koc Group	Iveco Fiat	27	Joint venture
Oyak Renault	1969	OYAK Group	Renault	50	Joint venture
Temsa	1988	Sabanci Group	Mitsubishi	–	Licence
Tofas	1971	Koc Group	Fiat	37.8	Joint venture
Toyota	1994	–	Toyota	100	Wholly owned
Türk Traktör	1954	Koc Group	Case New Holland	37.5	Joint venture
Uzel	1962	Uzel Group	Massey Ferguson	–	Licence

Source: *General and Statistical Information Bulletin of Turkish Automotive Manufacturers*, AMA Publications, various issues.

The Turkish automobile cluster

Turkey has seventeen different private automobile firms, which are registered under the Automobile Manufacturers Association of Turkey (AMA). Fourteen major automobile and many supplier firms, many technical universities, labour unions and trade associations have been established, in the so-called Detroit of Turkey (the triangle of Bursa-Sakarya-Istanbul), as shown in Figure 12.2. Many large Turkish manufacturing firms, comprising about 71 per cent of total manufacturing firms, have also invested in this industrial zone, to utilise the significant transportation opportunities, including its harbours and industrial infrastructures

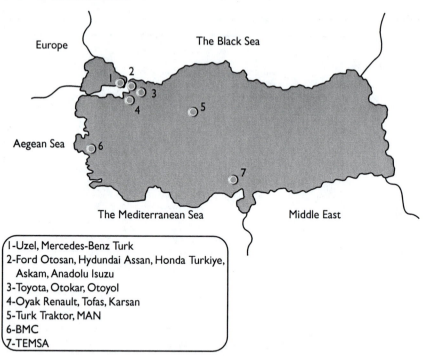

Figure 12.2 Manufacturing plants of Turkish automobile firms

that make the zone ideal for international trade. Such an effective and efficient logistics system will be a competitive advantage in the future. Also, the restructuring and training of the dealers and service personnel is absolutely necessary to compete with the well-organised networks of the current local producers and potential newcomers. Moreover, some of the most eminent technical universities and technical schools of Turkey are set up in this area, enabling automobile firms to find highly qualified labour, engineers and managers very easily. The majority of Turkish automobile supply firms are also established in this zone, for example, tyre manufacturers (Pirelli, Brisa), glass works (Sisecam, Pasabahce) and steel mills (Eregli and Karabuk), as well as other worldwide automobile equipment supplier giants, such as Bosch and Valeo.

As shown Figure 12.3, Turkish proximity to Europe is quite good for automobile manufacturers. This means that Turkish automobile firms can directly export to 27 European countries via seaway. On the other side, the Russian and Middle East market is quite close to Turkey.

Production

The total of 6 million vehicles in 2001 consisted of 75 per cent passenger cars and 25 per cent commercial vehicles, which means the market is far from the saturation point. However, the domestic automobile demand and production units of

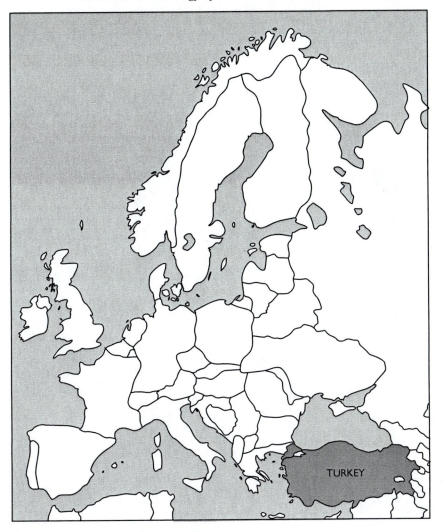

Figure 12.3 Turkey's condition in Europe

Turkey have showed fluctuation character in terms of inconsistent political decisions and indigenous Turkish economy since the 1960s. Automobile demand has
increased gradually in the last two decades and reached a peak level of 562.000
in 2003.

Although the domestic market seems to be expanding after two years of severe
contraction, the expansion is getting stronger in a low interest rate environment.
Due to higher confidence levels, backed by the government's commitment to the
economic reforms and EU-related reforms, domestic market auto sales rose significantly in 2003 (TAYSAD, 2004). Tables 12.3 and 12.4 explain that the total
automobile units and the number of automobiles per head are relatively low in

Table 12.3 Production in the automobile industry (1980–2003)

Units	Passenger car	Truck	Pick-up	Bus	Minibus	Midibus	Farm tractor	Total	Change (%)
1980	31.529	8.308	7.322	1.101	2.130	491	16.936	67.817	–
1981	25.306	12.486	5.454	1.584	2.040	378	25.358	72.606	7.1
1982	31.195	15.131	4.991	1.703	4.850	587	35.716	94.173	29.7
1983	42.509	17.514	6.822	1.964	6.712	1.382	41.799	118.702	26.0
1984	54.832	17.518	7.279	1.766	7.460	2.750	46.782	138.387	16.6
1985	60.353	18.162	7.888	1.637	7.397	2.191	37.830	135.458	-2.1
1986	82.032	13.646	6.605	1.813	7.318	1.508	28.053	140.975	4.1
1987	107.185	13.545	7.580	1.137	8.026	1.434	35.986	174.893	24.1
1988	120.796	12.842	7.196	1.078	6.401	1449	30.167	179.929	2.9
1989	118.314	11.763	7.250	1.069	5.898	1.984	18.077	164.355	-8.7
1990	167.556	16.933	10.553	1.689	7.898	4.288	30.098	239.015	45.4
1991	195.674	16.918	13.541	1.075	9.912	4.401	21.381	262.902	10.0
1992	265.245	21.266	16.984	1.415	11.450	6.399	21.723	344.482	31.0
1993	348.095	31.343	19.766	1.933	12.084	7.435	32.809	453.465	31.6
1994	212.651	12.108	9.602	1.034	4.924	2.855	25.169	268.343	-40.8
1995	233.412	19.759	16.808	1.279	7.645	3.537	44.068	326.508	21.7
1996	207.757	29.432	21.032	2.499	10.171	5.856	52.590	329.337	0.9
1997	242.780	43.693	32.435	3.499	12.935	9.060	55.565	399.967	21.4
1998	239.937	31.823	45.517	3.040	13.910	10.275	60.500	405.002	1.3
1999	222.041	13.096	37.551	2.327	12.894	9.953	27.435	325.297	-19.7
2000	297.476	28.348	68.807	4.213	20.597	11.506	37.434	468.381	44.0
2001	175.343	6.683	76.672	2.501	6.486	3.000	15.052	285.737	-39.0
2002	204.198	12.295	116.872	2.684	6.139	4.377	10.652	357.217	26.7
2003	294.116	19.041	195.606	4.490	13.625	6.794	28.794	562.466	57.7

Source: AMA Publications, various issues

Table 12.4 The automobile owner in comparison with some EU countries

Countries	Population	Automobile Owner (1/1000)
Germany	81,000,000	493
Italy	60,000,000	483
France	65,000,000	449
UK	56,000,000	432
Spain	45,000,000	353
Greece	10,000,000	192
Average of EU	380,000,000	400
Average of World	6,360,000,000	95
Turkey	70,000,000	54

Source: Automotive Manufacturers' Association (AMA) of Turkey, various issues.

Turkey in comparison to the world and the EU average respectively. For instance, while the rate is 483/1000 in Germany, it is 54/1000 in Turkey.

Due to huge demand, there is also an intensive competition in the automobile industry in Turkey. The competition is even more intense in the segments with medium size (C&D) and station wagon (W) cars, where the local producers mainly compete. There are many local producers that have made agreements with some of the biggest automobile giants in the world, such as Toyota, Renault, Hyundai and Honda.

The importance of the automobile industry

The Turkish automobile industry has become one of the big success stories of the country's economy, and plays a vital role in the Turkish economy today. In the first ten private firms ranked according to sales, four were automobile firms. The industry is defined as the locomotive sector of Turkish industrialisation and its contribution to the Turkish economy is as significant as the textile, food and tourism sectors, which means that the automobile industry is third with respect to turnover after the food and textile industries, and also the most rapidly growing sector with an average annual growth rate (SIS, 2003; SPO, 2003; AMA, 2003).

Due to its importance in terms of contribution to national product and development, export, employment, technology, etc., the automobile sector in Turkey is regarded as a strategic industry by a number of national institutions including the State Planning Organisation (DPT), Turkish Treasury, Small and Medium Industry Development Organisation (KOSGEB), and the Ministry of Industry and Commerce.

Contribution of Turkish automobile industry to external trade

The Turkish manufacturing industry accelerated to open the world market by adopting the ELG strategy and the CU Treaty, which gave a new horizon to Turkish automobile firms. Therefore, the external trade of the automobile sector increased dramatically. Although two economic crises badly affected the industry, as shown in Tables 12.5 and 12.6, export rate rocketed a record level of $6 billion during 2003, representing a growth of 68 per cent over the previous year. Principal exporters were Renault-Oyak, exporting vehicles worth $1 billion dollars (+47 per cent); followed by Ford-Otosan, worth $877 million (+163 per cent); Fiat-Tofas, worth $767 million (+8 per cent); and Toyota, worth $676 million. EU/EFTA has the majority rate of automobile export (AMA, 2003).

Contribution to Turkish transportation and logistics

The construction of Turkish roads started with the help of the Marshall Plan after WWII. Turkey is an important transit route from Europe to the Middle East, and long stretches of railroads were built by foreign powers through Turkish territory. The length of Turkish asphalt concrete roads increased from 336 km in 1950 to 8728 km in 2003 (AMA, 2003).

Nevertheless, the airway and airport facilities of Turkey have not developed in a similar way. Airfares are expensive relative to the average Turkish income. Turkish railways are insufficient and inefficient due to lack of investment and a poor infrastructure. Hence, people prefer to use motorway facilities. Motorway routes are vital for Turkish transportation. The motorways form the major transportation network in Turkey. Domestic transportation is realised chiefly by road (90 per cent).

Thus, roads provided a significant part of transportation of both industrial goods and agricultural products, which induced the Turkish economy to expand. Turkey has a rapid urbanisation rate of 4.58 per cent, and the majority of the Turkish population (57 per cent) live in cities. This means people need local transportation. In the large cities, railway, underground and seaway transportation

Table 12.5 Turkish foreign trade in automobile (US$)

		2000	**2001**	**2002**	**2003**
EU+EFTA	Import	6,558,913,641	2,157,208,724	3,263,113,605	6,048,183,259
	Export	2,155,973,247	2,412,163,998	2,806,147,357	4,090,375,412
	Total foreign trade	8,714,886,888	4,569,372,722	6,069,260,962	10,138,558,671
	Balance	−4,402,940,394	254,955,274	456,966,248	−1,957,807,847
Total	Import	8,275,930,780	2,573,788,825	3,908,220,371	7,345,408,458
	Export	3,274,874,483	3,475,090,252	4,319,298,558	6,095,219,893
	Total foreign trade	11,550,805,263	6,048,879,076	8,227,518,929	13,440,628,351
	Balance	−5,001,056,297	901,301,426	411,078,187	−1,250,188,565

Source: AMA, various publications.

Table 12.6 Production and export rate of Turkish automobile industry

	1995	1996	1997	1998	1999	2000	2001	2002	2003
Production	319,498	325,460	399,923	405,002	325,297	468,381	285,737	357,217	562,466
Export	35,544	39,252	31,174	37,926	92,051	104,744	202,158	261,934	359,685
Production (%)	11	12	8	9	28	22	71	73	64

Source: AMA, various publications.

have not been developed for local mass transportation due to the large investment requirements. Local transportation is realised mainly by coach, bus, midibus and minibus.

Contribution to technology and the attraction of foreign investment

The world automobile giants are pioneers of technology and technological innovations today. Investments of multinational firms also provide transfer of both technology and technological innovations to the Turkish automobile industry. Turkey is one of the major junctions of multinational JV automobile firms, including Mercedes, Honda, Hyundai, Ford, Fiat, Renault and Toyota. Such investments not only provide advanced technology for the automobile industry but also induce the development of the infrastructure of the aircraft and defence industries, which are an important part of the industrialisation progress of Turkey. Augmentation of potential domestic demand with the additional attractions excited new investments, modernisation and capacity expansion process. From the ELG strategy, liberalisation of the foreign investment regulations and provision of incentive packages have spurred both local and foreign capital investment into establishing automobile factories via strategic alliances.

Contribution to labour force

Turkey has the youngest population of Europe, and its population rate is still increasing (approximately 70 million). This means Turkey has a large educated labour pool. The working environment of the automobile industry is quite compatible to meet educated labour and intensive work. Today, the sector provides work for more than half a million people directly and indirectly with seventeen vehicle manufacturers and over 1,000 component manufacturers.

Therefore, the Turkish automobile industry has a large source of employment in manufacturing. It is the fifth largest in terms of employment and the seventh largest in terms of value added, accounting for 37 per cent of all value added of the total Turkish manufacturing industry. According to AMA and TAYSAD data (2000, 2001, 2002, 2003), about 30,000 people are employed by the industry and 100,000 workers are employed in the supplier industries. If tourism, marketing, services, insurance and transportation are taken into account this number increases to 1 million.

Macro-environmental factors in the Turkish automobile sector

Economic factors

The Turkish economy has been dominated by high inflation, fluctuating exchange rates, low purchasing power, budget deficits and high interest rates for years. Although GNP per capita increases every year at considerable rates due to the dynamic structure of the country, this, too, contributes to the increase in inflation. Economy is expanding but high economic uncertainty is a threat for both the buyers and the sellers. Also, Turkey experienced a few bitter economic crises within the last years. Thus, Turkey could not yet have a stable and reliable political and economic context. Nevertheless, Turkey shows heavy efforts to integrate its economy with the rest of the world and especially with the Western world.

Like other industries, the Turkish automobile industry has been also affected by the macro economic environment. During recession, the entire economy halted and automobile production rate decreased remarkably. For that reason, capacity utilisation of Turkish automobile firms has not been able to meet the desired level. Economic instability causes fluctuations in demand, which induce either a delay in investment or decreasing capacity utilisation. Thus, consumer demand in the Turkish automobile market is highly volatile and costs of financing projects have been quite high until recently. The domestic passenger car market is experiencing the worst year in the last decade, with a loss of consumer confidence, erosion in incomes and weak loan market conditions. Because of the high interest rate, domestic demand to those products was diminished and production decreased. Because of these facts, automobile companies, as well as other manufacturing firms whose entire operations rely on Turkish automobile market, are open to risks. But in 2000, the macroeconomic programme implemented in Turkey resulted in considerable increased demand to automotive products.

On the other side, one of the main issues of the Turkish automotive industry is the high level of purchasing taxes. Automobiles sold in the domestic market, either through importers or producers, are subjected to high taxes. Therefore, the complex and high tax rates diminish the domestic demand for the automobiles. The value added tax was increased from 25 per cent to 40 per cent for cars with an engine size of 1600–2000cc, to considerably control increase in domestic demand according to the implemented macroeconomic programme.

Moreover, there is a perception of high gasoline consumption. Turkish consumers use the most expensive gasoline price in Europe (1 litre gasoline = €1.2).

Political factors and green movement

For political and legal factors, tariffs on import cars have been reduced, but this advantage for importers is being offset by the depreciation of the Turkish lira against foreign currencies due to high inflation. The CU also dictates new quality standards for local producers. The environmental and safety requirements mandated by government are an example of shifting standards.

Thus, a large number of EU legislation is identified. Turkey is continuing its effort to prepare the relevant legal arrangements and some progress has been taken in this area. In this framework, the existing technical legislation relating to motor vehicles in Turkey is 'Regulation on Manufacturing, Modification and Assembly (AITM)', enforced by the Ministry of Industry and Trade, dated 3 February 1993. The regulation on 'Type Approval of Motor Vehicles (MARTOY)', which is mainly based on 70/156/EEC Directive, was enforced in 1997, and later amended in 1999 mainly based on the Directive 98/14/EC amending the Directive 70/156/EEC. According to this, EU motor vehicle directives are being adopted and the relevant AITM regulations are being repealed according to the harmonisation process. After the completion of the harmonisation efforts in this area, all regulations under AITM will be abolished and an EU-type approval system will be completely operational. A technical committee on motor vehicles (MARTEK) was established in 1997 by the Ministry of Industry and Trade after enforcement of MARTOY for monitoring harmonisation and implementation activities in this field. There are ten subcommittees working under MARTEK and representatives from the relevant public and private sectors meet regularly to perform the harmonisation of relevant legislation (SPO; Council of the European Union).

Moreover, the Turkish automobile market is gaining sensitivity about safety and environmental issues. The green movement is achieving popularity in Turkey. Consumer groups are established to attract public attention to these topics, and the media is promoting consumer rights and environmental pollution issues. Companies have to be careful about these trends since ignorance may lead to dramatic results for any company.

The major players and strategic movement in the Turkish automobile industry

The sector is comprised of privately owned firms as a whole. The seventeen active motor vehicle manufacturers in Turkey mainly operate under foreign licences or as subsidiaries of major international producers. As shown in Table 12.2, nine of these firms are JVs, five operate under licensing agreements, and two are fully foreign-owned FDIs.

Brands of European origin dominate foreign participation in the market. Capital partnerships between Fiat-Tofas, Renault-Oyak, Ford-Otosan and Toyota and the recent capital increases in their Turkish plants reveal the full integration of Turkey into the strategic market expansion plans of foreign firms. Since Turkey's entrance to the CU and its moves for the EU membership, Asian firms have sought to increase their investments in the Turkish automotive sector, which offers geographic advantages and strong Turkish counterparts to utilise export possibilities (DEIK, 2002: 6–7).

Fiat-tofas

Tofas is the automobile company of the largest Turkish Holding Group, the Koc Group. The group was founded in 1926 and is now one of the 500 biggest companies in the world and the largest conglomerate of Turkey. In 1969 a JV agreement was signed between Fiat Auto Spa and Koc Group, permitting the production of cars, engines and spare parts under the licence of Fiat in Turkey. Tofas was founded in 1971 as a JV between Fiat and Koc. The groups currently hold equal shares of the capital structure (37.86 per cent Koc Group, 37.86 per cent Fiat, 24.28 per cent public). The Tofas plant began production the same year with an initial annual capacity of 20,000 cars. The company now has an annual production capacity of 250,000 units. The company's most recently announced market shares for the PC (passenger cars) and LCV (light commercial vehicles) segments were around 13 and 19.5 per cent.

Tofas Oto Ticaret AS (later it was reorganised and its name changed to Birmot), which is a member of the Koc Group, was established in 1970 to carry out the marketing functions for the automobiles, components and other spare parts manufactured under Fiat licence by Tofas Turk Otomobil Fabrikasi. The company is the sole distributor of Tofas in Turkey and the distribution is realised through an extensive dealers' network, a majority of which are also members of the Koc group. In 1999 the company had a 36.4 per cent share of the market for locally manufactured automobiles and a 21 per cent share of the automotive market overall.

Until 1995, market shares of Tofas exceeded 40 per cent. Their decline has been striking in the second half of the decade: from about 50 per cent in 1994 to 18 per cent in 2000. Meanwhile, also the second largest car maker, Renault, has been losing market shares, from 32.5 per cent in 1995 to 16.0 per cent in 2000, but at a slower pace, at least up to 1999. This trend can be explained only to a limited extent by the increasing share of new producers (Opel, Toyota, Hyundai and Honda). The main feature shaping the market was the boom of imports. The sharp impact of trade liberalisation in 1996 is shown by the increase of imports share from less than 10 per cent in 1995 to about 54 per cent in 2000. Therefore, exporters to Turkey appear to be the true winners in the late 1990s in the Turkish market.

On the other side, Tofas has performed well in the past few years, particularly with passenger cars, unfinished completely-knocked-down (CKD), spare parts and engines, which are exported to a wide range of countries, extending from USA to Vietnam and Cuba to Ethiopia, covering 63 markets in total. Those countries became the customers of Tofas, thus the total revenues from export activities reached US$770 million by the end of 2003.

In the new system, TOFAS became the supplier of a region including Turkish Republics and the Middle East. This means that Tofas could be the production and distribution centre of the region. Tofas is now free to benefit from any opportunities in these countries, but when demand comes from other countries out of the region, Tofas is obliged to pass this demand to Fiat. Tofas will be selling engines and spare parts to European countries and Egypt, but these sales will be through Turin. The Turkish Republics and Middle Asian countries will have dealership arrangements as the sales structure. Arrangements will be performed by Tofas, but the facilities will not be owned by Tofas or Fiat.

For a period of more than two decades, Tofas was a good example of successful international partnership, oriented to penetrate a vast and protected market, transferring mature technologies, machinery and human resources from Italy. In the mid 1990s a strategic change took place: Fiat decided that Turkey should become one of the main production poles of the 178 project (Palio and Siena models).

The innovative idea was to produce a world car especially oriented to the needs of emerging countries in Eastern Europe, Latin America, Africa and Asia. Italy was the location of the new platform, where the models of this family have been developed, and the source of component exports, while production involved several main integrated poles and a number of assembly units in emerging or developing countries. In a first stage, the project was implemented in the Mercosur area (through a new Greenfield investment in Argentina and integration with pre-existent Brazilian facilities), with production starting in 1996. In 1997, Poland became another pole of this project, able to produce the Palio and Siena model and to export components within an integrated network of suppliers (Balcet and Enrietti, 1998).

Turkey was then chosen as a third production pole, whose importance was considered equal or superior to that of Poland, and second only to the Brazilian and Mercosur pole. The recent history of the Fiat group in Turkey reflects not only the strategic change by Fiat, but also the evolution of the macroeconomic context and the economic policies affecting the car market, including exchange rate devaluation, high inflation and subsequent stabilisation through restriction of demand.

In particular, the sharp liberalisation process that took place in 1996 deeply changed the strategic position of the main car makers in the country, Tofas and Renault. Stabilisation policies depressed the automotive market in the second half of the 1990s. Low wages still create cost advantages, if compared to Brazil, but in the second half of 1999 the real exchange rate revaluated, because of still high inflation rates, thus negatively affecting the international cost competitiveness of the country. One of the main issues in order to analyse the evolution of the competitive position of the Fiat group is how a JV can successfully support the transition from a domestic market-oriented strategy, in a highly protected context, to a globally or regionally integrated strategy. In the first context, the rules of the game are clear (Balcet, 1990). The local partner provides the access to the market and is responsible for the personnel and buying policies. The multinational partner transfers technologies and is responsible of the industrial management. The JV may be considered a learning instrument for both partners, which play complementary roles.

By contrast, the internationally integrated production requires a higher level of control on industrial processes, product quality, sourcing and trade flows by the multinational partner. The advantages of local partnership become less evident, and potential conflict can arise on the power of controlling international flows by the local partner. In any case, the process of international integration of the JV will be complex. This point is illustrated by Fiat's recent experience in Turkey.

Renault

Oyak-Renault was founded in 1969 with the JV agreement made with the Renault group of France to produce automobiles. Not only did the company help establish the domestic automobile industry, but it also encouraged Turkish firms to manufacture components and parts for its automobiles. Renault became the leading automaker in the Turkish market during the first half of 1998. One hundred and thirty domestic automobile suppliers provide anywhere between 50 and 85 per cent of its vehicles' components. Turkey represents Renault's sixth largest car market in Europe, and the French company was the second biggest foreign investor in Turkey after Japan's Toyota in 1996, according to a survey by the Foreign Investors Association (YASED).

In 1997, Oyak-Renault turned out 91,326 cars, controlling 38 per cent of Turkey's car production, according to the AMA of Turkey. It sells its cars through its distributor, Renault Mais, which has 230 dealers across the country. In 1996 the company was Turkey's ninth largest industrial company in terms of sales with a turnover of TL45.6 trillion (US$427 million), according to a survey by the Istanbul Chamber of Industry. Its export earnings in 1996 totalled US$35.5 million.

Initially devoted solely to the Turkish market, the site has come to focus on exports, which now account for over 80 per cent of production. Between 1998 and 2002, Oyak Renault increased its sales abroad ten fold. In 2003 the company was well on the way to being the market leader for passenger car sales for the sixth consecutive year, with 19.2 per cent market share at the end of July 2003. Despite the instability of the Turkish market, it has major growth potential in the medium term and Renault is determined to maintain its lead there.

The Bursa plant, which has introduced the quality standards and work organisation methods used in the Renault Production Way (French acronym SPR), is Renault's biggest manufacturing plant outside Europe, with a production capacity of 162,000 vehicles a year. It has the advantage of several international parts manufacturers working in partnership with Turkish companies.

Turkey is a vital part of Renault's profitable growth strategy, which aims to achieve half of all sales outside Europe by 2010. This is because of Renault's domination of the Turkish market and the country's high growth potential. Over the past two years, the Bursa plant has become a major production centre for exports to Western Europe, Eastern Europe, the Middle East and North Africa. In 2002, 40,635 Méganes and 46,564 Clio Symbols were exported, mainly to Western Europe, Central Europe and North Africa.

Despite the economic crisis plaguing the country since 2001, Turkey is still a strategic market for Renault, which has been the leading brand there since 1998. In 2002, Renault was the bestselling brand for passenger cars for the fifth year running, with a market share of 17.6 per cent, and is poised to keep its lead for a sixth year, having achieved 19.2 per cent penetration at the end of July 2003.

The Turkish automobile market took a sharp upturn from the 1980s, with more than 440,000 passenger cars sold in 1993, all brands combined. Since then it has been hit by three economic crises: in 1994, at the end of 1998 and in 2001. The most recent collapse slashed total sales to 135,000 after an all-time high of 456,000 in 2000. The market continued to fall in 2002, dipping below a total 95,000 cars sold.

However, 2003 brought some more hopeful signs, and by the end of July sales figures were back up to those recorded for the first eleven months of 2002. Although sales are still well below their 2000 level, the gradual recovery observed in recent months could bring the total market back up to 175,000 passenger cars in 2003 and 225,000 in 2004, probably reaching 500,000 before 2010.

Toyota

Toyota Motor Corporation (TMC) is one of the world's leading automakers, offering a full range of models, from mini vehicles to large trucks. Global sales of its brands, Toyota and Lexus, combined with those of Daihatsu and Hino, totalled 6.78 million units in 2003. Besides its own 12 plants and 11 manufacturing subsidiaries and affiliates in Japan, Toyota has 51 manufacturing companies in 26 locations, which produce Lexus- and Toyota-brand vehicles and components. Toyota markets cars worldwide through its overseas network, which consists of more than 160 distributors and numerous dealers. Toyota employs approximately 264,000 people worldwide and markets vehicles in more than 140 countries.

In Turkey, Toyota Motor Corporation reached an agreement with its strategic alliance partner, the Sabanci Group, to reorganise manufacturing and sales operations. In 1994 Toyota Motor Corporation agreed being a JV with Sabanci Group and Mitsui & Co. Ltd., and began by manufacturing operations in Turkey. This agreement involved assuming control of Toyota's jointly owned manufacturing plant. The Turkish plant, called Toyotasa, currently has an annual capacity of 100,000 units and is a major production centre for Europe. Turkey has always been an important market for Toyota Motor Corporation. Therefore, Toyota serves Turkish demand primarily through Corollas that it produces at a JV with the Sabanci Group in Istanbul. The first generation of Corolla was produced in 1994 and launched to market primarily in Turkish market.

Participation in a customs union with the European Union is integrating Turkey into the European economic sphere. This JV has presented huge opportunities for Turkey. But participation in the customs union also opened the nation's markets to escalating international competition. Thinking strategically, Toyota's challenge in Turkey, therefore, is to put in place an organisation that is internationally competitive. That includes structuring a solid sales-and-service network, as well as continuing to upgrade its manufacturing operations. It has also included working with Turkish suppliers to help them provide internationally competitive parts and materials.

Toyota Motor Manufacturing Turkey, Inc. (TMMT) has started exporting Corollas, establishing itself as a strategic Toyota manufacturing centre in Europe. TMMT, which has been producing Corollas as a TMC subsidiary since 1994, expects to ship over 40,000 Corolla sedans and station wagons annually abroad to 22 countries, mainly in Europe. With its new role, as being not only producer but also exporter, TMMT joins the ranks of Toyota Motor Manufacturing (UK) Ltd. and Toyota Motor Manufacturing France SAS, as Toyota continues to expand its European presence. TMC decided to transform TMMT into a European base location, after judging that it was well worth putting the faith in Turkey's potential in terms of its excellent and competitive labour force and gradually improving the domestic parts industry. Toyota bought the share of the Sabanci Group after the 2001 economic crisis, however, Toyotasa, has been going on its operations on marketing, sales, and after sales service with the partnership profile of 65 per cent of Sabanci Holding, 25 per cent of Toyota Motor Corporation and 10 per cent of Mitsui & Co. since 2000.

Ford Otosan

Ford Motor Company was incorporated in 1903 with Henry Ford as vice-president and chief engineer. In 1908 the company released the well-known T model, in which Henry Ford combined standardised and interchangeable parts. Ford Motor Company introduced the assembly line, which revolutionised mass production. In 1918 half of all cars in America were Model Ts. Ford's production of Model Ts made this company the largest automobile manufacturer in the world. Today, Ford Motor Company is a family of consumer-focused vehicle and service brands such as Ford, Mazda, Mercury, Lincoln, Aston Martin, Jaguar, Land Rover and Volvo. In addition, Ford operates Ford Financial, the world's largest finance company dedicated to serving the automotive industry, and Hertz, the world's first and largest car rental organisation.

Ford Otosan is a JV between Ford Motor Company and the Koç Group, each with 41 per cent share, with the remaining 18 per cent shareholding held publicly on the Istanbul Stock Exchange. The joint venture has its headquarters in Istanbul. The Koç Group has had a distribution agreement with Ford since 1928 and Otosan has sold Ford products in Turkey since 1959 when Otosan was established by Koç Group. Otosan Company made a licence agreement to produce D-1210 Ford trucks in 1976. Also, the company took the licence to produce Ford Taunus passenger cars between 1987 and 1993 and produced Ford Escorts until 1999. Ford Otosan is the sole distributor of Ford vehicles in Turkey. Ford Otosan now manufactures heavy and light commercial vehicles and imports other Ford automobiles.

Ford Otosan has two manufacturing plants. One of them is the Eskisehir factory that was established in 1984 by transferring the parts from the Istanbul factory. This factory is producing Cargo trucks, engine and transmission parts. In 2003 Ford Otosan self-achieved designing and producing Ford Cargo trucks and Ecotorq-named engines that belong completely to the company. The other factory is located at Kocaeli that started production in 2001 and has been chosen 'Best Plant in Europe' since 2002. Kocaeli Factory has had the annual capacity to produce 140,000 Transit Connect light commercial vehicle – Ford Motor Company and Ford Otosan hold the licence to produce Transit Connect – but after Ford Motor Company stopped producing Ford Transit Connect in Genk/Belgium, this factory increased its annual capacity to 200,000 by new investments. The company announced that if the demand for Transit Connect continues the company will increase its annual production capacity of Kocaeli Factory to 250,000 units in 2005 instead of in 2006 as planned before. Ford Otosan may become the European production centre for commercial vehicles by the production of Ford Transit Connect and Ford Cargo in these two plants in Kocaeli and Eskisehir.

According to Merkez Menkul AS research, the company had nearly US$2 billion revenue in 2003. Exports constituted 50 to 55 per cent of the whole sales of Ford Otosan in 2003. Ford Otosan especially exports to the European countries. Transit Connect had the 53 per cent of sales' volume in 2003 and the export of Transit Connect increased by 223 per cent and became 58,682 units in 2003 and domestic sale was 14,146 in 2003. AMA reports indicate that Ford Otosan has not produced passenger cars since 2000. Ford Otosan imports passenger cars and sells nearly 90 per cent of them to the domestic market. The company also imports Ranger commercial vehicles. Ford Otosan's Ford Cargo (heavy truck) production reached 3100 units in 2003. Ford Otosan has authorised dealers in fifty-two cities in Turkey. All of these dealers are also giving service and selling original spare parts. Ford Otosan is the 'Global Customer Satisfaction' special award winner in 2004 due to its well-organised, customer-oriented widespread dealer network. Also, the underlying reason behind the success of Ford Cargo depends on the customer orientation of Ford Otosan. Ford Otosan lets its most successful dealers visit the factory and make them learn about the production stage before trying to sell. Moreover, Ford Otosan declared that they will release the Transit Jumbo model, in addition to the Transit Connect and Cargo models. This implies that Ford Otosan is not only producing vehicles, but also contributes to creating new models.

Mercedes

Mercedes-Benz Turk was established in Istanbul in 1967 under the name 'Otomarsan' as a partnership between Daimler-Benz AG (36 per cent), Mengerler Ticaret TAŞ (32 per cent) and Has Otomotiv (32 per cent). The company started the production of 0302 type buses in 1968. In 1970, only two years after its foundation, the company started to export and of the 35,000 buses produced, over 12,500 buses have been exported to date. In 1984 the company was appointed as the general representative of Mercedes-Benz in Turkey, added with new partners to the enterprise and started a new investment necessary for production of trucks. In 1986, parallel to the growth potential of Turkey, the Truck Plant started production in Aksaray. In November 1990 the company name was changed to Mercedes-Benz Türk AşThe company currently employs 2800 personnel.

The shareholders of Mercedes-Benz Türk Aşare DaimlerChrysler AG (66.91 per cent), Overseas Lending Corporation (18.09 per cent), Koluman Holding Aş (7.04 per cent), Türk Silahlı Kuvvetlerini Güçlendirme Vakfı (5.00 per cent) and Makina ve Kimya Endüstrisi Kurumu (2.96 per cent).

Since its foundation, Mercedes-Benz Türk has sold approximately 35,000 buses, 35,000 trucks and 1000 midibuses from its own production, in addition to 22,000 cars since 1989 when the company activated the importation of passenger cars. Mercedes-Benz Türk currently produces intercity and municipality buses at Hoşdere and Davutpaşa plants and light, heavy duty trucks and semitrailer tractors at the Aksaray Plant. Mercedes-Benz Türk is the first company in the Turkish automotive industry to get the ISO 9002 quality certificate, obtained in 1994 for Aksaray and ISO 9001 quality certificate, obtained in 1995 for Davutpaşa and Hoşdere production plants. Furthermore, Mercedes-Benz Türk has held the certificate for ISO 14001 environment management standards since May 2000.

The main objectives of the company in setting up a second bus production plant in addition to the Davutpaşa plant, which has been in bus production since the beginning, are to increase the capacity and productivity to broaden the product range and to improve quality to the level required for exporting to west European markets.

The Hoşdere bus plant has been completed with an investment of DM65 million. This plant, comprising a paint shop, and assembling and finishing units, produces in cooperation with the Davutpaşa Plant. The bodies of the intercity and city type buses manufactured at Davutpaşa are conveyed to the Hoşdere facilities by special transport, where after the painting, assembling and finishing processes, they are ready to be delivered to the customers.

The Hoşdere plant has an initial production capacity of 3000 buses a year, and it is planned to increase this to 4000 at the final stage. Mercedes-Benz Türk currently employs 2200 personnel for bus manufacturing at the Hoşdere and Davutpaşa plants.

The Hoşdere plant, presently the most modern bus production facility of the world, has 52.500 m² covered area built on a total of 326.025 m² of land. The combination of conveyor belts and stationary working sites (boxes), instead of the conventional band production, provides the necessary flexibility to the plant to produce different models simultaneously and, moreover, time losses during manufacturing can be minimised.

Mercedes-Benz Türk, for the first time in the world, has applied at the Hoşdere plant air cushion technology in bus production. Having a very favourable effect on working conditions in ergonomic terms, the air cushions are used not only for conveyance of bodies between the assembling stations, but also for various stages of assembly. Storage and materials units are integrated to manufacturing halls with the purpose to provide optimum materials flow. The Hoşdere bus plant is a model facility with regard to both the technology and systems selected and environmental protection, owing to the special measures taken and the purification plants, the investment of which has been completed.

Being the sole bus production plant of Mercedes-Benz Türk from its establishment to the end of 1994, Davutpaşa plant has been completely reorganised to a body manufacturing plant with the most advanced body manufacturing technology after the start of operations at Hoşdere plant. Hoşdere and Davutpaşa Plants are working in cooperation and intercity and city type bus bodies manufactured at Davutpaşa are conveyed to Hoşdere for painting, assembling and finishing processes. Davutpaşa Plant has 24.314 m² closed area on a land area of 35.400 m².

Mercedes-Benz Türk's truck plant in the province of Aksaray started production in 1986. Since then, more than 35,000 trucks have been manufactured at the plant and sold primarily in the local market.

In addition to these vehicles, the chassis of city buses made in Germany have been produced and exported from Aksaray truck plant since 1991.

Mercedes-Benz Türk Aksaray Truck Plant was awarded ISO 9002 quality certificate for automobile industry and this was further enhanced through the award of VDA 6.1 by TÜV Südwest/Germany in 2000.

Mercedes-Benz started to implement its new truck strategy in 1998 and since then has invested approximately DM150 million in its Aksaray Truck Plant. The new truck strategy coincides with the existing bus strategy in the sense that productions are not solely for the home market. With a view to fulfilling the objective of renewing the product range through the introduction of ATEGO and AXOR trucks within the framework of the new truck strategy, investments were made to increase not only the quality of the products and the production facilities, but also to increase the output capacity from 8000 to 10,000 trucks. The investments included mainly the extension of the production area from 45,000 m² to 60,000 m², the introduction of a coating paint pool in compliance with the cathodic dipping system, and welding robots.

Producing trucks of the same quality as those produced in Germany, Mercedes-Benz Aksaray truck plant will soon start exporting, beginning with exports to central and east European countries. In addition, Aksaray Truck Plant is the same as its German counterparts in Wörth, in terms of product quality, and this has enabled Mercedes-Benz Türk's ancillary industries to export components to Mercedes-Benz truck plants in Germany. For the vehicles it produces and imports, Mercedes-Benz Türk supplies presales consultancy services to help with the selection of the most suitable vehicles for the customer's purpose, and after-sales maintenance, repairs and spare parts services. The company provides theoretical and practical training, guarantee and maintenance-repairs services to ensure economic and efficient utilisation of the vehicles it markets locally. Such services are also offered for foreign sales. The worldwide service stations of the brand Mercedes-Benz are at the service of all the vehicles exported by Mercedes-Benz Türk. Mercedes-Benz Türk opened its new spare parts warehouse in Hoşdere, Istanbul in 2000 with the purpose of supplying spare parts uninterruptedly. The central spare parts warehouse, occupying 21,000 m² of covered area has approximately 50,000 items of spare parts recorded in its inventory. With its nationwide urgent service network, Mercedes-Benz is able to deliver the original spare parts stocked at Hoşdere to any part of the country within 24 hours.

Hyundai

Hyundai Motor Company was founded in 1967 in Korea as a branch of Hyundai Business Group and in just 30 years was the eighth largest automaker in the world, with targeted annual sales of 1.5 million vehicles worldwide as of 2004 and with an annual production capacity of 2.4 million vehicles. One and a half million units of this production capacity is located in Korean plants, whereas the overseas production is led by plants in India and Turkey, with a total capacity of 500,000 vehicles.

During the early years of production, the company operated under the licence of Ford. However, in just seven years the company was able to build the necessary expertise to design, develop and produce an independent model, the Pony, which was unveiled at the 55th Turin Motor Show. In 1981, Hyundai Motor Company and Mitsubishi Motor Company of Japan signed a technical agreement, which enabled the technology transfer between these companies. As of 1991, Hyundai Motor Company designed and developed Korea's first proprietary engine and was fast becoming one of the world's elite motor companies.

The penetration of Hyundai cars to the Turkish market started with the foundation of Assan Hyundai MAS Inc. as a distributor of Hyundai cars towards the end of 1990. ASSAN Hyundai remained in charge of Turkish market operations until the forfeit of distribution rights to Hyundai Assan Otomotiv Sanayi ve Ticaret Aş(to be referred to as Hyundai Assan) in 1997, founded towards the end of 1994 as a 50 per cent equal share JV of Hyundai Motor Company and Kibar Group of Turkey, who are specialising in heavy industries. Hyundai Assan plant in Turkey started production in 1997 with a total annual capacity of 125,000 passenger cars and light commercial vehicles.

Hyundai Assan plant in Turkey not only serves the local market, but also serves as a 'strategic beachhead' for serving markets in Europe and the Middle East, as described by Hyundai Motor Company executives.

Although Hyundai Motor Company is the eighth largest auto-maker in the world as of 2004, as the world automobile industry continues to consolidate, the future of the company is still not perfectly clear. The current annual rate of production of Hyundai Motor Company is enough for the achieving economies of scale in the operations but without continuously pushing the sales figures to even higher levels, the consolidation trend might be too strong for Hyundai to resist. It is well known that the world's largest automobile markets are the United States, Europe and Japan, and, recently, Asia, and without establishing a strong position in these markets it is highly unlikely that an automobile company will survive given that the consolidation trend continues. Japanese and other Asian markets are very close to Korea and the operations in Japanese and Asian markets are mainly controlled directly by Korea. On the other hand, for the US operations Hyundai Motor America was founded in 1985. The only remaining major market is Europe and to penetrate into that market, Hyundai Motor Company established Hyundai Assan as their 'strategic beachhead'. From this perspective, that is, to resist against the consolidation trend in the automobile industry, it is easy to deduce the reasons for Hyundai investing into India, and into Turkey for Middle Eastern operations.

So far, only India, which is already founded as 100 per cent Hyundai Motor Company investment, is not a JV operation among all Hyundai operations in foreign countries. This can be attributed to Hyundai Motor Company's unwillingness to own 100 per cent of operations without establishing high enough sales figures and fully understanding the subtleties of operating in local markets, hence avoiding risk.

Honda

Honda Technical Research Institute was founded by Soichiro Honda and Taico Fujisawa in 1946. Originally, the company started by building power equipment and vehicle components. The company then started producing motorcycles and automobiles and lately it designed and developed a business jet. The motorcycle production began in 1949 and the automobile production began in 1963.

The company successfully penetrated into European and especially US markets in the last 20 years, which saw them going from the seventh largest auto-maker of Japan to the seventh largest automaker in the world. As of 2004, annual worldwide sales of motorcycles reach 6 million units, those of automobiles reach 3 million units and those of power equipment reach 12 million. The largest market for Honda is North America, with a sales volume of 1.5 million cars, which is followed by Japan and Europe, with sales volumes of 850,000 and 200,000 respectively.

Honda Motor Company's (HMC) operations in Turkey began in 1992 with the establishment of an equal share 50 per cent JV with Anadolu Group of Turkey. Initially, the operations only consisted of exporting, marketing and sales. In 1996 HMC and Anadolu Group of Turkey started the construction of a plant to produce Honda motorcycles and automobiles in Turkey. The plant started production in 1997 and became the second largest HMC plant in Europe. In 1998 HMC decided to increase their shares in the JV by raising capital, requiring Anadolu Group not to raise capital; and hence taking over the full control of all operations. In response, Anadolu Group proposed to sell their shares, which was accepted by HMC. Hence, Turkish operations were fully taken over by HMC. Such a move by HMC is not a surprise, as it has numerous subsidiaries around the world and without single exception it is the majority owner in all of those subsidiaries.

Despite the size of the company, HMC currently faces the same threat as Hyundai Motor Company: the consolidation trend in the automobile industry. HMC announced in 2003 that regardless of the mergers going on in the automobile industry, HMC will remain independent. Therefore, HMC focused on the fast-growing Asian markets and established high-capacity plants in India and China, which they expect to provide them with enough sales to achieve even better economies of scale in the consolidating automobile market. As of 2004, HMC considers the European economy to be weak, hence the Turkish plant is not going to be the major focus in the short run.

MAN

With its 76,000 personnel all around the world and its €16 billion of endorsement, MAN Holding is Europe's leading investment goods producer and system and service provider in the production of commercial vehicles, systems and machinery. MAN Turkey was founded in Istanbul in 1966 with the title of MAN Kamyon ve Otobüs Sanayi AŞ (MANAŞ), of which the one-third share belonged to MAN Nutzfahrzeuge AG, and its plant facilities started production within the same year. The truck plant was opened in 1984 and the engine plant in 1985 in Ankara. In the period from 1988 to 1991, production stopped temporarily. Management of MANAŞ was taken over by MAN Nutzfahrzeuge AG in 1995 and the Istanbul plant was sold. In this same year, the truck, commuter coach and travel bus production facilities were joined in Ankara. MANAŞ started the production of public transportation buses in Ankara in June 1995 and it started producing the S2000 model travel buses in April 1996.

An engine plant was purchased in 1996. The production capacity was increased to four buses per day in 1997 and the shares of MAN Nutzfahrzeuge AG increased to 81 per cent. The bus production capacity was increased twice in 2001. The spare parts and customer services buildings were opened. MAN Nutzfahrzeuge AG's share within MANAŞcapital structure increased to 99.9 per cent. The company title was changed to MAN Türkiye Aşin 2002. In MAN AG group, Man Türkiye A.S. became well known, particularly for its bus production, because of the quality and the increasing capacity of its production. With its third stage enlargement investment, MAN Türkiye AŞ aims to increase its daily bus production capacity with a rate of 50 per cent and to become MAN's Europe base for bus production in 2004.

Since 1994, MAN Turkey's exportation has continuously increased as it was planned. MAN Turkey aims to increase the portion of exportation among the total sales. It has completed 2001 with an enormous increase in exportation. With its intensive marketing activities in 2001, MAN Turkey reached an 82 per cent increase rate with the exportation of 679 buses, as compared to the previous year; and its level of income from exportation increased to €92.5 million. MAN Turkey exports to thirty-five countries, including Germany, France, Italy, Austria and Norway. MAN Turkey added Poland in 2000 and Hungary in 2001 to its present public transportation bus markets, such as Kazakhstan, Slovenia, Croatia, Czech Republic and Bulgaria. MAN Turkey's importance has increased among MAN Nutzfahrzeuge AG and the new NEOMAN formation; and it will become MAN's bus production base with its increasing bus production capacity.

MAN Turkey has started to increase its investments since 1995 and it aims to be active not only within the country, but abroad as well. The demand from abroad, the activity in the domestic market, German MAN AG's viewing MAN Turkey as a base in the region, and the plan of transferring the bus production to MAN Turkey have caused MAN Turkey to increase its production capacity. With MAN Turkey's increasing importance in the MAN group, a decision of carrying on the investments was reached; and together with an additional investment of €8 million euros, the daily bus production capacity will be increased by 50 per cent in 2003 and 2004.

BMC

BMC Sanayi ve Ticaret AS is one of the biggest commercial vehicle manufacturers in Turkey. Established in 1964, the company produces trucks, light commercial vehicles, buses and diesel engines on a site 11 km from Izmir, Turkey's third largest city. The company began with a partnership with the British Motor Corporation, producing Austin and Morris commercial vehicles under licence, progressing in 1966 to include a range of trucks, vans, agriculture tractors and diesel engines. Playing an important role in the development of the Turkish Automotive Industry, BMC has made a considerable contribution by accomplishing the production of the first diesel engines in Turkey, followed by the introduction of the adaptation from gasoline to diesel engines in 1976. In addition to the production of complete vehicles, BMC started to manufacture industrial engines, generators, marine engines and military products needed to support Turkey's fast-growing industry.

BMC Sanayi as an independent automobile company has invested heavily to establish its own foundry. In the initial stage, the foundry met the needs of its in-house production, but by increasing capacity over a period of time reached a point where it can now render service to the whole automobile industry. The foundry of BMC today is capable of rendering service to many automotive corporations not only in Turkey but also all over the world, established through its advanced mod-elling installation, superior technology, modern production facilities, its qualified staff – from its workers to its engineers – and its effective 'Quality Assurance System'. BMC Foundry today has a production capacity of 21,000 tonnes per annum. Important pieces such as engines, cylinder heads and brake drums have been casted since its start-up in 1975.

In 1989, a new growth strategy was determined after all the shares of the company had been acquired by Cukurova Holding, the biggest conglomerate of Turkey today. Consequently, BMC signed a cooperation agreement in 1990 with the pre-eminent Italian design house Pininfarina, the objective being to create a wholly domestic, purpose-built, unique cab. As a result of six years of intensive work and the investment of US$120 million, BMC introduced the new Profes-sional Range of trucks to the market in January 1997. The Professional series enabled BMC to be internationally recognised, providing a worldwide prestige to the Turkish Automotive Industry. Continuing to operate under the structure of Cukurova Holding, with its annual turnover of US$9.1 billion and total assets amounting to US$19.5 billion, employing 34,000 staff in 101 companies currently active in the sectors of banking, insurance, telecommunication, steel, textile, min-ing, paper, chemistry, transportation and construction, BMC is the only Turkish automotive corporation that is carrying out its own product design, development and engineering studies without relying upon any foreign companies.

BMC, which has been recognised worldwide since its foundation, is commit-ted to improving the quality of its products and services continuously. Each BMC product and part is produced at international quality standards. The quality of all BMC products has been registered with ISO 9001 quality system certificate. BMC, which demonstrates international quality in design, development, produc-tion, assembly, sales and services, exports its products to many countries. BMC, which is exporting to more than forty countries, signed technical licence agree-ments with Kenya, Tanzania, Nigeria, Ghana, Zimbabwe, Malaysia and South African Republic and issued production permission in these countries. BMC is the first and only Turkish company to provide licence to foreign countries in the commercial vehicle sector.

Türk Traktör

Türk Traktör was founded as Minneapolis Moline Turkish Tractor and Agricultur-al Machinery in 1954 to supply tractors for Turkish farmers. Located in Ankara, Türk Traktör company has been supplying tractors to the domestic market since 1954 and to the foreign markets since 1979. It is the first farm tractor manufac-turer of Turkey. From production of these 815 tractors in 1955, the company has improved its production capacity and now has an annual capacity of 30,000.

The company has always been affected by the macro environmental factors of Turkey, particularly from economic circumstances. For example, between 1956 and 1960, during the economic crisis, the company could produce only 367 tractors in total. This was mainly because of the foreign exchange deficit required to import production parts. In 1961 Minneapolis-Moline's share was taken over by Motec Industries Inc. Since this company was not producing small tractors that were suitable for Turkey, Türk Traktör cooperated with Fiat for producing new models and Fiat Turkey's general distributor, Egemak, became Türk Traktör's trade partner. With successful production years between 1961 and 1967, Türk Traktör won the confidence of Fiat and Koc group, and in 1967, Koc became a partner of the company. Minneapolis-Moline's share was taken over by White Motor Corporation. The local share of the company's production was increased to 46 per cent. In 1969 Fiat took over the shares of White Motor Corporation. In the 1970s Türk Traktör was again affected by the general economic crisis in the world and high inflation rate of Turkey, and the production was very low. The government policy of 'producing all motors of Turkey in a large company' forbid the company from producing its own motors and the company couldn't improve. In 1979 the first tractors in foreign markets were sold to Pakistan. After the military coup in 1980, the situation of the company got better. One of the cornerstones of tractor production in Turkey was the Gulf War in 1991 – only two tractor producers other than Türk Traktör could stand the crisis, Uzel and TZDK. In 1992 all public shares were taken over by Koc and the company became private. After this year, the company started using information technology in all departments. In 1994 Fiat transferred its share to New Holland NV. In 2000 New Holland took over the shares of Case and renamed as Case New Holland. As a result of economic crisis in Turkey, domestic tractor sales dropped drastically between 1999 and 2001.

After the merge, Türk Traktör has been meeting the demands for tractors as part of the global network of Case New Holland. Turk Traktor is a corporation of Koc Holding and New Holland today (equal share of 37.5 per cent). As a result of the new foreign trade opportunities led by the merge with New Holland as well as economical crises in the domestic market, the proportion of export products increased steadily. The sales organisation of CNH, New Holland's marketing office in England, receives orders from all over the world and transfers them to Türk Traktör. When all possible variations between the models are taken into account, the number of variants is almost 700. Increased variety in the preferences of foreign customers has pushed the company to a new period of adaptation to increased product variety. As the Turkish economy is recovering, the domestic demand for tractors also increases. The marketing of products that are produced for the domestic market is done by Trakmak Company under Koc Holding. Annual production capacity of the firms is 28,000 and approximately 37 per cent of the tractor park in Turkey belongs to Türk Traktör. Fifty-two per cent of its production is exported to more than fifty countries, including the USA, Canada and New Zealand. The company is continuously widening its production range with its customers' needs. Türk Traktör and New Holland Trakmak continue to be the local market leaders in the agricultural tractor sector.

Uzel

Uzel is one of the top ten biggest agricultural machinery manufacturers in the world in terms of production volume, and a leading manufacturer in the field of diesel engines and automotive systems. Uzel manufactures tractors under licence from US-based AGCO Corporation, which are marketed in Turkey under the Massey-Ferguson name. Moreover, the company produces diesel engines under a Perkins licence, and wheels under licences from Italian manufacturers Fergat and Gianetti. Uzel is 85 per cent owned by Uzel Holding, a company controlled by members of the Uzel family. The remaining 15 per cent of the company's shares are traded on the Istanbul stock exchange.

Massey Ferguson is a brand of AGCO Corporation, one of the world leaders in the design, development and manufacture of agricultural equipment, with annual sales of more than $2.3 billion. AGCO's portfolio of brands, as well as its worldwide distribution network, is the largest in the industry. These brands are marketed and sold through 7750 independent distributors and dealers in more than 140 countries. Massey Ferguson accounts for more than 50 per cent of AGCO Corporation's sales.

In 1935 the first steps towards the creation of the Uzel group of companies were taken. In 1961, Ibrahim Uzel & Partners Limited Company welcomed Massey Ferguson Limited, and a licensing agreement for the production of tractors was signed. In 1962, the first finished tractor came off the production line. Uzel has signed many agreements with foreign companies in order to exchange knowledge and production licences. In 1964 Uzel signed a licensing agreement with Perkins Engines Limited for the production of engines, and set up a diesel engine factory – another pioneering initiative in Turkey. In 1972 a know-how agreement was signed with Girling Ltd for the production of brake systems. In 1973 a know-how and technical cooperation agreement was signed with Burman & Sons for the production of steering boxes, and with Fergat SpA for the production of steel wheels for cars, trucks and tractors. Uzel took part in the formation of Döktaş and Asil Çelik, which were pioneering giant corporations in their fields of operation in Turkey.

Uzel continued its successful agreements and in 1994 a technical cooperation contract was signed with Rejna SpA to produce leaf springs and stabiliser bars and a licensing agreement was signed with Perkins Engines Limited to produce industrial engines. In 1996 Uzel's European regional centre, Pelico Industries SA, was founded. The Brussels-based company took charge of the import and export businesses of Uzel. In 1999 a distributorship agreement was signed with Canada-based Schulte for rock pickers, and a distributorship agreement was signed with the Italian firm Rimeco for sugar beet harvesters. In 2000 the Agricultural Machinery Unit became a partner of the London-based Farmec.com Limited, a company specialising in information services and used agricultural machinery supply, which is also one of the outstanding companies in Europe in this field. In 2001 Uzel has established a partnership with Deutz, one of the leading brands in engine manufacturing in Europe.

These strategic partnerships allowed Uzel to have competitive advantage in foreign markets. By its strategy of foreign trade, Uzel was successful in overcoming the economic crises in Turkey. In the last two years, Uzel's strategy included expansion in the European and US markets. Therefore, the company followed an export and acquisition plan in both markets.

Agco Corporation announced that as part of their global restructuring, increasing efficiency and strengthening their competitive position plan, they are closing down their factory in Coventry, UK, and transferring the production to three different facilities in the world. Along with Brazil and France, Uzel Makina Sanayi Aşwill be one of these facilities in Turkey. As a result of this, Uzel Makina Sanayi Aşis becoming one of the strategic centres of the world on tractor and tractor parts production and export.

Uzel Makine Sanayi AŞ, has increased the sales endorsement in the first quarter of 2004 by 157 per cent compared to the same period of 2003. At the same time the gross profit merge in the first quarter of 2004 has increased, compared to the same period of 2003, from 11 per cent to 24.5 per cent.

Conclusion

The roots of the Turkish automobile industry can be traced back to the industrialisation progress of Turkey in the 1950s. The Marshall Plan stimulated the industrialisation of Turkey, and this positively fuelled the Turkish automobile industry. Therefore, the Turkish automobile industry started with assembly operations via strategic alliances, for example, licence agreements and JVs, and was protected through high tariff barriers under the import substitution strategy (ISI) plan until 1980. After that date, Turkey adopted a new liberalisation policy and the export-led growth (ELG) strategy, which gave a new horizon to Turkish automobile industry and international trade as well as strategic alliances. The world automobile giants – Ford, Toyota and Honda – have introduced initiatives for new investments through JVs producing passenger cars and minibuses with a 100,000 unit capacity in Turkey since the last two decades. Turkey has also made a great step towards the globalisation process by signing a customs union treaty with the EU in 1995. The adoption of EU standards also enhanced the quality and efficiency of the sector, which reflected directly to export rate of automobile industry. Despite economic recessions, the export rate of the automobile industry increased gradually from $2 million in 1963 to $6 billion in 2003.

It is known that new initiatives for the automobile industry require heavy investments, which are especially well accepted by developing countries. Not only did strategic alliances invest financial asset but they also transferred the technology and know-how. Accordingly, production and export rate, efficiency and quality of the Turkish automobile industry enhanced gradually through strategic alliances.

As a result, Turkish manufacturing industries, including the automobile sector, has used strategic alliances all the way through its industrialisation process as a strategic development tool, for example, product development, technological enhancements, organisation of work, managerial techniques, profit strategies and investments since the 1950s. Thus, this aim has been reached somehow, and developments indicate that the Turkish automobile industry has lived through a period of rapid change to gradually become a production centre at the service of Europe. Particular geographical condition of a manufacturing site of the sector could hug the European market in which Turkish manufacturers can directly export to European, Middle East and Russian markets via seaway. The cluster formation of Turkish automobile manufacturers is quite suitable for international trade, in which the majority of the automobile and supply industries are based in the so-called Detroit of Turkey, the Marmara district, which provides excellent transportation opportunities, industrial infrastructure to firms. Many large Turkish manufacturing firms have also invested in this industrial zone, comprising about 71 per cent of total manufacturing. Accordingly, Turkey, along with a highly qualified young labour force and other potential opportunities, provide a new automobile manufacturing base for Europe.

References

AB Müktesebatinin Ustlenilmesine İliskin Türkiye Ulusal Programi.

Anadolu Isuzu Automotive Industry & Trading Co. (2006) Company website. www.isuzu.com.tr

Ansal, H. (1990) Technical change and industrial policy: the case of truck manufacturing in Turkey. *World Development* 18(11).

ASKAM Kamyon Imalat ve Tic. A. S. (2006) Company website. www.askam.com.tr

Association of Automotive Parts and Components Manufacturers (TAYSAD), various issues.

Association of Automotive Parts and Components Manufacturers (TAYSAD), Turkish Automotive Industry, 20 January 2004.

Automotive Manufacturers Association of Turkey (AMA) publications, various issues.

Balcet, G. (1990) *Joint Venture Multinazionali*. Milan: Etas Libri.

Balcet, A. and Enrietti, B.A. (1998) Global and regional strategies in the european car industry: the case of Italian direct investment in Poland. *Journal of Transnational Management Development* 1.

Banani, D. D. (2003) Reforming history: Turkey's legal regime and its potential accession to the European Union. *Boston College International & Comparative Law Review* 26(1).

BMC Cukurova Group (2006) Company website. www.bmc.com.tr

Duruiz, L. (1996) Getting organised for customs union: transformation efforts of Turkish automobile industry for the global markets. *Permanent Group for the Study Automobile Industry and Its Employees (GERPISA)*, June, Paris.

Export Promotion Centre of Turkey (IGEME) (2006) Monthly Statistical Bulletins. Retrieved from www.igeme.org.tr/introeng.htm

Export Promotion Centre of Turkey (IGEME), Research and Development Directorate, various issues.

Ford Otosan (2006) Company website. www.ford.com.tr

Foreign Economic Relations Board (DEIK) publications.

Fortune magazine, various issues.

Honda Türkiye (2006) Company website. www.honda.com.tr

Hyundai Assan (2006) Company website. www.hyundai.com.tr

Karsan Otomotiv Sanayii ve Ticaret A. Ş. (2006) Company website. www.karsan.com.tr

Koç Holding (2006) Company website. www.koc.com.tr

Kolasky, W. J., Jr. (1997) *Antitrust Enforcement Guidelines for Strategic Alliances*. Presented at the Federal Trade Commission's hearing on joint ventures, July.

Lee, H. S. (2003) *International Marketing Strategies by World Automobile Companies*. International annual conference, Global Business and Technology Association (GBATA), July, Budapest.

MAN Turkiye AS (2006) Company website. www.man.com.tr

Mercedes-Benz Turk A.S (2006) Company website www.mercedes.com.tr

Mossey Ferguson (2006) Company website. www.masseyferguson.com

OECD reports, various issues

Otokar A. S. (2006) Company website. www.otokar.com.tr

Otoyol Sanayi A. S (2006) Company website. www.otoyol.com.tr

Oyak-Renault A. S. (2006) Company website. www.renault.com.tr

Prime Ministry, Undersecretariat of Foreign Trade, Quarterly News Bulletin of Turkey's International Trade, various issues.

State Institute of Statistics, Prime Ministry, Republic of Turkey (SIS), Turkish Economy Statistics and Analysis, Printing Division.

State Planning Organisation (SPO) (2006) Monthly Statistical Bulletins. Retrieved from www.dpt.gov.tr/ing/

Syeda, A. U. and Ganeshe, S. R. (1992). new mores, new marriages: reconceptualising strategic alliances from an institution building perspective. *ASCI Journal of Management* 21.

TEMSA A. S. (2006) Company website. www.temsa.com.tr

Tezer, E. (1994) *The Turkish Automobile Industry*. In Turkish: Turkiye'deki Otomotiv Sanayii, AMA Publication 21.

TOFAS Turk Otomobil Fabrikalari A. S. (2006) Company website. www.tofas.com.tr

TOYOTA Otomotiv Sanyi Turkiye A. S. (2006) Company website. www.toyota.tr.com

Turk Traktor A. S. (2006) Company website. www.turktraktor.com.tr

Uzel Group (2006) Company website. www.uzelcorp.com

Winrow, G. (1995) *Former Soviet South Project: Turkey in Post-Soviet Central Asia*. Royal Institute of International Affairs.

Zaim, O. and Taskin, F. (1995) The sources of output growth and technical change in Turkish automotive industry. *Ninth World Productivity Congress* 1, June, Istanbul. Republic of Turkey, Ministry of Industry and Commerce. Council of the European Union, Brussels, 28 May 2001.

13 The effects of causal ambiguity on firm performance

An empirical analysis of Spanish manufacturing firms

Nuria González Álvarez and Mariano Nieto Antolín

The resource-based view (RBV) has become the dominant paradigm in research in strategic management (Peteraf, 1993). According to this perspective, variations in performance between firms from the same industry can be explained by the differences in their endowments of resources (Barney, 1986a, 1986b, 1991; Peteraf, 1993; Wernerfelt, 1984). Traditionally, it has been considered that firms with resources that are valuable, rare, non-substitutable and difficult to imitate can achieve and maintain over time a position of advantage with respect to their competitors (Barney, 1995: 56). Of these four characteristics, inimitability is the most important (Hoopes, Madsen and Walker, 2003: 890), and it is the most significant contribution of the RBV (Barney, 2001: 45).

In the framework of the RBV, resource characterisation and identification plays a key role. In the academic literature on the issue researchers tend to distinguish between resources, in their narrower sense, and capabilities (Barney and Arikan, 2001: 139). In this chapter we take account of this distinction, despite the fact that we recognise that these terms are often used synonymously (Makadok, 2001), and that some authors feel this distinction to be irrelevant (e.g., Wernerfelt, 1984; Barney, 1991; Barney and Arikan, 2001: 139). Capabilities – also called competencies – pose different problems with regards to the inimitability characteristic, and therefore we believe that they should be differentiated from resources.

Resources are assets, either tangible (e.g. machinery, buildings) or intangible (e.g. brands, reputation, licences) firms use to conceive of and implement their strategies (Barney and Arikan, 2001: 138). They are observable and can be easily valuated (Hoopes, Madsen and Walter, 2003: 890). Some researchers have pointed out that isolated resources cannot generate competitive advantages on their own; for that they need to be integrated and combined into groups forming capabilities (Hitt, Ireland and Hoskisson, 1999: 22). According to this view, capabilities are 'abilities of an organization to perform a coordinated set of tasks, utilizing organizational resource, for the purpose of achieving a particular end result' (Helfat and Peteraf, 2003: 999). Thus, they are intangible, they cannot be observed and are therefore difficult to evaluate. In general, the concept of capabilities is used to explain 'how' firms do things better and it conveys the notion that a firm possesses a degree of expertise and excellence in one or more particular areas compared to its competitors that results in a competitive advantage (De Carolis, 2003: 29).

An organisation's capability can be classified into two types: *operational capabilities* or *dynamic capabilities*. Operational capability can be defined as 'a high-level routine (or collection of routines), that, together with its implementing input flows, confers upon an organization's management outputs of a particular type' (Winter, 2000: 983). These capabilities comprise a series of routines enabling managers to execute and coordinate the group of tasks required to carry out an activity. In this context, the concept of routine should be understood in the sense used by Nelson and Winter (1982: 97) as a 'repetitive pattern of activities'. Dynamic capabilities build, integrate and reconfigure operational capabilities, and only affect indirectly, through the operational capabilities, the output of the firm (Teece, Pisano and Shuen, 1997). Managers use dynamic capabilities to administer the operational capabilities and to employ the resources of the organisation to generate new value-creating strategies (Grant, 1996; Pisano, 1994).

The RBV stresses that it is in both types of capabilities, and in the routines that make them up, that the potential resides for achieving competitive advantages (Eisenhardt and Martin, 2000; Grant, 1996; Teece *et al.* 1997). The stock of capabilities held by a particular firm will permit it to offer unique (and valuable) products, or achieve superior performance in such areas as quality, costs or time, and thereby be able to generate above-normal profits (Conner, 1991; Peteraf, 1993). In general, the duration of a particular advantage will depend on the degree to which the firm can protect the capabilities on which its advantage is based from imitation. In other words, the capabilities of a firm will lead to a competitive advantage when they are difficult to imitate. Thus, protecting capabilities against imitation becomes a crucial aspect to take into account for achieving a sustainable competitive advantage (Dierickx and Cool, 1989; Spender and Grant, 1996).

Capabilities tend to be protected by various isolating mechanisms. There is empirical evidence about the degree of use and the effectiveness of some of these mechanisms. Thus, scholars have verified that firms tend to protect their resources and capabilities with legal protection measures (such as patents), using secrecy, adopting leadership strategies (lead time), by moving quickly down the learning curve, or controlling certain complementary resources (complementary sales/service, complementary manufacturing) (Cohen, Nelson and Walsh, 2000; Geroski: 1995; Levin, Klevorick, Nelson and Winter, 1987; Teece, 1987). These barriers to imitation protect firms from the actions of their competitors, and permit them to maintain their position of competitive advantage.

Moreover, researchers have found a positive relation between the level of protection of the capabilities and the existence of causal ambiguity (Lippman and Rumelt, 1982; Barney, 1986a; Dierickx and Cool, 1989; Reed and Defillipi, 1990; Barney, 1991). In the literature, the concept of causal ambiguity is used to refer to the lack of knowledge that economic agents have about the sources leading to a sustainable competitive advantage. As firms use their capabilities, these reinforce each other and become more complex, which increases the level of causal ambiguity and hampers competitors' attempts to understand and imitate them (Rumelt, Shendel and Teece, 1994: 31).

Causal ambiguity derives from the very nature of the capabilities, and derives from the essentially tacit character of the knowledge bound up in routines (Nelson and Winter, 1982). Indeed, the knowledge needed to carry out organisational routines tends to be tacit (Itami, 1987; Rumelt, 1987; Winter, 1987). Even if the knowledge bound up in each of the tasks making up a particular routine is explicit, the routine as a whole may be unknown to the majority of the participants, and hence be tacit (Winter, 1987).

It might in principle be thought that causal ambiguity, like the other isolating mechanisms, in protecting a firm's capabilities from imitation by competitors will produce a positive effect on performance. However, some authors point out that causal ambiguity can also hamper managers' attempts to identify the core capabilities on which their firm bases its competitive advantage (Reed and Defillipi, 1990; King and Zeithaml, 2001). This ignorance will hinder the diffusion of routines inside the organisation (Szulanski, 1996) and in this case, causal ambiguity will have a negative effect on firm performance.

Which of these two effects will exert a bigger influence on firm performance? It has been noted that a capability, in order for it to be a source of competitive advantage, 'must not be so simple that it can be easily imitated, or so complex that it is difficult to use and control internally' (Schoemaker and Amit, 1994: 9). Causal ambiguity, which hinders the comprehension of capabilities, affects both competitors and the managers of the firm itself. While the first effect will positively impact on firm performance, the second will have a negative impact.

The objective of this chapter is to analyse how the causal ambiguity around capabilities influences firm performance. With this in mind, the rest of the chapter is structured as follows: in the next section, we establish the theoretical framework of the problem, based on a review of the main research on the phenomenon of causal ambiguity, and we advance the hypotheses to be tested; next, we describe the sample used and the empirical methodology followed; subsequently, in Part 4, we present our findings; finally, in Discussion and Conclusions, we advance a number of implications for management, at the same time as noting the main limitations of the study and suggesting some directions for future research.

Theoretical framework/effects of causal ambiguity

The concept of causal ambiguity was introduced by Lippman and Rumelt (1982) to reflect the basic ambiguity concerning the nature of the connections between actions and outcomes. Citing Demsetz (1972: 2), these authors describe this ambiguity in large and consolidated firms as follows:

> it is not easy to ascertain just why GM or IBM perform better than their competitors. The complexity of these firms defies easy analysis, so that the inputs responsible for their success may be often undervalued by the market for some time.

In this way, causal ambiguity reflects the inability of economic agents to understand fully the causes of efficiency differences between firms (Rumelt, 1984). Causal ambiguity is a consequence of the uncertainty of markets, and is therefore present in every process of competition between firms. There is ambiguity about what factors of production actually are and how they interact. In contrast to the assumption of neoclassical economics – whereby there is a finite and known group of factors of production – with causal ambiguity it is impossible to produce an unambiguos list of factors of production, much less measure their marginal contribution (Rumelt, 1984: 562).

Subsequently, in a seminal work, Reed and Defillipi (1990) analyse the relations between firm competencies, barriers to imitation and sustainable competitive advantage. They point out that certain characteristics of firm competencies, such as tacitness, complexity and specificity, generate – in isolation or in combination – causal ambiguity, and therefore create barriers to imitation. Thus, under conditions of causal ambiguity, firms that try to imitate others cannot identify precisely and use the resources which have led the first firm to obtain a competitive advantage (Reed and Defillipi, 1990; Barney, 1991). Causal ambiguity has been seen to be the most efficient isolating mechanism that firms have to protect themselves from imitation by competitors (Rumelt, 1984; Mahoney and Pandian, 1992).

The effects of causal ambiguity are not only felt between competitive firms, but also affect organisations participating in cooperation agreements. Causal ambiguity, in hindering an understanding of the logical linkages between actions and outcomes, inputs and outputs and causes and effects that are related to technological or process know-how, will also hold up the transfer of knowledge between alliance partners (Simonin, 1999). Thus, it will be difficult for the partners to determine which competencies have led each of them respectively to succeed. If they are unable to identify these resources, they will not be able to imitate and apply them in their own organisation either (Barney, 1991).

Traditionally, this reasoning has led scholars to assume that causal ambiguity is required for a sustainable competitive advantage, since it disincentivises potential imitators, acting as a protective mechanism of firm competencies. Under this perspective, by impeding imitation, causal ambiguity enhances performance (Lippman and Rumelt, 1982; Rumelt, 1984; Dierickx and Cool, 1989; Reed and Defillipi, 1990; Barney, 1991; Mahoney and Pandian, 1992).

Recently, however, some researchers have questioned the direction of the influence of causal ambiguity on firm performance (King and Zeithaml, 2001). They have pointed out that causal ambiguity, by hindering the identification of the competencies which lead firms to achieve superior performances, also restricts the transfer of the same competencies inside the organisation (Szulanski, 1996) and may block factor mobility (Lippman and Rumelt, 1982: 420; Reed and Defillipi, 1990: 90–91). In this way, causal ambiguity will impede the internal diffusion of knowledge and reduce its level of creation inside the organisation (Lin, 2003). Hence, in this case causal ambiguity exerts an adverse influence on performance.

Thus, at present there is a debate in the literature about the influence exerted by causal ambiguity on firm performance, since although on the one hand this variable slows the diffusion of superior practices and technologies across firms, on the other hand it impedes the creation of new knowledge within the firm (Mcevil, Das and Mccabe, 2000).

In their contribution to this debate, King and Zeithaml (2001) consider that causal ambiguity has been addressed in the literature in two different ways: linkage ambiguity and characteristic ambiguity. The first refers to the ambiguity about the link between competencies and competitive advantage (e.g. Lippman and Rumelt, 1982). The second refers to 'the characteristics of the competencies . . . which can be simultaneous source of advantage and of ambiguity'. This chapter will focus on the first of these forms, since its aim is to study the ambiguity that affects the relation between competencies and superior competitiveness, with the ultimate aim of determining the effect of ambiguity on firm performance. With this in mind, we distinguish between two types of causal ambiguity, depending on the economic agent that it affects.

First, *competitor ambiguity* refers to the causal ambiguity that a firm's competitors face when they attempt to identify the competencies that have helped the firm to achieve its superior competitive status in the market. Following the literature on the relation between causal ambiguity and imitation, the greater the causal ambiguity perceived by the competitors of a firm, the better the performance achieved by the firm, since the fact that the competitors do not know the causes of the firm's success protects it from potential imitators (Lippman and Rumelt, 1982; Barney, 1986a; Dierickx and Cool, 1989; Reed and Defillipi, 1990; Barney, 1991). On the basis of this reasoning, we advance the following hypothesis:

H1: Competitor ambiguity has a positive influence on firm performance.

Second, *manager ambiguity* refers to the ambiguity perceived by the managers of a firm when attempting to determine the relation between their competencies and competitive advantage. For firms, it is desirable that managers know which internal capabilities lead to particular results, so that they are able to take rational decisions about them, with a view to obtaining a competitive advantage. As Reed and Defillipi (1990: 90–91) suggest, 'where ambiguity is so great that managers do not understand intra firms causal relationships, or factor immobility exists, it may be impossible to utilize competencies for advantage'. Thus, the less ambiguity faced by the firm's management – that is, the more they understand the resources and capabilities required to achieve certain outcomes – the better the firm performance. This idea leads to our second hypothesis:

H2: Manager ambiguity has a negative influence on firm performance.

Methodology

Data and sample

The sample of firms we have used to test our two hypotheses comes from a directory of the largest Spanish firms (*Duns 50.000,* 2001 edition). The process of data selection and collection was as follows: first, we limited the sample to manufacturing firms (with SIC codes between 20 and 39), and large- and medium-sized companies (with a turnover of at least €20m in 1999). These criteria were applied to guarantee that the firms had developed a certain number of complex capabilities that might potentially cause problems of identification and comprehension on the part of both competitors and the firm's managers. Initially, the sample contained 1967 firms meeting these criteria.

Second, as the information provided by the above-mentioned directory was insufficient for the needs of our research, we sent a questionnaire to each of the 1967 firms. The questionnaire was directed at the chief executive officer (CEO), considered to be the person most qualified to respond to the questions and with easiest access to the information required. We received 258 usable responses, which represents a sampling error of ±5.80 per cent with a confidence level of 95 per cent.

Variable measures

To make the variables included in this research operative, we used mainly subjective measures provided by the responses from the questionnaire on a series of indicators. A seven-point Likert-type scale was used, with 1 representing 'totally disagree' and 7 'totally agree'. In Appendix 13A we present the indicators used to measure each of the variables considered in the research. We might mention that the indicators used to measure the competitor ambiguity were adapted from those used in the work of Simonin (1999) and Szulanski (1996); while the construct for manager ambiguity was especially built for this research.

With regards to firm performance, this was made operative using a multidimensional subjective measure. This measure included economic-financial as well as socio-organisational indicators, since only considering these in combination allows us to evaluate the success of an organisation (Robbins, 1990). Consequently, and following Naman and Slevin (1993), we built two scales of items. The objective of the first scale was for the managers to evaluate the importance of the indicators proposed. With the second scale, the aim was for the managers to express their level of satisfaction with respect to their expectations about these indicators during the past trading year. Subsequently, we calculated a weighted average of the satisfaction scores of the managers on the nine indicators, with the importance scores acting as weights.

In order to get unbiased estimators of the impact of the two types of ambiguity on firm performance, we selected some control variables considered to be related to the dependent variable of the model as well as to one at least of the independent variables. The control variables were: the size of the firm, the age of the firm, the period of time the CEO had been in the company and the sector to which the firm belonged.

For firm size we used the natural logarithm of the number of employees. For firm age, a question in the questionnaire asked respondents for the year the firm was founded. The longevity of the CEO was also requested in the questionnaire.

The firm age was included as a control variable, since it has been considered in the literature as a measure of the ambiguity which competitors face (Mosakowski, 1997). Mosakowski believes that the longer the firm has been operating in the market, the better its competitors will know it, and hence the lower the degree of causal ambiguity these agents will face. Similarly, the same argument applies to CEO longevity, so that this variable was also included as a control variable.

Moreover, it could be said that the performance of the firm will differ in function of the sector in which it operates, and the level of ambiguity of the competitors and managers may also differ between firms from different industries. Thus, we included in the model seventeen dummy variables representing eighteen different sectors to which the sample firms belonged according to their two-digit SIC codes. The number of sectors to which the firms from the initial population belonged was twenty, but this was reduced to eighteen for the final sample, since it was not possible to obtain any response from firms belonging to the sectors with SIC codes 21 and 25.

Table 13.1 shows the means, standard deviations and correlations for all the dependent and independent variables considered in this study.

Results

In order to analyse the data collected, initially we ran a factor analysis on the indicators used to measure competitor and manager ambiguity, with a view to summarising the original data with the least possible information loss. The analysis was carried out following the principal components method, and in order to obtain more easily interpretable results, we applied a factor rotation using the varimax method with Kaiser normalisation. In Table 13.2 we present the matrix of rotated components, the communalities, the initial eigenvalues, and the percentage of variance accounted for each component. As can be seen, the analysis resulted in two factors, each of which grouped the indicators corresponding to one type of ambiguity. Once these factors corresponding to the two types of ambiguity were detected, the factor scores of all the firms were noted for each factor.

Subsequently, with the scores obtained in the factor analysis we applied a regression analysis, with the aim of explaining the performance of the sample firms in function of the variables competitor ambiguity and manager ambiguity, once the effects of size, age, CEO longevity and sector had been controlled for. Table 13.3 shows the results of the hierarchical regression analysis carried out.

Table 13.1 Mean, standard deviations and correlations

Variable	N	Mean	s.d.	1	2	3	4	5
1 Firm performance	236	4.00	1.99					
2 Competitor ambiguity	256	0.00	1.00	0.14[a]				
3 Manager ambiguity	256	0.00	1.00	−0.37[b]	0.00			
4 Firm size	253	5.68	1.31	0.06	−0.11	−0.17[b]		
5 Firm age	258	3.50	0.72	−0.01	−0.06	−0.04	0.18[b]	
6 CEO longevity	248	2.29	1.01	0.14[b]	−0.08	0.04	0.08	0.08

Note
a $P<0.05$
b $P<0.01$

Table 13.2 Factorial analysis: types of ambiguity

Item	Components		Communalities
	1	*2*	
MA1	0.63	0.01	0.39
MA2	0.55	0.02	0.30
MA3	0.80	−0.03	0.64
MA4	0.82	−0.02	0.68
MA5	0.63	0.07	0.40
MA6	0.74	−0.06	0.56
CA1	−0.04	0.66	0.45
CA2	0.05	0.76	0.58
CA3	0.12	0.67	0.46
CA4	−0.12	0.73	0.55
% of variance accounted for	30.07	50.28	
Eigenvalue	3.007	2.02	

In the first model, only the control variables were included as independent variables. The second model added the ambiguity faced by the competitors. The third model added the ambiguity faced by the firm's managers as explicative variable to the above-mentioned variables.

With regards to the control variables, some turned out to be marginally significant, indicating that they exert an influence on the dependent variable. Thus, the coefficient associated with CEO longevity was significant at the 95 per cent level of confidence in the first model, and at 90 per cent in the other two models. It was positive in the three models, indicating that the longer the CEO had been in the firm, the better the firm performance. On the other hand, the parameter for the age of the firm was positive and significant in the third model at the 90 per cent confidence level, indicating that the longer the firm had been operating in the market, the worse its performance. This may, according to Mosakowski (1997), be because the longer the firm had been operating, the more its competitors know it, and hence the less causal ambiguity they face. Its competitors can then appropriate its competencies, which will lead the firm to achieve worse results.

Hypothesis 1 proposes that the ambiguity perceived by the competitors of a firm will be positively related to the performance achieved by the firm. The significance and positive sign of the coefficient of this variable in both Models 2 and 3 supports this hypothesis. Similarly, Hypothesis 2 predicts that the ambiguity faced by the firm's own managers is negatively related to the firm's performance. The negative sign of the coefficient of this variable in Model 3, along with its significance, supports this hypothesis too.

Moreover, in the third model it can be seen that the parameter associated with the manager ambiguity is greater in absolute terms than that of the competitor ambiguity, which means that the effect exerted on firm performance by manager ambiguity is greater than that exerted by competitor ambiguity.

Table 13.3 Results of hierarchical regression analysis for firm performance

Variables	Model 1		Model 2		Model 3	
	b	*s.e.*	*b*	*s.e.*	*b*	*s.e*
Intercept	4.11[c]	1.24	3.78[c]	1.23	4.04[c]	1.14
Firm size	0.15	0.13	0.18	0.12	0.13	0.12
Firm age	−0.25	0.20	−0.26	0.20	0.31[a]	0.19
CEO longevity	0.27[b]	0.13	0.26[a]	0.13	0.22[a]	0.12
Sector sic20	−0.52	0.92	−0.29	0.91	−0.01	0.85
Sector sic22	0.53	1.10	0.78	1.09	1.30	1.02
Sector sic23	0.66	1.64	1.22	1.64	0.87	1.52
Sector sic24	−2.74[a]	1.61	−2.36	1.60	−1.08	1.50
Sector sic26	0.67	1.29	0.89	1.28	1.29	1.19
Sector sic27	−0.67	1.11	−0.39	1.11	−0.68	1.03
Sector sic28	−1.02	0.92	−0.75	0.92	−0.55	0.85
Sector sic29	−0.15	2.12	0.37	2.10	0.61	1.95
Sector sic30	−1.32	1.06	−1.24	1.04	−0.99	0.97
Sector sic31	0.17	1.63	0.54	1.62	1.09	1.50
Sector sic32	−0.70	0.98	−0.49	0.98	−0.15	0.91
Sector sic33	−2.13[a]	1.08	−1.84[a]	1.08	−1.29	1.00
Sector sic34	−0.31	1.02	0.03	1.01	0.32	0.94
Sector sic35	−0.29	0.95	0.12	0.94	−0.07	0.88
Sector sic36	−1.10	0.97	−1.02	0.96	−0.69	0.90
Sector sic37	−1.08	0.97	−0.95	0.96	0.60	0.89
Sector sic38	−0.26	1.17	−0.16	1.16	−0.28	1.07
Competitor ambiguity			0.33[b]	0.14	0.35[c]	0.13
Manager ambiguity					−0.77[c]	0.13
R^2	0.12		0.14		0.27	
F	1.33		1.56[a]		3.28[c]	
N	258		258		258	

Notes
a $P<0.10$
b $P<0.05$
c $P<0.01$

Discussion and conclusions

Our findings allow us to confirm that causal ambiguity exerts a double-edged influence on the performances of large- and medium-sized Spanish manufacturing
firms. Thus, we have shown, on the one hand, that causal ambiguity constitutes
one of the mechanisms which firms can use to defend themselves from the actions
of their rivals, since we have tested that there is a positive association between
the causal ambiguity faced by a firm's competitors and the performance of the

firm. Thus, and as is suggested by a number of previous studies, causal ambiguity protects firms from imitation, which contributes to the sustainability of their competitive advantage (Lippman and Rumelt, 1982; Barney, 1986a; Dierickx and Cool, 1989; Reed and Defillipi, 1990; Barney, 1991; King and Zeithaml, 2001).

On the other hand, we have demonstrated that the causal ambiguity that is faced by the firm's own managers has an adverse effect on firm performance. This finding is consistent with the authors that have questioned the effect of causal ambiguity on firm performance, arguing that although it impedes the diffusion of a firm's competencies outside the firm, thereby protecting the firm from the risk of imitation, it also blocks the transfer of these competencies inside the firm itself (Szulanski, 1996; Mcevil, Das and McCabe, 2000; King and Zeithaml, 2001; Lin, 2003).

Moreover, we have found that the effect on firm performance of manager ambiguity is greater than the effect of competitor ambiguity. This last finding contributes to resolving the debate in the literature, and is consistent with those studies stressing the need for knowledge to flow within organisations (Szulanski, 1996; O'Dell and Grayson, 1998; Hansen, 1999; Argote and Ingram, 2000; Lin, 2003), since manager ambiguity will only be reduced by the transfer of competencies within organisations. Only in this case will the firm be able to achieve superior performance.

Thus, and trying to summarise our findings, both competitor ambiguity and manager ambiguity determine firm performance, with the second effect being greater. Hence, the two types of causal ambiguity we have considered should be added to the list of factors that help firms achieve and sustain a competitive advantage.

We should point out that this work has some limitations. First, we have to recognise that there are clearly many other factors that can explain firm performance apart from causal ambiguity. However, as the main objective of the present work was to study the relations between causal ambiguity and firm performance, it did not seem wise, for operational reasons, to complicate the analysis by including other variables. Moreover, the measures of some of the variables used may be less precise than would be desirable, which may blunt some of the power of our tests on the two hypotheses proposed. In this context, it would have been desirable for the competitors themselves to evaluate the causal ambiguity that they face when attempting to imitate a firm. This was not possible as it proved impossible to determine which firms were rivals of which other firms.

Finally, from our findings we might advance two suggestions to help firms sustain a position of competitive advantage and obtain superior performances to their competitors. On the one hand, by protecting their capabilities from imitation by their rivals. One way of doing this is to attempt to project to the outside the greatest level of ambiguity possible. If a firm manages to hide its sources of competitive advantage from its competitors, these will not easily be able to imitate it. Additionally, the firm should make great efforts to identify the capabilities that contribute most to its success, and at the same time diffuse this knowledge to all the management, thereby reducing the level of causal ambiguity inside the organisation.

This poses a number of questions: what kinds of factor contribute to both types of ambiguity? Can firms effectively control these factors, and hence the effects of causal ambiguity, such that the causal ambiguity affects competitors more than the firm's managers? How can a firm protect its capabilities from a competitor's actions at the same time as spreading knowledge about them throughout the organisation? Research on various aspects of human resource management, focusing on the creation of a climate favouring the transfer of competencies within organisations and impeding imitation, may shed some light on these issues. All these are promising directions for future research.

Appendix 13A Items included in questionnaire

Variable	Measures
Manager ambiguity $\alpha = 0.79$	Top and middle managers in our firm know what specific actions and decisions they should take to achieve a superior performance to our competitors (MA1)
	Top and middle managers in our firm can determine the causes of failures of our firm (MA2)
	Top and middle managers in our firm know the strategy adopted by the firm (MA3)
	Top and middle managers in our firm are generally informed about any change in the strategy (MA4)
	The majority of the top and middle managers in our firm know when a new product is going to be launched (MA5)
	Our firm has the policy of explaining to top and middle managers the causes of rises or falls in profits (MA7)
Competitor ambiguity $\alpha = 0.66$	Our competitors are unable to imitate immediately the knowledge and capabilities used by our firm (CA1)
	Our competitors do not know the keys of our success (CA2)
	Our competitors do not know the causes of rises or falls in the profits of our firm (CA3)
	Our competitors find it difficult to establish the specific actions carried out by our firm to achieve a superior performance (CA4)
Results	Operating profit
	Sales growth
	Growth in profits
	Market share
	Return on investment
	New product development
	Market development
	Absence of conflict in firm
	Productivity

References

Argote, L. and Ingram, P. (2000) Knowledge transfer in organizations: a basis for competitive advantage in firms. *Organizational Behavior and Human Decision Processes* 82, 150–169.

Barney, J. B. (1986a) Strategic factor markets: expectations, luck and business strategy. *Management Science* 32, 1231–1241.

Barney, J. B. (1986b) Organizational culture: can it be a source of sustained competitive advantage?. *Academy of Management Review* 11, 656–665.

Barney, J. B. (1991) Firm resources and sustained competitive advantage. *Journal of Management* 17, 99–120.

Barney, J. B. (1995) Looking inside for competitive advantage. *Academy of Management Executive* 9, 49–61.

Barney, J. B. (2001) Is the resource-based 'view' a useful perspective for strategic management research? Yes. *Academy of Management Review* 26, 41–56.

Barney, J. B. and Arikan, A. M. (2001) 'The resource-based view: origins and implications', in M. A. Hitt, R. E. Freeman and J. S. Harrison (eds), *Handbook of Strategic Management*. Oxford: Blackwell.

Cohen, W. M, Nelson R. N. and Walsh, J. P. (2000) Protecting their intellectual assets: appropriability conditions and why U.S. manufacturing firms patent (or not). National Bureau of Economic Research, working paper no. 7552.

Conner, K. R. (1991) A historical comparison of resource based theory and five schools of thought within industrial organization economics: do we have a new theory of the firm?. *Journal of Management* 17, 121–54.

De Carolis, D. M. (2003) Competencies and imitability in the pharmaceutical industry: an análisis of their relationship with firm performance. *Journal of Management* 29, 27–50.

Demsetz, H. (1972) Industry structure, market rivalry and public policy. *Journal of Law and Economics* 16, 1–9.

Dierickx, I. and Cool, K. (1989) Asset stock accumulation and sustainability of competitive advantage. *Management Science* 35, 1504–1511.

Duns and Bradstreet España (2001). *Duns 50.000 Principales Empresas Españolas*. Madrid.

Eisenhardt, K. M. and Martin, J. A. (2000) Dynamic capabilities: what are they?. *Strategic Management Journal* 21, 1105–1121.

Geroski, P. A. (1995) What do we know about entry?. *International Journal of Industrial Organization* 13, 412–440.

Grant, R. M. (1996) Toward a knowledge-based theory of the firm. *Strategic Management Journal* 17, Winter special issue, 109–122.

Hansen, M. T. (1999) The search- transfer problem: the role of weak ties in sharing knowledge across organization subunits. *Administrative Science Quarterly* 44, 82–111.

Helfat, C. E. and Peteraf, M. A. (2003) The dynamic resource-based view: capability lifecycles. *Strategic Management Journal* 24, special issue, 997–1010.

Hitt, M. A., Ireland, R. D. and Hoskisson, R. E. (1999) *Strategic Management: competitiveness and globalisation*. Cincinnati: South Western College Publishing.

Hoopes, D. G., Madsen, T. L. and Walker, G. (2003) Why is there a resource-based view? Toward a theory of competitive heterogenity. *Strategic Management Journal* 24, special issue, 889–902.

Itami, H. (1987) *Mobilizing invisible asset*. Cambridge, MA: Harvard University Press.

King, A. W. and Zeithaml, C. P. (2001) Competences and the firm performance: examining the causal ambiguity paradox. *Strategic Management Journal* 22, 75–99.

Levin, R. C., Klevorick, A. K., Nelson, R. S. and Winter, S. G. (1987) Appropiating the returns from industrial research and development. *Brooking Papers on Economic Activity* 3, 783–820.

Lin, B. W. (2003) Technology transfer as technological learning: a source of competitive advantage for firms with limites R&D resources. *R&D Management* 33, 327–341.

Lippman, S. A. and Rumelt, R. P. (1982) Uncertain imitability: an analysis of interfirm differences in efficiency under competition. *Bell Journal of Economics* 13: 418–438.

McEvily, S. K., Das, S. and Mccabe, K. (2000) Avoiding competence substitution through knowledge sharing. *Academy of Management Review* 25, 294–311.

Mahoney, J. T. and Pandian, J. R. (1992) The resource-based view within the conversation of strategic management. *Strategic Management Journal* 13, 363–380.

Makadok, R. (2001) Towards a synthesis of resource-based and dynamica capability views of rent creation. *Strategic Management Journal* 22, 387–402.

Mosakowski, E. (1997) Strategy making under causal ambiguity: conceptual issues and empirical evidence. *Organization Science* 8, 414–442.

Naman, J. L. and Slevin, D. P. (1993) Entrepreneurship and the concept of fit: a model and empirical tests. *Strategic Management Journal* 14, 137–153.

Nelson, R. R. and Winter, S. G. (1982) *An evolutionary theory of economic change*. Cambridge, MA: Harvard University Press.

O'Dell, C. and Grayson, C. (1998) If only we knew what we know: identification and transfer of internal best practices. *California Management Review* 40(3), 154–174.

Peteraf, M. A. (1993) The cornerstones of competitive advantage: a resource based-view. *Strategic Management Journal* 14, 179–191.

Pisano, G. P. (1994) Knowledge, integration, and the locus of learning: an empirical analysis of process development. *Strategic Management Journal* 15, Winter special issue, 85–100.

Reed, R. and DeFillipi, R. (1990) Causal ambiguity, barriers to imitation and sustainable competitive advantage. *Academy of Management Review* 15, 88–102.

Robbins, S. P. (1990) *Organization theory: sctructure, designs and applications*. 3rd edn. Englewood Cliffs: Prentice Hall International Editions.

Rumelt, R. (1984) 'Toward a strategic theory of firm', pp. 556–570 in R. Lamb, *Competitive strategic management*. Englewood Cliffs: Prentice-Hall.

Rumelt, R. (1987) 'Theory, strategy and entrepreneurship', pp. 137–158 in D. Teece (ed.), *The Competitive Challenge*. Cambridge, MA: Ballinger Publishing.

Rumelt, R. P., Schendel, D. E. and Teece, D. J. (eds) (1994) *Fundamental Issues in Strategy*. Boston, MA: Harvard Business School Press.

Schoemaker, P. J. H. and Amit, R. (1994) Investment in strategic assets and firm-level perspectives, pp. 3–33 in P. Shrivastava, A. Huff and J. Dutton (eds), *Advances in Strategic Management*, 10A. Greenwich: JAI Press.

Simonin, B. (1999) Ambiguity and the process of knowledge transfer in strategic alliances. *Strategic Management Journal* 20, 595–623.

Spender, J. C. and Grant, R. (1996) Knowledge and the firm: overview. *Strategic Management Journal* 17, Winter special issue, 5–9.

Szulanski, G. (1996) Exploring internal stickiness: impediments to the transfer of best practice within the firm. *Strategic Management Journal* 17, 27–43.

Teece, D. (1987) 'Profiting from technological innovation: implications for integration, collaboration, licensing and public policy', pp.185–219 in D. Teece (ed.), *The Competitive Challenge*. Cambridge, MA: Ballinger Publishing.

Teece, D., Pisano, G. and Shuen, A. (1997). Dynamic capabilities amd strategic management. *Strategic Managament Journal* 18, 509–533.

Wernerfelt, B. (1984) A resource-based view of the firm. *Strategic Management Journal* 5, 171–180.

Winter, S. G. (1987) 'Knowledge and competence as strategic assets', pp. 159–183 in D. Teece (ed.), *The Competitive Challenge*. Cambridge, MA: Ballinger Publishing.

Winter, S. G. (2000). The satisficing principle in capability learning. *Strategic Management Journal* 21, 981–996.

14 A firm's strategic orientation and performance

Exploring the moderating factors

Alejandro Escribá-Esteve, Luz Sánchez-Peinado and Esther Sánchez-Peinado

Introduction

Over the last few years the need for firms to adopt a strategic and entrepreneurial behaviour has been accentuated due to the acceleration of technological change and growing international competition. This new competitive landscape has led strategic management scholars to concern with the relationship between performance and the strategic posture adopted by firms on aspects such as information planning processes, competitive aggressiveness, future orientation, risk taking or proactiveness. Despite efforts to explain this relationship, there is no consensus regarding how to characterise firm strategic orientation and its actual effect on performance. In this sense, recent studies have highlighted the need to control some contingency factors, such as managerial, organisational, environmental and strategic factors, in theorising about this relationship (e.g. Covin and Slevin, 1991; Zahra, 1993; Lumpkin and Dess, 1996, 2001; Matsuno and Mentzer, 2000; Miles *et al.*, 2000; Entrialgo *et al.*, 2001, among others).

The nature of such a contingent perspective implies that the firm's product competitive strategy, growth initiatives, organisational practices and environmental dimensions will moderate the relationship existing between the firm's strategic orientation and its performance. Nevertheless, such moderating effects have not been well documented empirically in the literature. To address this question, we provide a contingent framework for analysing the relationship between strategic orientation and performance, and we present empirical evidence about the moderating effects of strategic, organisational, managerial and environmental characteristics over this relationship. A mail survey was used to collect primary data from 295 firms pertaining to seven industries (furniture; textiles; tiles and ceramics; road transportation; food processing; machine-tool producers; and shoes manufacturing).

The chapter is structured as follows. Section one gives a short overview of firm strategic orientation–performance relationship, justifying the need for adopting a contingent approach to analyse this relationship. Section two develops the specific hypotheses of the moderating effects.

Subsequently, we offer a description of the methodology and the statistical study, and we discuss the empirical results. Finally, we present the main conclusions and suggest further research areas.

Strategic orientation and performance relationship

Entrepreneurship, which typically leads to new product introduction or market entry, creates value through association with the discovery and exploitation of profitable business opportunities (Lumpkin and Dess, 1996; Shane and Venkataraman, 2000; Zahra and Dess, 2001). In addition, entrepreneurial activities also create value when they facilitate access to resources and capabilities that are strategic to competitiveness and performance (Stuart, 2000).

Much of the empirical entrepreneurship research has focused on the entrepreneurial posture of firms, trying to respond how firms should behave in order to be entrepreneurial. Literature argues that entrepreneurial organisations, that is, organisations with entrepreneurial postures, are risk taking, innovative and proactive (Miller, 1983; Covin and Slevin, 1989, 1991; Wiklund, 1999; Kreiser, Marino and Weaver, 2002). They are willing to take on high-risk projects with chances of very high returns, often initiate actions to challenge its competitors and are first-to-market with new product offerings.

However, a new stream of research is trying to reconcile entrepreneurship perspective with strategic perspective (Hitt and Ireland, 2000; Ireland *et al.*, 2001; Venkataraman and Sarasvathy, 2001). Researchers argue that entrepreneurship involves identifying and exploiting entrepreneurial opportunities but, to create the most value, entrepreneurial firms also need to act strategically (Hitt *et al.*, 2001). Entrepreneurial actions entail creating new resources or combining existing ones in new ways to develop new products or enter new markets before competitors (Ireland *et al.*, 2001), whereas strategic management entails the set of decisions and actions designed to produce a competitive advantage (Hitt, Ireland and Hoskisson, 2001). Therefore, value creation depends not only on opportunity-seeking behaviour (entrepreneurship approach) but also on advantage seeking behaviour (strategic management approach) (Hitt *et al.*, 2001).

Given the strategic nature of firm attitude we assume that this posture is a multidimensional construct that involves entrepreneurial orientations (innovative, proactive and aggressive) and, also, strategic postures (information analysis process and future orientations), as it is proposed by Venkatraman (1989).

A significant portion of prior strategic/entrepreneurial research has focused on its performance implications (Covin and Covin, 1990; Zahra, 1991; Zahra, 1993; Zahra and Covin, 1995; Lumpkin and Dess, 1996; Wiklund, 1999, among others). Although many researchers suggest a positive relationship between a firm's strategic orientation and performance, the sustainability of this relationship remains to be determined. Strategic orientation is claimed to be a resource-consuming orientation requiring extensive investments by the firm (Covin and Slevin, 1991), thus some studies could evidence just a short-term effect (Wiklund, 1999).

The positive influence of strategic orientation on performance is based on the first-mover advantages and the tendency to take advantage of emerging opportunities implied by strategic orientation (Wiklund, 1999). Firms with strategic orientation can introduce new goods and services ahead of their competitors, establish industry standards and control access to the market by dominating distribution channels. These actions should help first-movers to acquire sustained rather than temporary high performance (Zahra and Covin, 1995).

Zahra (1991) found a positive and growing correlation between strategic orientation and performance during three consecutive years. Zahra and Covin (1995) showed that strategic orientation influenced performance during each of the five years studied, increasing over time. So, these results suggest that the effect of strategic orientation on performance could be long term rather than short term.

Other studies, such as Zahra's (1993), suggest that firm strategic orientation does not always lead to improvements in growth and profitability. Some entrepreneurship activities fail to produce their intended financial results, focusing on preserving the existence of the firm, rather than improving its revenues and profitability. Thus, other arguments are based on non-financial implications of strategic orientation. Literature mentions several possible non-financial outcomes: increasing employee motivation and task involvement, and creating a positive organisational culture that encourages the integration of employee and organisational needs, reputation, public image, etc. (Peters and Waterman, 1982; Lumpkin and Dess, 1996).

In this sense, Lumpkin and Dess (1996) recognise the multidimensional nature of firm performance and suggest that traditional accounting measures (sales growth, market share and profitability) and non-financial measures should be incorporated when we assess how strategic orientation is related to firm performance.

Consequently, the relationship between strategic orientation and firm performance has inspired discussion in the literature. In order to solve this controversy, other authors claim that the role of contingent variables should be considered when we assess the strategic orientation–performance relationship (Covin and Slevin, 1989, 1991; Zahra, 1993; Lumpkin and Dess, 1996, among others). They argue that *environmental* factors, such as dynamism and complexity; *organisational* factors, such as centralisation of decision-making; *strategic* factors, such as firm competitive strategy and growth initiatives; and *top management team characteristics*, such as level of education and experience in other firms or sectors, may influence the performance of firms with a strategic orientation. So, there exists another stream of research that stresses the importance of viewing the strategic orientation–performance relationship in a contingency framework.

Contingency theories recognise the importance of the fit among key constructs of interest (Lawrence and Lorsch, 1967). Organisational effectiveness results from fitting certain organisational characteristics to contingencies that reflect the situation of the organisation (Galbraith, 1973). These contingencies include the environment, firm organisational characteristics and strategy.

In sum, despite the controversy concerning appropriate measures of firm performance and the long-term effects of strategic orientation, much empirical evidence supports that strategic orientation leads to superior firm performance.

So, in our study, we propose a positive relationship between firm strategic orientation and performance, and defend the need to control moderator effects over this relationship. We consider it necessary to investigate the role of environmental, organisational, strategic and managerial variables to further understand how strategic orientation contributes to performance outcomes. We hypothesise that:

H1: Strategic orientation is positively associated with firm performance.

Contingency effects of strategic orientation–performance relationship

External variables

The concept of external environment is intended to include those forces and elements external to the organisation's boundaries that affect its actions. There are some empirical and conceptual arguments to suggest that strategic orientation is not equally suitable in all environments (Covin and Slevin, 1989). Organisations often respond to challenging environmental conditions by taking risks, exhibiting proactive behaviours and planning in order to effectively cope with the adverse forces prevalent in dynamic and complex environments. However, in benign environments, the assumption of risk and aggressive behaviour in order to gain or maintain a competitive advantage is not necessary for survival in this type of environment.

On the other hand, strategic postures may also lead to changes in environmental conditions. Entrepreneurial firms may be partly responsible for making the environment dynamic by contributing challenging product innovations and, thus, promoting imitation (Miller and Friesen, 1982). The argument for a bidirectional relationship between entrepreneurial posture and environmental conditions has been supported by multiple authors (Miller and Friesen, 1982; Covin and Slevin, 1991; Zahra, 1993, among others).

Several studies indicate that the relationship between strategic posture and firm performance is moderated by environmental conditions (Covin and Slevin, 1989, 1991; Covin and Covin, 1990; Zahra, 1993; Lumpkin and Dess, 1996; Miles, Covin and Heeley, 2000). In highly complex, dynamic and hostile environments, strategic orientations appear to promote high levels of firm performance because the assumption of risk and proactiveness may be necessary for survival in those environments (Covin and Slevin, 1989). Similarly, Mintzberg (1973) has argued that uncertain environments are suitable contexts for the use of entrepreneurial strategy-making modes, implying the existence of an environmental contingency effect.

Based on the arguments presented above, we hypothesise that:

H2: The relationship between strategic orientation and firm performance will be moderated by the environment turbulence. Firms with strategic orientation that operate in more turbulent environments will have higher performance relative to those that operate in less turbulent environments.

Organisational variables

Organisational structure represents communication and authority relationships within an organisation and it can be defined in terms of its centralisation. Centralisation may indicate the extent to which the firm is organic or mechanistic, and, thus, it is an indicator of firm flexibility to accept innovations and new market opportunities. Organic organisations are decentralised and informal whereas mechanistic organisations tend to be highly centralised and formal. Covin and Slevin (1988) argue that a strategic orientation should be associated with decentralisation and low complexity in order to adapt innovations and new business areas within the firm. In fact, their empirical results show that organicness of the firms' structure was found to moderate the relationship between an entrepreneurial decision-making style and performance. Similarly, Khandwalla (1977) considers that wherever there is a strong strategic orientation there ought to be an organic structure in order to be able to adapt itself to new environmental opportunities and risk-taking behaviours.

On the other hand, behaving in an entrepreneurial manner implies aggressive postures in order to respond to others' actions. Therefore, entrepreneurial firms often adopt structures that allow flexibility and rapid decision-making (Covin and Slevin, 1988). From a contingent approach, a strategic posture will be most positively related to firm performance when is accompanied with the appropriate organisational structure (Covin and Slevin, 1991), which means that decentralisation of the decision-making process will strengthen the positive relationship between strategic orientation and performance.

In sum, organisation structure must be included in order to correctly specify the strategic orientation–performance relationship. Based on the existing theoretical arguments, we hypothesise that:

> H3: The relationship between strategic orientation and firm performance will be moderated by centralisation. Firms with a strategic orientation that use a more decentralised structure will have a higher performance relative to those that use a more centralised structure.

Strategic variables

We have introduced the firms' strategic orientation as an attitude oriented to the discovery and exploitation of profitable business opportunities (Lumpkin and Dess, 1996; Shane and Venkataraman, 2000). In this sense, firms looking for new opportunities should be implementing growth and competitive initiatives that provide access to such opportunities. Firms doing so should be achieving higher levels of performance than firms that do not implement the 'appropriate' strategies to take profit of new business opportunities. Hence, from a contingency perspective, we also address the potential moderation of the strategy initiatives of the firms over the relationship existing between the firms' strategic orientation and their performance.

Growth initiatives, defined in terms of propensity of entering into new markets or businesses, may be related to proactive behaviours by seeking new opportunities and creating demand. In fact, entrepreneurship literature argues that proactiveness is accompanied by new venturing activity (Miller, 1983), which may imply a diversification or internationalisation strategy for the firm.

As we have stated above, strategically oriented firms are proactive and dynamic firms in aspects related to the search and exploitation of profitable business opportunities. These new opportunities enrich a company's performance by creating new knowledge that becomes a foundation for building new competencies or revitalising existing ones (Burgelman, 1984; Lumpkin and Dess, 1996; Zahra, Jennings and Kuratko, 1999; Shane and Venkataraman, 2000).

Moreover, firms with a high strategic orientation are prone to product and process innovation and, thus, such firms have an important technological knowledge base that allows them to diversify towards a wide range of markets (Kitching, 1967; Reed and Luffman, 1986; Silverman, 1999).

Therefore, the impact of the firms' strategic orientation over their performance should by amplified by the implementation of initiatives that take profit of new opportunities existing within new businesses (diversification) or new markets (internationalisation), where they can exploit capabilities as well as access new ones. In this sense, Covin and Slevin (1991) suggest that ambitious growth strategies require a higher strategic posture in order to facilitate the achievement of growth goals and, subsequently, improve the firm's performance. In contrast, managers with more conservative styles will be more effective following maintenance strategies rather than active growth strategies.

Following a contingent approach, the effectiveness and, thus, outcomes of a strategic orientation may be contingent upon firm growth initiatives. Consequently, strategic orientation should be more positively related to firm performance among firms with active growth strategies than among firms with less ambitious growth strategies.

H4: The relationship between strategic orientation and firm performance will be moderated by growth orientation. Firms with a strategic orientation that use more ambitious growth strategies will have higher performance relative to those that use less ambitious growth strategies.

On the other hand, competitive orientation indicates the focus of firm strategy on cost leadership or differentiation. The competitive strategy literature based on Porter's seminal contributions and Miles and Snow's (1978) typology focuses on the competitive positioning part of strategy and is a useful framework in distinguishing different strategic orientations of firms (Borch, Huse and Senneseth, 1999). Miles and Snow's typology includes four types: prospector, defender, analyser and reactor types. Prospectors create changes in an industry by product development, introduction of new technologies, etc. Analysers are interested in developing business ideas and locating and exploiting new product and market opportunities. Their innovation source is most often imitation. Defenders try to create a stable domain. They do so by being cost efficient. Reactors are organisations in which top managers frequently perceive change and uncertainty occurring in their organisations but are unable to respond effectively.

The major contribution in understanding competitive strategy is Porter's (1980) typology: differentiation and cost leadership strategy. Segev (1989) found that differentiation could be compared with Miles and Snow's (1978) prospectors, and cost leadership could be compared to defenders. Both analysers and reactors would be in the middle of a continuum between prospectors and defenders.

The review of the literature suggests the existence of moderating effects of strategy types. The central logic is that implementing a particular strategy is essentially a process of organisational adaptation to the market environment (Miles and Snow, 1978) in which a strategic orientation should play a fundamental role. In fact, strategies that emphasise innovation and new product introduction (differentiation strategies) are generally associated with an entrepreneurial orientation, whereas strategies based on cost leadership tend to be in the domain of firms seeking to sustain advantage by erecting scale economy barriers. Differentiation strategies rely on strong marketing abilities, innovations and creative ideas, which are related with some dimensions of strategic orientation such as proactiveness, whereas cost leadership strategy emphasises process engineering skills, tight cost controls and efficient distribution systems. This idea suggests that firms seeking to renew or strengthen themselves by being more entrepreneurial should adopt differentiation strategies rather than cost leadership strategies in order to achieve a better performance (Entrialgo *et al.*, 2001). So, firms with strategic orientation employing cost leadership strategies will have relatively lower performance (Dess *et al.*, 1997).

Thus, our fifth hypothesis establishes that:

> H5: The relationship between strategic orientation and firm performance will be moderated by competitive orientation. Firms with a strategic orientation that use differentiation strategies will have higher performance relative to those that use cost leadership strategies.

Managerial variables

There is a divergence of previous research into two different substreams. On the one hand, some researchers examine the linkage between managerial characteristics and performance (Child, 1974; Norburn and Birley, 1988; Virnay and Tushman, 1986), while some others have emphasised the link between specific managerial characteristics and the strategic behaviour of the firm (Hofer and Davoust, 1977; Kerr, 1982; Wiersema, Van der Pol and Messer, 1980). However, not much research has integrated these approaches.

It is generally acknowledged that strategic decisions are influenced by the beliefs, value structures and management philosophies of the strategists (Covin and Slevin, 1991). As the decision to adopt a strategic posture must be considered a strategic choice (Khandwalla, 1987), firms' strategic orientation may reflect top managers' beliefs of how a firm should be managed.

The level of formal education indicates an individual's knowledge and skill base (Hambrick and Mason, 1984). Firms managed by executives with a high level of education have cognitive abilities and qualities that reflect a high ability to process information and to discriminate between an extensive variety of alternatives (Wiersema and Bantel, 1992). Furthermore, managers with experience in other firms or sectors tend to make more changes in structure, procedures and people than do chief executives promoted from within the firm. Managers who have developed their careers in one organisation can be assumed to have relatively limited perspectives when faced with an unprecedented problem (Cyert and March, 1963). Therefore, the highest levels of education and experience from outside the firm tend to be associated with receptivity to innovation (Kimberly and Evanisko, 1981) and, thus, individuals are more likely to adopt strategic behaviours.

On the other hand, manager teams that demonstrate a preponderance of experience and wider education training will outperform those which do not (Norburn and Birley, 1988). Managers with higher levels of education and experience in other firms or sectors are expected to generate a wider range of creative solutions when faced with complex problems and, thus, they will outperform firms lacking such education and experience (Hambrick and Mason, 1984; Hitt and Tyler 1991).

Moreover, performance would be associated with firms that more completely align the characteristics of their managers with their strategic orientation. The absence of this coalignment will result in a conflict between the firm's resources and capabilities and managerial decisions, which would have a negative impact on performance (Entrialgo, 2002). Thus, firms with strategic orientation that are managed by leaders with high levels of education and experience will perform better than firms managed by leaders without such characteristics.

We hypothesise that:

> H6: The relationship between strategic orientation and firm performance will be moderated by managers' level of education. Firms with strategic orientation that possess managerial teams with high level of education will have higher performance relative to those that do not possess managers with high level of education;

and

> H7: The relationship between strategic orientation and firm performance will be moderated by managers' experience. Firms with strategic orientation that possess managers' teams with high experience in other firms or sectors will have higher performance relative to those that do not possess managers with such experience.

Methodology

Selection of sample

Data was generated from a mail survey of firms pertaining to seven sectors that have an important economic and employment contribution in the area of the Valencian Community in Spain. The study was introduced by a letter from the Chamber of Commerce of Valencia explaining the objectives of this research and asking managers to collaborate by responding a questionnaire. The survey instrument consisted of an extensive mail questionnaire, which was mailed to 2000 senior-level managers (who were most likely to be involved in the decision-making process in their firms). During three months, a series of phone reminders were carried out to increase the response rate.

Finally, we obtained primary data from 301 firms pertaining to seven industries (furniture; textiles; tiles and ceramics; road transportation; food processing; machine-tool producers; and shoes manufacturing). Six questionnaires were ineligible because the research instrument was inadequately completed. Thus, a total of 295 questionnaires were deemed usable for our analyses. The yielded response rate (14.75 per cent) is comparable with other studies adopting a similar research design (Entrialgo, 2002).

The sample was composed by small- and medium-sized firms pertaining to traditional industries of the Valencian Community, which are mature and fragmented in nature. Hence, our firms operate in saturated markets, with low growth rates.

Method

The importance of strategic orientation in predicting performance and moderator influences over this relationship were tested with a covariance structure model. Although moderated regression analysis is the most widely used technique used to assess interaction effects, it has potential pitfalls, such as multicollinearity or the absence of measurement error. Moreover, it is notorious that the lower statistical power may lead a researcher to conclude that there is no interaction effect in the sample when there actually is an interaction effect in the relevant population (Aguinis, 2002).

We ran a structural equation model in order to solve potential computational problems which might be caused by multicollinearity.[1]

The analysis was conducted using EQS and we used the generalised least squares method of estimation.

Variables

Strategic Orientation Scale (SOS) conceptualisation is based on an initial list of twelve items related to the five dimensions included in Venkatraman's (1989) study (aggressiveness, analysis, futurity, proactiveness and riskiness). The basic choice for the assessment of measurement properties is between the use of Exploratory Factor Analysis (EFA) and the Confirmatory Factor Analysis (CFA). In EFA the factor loadings for the items included in SOS indicated the existence of four dimensions. We observed two items with factor loadings lower than 0.60 and we thus decided to drop these items from our scale. CFA was used to assess the validity and the overall model fit for four-factor solution. A diagram of the final scale appears in Figure 14.1. Tables 14.1 and 14.2 also list the items included in each dimension and the fit indices for SOS.

With regard to performance variable, we used a subjective approach. Subjective measures of performance were chosen over objective data because small and medium-sized firms are often very reluctant to provide financial data. This type of measure has been used in multiple studies focused on strategic orientation–performance relationship (Covin and Covin, 1990; Miles, Covin and Heeley, 2000; Kumar, Subramanian and Strandholm, 2001; Jennings, Rajaratnam and Lawrence, 2003). Moreover, previous studies that have used both subjective and objective measures have found a strong correlation between the two approaches (see, e.g. Venkatraman and Ramanujam, 1986).

Our performance construct includes five items that reflect the financial and non-financial nature of this variable. Some authors recognise the multidimensional nature of firm performance and suggest that traditional accounting measures (sales growth, market share and profitability) and non-financial measures should be incorporated when we assess how strategic orientation is related to firm performance (Lumpkin and Dess, 1996; Zahra, 1993).

In Table 14.3 we present the multiple-item measures of dependent and inde-

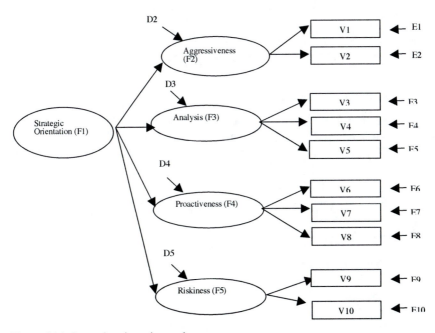

Figure 14.1 Strategic orientation scale

Table 14.1 Strategic orientation scale's measurement

Dimensions	Managers' perceptions about… (1, strongly disagree; 2, disagree; 3, indifferent; 4, agree; 5, strongly agree)
Aggressiveness	Sacrificing profitability to gain market share (V1)
	Cutting prices to increase market share (V2)
Analysis	Establish deliberated plans to cope with environment opportunities and threatens (V3)
	Emphasise effective seeking and key information registration for decision-making (V4)
	Following formal proceedings to coordinate decisions in different areas (V5)
Proactiveness	Emphasise innovation to anticipate future market needs (V6)
	Constantly seeking new products and markets (V7)
	Usually the first ones to introduce new brands or products in the markets (V8)
Riskiness	Sometimes decisions in the firm have produced important changes in the way to operate as an organisation (V9)
	The firm develops less risky investment projects than competitors, although income expectations are lower (V10)

pendent variables and their construct reliability. Cronbach's alpha was used to measure the construct reliability of some variables.

Statistical analysis and discussion

Prior to running the statistical analysis, the correlation matrix was examined. Most of the correlations among the variables are small. Further, the variance-inflation factor (VIF) reveals that most of these are close to 1. The largest VIF value is

Table 14.2 Goodness of fit (Strategic orientation scale)

Indices	Levels of an acceptable fit	Level of our scale
Bentler-Bonett normed fit index	Close to 0.9	0.932
Bentler-Bonett non-normed fit index	Close to 0.9	0.952
Comparative fit index	Close to 1	0.967
Lisrel GFI fit index	Close to 0.9	0.960
Lisrel Agfi fit index	Close to 0.9	0.929
Standardised RMR	Lower than 0.08	0.041

Table 14.3 Variables' measurement

Variables	Measure	Cronbach's alpha
Performance	Managers' assessment about: (a) profitability of sales; (b) market share; (c) loyalty degree of customers; (d) annual growth sales rate in the last five years; and (e) product improvement and development costs	0.6154
Strategic orientation	See scale's measurement below (Figure 14.1; Tables 14.1 and 14.2)	See Tables 14.1 and 14.2
Managers' level of education	Percentage of managers with high level of education	n/a
Managers' experience	Percentage of managers with experience in other firms and other sectors	n/a
Competitive orientation	Managers' perception about: (a) production costs; (b) marketing costs; (c) quality control costs; and (d) after-sales services costs	0.6264
Growth orientation	Index that includes the sum of the importance given by managers to diversification and internationalisation growth strategies divided by the sum of highest levels of importance	n/a
Turbulence	Managers' perception about: (a) quickness and frequency of technological changes; (b) quickness and frequency of customer needs; (c) difficulty to predict changes that will happen in the future; (d) impact of other firms' actions over the firm; and (e) variety of external factors that influence over firm's decisions	0.7174
Centralisation	Extent to which important decisions are taken by the managing director	n/a

Note
n/a: not applicable

1.468, which is well below the cut-off at 10 (Hair *et al.*, 1999). This evidence reduces concerns about multicollinearity problems. Table 14.4 shows the correlation matrix and some descriptive statistics.

The importance of strategic orientation in predicting performance and the moderator influences over this relationship were tested with a covariance structure model. The analysis was conducted using EQS and we used the generalised least squares method of estimation. A diagram of moderator effects in structural equations model appears in Figure 14.2.

Our model includes seven equations, one corresponding to each endogenous variable in the model. These equations were tested simultaneously. The results are shown in Table 14.5.

The overall fit of the model to the data is tested with a chi-square goodness of fit statistic, which tests the null hypothesis that the observed covariance matrix is equal to the covariance matrix estimated by our model (Bentler, 1980). Chi-square

Table 14.4 Descriptive statistics and correlation matrix

Variables	Mean	Standard deviation	1	2	3	4	5	6	7	VIF
Education	39.7937	33.62	1.000							1.102
Strategic orientation	3.2535	0.5442	0.168[a]	1.000						1.468
Turbulence	3.3779	0.6569	0.041	0.229[a]	1.000					1.110
Competitive orientation	3.0830	0.5676	0.129[b]	0.456[a]	0.133[b]	1.000				1.287
Centralisation	3.3496	0.7671	−0.044	−0.108	0.163[a]	−0.125[b]	1.000			1.070
Growth orientation	1.5036	1.1686	0.259[a]	0.305[a]	0.040	0.206[a]	0.015	1.000		1.176
Experience	20.6564	23.8730	0.176[a]	0.270[a]	0.130[b]	0.125[b]	−0.067	0.151[a]	1.000	1.112

Notes
a correlations are significant at 0.01 level
b correlations are significant at 0.05 level

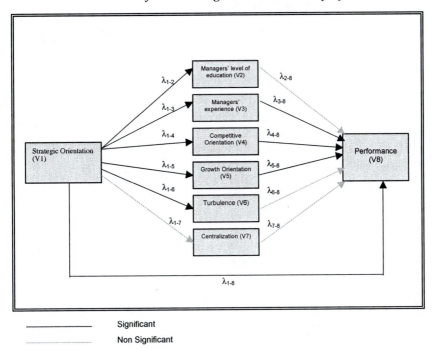

Figure 14.2: Predicted contingency model of strategic orientation and performance relationship

statistic provides a test of the null hypothesis that the theoretical model fits the data. So, if the model provides a good fit, we expect to see a small value of chi-square and a large *p* value. In the present analysis, chi-square was 14.621 with 13 degrees of freedom, which was not significant ($P=0.33162>0.05$), so we can't reject the null hypothesis of good model fit. In other words, this test supported our model. We selected seven additional measures of fit, as shown in Table 14.6. All indices provide additional evidence of the validity of our model.

The first hypothesis established that firms with a higher strategic orientation should be achieving a higher performance than firms with a lower strategic orientation. Accordingly with prior studies (Zahra and Covin, 1995; Wiklund, 1999), our results show that there is a significant, direct and positive relationship among strategic orientation and performance (coefficient $\lambda_{1-8}>0$ [$P<0.05$]), supporting Hypothesis 1. Hence, the findings indicate the positive effects of strategic orientation during a period of time and provide insights about the sustainability of the strategic orientation–performance relationship.

From a contingency perspective, we have addressed the factors that could be moderating such a relationship.

Thus, our second hypothesis focused on the effect of environmental variables over the relationship existing among strategic orientation and performance. It has been argued that strategic orientation is especially well suited to turbulent and

Table 14.5 Moderator influences over strategic orientation and performance relationship

Parameters	Standardised coefficients	t-value	p-value
λ_{1-2}	0.168	2.915	< 0.01
λ_{1-3}	0.270	4.805	< 0.001
λ_{1-4}	0.456	8.796	< 0.001
λ_{1-5}	0.305	5.494	< 0.001
λ_{1-6}	0.229	4.029	< 0.001
λ_{1-7}	−0.075	−1.284	Non sign
λ_{1-8}	0.141	2.273	< 0.05
λ_{2-8}	0.001	0.011	Non sign
λ_{3-8}	0.137	2.625	< 0.01
λ_{4-8}	0.336	5.945	< 0.001
λ_{5-8}	0.129	2.384	< 0.05
λ_{6-8}	−0.058	−1.097	Non sign
λ_{7-8}	−0.588	−0.030	Non sign

$t > 1.96; P < 0.05$
$t > 2.576; P < 0.01$
$t > 3.291; P < 0.001$

hostile environments (Covin and Slevin, 1989, 1991). Accordingly to these contributions, we expected that firms with strategic orientation that operate in more turbulent environments will have higher levels of performance relative to those operating in less turbulent environments. Our results, however, do not allow us to support this hypothesis. Although there is a positive relationship among strategic orientation and turbulence ($\lambda_{1-6} > 0$ [$P < 0.001$]) the moderating effect is not supported (λ_{6-8}; $P > 0.05$). It is possible that firms with a higher strategic orientation perceive a more turbulent environment than firms with lower levels of strategic orientation, because the former are more aware of the need to monitor for changes in the environment (analysis and proactiveness orientation). Nevertheless, our sample is composed of firms competing in mature business. So, independently of the manager perceptions, it is possible that the differences in the level of turbu-

Table 14.6 Indices of goodness of fit (overall model)

Indices	Levels of an acceptable fit	Levels of our model
Bentler-Bonett normed fit index	Close to 0.9	0.947
Bentler-Bonett non-normed fit index	Close to 0.9	0.986
Comparative fit index	Close to 1	0.993
Lisrel GFI fit index	Close to 0.9	0.988
Lisrel AGFI fit index	Close to 0.9	0.967
Standardised rmr	Lower than 0.08	0.029
Root mean sq. error of app. (rmsea)	Lower than 0.08	0.021

$\chi^2 = 14.621$ with 13 degrees of freedom; $P = 0.33162 > 0.05$

lence that they are facing were not important enough to moderate the relationship among the firms' strategic orientation and their performance.

With regard to the moderating effects of organisational variables, Hypothesis 3 argued that the impact of strategic orientation over the firm performance should be greater when the firm uses a more decentralised organisational structure. Our results, however, don't corroborate this hypothesis (λ_{1-7}; $P > 0.05$; λ_{7-8}; $P > 0.05$). Even if a decentralised structure can make easier the adaptation to the environmental changes, our evidence suggests that, in the case of small- and medium-sized firms (our sample is mainly composed of SME), whether the decisions are being taken only by the managing director (centralisation) or by the functional executives (decentralisation) may not be essential to the firm to take profit of the opportunities and to deal with the threats of the environment. These results can also been explained by the measure of the organisational characteristics that has been used in our study. An organic structure, which makes easier and faster the needed adaptation of the firm to the opportunities and changes faced in the environment, is related to other dimensions apart from the degree of decentralisation of the decision-making authority. Covin and Slevin (1989) used a broader scale considering five items related to: the type of communication channels; the degree of formalisation of the managing style, expertise versus hierarchic basis on decision-making, organisational routines and inertia, and behaviour procedures weight. It is possible that some small firms could maintain a high centralisation of decision-making in the person of the managing director, but could still achieve an organic and flexible structure by means of open channels of communication, changing managerial styles depending on the circumstances, lower weight of procedures in comparison with getting things done, etc.

We also explored the moderating effects of the growth initiatives and the competitive orientation of the firms over the relationship existing among the firms' strategic orientation and performance. We expected that firms characterised by a strategic orientation that were using active growth strategies should be achieving higher levels of performance that firms that were not using such growth initiatives (Hypothesis 4). Our evidence supports such a hypothesis ($\lambda_{1-5} > 0$ [$P < 0.001$]; $\lambda_{5-8} > 0$ [$P < 0.05$]). When operating in mature business, which is characterised by saturated markets and low growth rates, firms with strategic postures seem to look for new opportunities by means of new product and new market expansion (diversification and internationalisation strategies) in order to increase their performance.

On the other hand, innovation and differentiation strategies have been usually related to an entrepreneurial and strategic orientation. Moreover, in mature and fragmented sectors, like those included in our sample, cost advantages are difficult to achieve and maintain because of the lack of economies of scale. In addition to this, technologies and know-how are widely disseminated, which makes difficult to develop process innovations that could provide significant cost advantages. In fragmented industries, efficiency is a key factor, but rarely an important source of competitive advantages. So, strategically oriented firms (operating in mature and fragmented industries) that use their proactiveness to develop strategic and marketing innovations (differentiation competitive strategies) should be achieving higher levels of performance than firms following cost leadership strategies based on improvements in production processes and scale economies (Hypothesis 5). Again, the evidence yielded in our research corroborates such a hypothesis.

Finally, with regard to the moderating effect of managerial variables, we hypothesised that the level of education (Hypothesis 6) and the previous experience in other firms or sectors (Hypothesis 7) of the firm's managerial team should amplify the relationship among the firm's strategic orientation and its performance. Our results partially support the moderating effect of the managerial variables. While the previous experience of the managers in other firms or industries seems to strengthen the positive relationship among the strategic orientation of the firm and its performance ($\lambda_{1-3} > 0$ [$p<0.001$]; $\lambda_{3-8} > 0$ [$p < 0.01$]), the educational level of the managerial team doesn't seem to moderate the above mentioned relationship ($\lambda_{1-2} > 0$ [$p<0.001$]; λ_{2-8} [$p > 0.05$]). Firms competing in mature and fragmented business behave by following some industry recipes, which usually limit their ability to look for new opportunities beyond the limits of the industry routines and commonly accepted practices. Our evidence suggests that managers with previous experience in other firms or in other industries may be more aware of the opportunities existing in new business and markets, and may have a higher proclivity to behave in a more innovative way, which allow them to have access to new opportunities and improve their firm's performance in comparison to those firms following the traditional industry recipes and norms.

However, although educational level has been positively associated to cognitive abilities (information processing, ambiguity toleration, etc.), which should increase the entrepreneurial behaviour of the managers, our results do not show a moderating factor of such managers' educational level over the existing relationship among the firms' strategic orientation and their performance.

Conclusions, limitations and further research areas

Our main objective was to analyse the impact of the firm's strategic orientation over its performance, and to explore the moderating effects of several factors that had been pointed out by previous theoretical and empirical works.

In recent years, some authors have highlighted the need to control whether the relationship among strategic orientation and performance of the firms is moderated or not by some contingency factors (Miller, 1988; Covin and Slevin, 1991; Zahra, 1993; Lumpkin and Dess, 1996). Contingency approach suggests that fit among key variables, such as environment, strategic orientation, structural and managerial characteristics of a firm influence how an strategic orientation will be configured to achieve high performance. In some cases, the moderating role of such contingency factors has been proposed only from a theoretical perspective (i.e. the moderating role of the growth and competitive orientation of the firms' managerial characteristics). In other cases, there is some empirical evidence of such moderating effects (i.e. environmental hostility and organisational structure characterisation). However, such moderating effects have not been well documented empirically in the literature yet.

With the aim to contribute to settling this lack of empirical evidence, we have set up a contingency model that has been built upon the previous propositions and findings of other authors with regard to the moderating role of variables related to (1) the managerial characteristics of the firms; (2) the competitive and growth initiatives implemented by them; (3) the environmental conditions faced by firms; and (4) the degree of decentralisation of the decision-making authority in firms. We have tested our model, using a covariance structure model, in a sample of 295 firms operating in mature and fragmented industries.

Our findings confirm that the strategic orientation of a firm has a positive and significant impact on the firm's performance. Second, such a relationship is moderated by the strategic behaviour of the firm (such as the type of growth and competitive orientation of the firm) and by the manager's tenure (prior experience in other firms or sectors). These moderating effects had not been empirically tested previously. Third, although the existing literature had proposed a moderating role of the turbulence of the environment, as well as of the degree of decentralisation of the decision-making authority, our results do not allow us to support such moderating effects in the case of SMEs operating in mature and fragmented sectors.

Additionally, we have conceptualised and developed a valid scale to measure a firm's strategic orientation. Operational measure was developed and validated through the use of CFA. We have identified four subdimensions that reflect the strategic posture adopted by firms on aspects such as information planning process, competitive aggressiveness, risk-taking or proactiveness. Although this measure would provide initial steps for replications, extensions and refinements in future studies, it should be useful for researchers in their efforts to test theoretical relationships.

Despite these contributions, the present study has some limitations. First, our study was conducted with empirical data collected in 2003 from SMEs operating in mature and fragmented industries in Spain. Thus, generalisations to other countries and industries should be made with caution, especially for those aspects that could vary in different settings, such as the characteristics of the environment faced by firms or the managerial tenure influence over different kinds of firms and industries.

Second, due to the absence of objective data, this study relied on subjective measures of key variables. Although efforts were taken to guard against biased responses, this study is subject to the potential weaknesses associated with the use of perceptual data. In a retrospective view, however, the use of multiple respondents per organisation might have been preferable if that interrater reliability could have been assessed. Moreover, the measurement of the organisational variables could have been improved, including having more items in the survey instrument. In this way, a more reliable assessment of the organic structure of the firms could have been obtained.

Finally, some of the limitations of this study suggest further research areas.

We have used an aggregated measure of strategic orientation. Future research should analyse the link between the various subdimensions of strategic orientation (aggressiveness, analysis, proactiveness and riskiness) and firm performance. This study would help assess which configurations of strategic orientation are most important in particular situations.

With regard to future studies that will be focused on the moderating role of organisational variables, we suggest considering more complex measures of structural characteristics of firms by including the type of communication channels; the degree of formalisation of the managing style; expertise versus hierarchic basis on decision-making; organisational routines and inertia; and behaviour procedures weight.

This study relies on subjective measures of a firm's performance. In future studies, we suggest using objective measures of performance of the participating firms from secondary data sources. Such measures could include accounting indicators such as sales growth, market share and profitability, as well as other elements of customer satisfaction. This will allow us to compare results of objective and subjective measures of performance, as well as to analyse the different impacts of strategic orientation on financial and non-financial outcomes.

Some authors have highlighted the need to control the impact of the firm's strategic orientation over performance during a period of time (Zahra, 1991; Zahra and Covin, 1995). Although we have measured firms' performances during the last five years, a longer period would have been preferred in order to capture the long-term effect of strategic orientation over firms' successes.

Furthermore, the contingency model should also be tested in different geographic locations and industries. The comparison of our results with the findings in other settings can provide interesting contributions to the understanding of the context in which strategic postures lead to a better performance.

This study has highlighted some interesting relations that should also be studied more in depth in future research. Consideration of firms' competitive and growth orientations should be incorporated to the analysis of the impact of entrepreneurial orientation over firms' performances. Further research on other growth initiatives, such as the use of strategic alliances, mergers and acquisitions, or internal growth, could provide interesting conclusions to the understanding of the moderating role of strategic variables over firms' strategic orientation and performance relationships. Additionally, we intend to go further in the study of the influence of the competitive orientation of the firms by developing new and more accurate measures of such orientation.

Note

1 We also ran a moderated regression analysis in order to test contingency effects over strategic orientation–performance relationships. We used mean-centred data (subtracting the mean of all variables from all observations) in order to interpret regression parameters. We obtained the same results as those obtained using the structural equation model.

References

Aguinis, H. (2002) Estimation of interaction effect in organization studies. *Organizational Research Methods* 5(3), 207–211.

Bentler, P. M. (1980) 'Multivariate Analysis with Latent Variables: Causal Modelling', pp. 419–456 in M. R. Rosenzweig and L. W. Porter (eds), *Annual Review of Psychology, vol. 31*. Palo Alto, CA: Annual Reviews.

Borch, O. J., Huse, M. and Senneseth, K. (1999) Resource configuration, competitive strategies, and corporate entrepreneurship: an empirical examination of small firms. *Entrepreneurship Theory and Practice* 24(1), 49–70.

Burgelman, R. A. (1984) Designs for corporate entrepreneurship in established firms. *California Management Review* 26(3), spring, 154–166.

Child, J. (1974) Managerial and organizational factors associated with company performance. *Journal of Management Studies* 11, 13–27.

Covin, J. G. and Covin, T. J. (1990) Competitive aggressiveness, environmental context, and small firm performance. *Entrepreneurship Theory and Practice*, summer, 35–50.

Covin, J. G. and Slevin, D. P. (1988) The influence of organization structure on the utility of an entrepreneurial top management style. *Journal of Management Studies* 25, 217–234.

Covin, J. G. and Slevin, D. P. (1989) Strategic management of small firms in hostile and benign environments. *Strategic Management Journal* 10, 75–87.

Covin, J. G. and Slevin, D. P. (1991) A conceptual model of entrepreneurship as firm behavior. *Entrepreneurship: Theory and Practice* 16(1), 7–24.

Cyert, R. M. and March, J. G. (1963) *A Behavioral Theory of the Firm*. Englewood Cliffs, NJ: Prentice Hall.

Dess, G., Lumpkin, G. T. and Covin, J. G. (1997) Entrepreneurial strategy making and firm performance: test of contingency and configurational models. *Strategic Management Journal* 18(9), 677–695.

Entrialgo, M. (2002) The impact of the alignment of strategy and managerial characteristics on Spanish SMEs. *Journal of Small Business Management* 40(3), 260–270.

Entrialgo, M., Fernández, E. and Vázquez, C. J. (2001) The effect of the organizational context on SME's entrepreneurship: some Spanish evidence. *Small Business Economics* 16(3), 223–236.

Galbraith, J. R. (1973) *Designing Complex Organizations*. Reading, MA: Addison-Wesley.

Hair, J., Anderson, R., Tatham, R. and Black, W. (1999) *Multivariate Data Analysis*. Madrid: Prentice Hall Ibérica.

Hambrick, D. C. and Mason, P. A. (1984) Upper echelons: the organization as a reflection of its top managers. *Academy of Management Review* 9(2), 193–206.

Hitt, M. A. and Ireland, R. D. (2000) 'The intersection of entrepreneurship and strategic management research', pp.45–63 in. D. L. Sexton and H. A. Landstrom (eds), *Handbook of Entrepreneurship*. Oxford: Blackwell.

Hitt, M. A. and Tyler, B. B. (1991) Strategic decision models: integrating different perspectives. *Strategic Management Journal* 12, 327–351.

Hitt, M. A., Ireland, R. D. and Hoskisson, R. E. (2001) *Strategic Management: competitiveness and globalisation*. Cincinnati, OH: Southwestern.

Hitt, M. A., Ireland, R. D., Camp, S. M. and Sexton, D. L. (2001) Guest editor's introduction to the special issue strategic entrepreneurship: entrepreneurial strategies for wealth creation. *Strategic Management Journal* 22, 479–491.

Hofer, C. W. and Davoust, M. (1977) *Successful Strategic Management*. Chicago, IL: A. T. Kearney.

Ireland, R. D., Hitt, M. A., Camp, S. M. and Sexton, D. L. (2001) Integrating entrepreneurship actions and strategic management actions to create firm wealth. *Academy of Management Executive* 15(1), 49–63.

Jennings, D. F., Rajaratnam, D. and Lawrence, F. B. (2003) Strategy-performance relationships in service firms: a test for equifinality. *Journal of Managerial Issues* 15(2), summer, 208–220.

Kerr, J. (1982) Assigning managers on the basis of the life cycle. *Journal of Business Strategy* 2(4), 58–65.

Khandwalla, P. (1977) *The Design of Organizations*. New York: Harcourt Brace Jovanovich.

Khandwalla, P. (1987) Generators of pioneering innovative management: some Indian evidence. *Organization Studies* 8(1), 39–59.

Kimberly, J. R. and Evanisko, M. J. (1981) Organizational innovation: the influence of individual, organizational, and contextual factors on hospital adoption of technological and administrative innovations. *Academy of Management Journal* 24, 689–713.

Kitching, J. (1967) Why do mergers miscarry?, *Harvard Business Review* 45(6), 84–101.

Kreiser, P. M., Marino, L. D. and Weaver, K. M. (2002) Assessing the psychometric properties of the entrepreneurial orientation scale: a multi-country analysis. *Entrepreneurship Theory and Practice*, summer, 71–94.

Kumar, K., Subramanian, R. and Strandholm, K. (2001) Competitive strategy, environmental scanning and performance: a context specific analysis of their relationship. *International Journal of Commerce and Management* 11(1), 1–33.

Lawrence, P. and Lorsch, J. (1967) *Organization and Environment*. Cambridge, MA: Harvard University Press.

Lumpkin, G. T. and Dess, G. G. (1996) Clarifying the entrepreneurial orientation construct and linking it to performance. *Academy of Management Review* 21(1), 135–172.

Lumpkin, G. T. and Dess, G. G. (2001) Linking two dimensions of entrepreneurial orientation to firm performance: the moderating role of environment and industry life cycle. *Journal of Business Venturing* 16(5), 429–451.

Matsuno, K.. and Mentzer, J. T. (2000) The effects of strategy type on the market orientation–performance relationship. *Journal of Marketing* 64(4), 1–16.

Miles, M. P., Covin, J. G. and Heeley, M. B. (2000) The relationship between environmental dynamism and small firm structure, strategy and performance. *Journal of Marketing Theory and Practice*, spring, 63–74.

Miles, R. E. and Snow, C. C. (1978) *Organizational Strategy, Structure, Process*. New York: McGraw-Hill.

Miller, D. (1983) The correlates of entrepreneurship in three types of firms. *Management Science* 29, 770–791.

Miller, D. (1988) Relating Porter's business strategies to environment and structure: analysis and performance implications. *Academy of Management Journal* 31, 280–308.

Miller, A. and Friesen, P. H. (1982) Innovation in conservative and entrepreneurial firms: two models of strategic momentum. *Strategic Management Journal* 3, 1–25.

Mintzberg, H. (1973) Strategy making in three modes. *California Management Review* 16(2), 44–53.

Norburn, D. and Birley, S. (1988) The top management team and corporate performance. *Strategic Management Journal* 9(3), 225–237.

Peters, T. J. and Waterman, R. H., Jr. (1982) *In Search of Excellence: lessons from America's best-run companies*. New York: Harper & Row.

Porter, M. E. (1980) *Competitive Strategy*. New York: Free Press.

Reed, R. Y. and Luffman, G. A. (1986) Diversification: the growing confusion. *Strategic Management Journal* 7(1), 29–35.

Segev, E. (1989) A systematic comparative analysis and synthesis of two business-level strategic typologies. *Strategic Management Journal* 10, 487–505.

Shane, S. and Venkataraman, S. (2000) The promise of entrepreneurship as a field of research. *Academy of Management Review* 25(1), 217–226.

Silverman, B. S. (1999) Technological resources and the direction of corporate diversification: toward an integration of the resource-based view and transaction cost economics. *Management Science* 45(8), 119–124.

Stuart, T. (2000) Interorganizational alliances and the performance of firms: a study of growth and innovation rates in a high-technology industry. *Strategic Management Journal* 21(8), 791–811.

Venkataraman, S. and Sarasvathy, S. D. (2001) 'Strategy and entrepreneurship: outlines of an untold story', in M. A. Hitt, E. Freeman and J. S. Harrison (eds), *Handbook of Strategic Management*. Oxford: Blackwell.

Venkatraman, N. (1989) Strategic orientation of business enterprises: the construct, dimensionality, and measurement. *Management Science* 35(8), August, 942–962.

Venkatraman, N. and Ramanujam, V. (1986) Measurement of business performance in strategy research: a comparison approach. *Academy of Management Review* 11(4), 801–814.

Virnay, B. and Tushman, M. L. (1986) Executive succession: the changing characteristics of top management teams. *Academy of Management Best Paper Proceedings*, 155–159.

Wiersema, M. F. and Bantel, K. A. (1992) Top management team demography and corporate strategic change. *Academy of Management Journal* 35(1), 91–122.

Wiersema, J. G., Van der Pol, H. W. and Messer, H. M. (1980) Strategic management archetypes. *Strategic Management Journal* 1, 37–47.

Wiklund, J. (1999) The sustainability of the entrepreneurial orientation-performance relationship. *Entrepreneurship Theory and Practice*, Fall, 37–48.

Zahra, S. A. (1991) Predictors and financial outcomes of corporate entrepreneurship: an explorative study. *Journal of Business Venturing* 6(4), 259–285.

Zahra, S. A. (1993) A conceptual model of entrepreneurship as firm behavior: a critique and extension. *Entrepreneurship Theory and Practice*, Summer, 5–21.

Zahra, S. A. and Covin, J. G. (1995) Contextual influences on the corporate entrepreneurship–performance relationship: a longitudinal analysis. *Journal of Business Venturing* 10( ), 43–58.

Zahra, S. A. and Dess, G. G. (2001) Entrepreneurship as a field of research: encouraging dialogue and debate. *Academy of Management Review* 26, 8–10.

Zahra, S. A., Jennings, D. F. and Kuratko, D. F. (1999) The antecedents and consequences of firm-level entrepreneurship: the state of the field. *Entrepreneurship Theory and Practice* 24(2), 45–66.

15 Strategies for best practice in project management

A global perspective

John Saee

Introduction

Globalisation of the world economy has had far-reaching implications for existing organisational structures and, hence, their management practices around the world. As a result, many organisations now recognise that they can increase their flexibility and responsiveness in globally competitive market environments through deployment of transnational project teams – powerful vehicles to develop innovation and change within their companies. Such teams consist of membership with multiple nationalities, working on activities that transcend national borders (46; 47; 16).

In this organisational setting, specialists from various functional areas across the organisations located in different geographical areas work together jointly and in ad hoc project teams from inception to completion of projects for which they are wholly responsible. These project teams are empowered to act on behalf of their company (36).

Meanwhile, it is argued that international project teams are where most of the boundary-spanning work in international enterprise goes on, making them a key factor in organisational success and an important catalyst for individual and organisational development. In particular, the ability to learn in and through international project teams is seen as a key developer of a more international outlook. Project teams also help the organisation share information, knowledge and resources across boundaries, transmit and recreate corporate culture, and provide examples of best practice (15; 16).

Similarly, project management provides an organisation with powerful tools that improve its ability to plan, organise, implement and control its activities and the way it uses its people and resources.

The need for project management arose as a result of a number of emerging environmental forces in modern society. Of the many emerging environmental forces involved, three feature most prominently:

- the growing demand for complex, sophisticated, customised goods and services;
- the exponential expansion of human knowledge; and

- intense competition among firms for profit maximisation and provision of quality service fostered by the globalisation of the contemporary market economy.

This has, in turn, put extreme pressure on modern organisations to make their complex, customised outputs available as quickly as possible. Responses must be made faster, decisions must be made sooner and results must occur more quickly (30).

Project management, including international project management, is not simply regarded as an interesting application of previously expounded theory; it is regarded as very much the future of management (19).

In this research article an attempt has been made to understand the dynamics of international project management and to identify various factors which are crucial in the context of project management across cultures. An effort has been made to understand how these factors affect the performance of a project across cultural, economical and political divides in an international setting. This research article also discusses what strategies and tactics should be adopted to render the project successful. It has been emphasised that the factors identified as crucial must be considered by management in order to develop appropriate strategies to follow the best practice in international project management (22).

Project management

A project is a set of activities with a defined start and a defined end state, which pursues a defined goal and uses a defined set of resources (43: 515).

Project management serves a number of functions. The functions can be identified in three categories:

1   general project management processes (project integration, strategic planning and resource allocation);
2   basic project management functions (scope management, quality management, time management and cost management); and
3   integrated project management functions (risk management, HR management, contract management, and communication management) (12).

The fundamentals of project management

The primary objective of project management is designed to meet and exceed the expectations of the sponsors of the project. These expectations can be categorised in three different ways:

1   quality (the project produces desired outcomes with minimum defects);
2   cost (the project produces desired outcome for the anticipated cost); and
3   schedule (the project produces the desired outcome within the anticipated time frame) (25).

With that in view, the question arises as to what constitutes the factors underlying project management. Review of literature (12) points to ten factors that form the foundation for project management, which managers have to carefully consider and implement in their overall project management so as to ensure its success:

1   *Concentrate on interfacing.* This involves both defining frontiers and making efforts at bridge building among various areas that have interdependent relationships with the project in question.

2   *Organise the project team.* This calls for selecting qualified team members for the project as well as sound management practices in so far as to ensure high-level motivation of project team members through the appropriate incentive programmes coupled with the increased delegation of responsibility for the team members.

3   *Plan strategically and technically.* Use a top down planning approach while breaking the project down into component parts using a work breakdown structure or other project logic.

4   *Remember 'Murphy's law'.* According to Murphy, 'If anything can go wrong, it will.' Thus, strategies, plans and systems should be tested to ensure fail-safe implementation.

5   *Identify project stakeholders.* Identify who has a stake and influence regarding project outcome – such as clients, users, managers, financiers, suppliers of technology and higher management – and create systems for involving and satisfying their needs and expectations.

6   *Be prepared to manage conflicts.* Apply conflict management techniques: negotiate when interests clash, promote collaboration when talents and capabilities are complementary, force the issue when important principles are at stake, and finally set off conflict, if necessary, to realise project goals.

7   *Expect the unexpected.* Reducing the unexpected helps keep projects on track. In project environments, surprises can be minimised by participative planning, contingency allowances, use of expert opinion and statistical comparisons with similar prior projects.

8   *Listen to intuition as part of project decision-making.* Intuition reflects the gut feeling formed by the experiences logged over the years.

9   *Apply behavioural skills.* This involves application of sound interpersonal skills on the part of project managers to influence their team members in a positive manner.

10 *Follow up and take remedial action.* Create a system for measuring progress, then estimate that progress against initial plans and take remedial action.

The distinction between line and project management

Research (19) shows that many of the competencies required of project managers are similar in many ways to those required of line managers. There are, nonetheless, some differences. While it is a truism that project managers, like line managers, do indeed work to tight schedules and for specific objectives, line management practice is predicated on a 'business as usual' approach, whereas project managers have a 'one off' finite deadline.

Overall, project managers are expected to:

- convert business objectives to project objectives;
- obtain value for money through planning and controlling both physical and human resources over a set period of time;
- integrate complex effort and multiprofessional growth of people, often across cultural divides;
- communicate with all levels of management, upward and across;
- react to continual change;
- accelerate innovation and change;
- restructure new teams and develop attitudes and facilitate working relationships, often in a very short space of time; and
- work with and satisfy the needs of a client (19: 318).

Meanwhile, research (52) shows that for a project manager to be effective, they would need to possess five demonstrable attributes and qualifications:

1 background and experience relevant to the project;
2 leadership and strategic expertise;
3 technical expertise in the area of the project in order to make sound technical decisions;
4 interpersonal competence and the people skills to take on such roles as project champion, motivator, communicator, facilitator and politician; and
5 proven managerial competencies in relation to a track record of getting things done.

Key success factors of international project management

Project management has provided a sound foundation for the change in management in recent decades – for example, in the integration and reorganisation of major businesses and developing new initiatives between a company and its customers, suppliers and partners. Even so, there are opportunities for making it a more effective tool. Many organisations will admit to having problems or issues that limit their use of project management for managing change (9; 23). By understanding these issues and working to eliminate them, it may be possible to improve the effectiveness of project management.

As with many managerial responsibilities, the management of an international project involves planning, organisation and control of a large number of complex factors, activities and their interrelations. Managing them simultaneously and giving them all equal attention is virtually impossible. However, by adapting the Pareto rule of separating out the important few from the trivial many helps to focus attention on the key factors that are critical for achieving success (33).

There is ample evidence in the literature to support the existence of critical or key success factors for project management. Baker *et al*. (1983) postulated that the perceived project success or failure is not a function of time and cost. Kerzner (24) has identified six critical success factors for successful projects:

- corporate understanding of project management;
- executive commitment to project management;
- organisational adaptability;
- sound project manager selection criteria;
- project manager's leadership style; and
- commitment to planning and control.

Meanwhile, additional research (39) identified the following factors as being critical to the success of the projects:

1 *Project mission*. This involves determination of a clearly defined project's goals and mission by management with clear indications that the project is necessary and why.
2 *Competent project manager*. A skilled project leader who possesses the essential interpersonal, technical and administrative competencies.
3 *Top management support*. No project is likely to succeed unless it enjoys the full support of the senior management within the organisation. Thus, acquiring support for the project while communicating top management support for the project to every employee within the organisation is critical.
4 *Project plan*. All activities surrounding the projects have to be meticulously planned for and the necessary resources required to carry out the project have to be fully allocated. There also has to be ways of monitoring of its progress in terms of the specific stage deadlines. Managers have to consider: if the plan is workable; if the amount of time and money, and people allocated is sufficient; if the funds are guaranteed; if the organisation will carry through the project; and if there is flexibility in the plans allowing for over-running the schedule.
5 *Client consultation*. A detailed understanding of your client requirement is a must for a project manager, thus regular meetings between client and the project manager are deemed necessary at all stages of the project.
6 *Competent project team*. Recruitment and selection of competent staff backed by their training is critical in order to ensure the success of the project.
7 *Technical task*. Technical skills have to be matched with the right people in terms of qualifications and expertise.
8 *Client acceptance*. Gaining acceptance from one's client for any given project is critical. Thus, a project manager needs to develop a sound selling strategy at an early phase of the project in order to sell the project to the client. Developing a good interpersonal relationship with the client is deemed necessary so that the project manager can negotiate with the client where appropriate (19).

9 *Monitoring and feedback.* Obtaining feedback throughout the project from key individuals is necessary to ensure quality outcome for the project. This obviously involves establishing sound monitoring procedures to capture a systematic feedback on all aspects of the project.

10 *Communication.* The concept of communication in project management refers to the spoken and written documentation, plans and drawings used in the processes of an international project.

11 *Trouble-shooting mechanisms.* A system or set of procedures capable of tackling problems when they arise, trace them back to the their root cause and resolve them. All team members should act as 'look-outs' for the project, and all team members should monitor the project, and when a problem is identified by a team member, action needs to be taken at once to remedy the problem (19).

Rosenau (41) suggested that the essence of successful project management consisted of satisfying the triple constraints of time, cost and performance.

One of the most important findings arising from the preliminary literature survey is that the factors expounded could not explain the reasons why the project could be considered as successful by one party and at the same time be considered a failure by another. However, it is argued that there are two possible viewpoints of project success. The first is the macro viewpoint, which takes care of the question 'does the original concept tick?'. The users and stakeholders are usually the ones looking at project success from the macro viewpoint. The second is the micro viewpoint, which usually concerns the implementation parties (29).

Best practice in project management

Research (37) shows that other things being equal, utilisation of best practice can lead to competitive advantage for a firm and/or project management. Best practice means adopting managerial practices of the most successful organisations and/or through benchmarking.

Given increasing application of projects worldwide, it becomes necessary to understand the project management system and consider its unique attributes within the international setting. It is within this framework that the best practices for international project management are required to be developed (45). Thus, the important factors, critical for success and therefore needed to be considered for adopting the best practice in project management, are described below.

Conceptualisation and initiation

This stage involves identifying the business needs for the setting of goals and specific objectives, and gaining support for the project from the key stakeholders by identifying and communicating the benefits of the project (19).

Planning

Planning is broadly defined as determining what needs to be done, by whom and when, in order to accomplish one's assigned responsibility. It is a process involving the assessment of the environment for opportunities, threats, strengths and weaknesses (24).

The components of planning normally include objective, programme, schedule, budget, forecast, organisation, policy, procedure and standards. However, in an attempt to plan the work of a project management team, Johns has further simplified the process of planning to include only five fundamental management tools, namely:

- Determination of clear and measurable project objectives.
- Work-breakdown structure – this component of planning enables personnel and clients to get a general overview of the project as a whole entity.
- Project organisation – the organisation of the project requires the accountability and ownership of tasks to be clearly defined and placed on key personnel. 'The participation of workers in objective setting is fundamental to all current management ideologies as well as classic management ideologies' (21: 34).
- Project schedule – scheduling of project accomplishments is a necessary tool for the success of the programme, and for this to be successful, the schedule must be communicated in a simple and comprehensible form, so that all may easily acknowledge the direction in which the project is heading.
- Budget – an effective method in which managers can control financing and task duration is through the determination of resource requirements used by each personnel in each task, and the interdependence of each product onto others used in those individual tasks.

Furthermore, it is argued that:

> the extent to and rigor with which these tools are used must be allowed to differ in a company, because the sizes and natures of projects differ, the natural styles and cultures of the people involved differ, and the business situations differ.
>
> (21: 35)

Meanwhile, Pinto and Slevin (39) consider a project plan as one of the key factors for success of a project, as it involves scheduling of all the activities along with the resources required. They suggested that at plan stage it is to be seen that the plan is workable; the amount of time, people and money allocated is sufficient; the organisation is ready to carry through the plan; and the funds are guaranteed.

Project management: an international perspective

International project management plans are subject to the same threats and opportunities as domestic ones. However, there are a number of additional constraints that shape objectives, goals and strategies. Factors such as political instability and risk, currency instability, competition, pressures from national government and nationalism can all interfere with project management planning (45). Strategy development therefore requires that the companies:

- evaluate opportunities, threats, problems and risks;
- assess the strengths and weaknesses of its personnel to carry out the job;
- define the scope of its global business involvement;
- formulate its global corporate objectives; and
- develop specific corporate strategies in the organisation as a whole (38).

Overall, the project manager needs to develop a thorough understanding of the environmental factors that will impinge upon the individual project, for example, in a particular country, including:

- knowledge of geography about the country in question;
- finance;
- local politics, which has a bearing on the successful completion of a project;
- national culture. Developing an understanding of the host culture is crucial, which obviously has a major impact on the way a project is conducted; and
- local laws, which can vary considerably and influence the resources needed for a project. For instance, in Francophone African countries, local labour law allows employees to take three days' leave of absence when a close relative dies. With large families this can cause serious disruption to staff availability (43).

Communication

The critical importance of communication in organisations, in particular its influence on the acceptance of something new, is well documented (50; 51), as is the critical importance of intercultural communication competence in an organisation/project based on cultural diversity (30).

Lack of communication has been cited as the biggest reason for the failure of many changed projects to meet their expectations (35). Successful communication needs to be focused and the timing is of crucial importance. Used effectively, it can reduce non-productive effort, avoid duplication and help eliminate mistakes (4). Time, cost and performance vary considerably within the international areas. Time is a communication system, just like words and language. For example, Western culture views time as a resource: 'time is money'. Eastern and Middle Eastern cultures view time quite differently, as do most Mediterranean people. Consequently, concepts such as schedules and deadlines, which are essential to project management, are not held in the same regard and therefore are not followed as conscientiously as in Western cultures. Another communication factor to be considered is directness. In the USA, one is direct and gets straight to the point. In other cultures, the direct route is avoided and even disliked. Arabs, some Europeans and Asians do not go straight to a point (45).

Control systems

This is an important project managerial function. Moder conceives controlling as 'the process of making events conform to schedules by coordinating the action of all parts of the organization according to the plan established for attaining the objective' (31: 324). It is for this reason that control is essential to any project managers, especially for those who are dealing within an international context.

The process of project control involves three sets of decisions. These include monitoring/measuring, evaluating and action. Through the use of an agreed metric towards the accomplishment of established objectives, a measurement of actual project progress is compared to that of planned directions. Evaluating relates to the process of determining causes and their solutions to notable variations in performance within the project. The course of acting often involves a manager briefing appropriate individuals of progress in the project, taking corrective action in light of unfavourable situations, and exploiting opportunities to benefit from, and take advantage of it. These control processes are a necessity for any international project management, although without the presence of project execution plans, procedures for analysing, reporting and reviewing performance against baselines, and the disciplined process for considering, approving and implementing change, the project will certainly lose control (21: 36).

Basic to any project management system is a control subsystem, comprising standards, comparisons and corrective actions. Control and its associated problems in international projects are much more complex than in domestic ones as a result of differing political, cultural, economic and legal environments. Geographic distance, language barriers, communication habits, culture and differing frames of reference all influence the control subsystems (38).

Criticism and how it is expressed can seriously affect managerial control; detailed reporting and tight control are not accepted in some cultures. For example, in Japanese culture, maintaining group cohesiveness is more important than reporting a problem to a supervisor; supervisors tend to solve the problems at the group level before referring them to upper management (11).

Essentially, the project manager must be able to negotiate a successful balance between project control imperatives and the reality of cultural diversity milieu in which the project operates. This calls for an effective intercultural communication competence on the part of the international project manager.

Organisational designs in different cultures

Authority, responsibility and accountability vary by project, culture and company's priorities and preferences. For example, technically and security sensitive projects tend to be more centralised and more tightly controlled. Group decision-making seems to work well in Japan. But it is not prevalent in other societies (3). French companies show more autocratic behaviour, while large and experienced companies in the USA and most of Western Europe exhibit the highest level of management delegation (6). These findings are germane to project success, for while there are many reasons for the failure of projects in the international environment, the most significant is the inability to get the maximum performance out of people. Each culture has different expectations of the superior-subordinate relationships.

Position, rank, authority and respect are supported in many foreign countries by informal and formal codes of dress, behaviour and attitudes. While delegation and participative management are practised and supported in Scandinavian countries, this is not the case in many other countries. Clearly these organisational and operational patterns significantly affect project management (45).

Organisational support

Jones (21) maintains that as companies experiment with project-based organisations, what executive managers frequently find missing is instinctive knowledge pertaining to how to create an organisational management culture. The questions and challenges facing executives are how to:

- create explicit senior management goals that support and encourage cross-functional project teams;
- work with one another as a senior management team and how to mutually support cross-functional project teams; and
- establish clearly communicated priorities for work done by cross-functional project teams in relation to other work.

The main steps senior management must take in creating a project-based organisational culture are to:

- write a clear policy stating the support of the project team's responsibility and authority to accomplish their missions, goals and objectives; and
- continually repeat the message that the project teams are empowered to act as long as their actions are in the best interests of the organisation.

In a recent and ongoing survey of senior managers from international companies being conducted at the Management Centre in Europe, it was found that all of these companies use cross-functional project teams as a primary way of conducting their business. These companies have also exhibited organisational support for project management in the areas of frequent use of management committees for reviewing project teams' performance, establishment of priorities between projects, periodic review of project team members' performance and the existence of planning and control processes. Weak organisational support was exhibited by these companies in areas such as resource planning and replanning project management training for project team members and absence of management support of project (21).

Jones (21) maintains that a prerequisite for effective organisational support is the existence of a specific management form where the project team can openly and regularly discuss problems they are encountering so that appropriate strategies could be developed to address these perceived problems at all levels.

People as subsystems

Human subsystems in international project management are by their very nature far more complex and complicated than in the management of domestic projects. For example, in the case of motivation, with little job security, American workers are motivated to work hard in order to earn money. But motivation varies widely by country and culture. To the French, quality of life is what matters most. In Japan, society and companies come first, and workers are motivated by permanent or lifetime employment, bonuses and fringe benefits based on the company's performance as a whole (5).

Another aspect in human subsystems is negotiations, which, within the international context, are made all the more difficult by differences in culture, trade customs and legal order. Language barriers can complicate negotiations. Interpreters can slow the pace of negotiations and/or take the unwanted active roles. However, the successful negotiator in international project management sees and understands the world as others do; manages stress and copes with ambiguity; sells the merits of the proposal in meaningful terms that express ideas clearly; and demonstrates cultural sensitivity and flexibility (8).

Smith and Haar (45) further advocated that no prescription can demonstrably be iron clad. Moreover, the human dimension in project management is of the utmost importance in international projects. Many projects that are technically, financially and organisationally strong have failed as a result of cross-cultural factors, that is, the inability of managers and supervisors to comprehend and respond to foreign environments.

Guidelines for best practice in international project managers

Research (24) identified the following guidelines for foreign executives involved in initiation, planning and implementation of projects:

- be aware of the environment of the host country;
- study the host company's developing plans and develop long-range plans for future cooperation;
- survey the financial institutions involved in the project and study the investment laws if applicable;
- before undertaking a project, study its feasibility from a technical, economic and operational point of view. Also, study the contribution of the project to the development of the host country;
- develop relationships with governmental and business leaders and develop special relationship with the project's local 'godfather';
- choose the right project manager for managing and implementation of the project and assign him to the project at an early stage;
- communicate with the client and learn how to deal with the counterpart effectively;
- study the different stages and phases of the project: preparation and initiation,

implementation and operation; and

- study the decision-making process and the different organisations responsible for project implementation and operation.

Project personnel management

Within the operations of an international project management team there are often a wide variety of positions held by personnel from different nations around the globe. It is for this reason that the manager should explore the conditions and benefits, then define clear standards which outline the working conditions before recruiting personnel. International projects vary in working conditions, which relate uniquely to each individual work site involved, and the duration of the working week is also contingent upon the work nature and/or location of the project.

With these factors of international project management in mind, selected personnel, including project managers, must meet certain criteria in ensuring that the most suitable individuals are employed for work overseas in different cultures:

- technical and managerial skills and abilities;
- cultural empathy;
- adaptability and flexibility;
- diplomatic skills;
- family factors;
- emotional stability and maturity; and
- motivation and aspiration.

As regards to employment strategy, it is highly unlikely that the availability of qualified and experienced local nationals will obviate the need for expatriate managers in foreign subsidiaries. According to Robinson (40), it may be that some of the well-established multinational and transnational corporations actually plan on recruiting and maintaining between 5 and 10 per cent expatriates or third country nationals in local subsidiary management. The reason behind this managerial strategy is based on the assumption that there are benefits that can arise from this international human resource management practice, such as providing multinational experience and intensifying corporate socialisation process for all parties involved in the project.

Client consultation and acceptance

As previously discussed, the client should be clearly identified, usually as the one who will be 'using' the completed project. Close consultation with the client is necessary for outside projects. Client acceptance is usually the 'bottom line' which should be backed up with perceived and tangible benefits, and involves good communication. Hence, the following points are important to consider:

- know the client and what he or she requires;
- schedule regular meetings with the client;

- ascertain whether the client is accepting or resisting; and
- develop a sound interpersonal relationship with the client so that you can negotiate with them where necessary (19).

Training and education

Inadequate training and education for the international setting results in a group of managers who do not understand and, therefore, can not master adequately the technical aspects of project management. Successful project management requires extensive and intensive training in techniques and methodologies of project operations (45).

The training strategy, as identified by research (24), should include:

- training based on transcultural management in the context of the specifics of the job;
- educational approach to training that enables the managers to analyse case studies;
- training based on host national's perceptions;
- training that sensitises managers to awareness of his or her impact on host national workforce; and
- training for the purpose of acquiring technical knowledge for performing the job.

The use of scheduling, costing, modelling and programming techniques and methodologies should be much the same in large international projects. However, because of variation in education and availability of hardware and software, adjustment must be made in the project management systems.

Breaking the project into bite-size chunks

Breaking large projects down into subprojects or work packages is regarded as one of the most important tasks in the development of projects (27). It ensures greater ownership by all those owning a 'chunk' of the project, spreading responsibility and accountability across a greater number of people. Furthermore, it is easier to manage in a number of ways: delegating responsibilities to the project team, monitoring against the objectives, communicating progress of the project, identifying problems upfront and making modifications to the project (9).

Product perspective

The ultimate outcome of a project is an artefact with technological complexities and many years of operational life. In addition, it is the result of a distributed collaboration not only during the engineering phase but also during the production and assembly phases. Thus, the product perspective emphasises the role of configuration management, which essentially concerns the control of specification changes and the work/information/data flow during engineering and manufacturing process (49). Further, the role of product data management will become even more important in project management areas. The reasons are that technological complexity of the products is continuously increasing; the duration of projects tend to be lengthening all the time; the number of geographically distributed collaborators is increasing due to diversity of skills needed; the economic benefits of outsourcing growing exponentially; the needed investments are increasing; and the economic environment requires expeditious and flexible performance. Hence, ensuring the consistency of the product configuration is of the utmost importance to succeeding in international project management (14).

Risk management

Given the many differences, complexities and uncertainties that distinguish international project management from domestic project management, a number of risk factors are needed to be considered for ensuring success in international project management. The risks could emerge from political, economic, social, technological and regulatory environments of the project (45).

According to Kerzner (24), it is important that risk management strategy is established early in a project and that risk is continually addressed throughout the project life cycle. He further emphasises that risk management includes several related actions, detailed below.

The distinction between project strategy and tactics

There is a major difference between strategy and tactics in project management.

Project strategy defines, in a generalised rather than a specific way, how the organisation is going to achieve its project objectives and to meet the related measures of performance. It accomplishes in two distinct manners: (1) it defines the phases of the project. Phases break this project down into time based sections; and (2) the project strategy set milestones, which are important events during the project's life at which specific reviews of time, cost and quality are made (43).

Tactics, on the other hand, refers to client consultation, personnel recruitment and training, identification of tasks, gaining client acceptance, monitoring and feedback, communication and trouble-shooting.

Projects are often typified by a weakness in either strategy or tactics, and this may lead to four different types of errors:

- failing to take an action when one should be taken;
- taking an action when one should not have been taken;
- taking the wrong action or solving the wrong problem; and
- solving the right problem but the solution is not used (44; 19).

Concluding remarks

In this chapter, it was established that as a result of increasing competition in rapidly changing and financially challenging international environments, firms are adopting flexible strategies and structures such as project management methods in order to speed improved quality products and services to their market segments and to provide quality customer service (21). Project management across professional, national and cultural frontiers is highly complex. The project manager's responsibility is to manage across these systems in order to meet specific business objectives within a finite timeline. The need to identify, distinguish and respond effectively to a distinct set of managerial requirements, thus, becomes the foremost challenge facing international project managers. Consequently, in this chapter, various factors were identified that are crucial in the context of project management across cultures and must be considered in order to develop appropriate strategies to follow the best practice in international project management. The conclusion that may be drawn in this chapter is that in order for the firms to excel in international project management, they have to carefully consider and implement appropriate strategies relating to the following critical factors: conceptualisation and initiation; project plan; communication; organisation; organisational support; human subsystems; breaking the project into bite-size chunks; client consultation and acceptance; education and training; and the product perspective.

Finally, most international projects are often identified by a weakness in either strategy or tactics that leads to different types of errors. Thus, the major challenge facing international project managers is to ensure that the tactics pursued in an international project are entirely complementary to the overall project management strategy. Furthermore, international project managers will greatly benefit from developing high-level intercultural communication competence, deemed an essential ingredient in managing successfully a culturally diverse project management team.

Bibliography

1   Baker, B. N., Murphy, D. C. and Fisher, D. (1983) 'Factors affecting project success' pp. 669–685 in D. I. Cleland and D. R. King (eds), *Project Management Handbook*. New York: Van Nostrand.

2   Barham, K. and Oates, D. (1991) *Developing the International Manager*. London: Business Books.

3   Bass, B. M. (1979) *Assessment of Managers: an international comparison*. New York: MacMillan.

4   Beavers, D. (1997) Communication breakdown. *Supply Management* 2(12), 34–35.

5   Bello, J. A. (1986) 'Behavioral problems of operational research implementation in developing countries', in U. G. Damachi and H. D. Seibel (eds), *Management Problems*. New York: St. Marlin's.

6   Berenbim, R. E. (1989) *Operating foreign subsidiaries: how independent can they be?* New York: Conference Board.

7   Burns, A. C. (1989) 'Executing the international project', in R. L. Kimmons and J. H. Loweree (eds), *Project Management*. New York: Marcel Dekker Inc.

8   Casse, P. (1979) *Training for the Cross-cultural Milieu.* Washington DC: Sietar.

9   Clarke, A. (1995) The key success factors in project management. *Proceedings of a Teaching Company Services.* London, December.

10 Clarke, A. (1999) A practice use of key success factors to improve the effectiveness of project. *International Journal of Project Management* 17, 139–145.

11 Clutterbuck, D. (1989) Breaking through the cultural barriers. *International Management*, December, 41–42.

12 Dinsmore, C. P. (ed.) (1993) *The AMA Handbook of Project Management.* New York: American Management Association.

13 Fatehi, K. (1996) *International Management: a cross cultural and functional perspective.* New Jersey: Prentice Hall.

14 Hameri, A. P. (1997) Project management in a long-term and global one-of a kind projects. *International Journal of Project Management* 15, 251–257.

15 Heimer, C. (1994) Paper presented to conference on Training for Change, IAE, Aix-en-Provence, France, March.

16 Iles, P. H. and Paromjit, K. (1997) Managing diversity in transnational project teams. *Journal of Managerial Psychology* 12(2), pp. 95–117.

17 Irvine, D. and Ross Baker, G. (1994) 'The impact of cross-functional teamwork on workforce integration'. Paper submitted to the ninth workshop on strategic human resource management, St Gallen, Switzerland, March.

18 Jackson, S. E. (1992) 'Team composition in organizational settings: issues in managing an increasingly diverse workforce', pp. 138–176 in S. Worchel, W. Wood and J. A. Simpson (eds), *Group Process and Productivity.* Newbury Park, CA: Sage.

19 Jackson, T. (1993) *Organizational Behavior in International Management.* London: Butterworth Heinemann.

20 Johns, T. G. (1999) Managing the behavior of people working in teams: applying the project management method. *International Journal of Project Management* 13(1).

21 Johns, T. G. (1999) On creating organizational support for the project management method. *International Journal of Project Management* 17, 47–53.

22 *Journal of Management Systems (Association of Management Flagship).* A slightly different version of this chapter was initially published under the title of 'Best practice in international project management' in the *Journal of Management Systems (Association of Management Flagship)* and is now revised and reprinted with permission from the same journal.

23 Kahn, W. A. (1993) Facilitating and undermining organizational change: a case study. *Journal of Applied Behavioral Science* 29(1), 32–55.

24 Kerzner, H. (1998) *Project Management: a systems approach to planning, scheduling and controlling.* New York: John Wiley and Sons.

25 Kress, R. E. (2001) Quality project management: key to success factor to exceeding buyer values. *Journal of Industrial Management* 36(6), 22.

26 Lerpold, L. (1996) 'Multinational teams in strategic alliances: a case study of problems, their origins and their manifestations'. Paper presented at the eleventh workshop on strategic HRM, Brussels, Belgium, 13–15 March.

27 Lewis, R. (1996) Take the 'big' out of big projects: break them into manageable chunks. *Infoworld* 18(20), 24.

28 Lewis, R. D. (1996). *When Cultures Collide: managing successfully across cultures.* London: Nicholas Brealey Publishing.

29 Lim, D. S. and Mohamed, M. Z. (1999) Criteria of project success: an exploratory re-examination. *International Journal of Project Management* 17(4), 243–248.

30   Meredith, J. and Mantel, S. J. (1985) *Project Management: a managerial approach.* New York: Wiley & Sons.

31   Moder, J. J. (1988) 'Network techniques in project management', pp. 324–373 in D. I. Cleland and W. R. King (ed.), *Project Management Handbook.* New York: Van Nostrand Reinhold.

32   Monye, S. O. (1997) *The International Business Blue Print.* Oxford: Blackwell Publishers Ltd.

33   Morris, C. (1996) *Quantitative Approaches in Business Studies.* 4th edn. London: Pitman Publishing.

34   Oakland, J. (1989) *Total Quality Management.* London: Butterworth Heinemann.

35   Pardu, W. (1996) Managing change in a project environment. *CMA Magazine,* May.

36   Peters, T. (1994) *The Tom Peter Seminar.* New York: Random House.

37   Pfeffer, J. (1994) *Competitive Advantage Through People.* Boston, MA: Harvard Business School Press.

38   Phatak, A. V. (1997) *International Management: concepts and cases.* Cincinnati, OH: South-Western College Publishing.

39   Pinto, J. K. and Slevin, D. P. (1987) Critical success factors in successful project implementation. *IEEE Transactions on Engineering Management* 3(1).

40   Robinson, R. D. (1978) *International Business Management: a guide to decision.* 2nd edn. Hinsdale: The Dryden Press.

41   Rosenau, M. D., Jr (1984) *Project Management for Engineers.* New York: Van Norstrand Reinhold.

42   Schroder, H. M. (1989) *Managerial Competence: the key to excellence.* Dubuque, IA: Kendall/Hunt.

43   Slack, N., Chambers, S. and Johnston, R. (2001) *Operations Management.* 3rd edn. Harlow: Pearson Education Limited.

44   Slevin, D. P. (1989) *The Whole Manager.* New York: American Management Association, AMOCOM.

45   Smith, L. A. and Haar, J. (1993) 'Managing international projects', pp. 441–448 in P. C. Dinsmore (ed.), *The AMA Handbook of Project Management.* New York: American Management Association.

46   Snell, S. A., Davison, S. C., Hamrick, D. C. and Snow, C. C. (1993) 'Human resource challenges in the development of transnational teams'. Working paper, International Consortium for Executive Development Research, Lexington, MA.

47   Snow, C. C., Davison, S. C., Snell, S. A. and Hambrick, D. C. (1996) Use transnational teams to globalize your company. *Organizational Dynamics* 24.

48   Stallworthy, E. and Kharbanda, O. (1987) The project manager in the 1990s. *Industrial Management and Data Systems* 7(5), 10–43.

49   Stark, J. (1992) *Engineering Information Management System: beyond CAD/CAM to concurrent engineering.* New York: Van Nostrand Reinhold.

50   Timm, P. (1980) *Managerial Communication: a finger on the pulse.* Englewood Cliffs, NJ: Prentice Hall.

51   Timm, P. R. (1989) *Managerial Communication.* Englewood Cliffs, NJ: Prentice-Hall.

52   Weiss, J. W. and Wysocki, R. K. (1992) *Five-Phase Project Management: a practical planning and implementation guide.* New York: Addison-Wesley.

53   Wills, S. and Barham, K. (1994) Being an international manager. *European Management Journal* 12(1), 49–58.

16 Organisational size, distinctive competencies and performance[1]

César Camisón and Montserrat Boronat

Introduction

The business administration literature accords great importance to the study of the relation between organisational size and performance (Gooding and Wagner, 1985; Szymanski, Bharadwaj and Varadarajan, 1993). Certain theoretical approaches, such as firm theory, industrial organisation and the contingent approach, have established the importance of organisational size. Nevertheless, the researcher's theoretical background influences how the relation between size and performance is estimated. Results from a meta-analytical review of the relation between these variables, undertaken by Camisón (2001) revealed a positive, though not very high (0.155), correlation between the two. However, the relation may be affected by other methodological or theoretical factors. The measurement of variables and certain sample characteristics are included in the methodological factors. With regard to the theoretical factors, results showed the influence of variables relative to the firm's portfolio of resources and capabilities. The study of the influence of this kind of variable in the relation between size and performance could represent a fundamental point in the analysis of competitiveness in small and medium enterprises (SMEs).

The theoretical approach adopted in the present study is the resource-based view (RBV) (Wernerfelt, 1984; Barney, 1986, 1991; Dierickx and Cool, 1989; Amit and Schoemaker; 1993; Peteraf, 1993). The RBV marked a shift from previous predominant approaches. Under the influence of Porter's (1990) competitive advantage theory and through various empirical studies based on the PIMS database, industry analysis and competitors became a major subject of study in the understanding of competitive success in previous decades. However, differences between firms belonging to the same industry have also been observed. Moreover, in many sectors there are often no economies of scale (Scherer, 1970), that could present sources of competitive advantages as previous theoretical approaches stated. Hence, the RBV considers organisations as a bundle of resources and capabilities (Wernerfelt, 1984), rather than defining them according to their products, competitive position and market share. As such, it provides an approach that is particularly appropriate for the study of SME competitiveness, since the lack of consensus in empirical studies on the influence of organisational size on performance leads us towards a discussion about the role of these companies (SMEs) in our economy.

The aim of this study is to determine whether there is an indirect relation between organisational size and performance. This indirect influence is tested through the association of size and organisational distinctive competencies. We attempt to discover whether there is a relation between size and distinctive competences, and if so, whether it affects performance positively or negatively. Moreover, the model allows us to observe the nature of any direct influence. This analysis will enable us to draw conclusions about whether certain types of organisations, SMEs or large companies, have an advantage due to the size characteristic, or, on the contrary, whether organisational size does not affect the relation between distinctive competencies and performance.

The study is structured as follows: first, we briefly explain the RBV and the main variables that we consider from this approach, to later introduce them into our model. We also review the problem of organisational size from this perspective and introduce the importance of the variable in other theoretical approaches; we then present the model by introducing the joint effect of size and distinctive competencies; this is followed by an explanation of the methodology and the results of our model; the chapter ends with conclusions, limitations and recommendations for future research.

Resource-based view

The RBV shows a distinct contrast to the dominant approach of the 1980s, in which monopolistic rents deriving from the power of control and from market position were the source of competitive advantages. According to this approach, divergences in business performance can be explained by *Ricardian* rents, which derive from the difference in quality of resources and conditions of scarcity, and *Shumpeterian* rents, or the difference between the ex post value of an innovation and ex ante cost of the combined resources needed to carry it out (Montgomery and Wernerfelt, 1988; Peteraf, 1993).

Different theoretical approaches grouped in the same way also exist. All of them stress the importance of distinctive competencies in organisational success, and various authors (Foss, 1996) have referred to the body of work that emphasises these distinctive competencies as the competence-based perspective (Camisón, 2002a). On the whole, they distinguish between two kinds of approaches (Foss, 1996; Schulze, 1994): the RBV and the dynamic capabilities approach. The former has a more static view, as it focuses on the study of the properties of resources to become sources of competitive advantage and on the conditions under which it is possible to create and maintain superior rents in competitive equilibrium. The latter approach deals with the generation process of these resources and capabilities. However, the target of both approaches is for organisations to obtain superior competitive advantage when they achieve a set of distinctive competencies that are not shared with other market players, thus enabling them to provide products that are more successful in satisfying consumers than those of their competitors (Grant, 1991).

According to the RBV (Peteraf, 1993; Amit and Schoemaker, 1993; Barney, 1986, 1991; Wernerfelt, 1984), the main source of competitive advantages in organisations is the possession of certain assets, which are specific attributes that each organisation is capable of creating, developing, maintaining and controlling. These assets must have certain properties that allow them to be defined as strategic assets (Barney, 1991; Amit and Shoemaker, 1993), and thus become a source of competitive advantage. According to Barney (1991), these resources must be valuable, rare, imperfectly imitable and non-substitutable. The first property is that which enables the organisation to take advantage of opportunities or to reduce threats from the market, and therefore, to generate benefits or to minimise losses (Miller and Shamsie, 1996). The second property is determined by the number of organisations that have, or could have, the resource. The last two characteristics enable these resources to become a source of sustainable competitive advantages. Inimitability depends on three conditions: path dependence, or the company's particular history that provides it with a location, a causal ambiguity that makes it difficult to identify the specific assets that allow superior rents to be attained; and the creation of these resources by way of a social complexity that makes imitation by other companies more complex. Finally, the fact that they are non-substitutable implies that equivalent strategic resources do not exist, that is to say, the same strategy cannot be carried out.

In order to measure these assets, they must be classified. However, as Barney (2001) points out, it is precisely the measurement of concepts that requires further research, since the same conditions that give these resources and capabilities their strategic dimension are those that place obstacles to their identification and therefore their measurement.

First, we turn to the distinction between tangible and intangible resources. Physical or financial assets are found within the first group, whereas the intangible classification includes resources such as reputation, know-how, culture or patents. The main difference between the two types is that the former are more observable, which leaves them more open to imitation. Moreover, the characteristic of tangibility makes them more susceptible to trading, since they are easy to evaluate. The main source of competitive advantage is therefore found within the intangible resources.

We could also group these assets into physical assets, which include technology, plant, equipment, location and access to raw materials; human capital, comprising characteristics such as learning, experience, and relations between workers; and organisational capital, which covers formal structure, coordination and control systems, and informal relations between human groups within the organisation and between the organisation and its environment (Barney, 1991; Rangone, 1999). However, the same author (Barney, 1991) points out that not all these assets will always become strategic resources, although they may hold the abovementioned properties. Grant (1991), and Azzone and Rangone (1996) make further subdivisions, obtaining a functional classification: financial, physical, technological, human, reputation and organisational resources. Other classifications that cover the activities of the value chain are those of Lado, Boyd and Wright (1992) and Lado and Wilson (1994).

On the other hand, some authors claim that these classifications do not gather all the dimensions of the distinctive competencies (McGee and Peterson, 2000), since a distinction should be made between functional competencies, which concern the combination of knowledge and abilities related to different functional areas, and interfunctional or coordination competencies, which integrate all capabilities, and are concerned with the general management and its function of integrating all other capabilities. In this study, we consider this distinction between functional and coordination competencies.

Moreover, the main divergence between the more dynamic approach of the theory (Teece and Pisano, 1994; Teece, Pisano and Schuen, 1997) and the more static approach is based on the fact that the former examines the reasons from organisational heterogeneity rather than analysing the characteristics of strategic resources. This dynamic approach takes its starting point from the *Schumpeterian* notion of economic change, in which competition is seen as a process of creative destruction, and where innovations are continuously introduced (Schumpeter, 1934). From this approach, the market is dynamic (Teece, Pisano and Schuen, 1997), with fast and unpredictable changes. Therefore, competition is like a process in continuous evolution, and in which it is very difficult to reach competitive equilibrium (Nelson and Winter, 1982).

Thus, dynamic capabilities are those that will enable the organisation to renew the resources and capabilities it already has (Kogut and Zander, 1992; Henderson and Cockburn, 1994). They have been variously called higher order integration capabilities (Fuchs *et al.*, 2000; Lawson and Samson, 2001), combinative capabilities (Kogut and Zander, 1992), competencies based on transformation (Lado, Boyd and Wright, 1992), or integration capabilities (Yeoh and Roth, 1999). Therefore, in a dynamic environment, with rapidly changing market conditions, these competencies will be essential to obtain competitive advantages (Eisenhardt and Martin, 2000).

This process of creation, integration and reconfiguration gives rise to concepts such as the generation and transference of knowledge (Nonaka, 1994; Nonaka and Takeuchi, 1995) and organisational learning (Argyris and Schön, 1978, 1996; Leonard-Barton, 1995). Distinctive competencies in knowledge refer to cognition, and those of learning to behaviour. The importance of the study of these capabilities has led to the development of theoretical frameworks for each one. However, here we do not enter into an analysis of this different perspective, since we consider them to be included in the same dynamic approach and thus consider them together.

Organisational size

With regard to the relation between organisational size and performance, the competence-based perspective does not affirm that organisational size is the most important variable for generating distinctive competencies. In fact, it is an approach that focuses on internal aspects of the organisation. Because of this, it will become the most suitable framework to study the competitiveness of small and medium companies. This type of organisation must look for the resources and capabilities that also give them the chance to attain superior competitive advantages. These resources may or may not be different from those held by larger organisations. Despite this, Barney, Wright and Ketchen (2001) and McGee and Peterson (2000) point to the existence of studies focused on the RBV in larger organisations. However, SMEs need critical resources to be able to obtain competitive advantages. The same notion may be extended to the more dynamic perspective of this approach. The competence approach must therefore also be developed in this field because it is precisely within organisations that the differences between the two types of firms lie. Some exceptions of studies that have applied the RBV to small and medium companies include the works of Borch, Huse and Senneseth (1999), Rangone (1999) and McGee and Peterson (2000).

On the other hand, some theoretical approaches, such as firm theory, industrial organisation and the contingent approach, have granted particular importance to the variable of organisational size. In firm theory, the company is a place where productive factors are combined to produce output, taking into consideration restrictions derived from the stock of given production techniques. The company must choose the most profitable of these techniques according to the relative prices of inputs that are fixed parameters. Therefore, with respect to the relation between organisational size and performance, this theory considers that size of the productive plants of a given sector is explained only by considering the existing technology. This technology will determine the cost curves through which the equilibrium is analysed. If conditions of cost in an industry with homogenous production determine a curve of average costs in the long term, based on the volume of production, the scale of more efficient production will be the size that corresponds to the minimum unit cost. Therefore, economies of scale and the productive requirements of capital will determine the efficient minimum volume, and consequently, the average dimension of a certain activity.

With respect to industrial organisation (Mason, 1949; Bain, 1959, 1972; Demsetz, 1973; Scherer, 1970; Schmalensee, 1982) and the role of organisational size, both the new industrial economy and the classic economy state that the improvement of competitiveness of an industry in a global market requires large companies and concentrated market structures. Therefore, the bulk of the growth would lie in large industrial companies as these would be able to take advantage of costs derived from the learning curve and of scale economies. As a result, the central paradigm of this theory assumes that, except for differences in scale, all companies of the same industry are equal (Hill and Deeds, 1996). Numerous empirical works within this approach have studied the relation between organisational size or the level of existing concentration in an industry, and benefits (Hall and Weiss, 1967; Gale, 1972). However, it should be pointed out that the results in this field are not conclusive (Conner, 1991).

The contingent approach (Bernasconi, 1983; Mintzberg, 1985) breaks with the mechanist view of industrial organisation, and does not accept the existence of a universally optimal strategy, since it admits the diversity of the environment and variety in enterprise strategies. But it also shows a bias in identifying the sources of competitive advantages, towards the size variable, decisive in the configuration of the strategy and the structure of the company. Along with uncertainty and technology, size is one of the most widely studied variables in the contingent approach. Although many works have established the importance of size as a determining factor of organisational structure (Hickson, Pugh and Pheysey, 1969; Child, 1973; Blau *et al.*, 1976), there is a lack of consensus about this importance, and other authors have confirmed that this relation does not exist (Woodward, 1965).

The study of the direction and intensity of the relation between size and performance is therefore still very much open. There are contradictory results in the literature. In a meta-analytical study, Camisón (2001) found that this relation was positive, although its magnitude was not very high. He pointed out that it was moderate by methodological aspects (forms of measurement, nature of the sample), and by some theoretical variables. In this study, Camisón (2001) proposes that resources and capabilities are variables that may influence the relation between size and performance. Thus, in our model, we introduce the direct effect between both variables, and also the indirect effect through the interaction between distinctive competencies and organisational size, and we analyse whether this interaction has a significant effect on performance.

We have already pointed out the lack of any resolute contradictions in empirical results relative to the relation between size and performance. These contradictions can be extended to the association between size and distinctive competencies. Traditionally, the advantages of large companies have been defended because of their access to scale economies, the greater availability of financial and productive resources, and bargaining power against suppliers and buyers. The advantages of the SME thus include their greater flexibility, greater adaptability, lower levels of bureaucracy, greater proximity to the customer, and greater management control. These divergences suggest that distinctive competencies in large and small companies may be different, although this does not mean that small companies are less competitive. The success of *international new ventures* or of *high-technology start-ups*, widely studied in the literature, confirms that small organisations may develop different distinctive competencies from those developed by larger companies. In the study of exporting behaviour, the tendency to export and performance, Moen (1999) found that advantages of small and big exporting companies are different, and clarified that this difference does not necessarily involve less competitiveness on the part of small firms. Moreover, in a meta-analytical review of the relation between size and innovation, Camisón-Zornoza *et al.* (2004) found that although the relation between the two variables is positive, it is affected by other theoretical and methodological variables that studies must take into consideration. Therefore, we consider it important to test whether a moderator effect of the relation between size and distinctive competencies exists.

Methodology

Model

The estimation of a multiple regression model allows us to observe the effect of the independent variables on the performance. The independent variables include distinctive competencies and organisational size. However, the competence perspective focuses on internal organisational variables, but it is not closed to the influences of environmental variables that other theoretical approaches propose. Therefore, two control variables are included in the model in order to introduce the valuable contributions from industrial organisation (Mason, 1949; Bain, 1959, 1972; Scherer, 1970; Demsetz, 1973; Caves and Porter, 1977; Schmalensee, 1982; Porter, 1980, 1985) and from the contingent approach (March and Simon, 1958; Burns and Stalker, 1961; Lawrence and Lorsch, 1967; Tushman and Nadler, 1978; Venkatraman and Camillus, 1984). These variables are the opportunity of the competitive environment and uncertainty of the environment. Because the sample data refers only to one area of the country, variables relative to country effect are not included.

We then introduce multiplicative terms in the regression model in order to analyse the association between distinctive competencies and organisational size, and its effects on performance. To do so, we follow the methodology developed, among others, by Cohen and Cohen (1983) and Jaccard *et al.* (1990), of the interaction effects on multiple regression analysis.

Database

The data used in this study was taken from a questionnaire on competitiveness of industrial companies in one Spanish region. Our sample consists of 401 industrial companies, randomly selected from 3394 companies (ARDAN database), with a ±95 per cent confidence interval and a ±5 per cent error. Interviews with managers took place in 1998 through a structured questionnaire. It should be noted that this database was created by the Universitat Jaume I Business department, and that only a selection of its total number of questions was used here. Table 16.1 shows the basic information from this database.

Table 16.1 Database

Population	3394 industrial companies in the Valencian region of Spain
Sample	401 companies
Confidence interval and error	95% 5%
Data support	Interview with a structured questionnaire
Time	November–December 1998

Measurement

Measurement of variables, except for organisational size, was carried out using multi-item scales that had already been validated in previous studies (Camisón, 1999, 2002b, 2004). We also used the Cronbach coefficient (Cronbach, 1951) in this study. It is one of the most widely used measures of the internal consistency of scales. The questionnaire, which enabled us to construct these scales, gathers managerial perception of the aspects that the literature considers excellent to reflect the dimensions that form each one of the variables. Managers answer the questions in relation to their own company, but in comparison with its competitors. These subjective measures reflect the potential of the company, since they go beyond pure accounting data. Their use has been justified in the literature (Lawrence and Lorsch, 1967; Powell, 1992) and there are a number of studies that have used it (Snow and Hrebiniak, 1980; Dess, 1987; Conant, Mokwa, Varadarajan, 1990; Powell, 1992, 1996; Gadenne, 1998). Some studies have even compared it with objective data on market share and profitability, among others, in order to test the high correlation between both kinds of measures (Dess and Robinson, 1984; Venkatraman and Ramanujam, 1987) and the non-existence of bias in subjective measures (Camisón, 1999; Entrialgo, Fernández and Vázquez, 2001). In this study the absence of good proxies to the variables and of the objective data prevented this type of test from being carried out. Thus, final measures were made by means of the arithmetic mean of the items included in each one of the variables, which are available from the authors on request.

Regarding the dependent variable, consensus on the way performance should be measured has been the subject of constant re-evaluation (Venkatraman and Ramanujam, 1987; Capon, Farley and Hoenig, 1990), and is of great importance in the strategic literature. Following other works (e.g. Peters and Waterman, 1982; Puig, 1996; Camisón, 1999; Peng and Luo, 2000), we consider it as a multidimensional construct. Our scale measures performance not only by financial or economic dimensions, but also by qualitative and strategic dimensions. The latter allows us to reflect the competitive potential of the company. We make use of a multi-item scale (Camisón, 1999, 2004), which gathers the different dimensions that reflect those pointed out in the literature: customer and employee satisfaction, financial results, operative efficiency, social impact and capacity to compete. It is a validated scale and it is constructed according to the methodological guidance proposed by several authors (Lazarsfeld, 1965; Churchill, 1979), already applied in our previous studies. It is made up of 24 items, with a Cronbach's alpha of 0.87.

With regard to the variables related to distinctive competencies, we first introduce the variable that reflects functional distinctive competencies. Here, previous research (Camisón, 2002b) is also followed. This scale has been created by following the approaches from Snow and Hrebiniak (1980), Hitt and Ireland (1985), and Conant, Mokwa and Varadarajan (1990). Items from this scale measure competencies that facilitate strategy implementation and the effectiveness of the effort made in each one of the functional activities. Thus, we take into consideration different scales relative to marketing, production, and financial competencies. The global scale has a Cronbach's alpha of 0.92.

Competencies on coordination reflect resources and capabilities related to organisational integration and coordination. They are therefore the base on which all other abilities will be developed. They include both capacities linked to the integration of functional activities, and those relative to the coordination of the whole organisation. Camisón (2002) explains how to construct an instrument to measure this type of competencies and he also validates this scale. In the present study, our scale also comes from other works that have already dealt with the subject (Ansoff, 1985; Lado, Boyd and Wright, 1992). The final Cronbach's alpha coefficient has a value of 0.93.

Another previously validated instrument (Camisón, 2002b) is used to measure dynamic competencies. Items that comprise this scale were created following a wide set of excellent works in the field (Goh and Richards, 1997; Brown and Eisenhardt, 1998; Helfat and Raubitschek, 2000; Schulz, 2001; Takeishi, 2001). With regard to knowledge capabilities, it reflects capacities and abilities related to the knowledge management system, internal capacity of growth of the knowledge stock and knowledge transfer and application, and the knowledge stock. Concerning learning capabilities, it contains dimensions relative to the managerial attitude towards change and learning, culture of innovation and learning, development of competencies and whether organisational design is open to change. Finally we obtain a Cronbach's alpha of 0.96.

Measurement of organisational size has also been the subject of debate, and it can be measured in many ways; number of employees, sales volume, and market share among others. Number of employees is the most frequently used in the literature, and because our database includes this information, we used it in this study.

With regard to the control variables, those related to the opportunities of the competitive environment are also measured with a multi-item scale. It shows the following dimensions: bargaining power of buyers and suppliers, threat of new entrants, threat of substitute products, and rivalry among existing competitors. It thus reflects Porter's Five Competitive Forces Model (Porter, 1980). It is also a previously validated scale (Camisón, 2004). In this case, Cronbach's alpha has a value of 0.59. It is not high, but it is near the limit of 0.60 that some authors have proposed.

Finally, environmental uncertainty is measured through the dimensions pointed out by Dess and Beard (1984), which other studies have also utilised (Lawless and Finch, 1989; Ketchen, Thomas and Snow, 1993): dynamism, munificence and complexity of the population environment. The Cronbach's alpha coefficient of this scale, which has been used in other studies (Camisón, 2004), has a value of 0.77.

Results

Results are shown in Table 16.2. First, we can see the model without interaction terms, followed by results of the model with interactions between organisational size and distinctive competencies.

In the first model, we can see (Table 16.2) that the value of the F statistic is high ($F=52.0402$) with a level of significance of 0.000. The adjustment of the model is also good (R^2 adjusted$=0.4349$). Beta-standardised coefficients remove problems of different units of measurement and they reflect the relative impact of the independent variables, of a change in a deviation standard unit of the independent variables on the dependent one. Significance of beta coefficients (signif. column) is verified by means of the t statistic, and the coefficients are all significant as they show a level below 5 per cent.

In this model without interaction terms, we can observe the positive and significant effect on performance of functional distinctive competencies ($\beta=0.3028$, $P<0.001$), of distinctive competencies on coordination ($\beta=0.0996$, $P<0.05$), and of dynamic distinctive competencies ($\beta=0.2713$, $P<0.001$). The size variable is also positive and significant ($\beta=0.1371$, $P<0.001$). With regard to control variables and according to the literature, they also show a significant and positive effect of attractiveness of competitive environment, and a significant and negative effect of environmental uncertainty.

In the model with interactions terms (Table 16.2), we test the significance of the t-statistic related to these interaction terms (Jaccard *et al.*, 1990). If interaction terms are introduced, the interpretation of regression coefficients changes (Jaccard,

Table 16.2 Results

Variables	Model without interaction effects		Model with interaction effects	
	Beta	Signif.	Beta	Signif.
Constant/Intersec.		0.0000	−0.0246	0.5265
Industry attractiveness	0.1226	0.0044	0.1152	0.0071
Environmental uncertainty	−0.1479	0.0006	−0.1438	0.0008
Number of employees	0.1371	0.0005	0.1346	0.0022
Functional competencies	0.3028	0.0000	0.2768	0.0000
Competencies of coordination	0.0996	0.0496	0.0929	0.0669
Dynamic competencies	0.2713	0.0001	0.2913	0.0000
Number of employees × functional competencies			0.1603	0.0441
Number of employees × competendes of coordination			0.0140	0.8648
Number of employees × dynamic competencies			−0.0794	0.2358
Model adjustment				
R	0.6659			
R^2	0.4434		0.454	
Adjusted R^2	0.4349		0.442	
F statistic	52.0402			
F signif.	0.0000			

et al., 1990; Hair *et al.*, 1999). The value of *b* of the interactive term represents the effect of one of the interactive variables on the dependent variable when the other interactive variable changes in a unit. The coefficients of a regression without interaction effects indicate the effect of each one of the independent variables when the rest of them equal zero. In this case, non-standardised coefficients appear, since the analysis of standardised coefficients can become difficult when the interactive term is introduced (Jaccard *et al.*, 1990). As we can see in Table 16.2, the interaction between organisational size and functional distinctive competencies is significant ($b=0.1603$, $P<0.05$). Nevertheless, the rest of the multiplicative terms are not significant in the case of competencies in coordination ($b=0.0140$, $P>0.1$) or dynamic distinctive competencies ($b=-0.0794$, $P>0.1$).

Conclusion

We can only confirm an indirect effect of organisational size through functional distinctive competencies. Moreover, this effect is positive, which indicates that greater size benefits functional competencies and then performance. However, whether the effect on performance of coordination and dynamic competencies is more positive or negative does not depend on organisational size. As we stated above, one possible explanation may be that both large and small companies enjoy advantages. These advantages may be different, but both can favour the generation of distinctive competencies. This could represent an important advance in the defence of SMEs, and must therefore be tested in future research. These coordination and dynamic competencies may become more necessary in the future, and they can be attained not only by large organisations but also by small ones.

In the question of how organisational size is important to the creation of advantages and disadvantages, the literature shows the strengths and weaknesses of large and small organisations. The competitive advantages of large companies lie in a greater resource base, superior opportunities for growth, higher employee expectance and greater power of control over the environment. This may be the reason for a significant interactive effect of functional competencies and size on performance, since the functional variable includes financial, production and marketing capabilities. However, SMEs have greater flexibility and capacity for change and adaptation, are less bureaucratic and have a more human organisational environment. These advantages could be a suitable framework for the development of coordination and dynamic competencies. Our results also seem to point in this direction.

Although the interaction between dynamic competencies and size is negative, we cannot draw conclusions because it is not significant. Nevertheless, this negative sign could point to the direction for future research to improve the competitiveness of small- and medium-sized companies. These kinds of competencies could become the most essential ones in the future. The fact that these multiplicative terms are not significant could also be an argument in favour of SMEs, since small size does not represent a restriction to the positive influence of distinctive competencies on performance. But it should be tested in future research.

We should also comment on the direct influence of organisational size on performance. This effect is positive and significant. Hence, hypothetically, this influence could be a disadvantage in defending small organisational size. Results from a previous study (Camisón, 2001) pointed out that there were different moderator variables in the relation between size and performance. However, in the present study, only one interaction proposed is significant. This fact is also a starting point to analyse other possible moderating effects.

Finally, we must mention the limitations of the present work. They are related to the nature of the database. Data is relative to a single period, and therefore a wider database is required. The study should also be extended with objective data.

Note

1 The present study is part of a wider research, which has received financial support by grant from the Spanish Ministry of Science and Technology and FEDER (European Fund for Regional Development) (SEC2003–01825/ECO).

References

Amit, R. and Schoemaker, P. (1993) Strategic assets and organizational rent. *Strategic Management Journal* 14(1), 33–46.

Ansoff, H. I. (1985) '¿Qué es la estrategia de la empresa?', pp. 21–40 in *Enciclopedia de Dirección y Administración de la Empresa. Volumen V: Dirección general y política de empresa*. Barcelona: Ediciones Orbis.

Argyris, C. and Schön, D. (1978) *Organizational learning: a theory of action perspective*. Reading, MA: Addison-Wesley.

Argyris, C. and Schön, D. (1996) *Organizational learning II. Theory, method and practice*. Reading, MA: Addison-Wesley.

Azzone, G. and Rangone, A. (1996) Measuring manufacturing competence: a fuzzy approach. *International Journal of Production Research* 34(9), 2517–2532.

Bain, J. S. (1959) *Industrial Organization*. New York: Wiley.

Bain, J. S. (1972) *Essays on Price Theory and Industrial Organization*. Cambridge, MA: Harvard University Press.

Barney, J. (1986) Strategic factor markets: expectations, luck, and business strategy. *Management Science* 42(10), 1231–1241.

Barney, J. (1991) Firm resources and sustained competitive advantage. *Journal of Management* 17(1), 99–120.

Barney, J. B. (2001) Is the resource-based view a useful perspective for strategic management research? Yes. *Academy of Management Review* 26(1), 41–56.

Barney, J., Wright, M. and Ketchen, D. J. (2001) The resource-based view of the firm: ten years after 1991. *Journal of Management* 27, 625–641.

Bernasconi, M. (1983) Strategie: Une Analyse Comparèe des Travaux du BCG, du PIMS et de Porter. *Revue Française de Gestion* 42, 13–17.

Blau, P. M., Flabe, C. M. *et al.* (1976) Technology and organization in manufacturing. *Administrative Science Quarterly* 21 (March), 20–40.

Borch, O. J., Huse, M. and Senneseth, K. (1999) Resource configuration, competitive strategies, and corporate entrepreneurship: an empirical examination of small firms. *Entrepreneurship: Theory and Practice* 24(1), 49.

Brown, S. L. and Eisenhardt, K. M. (1998) *Competing on the Edge: strategy as structured chaos*. Boston, MA: Harvard Business School Press.

Burns, T. R. and Stalker, G. M. (1961) *The Management of Innovation*. London: Tavistock Institute.

Camisón, C. (1999) La medición de los resultados empresariales desde una óptica estratégica: construcción de un instrumento a partir de un estudio Delphi y la aplicación a la empresa industrial española en el período 1983–96. *Estudios financieros* 199 (October), 201–264.

Camisón, C. (2001) La investigación sobre la PYME y su competitividad: balance del estado de la cuestión desde las perspectivas narrativa y meta-analítica. *Papeles de Economía Española* 89/90, 43–86.

Camisón, C. (2002) *A proposal of conceptualization for organization distinctive competences stock*. Working paper 3/02, Universitat Jaume I, Research group on strategy, knowledge management and organizational learning, Castellón.

Camisón, C. (2004) Shared, competitive, and comparative advantage: a competence-based view of industrial-district competitiveness. *Environment and Planning A* 36(12), 2227–2256.

Camisón-Zornoza, C., Lapiedra-Alcamí, R., Segarra-Ciprés, M. and Boronat-Navarro, M. (2004) A meta-analysis of innovation and organizational size. *Organization Studies* 25(3), 331–361.

Capon, N., Farley, J. and Hoenig, S. (1990) Determinants of financial performance: a meta-analysis. *Management Science* 36(10), 1143–1159.

Caves, R. E. and Porter, M. E. (1977) From entry barriers to mobility barriers: conjectural decisions and contrived deterrence to new competition. *Quarterly Journal of Economics* 91, 241–262.

Child, J. S. (1973) Predicting and understanding organization structure. *Administrative Science Quarterly* 18, 1–17.

Churchill, G. A. (1979) A paradigm for developing better measures of marketing constructs. *Journal of Marketing Research* 16(1), 64–73.

Cohen, J. and Cohen, P. (1983) *Applied Multiple Regression/Correlation Analysis for the Behavioral Sciences*. 2nd edn. Hillsdale, NJ: Lawrence Erlbaum Associates.

Conant, J. S., Mokwa, M. P. and Varadarajan, P. R. (1990) Strategic types, distinctive marketing competencies and organizational performance: a multiple measures-based study. *Strategy Management Journal* 11, 365–383.

Conner, K. R. (1991) A historical comparison of resource-based theory and five schools of thought within industrial organization economics: do we have a new theory of the firm?. *Journal of Management* 17(1), 121–154.

Cronbach, L. (1951) Coeficient alpha and the internal structure of tests. *Psychometrica* 16, 297–334.

Demsetz, H. (1973) Industry structure, market rivalry and public policy. *Journal of Law and Economics* 16(1), 1–9.

Dess, G. G. (1987) Consensus on strategy formulation and organizational performance: competitors in a fragmented industry. *Strategic Management Journal* 8(3), 259–277.

Dess, G. G. and Beard, D. W. (1984) Dimensions of organizational task environments. *Administrative Science Quarterly* 29, 52–73.

Dess, G. G. and Robinson, R. B. (1984) Measuring organizational performance in the absence of objective measures: the case of the privately-held firm and conglomerate business unit. *Strategic Management Journal* 5, 265–273.

Dierickx, I. and Cool, K. (1989) Asset stock accumulation and sustainability of competitive advantage. *Management Science* 35(12), 1504–1511.

Eisenhardt, D. M. and Martin, J. A. (2000) Dynamic capabilities: what are they?. *Strategic Management Journal* 21(10/11), 1105–1121.

Entrialgo, M., Fernández, E. and Vázquez, C. J. (2001) El comportamiento emprendedor y el éxito de la PYME: modelos de contingencia y configuracionales. *Dirección y Organización* 25, 47–58.

Foss, N. J. (1996) Research in strategy, economics and Michael Porter. *Journal of Management Studies* 33(1), 1–24.

Fuchs, P. H., Mifflin, K. E., Miller, D. and Whitney, J. O. (2000) Strategic integration: competing in the age of capabilities. *California Management Review* 42(3).

Gadenne, D. (1998) Critical success factors for small business: an inter-industry comparison. *International Small Business Journal* 17(1), 36.

Gale, B. T. (1972) Market share and rate of return. *Review of Economics and Statistics* 54(4), 412–423.

Goh, S. and Richards, G. (1997) Benchmarking the learning capability of organizations. *European Management Journal* 15(5), 575–584.

Gooding, R. Z. and Wagner, J. A. (1985) A meta-analytic review of the relationship between size and performance, the productivity and efficiency of organizations and their subunits. *Administrative Science Quarterly* 30(4), 462–481.

Grant, R. M. (1991) The resource-based theory of competitive advantages: implications for strategy formulation. *California Management Review* 33(3), 114–135.

Hall, J. and Weiss, L. (1967) Firm size and profitability. *Review of Economics and Statistics* 44, 319–331.

Hair, J. F., Anderson, R. E., Tatham, R. L. and Black, W. C. (1999) *Análisis Multivariante*. 5th edn. Madrid: Prentice-Hall.

Helfat, C. E. and Raubitschek, R. S. (2000) Product sequencing: co-evolution of knowledge, capabilities and products. *Strategic Management Journal* 21 (10/11), 961–979.

Henderson, R. and Cockburn, I. (1994) Measuring competence?: exploring firm effects in pharmaceutical research. *Strategic Management Journal* 15 (Winter special issue), 63–84.

Hickson, D. J., Pugh, D. S. and Pheysey, D. C. (1969) Operations technology and organization structure: an empirical reappraisal. *Administrative Science Quarterly* 14, 378–398.

Hill, Ch. W. L. and Deeds, D. L. (1996) The importance of industry structure for the determination of firm profitability: a neo-Austrian perspective. *Journal of Management Studies* 33(4), 429–451.

Hitt, M. A. and Ireland, R. D. (1985) Corporate distinctive competence, strategy, industry and performance. *Strategic Management Journal* 6(3), 273–294.

Jaccard, J., Turrisi, R. and Wan, Ch. I. (1990) Interaction effects in multiple regression. *Sage University Papers Series: quantitative applications in the social sciences* 72. Sage Publications.

Ketchen, D. J., Thomas, J. B. and Snow, C. C. (1993) Organizational configurations and performance: a comparison of theoretical approaches. *Academy of Management Journal* 36(6), 1278–1313.

Kogut, B. and Zander, U. (1992) Knowledge of the firm, combinative capabilities, and the replication of technology. *Organization Science* 3(3), 502–518.

Lado, A. A., Boyd, N. G. and Wright, P. (1992) A competency-based model of sustainable competitive advantage: toward a conceptual integration. *Journal of Management* 18(1), 77–91.

Lado, A. and Wilson, M. (1994) Human resource systems and sustained competitive advantage: a competency-based perspective. *Academy of Management Review* 19(4), 669–727.

Lawless, M. W. and Finch, L. K. (1989) Choice and determinism: a test of Hrebiniak and Joyce's framework on strategy-environment fit. *Strategic Management Journal* 10(4), 351–365.

Lawrence, P. R. and Lorsch, J. W. (1967) *Organization and Environment: managing differentiation and integration*. Boston, MA: Harvard University Press.

Lawson, B. and Samson, D. (2001) Developing innovation capability in organisations: a dynamic capabilities approach. *International Journal of Innovation Management* 5(3), 377–400.

Lazarsfeld, P. F. (1965) 'De los conceptos a los índices empíricos', in P. F. Lazarsfeld and R. Boudon (eds.), *Metodología de las Ciencias Sociales* vol. I, pp. 35–62. Barcelona: Laia.

Leonard-Barton, D. (1995) *Wellsprings of Knowledge*. Boston, MA: Harvard Business School Press.

March, J. G. and Simon, H. A. (1958) *Organizations*. New York: Wiley.

Mason, E. (1949) The current state of the monopoly problem in the US. *Harvard Law Review* 62, 1265–1285.

McGee, J. E. and Peterson, M. (2000) Toward the development of measures of distinctive competencies among small independent retailers. *Journal of Small Business Management* 38(2), 19.

Miller, D. and Shamsie, J. (1996) The resource-based view of the firm in two environments: the Hollywood film studios from 1936 to 1965. *Academy of Management Journal* 39(3), 519–543.

Mintzberg, H. (1985) A review of positioning school of strategic management. *The Fifth Annual Strategic Management Society Conference*, Barcelona, October.

Moen, O. (1999) The relationship between firm size, competitive advantages and export performance revisited. *International Small Business Journal* 18(1), 53–72.

Montgomery, C. and Wernerfelt, B. (1988) Diversification Ricardian rents and Tobin's q. *Rand Journal of Economics* 19, 623–632.

Nelson, R. R. and Winter, S. G. (1982) *An Evolutionary Theory of Economic Change*. Cambridge, MA: Harvard University Press.

Nonaka, I. (1994) A dynamic theory of organizational knowledge creation. *Organization Science* 5(1), 14–24.

Nonaka, I. and Takeuchi, H. (1995) *The Knowledge-Creating Company. How Japanese companies create the dynamics of innovation*. Oxford: Oxford Univerity Press.

Peng, M. W. and Luo, Y. (2000) Managerial ties and firm performance in a transition economy: the nature of a micro-macro links. *Academy of Management Journal* 43(3), 486–501.

Peteraf, M. A. (1993) The cornerstone of competitive advantage: a resource-based view. *Strategic Management Journal* 14, 179–191.

Peters, T. J. and Waterman, R. H. (1982) *In Search of Excellence: lessons from America's best-run companies*. New York: Harper & Row Publishers. Spanish edition (1984): *En busca de la excelencia. Lecciones de las empresas mejor gestionadas de los Estados Unidos*. Madrid: Plaza & Janés.

Porter, M. E. (1980) *Competitive Strategy: techniques for analyzing industries and competitors*. New York: Free Press.

Porter, M. E. (1985) *Competitive Advantage*. New York: Free Press.

Porter, M. E. (1990) *The Competitive Advantages of Nations*. New York: Free Press.

Powell, T. C. (1992) Organizational alignment as competitive advantage. *Strategic Management Journal* 13(2), 119–134.

Powell, T. C. (1996) How much does industry matter? An alternative empirical test. *Strategic Management Journal* 17, 323–334.

Puig, P. (dir., 1996) *La competitivitat de l'empresa industrial a Catalunya. Anàlisi de l'entron econòmic i de les estratègies competitives en un context de modernització del sector públic*. Barcelona: ESADE

Rangone, A. (1999) A resource-based approach to strategy analysis in small-medium sized enterprises. *Small Business Economics* 12, 233–248.

Scherer, F. M. (1970) *Industrial Market Structure and Economic Performance*. Chicago: Rand MacNally (first edition published in 1970).

Schmalensee, R. (1982) 'The new industrial organization and the economic analysis of modern markets', pp. 253–285 in W. Hildenbrand (ed.) (1982).

Schulz, M (2001) The uncertain relevance of newness: organizational learning and knowledge flows. *Academy of Management Journal* 44(4), 661–682.

Schulze, W. S. (1994) The two schools of thought in resource-based theory: definitions and implications for research. *Advances in Strategic Management* 10, 127–151.

Schumpeter, J. A. (1934) *The Theory of Economic Development*. Cambridge, MA: Harvard University Press.

Snow, C. C. and Hrebiniak, L. G. (1980) Strategy, distinctive competence and organizational performance. *Administrative Science Quarterly* 25(2), 317–336.

Szymanski, D. M., Bharadwaj, S. G. and Varadarajan, P. R. (1993) An analysis of the market share-profitability relationship. *Journal of Marketing* 57(3), 1–18.

Takeishi, A. (2001) Bridging inter- and intra-firm boundaries: management of supplier involvement in automobile product development?. *Strategic Management Journal* 22(5), 403–434.

Teece, D. J. and Pisano, G. (1994) The dynamic capability of firms: an introduction. *Industrial and Corporate Change* 3(3), 537–556.

Teece, D. J., Pisano, G. and Shuen, A. (1997) Dynamic capabilities and strategic management. *Strategic Management Journal* 18(7), 509–533.

Tushman, M. L. and Nadler, D. A. (1978) Information processing as an integrating concept in organization design. *Academy of Management Review* 3, 613–624.

Venkatraman, N. and Camillus, J. (1984) Exploring the concept of fit in strategic management. *Academy of Management Review* 9, 513–525.

Venkatraman, N. and Ramanujam, V. (1987) Measurement of business economic performance: an examination of method convergence. *Journal of Management* 13, 109–122.

Wernerfelt, B. (1984) A resource-based view of the firm. *Strategic Management Journal* 5(2), 171–180.

Woodward, J. (1965) *Industrial Organization: theory and practice*. London: Oxford University Press.

Yeoh, P. and Roth, K. (1999) An empirical analysis of sustained advantage in the US pharmaceutical industry: impact of firm resources and capabilities. *Strategic Management Journal* 20(7), 637–653.

17 Strategies for developing an excellence paradigm of intraorganisational marketing culture and quality management

John Saee and Zahid Mahmood

Introduction

The main purpose of this paper is to develop a theoretical framework concerning the use of internal marketing (IM) as a vehicle for the successful implementation of quality management (QM). The ultimate goal in this context is to present IM as a technique for gaining the acceptance of the employees or departments that are critical to the successful implementation of QM programmes (Lewis, 1996). The argument presented in this article is based upon the view that the internal market consists of groups of workers and managers communicating and interacting with other groups of workers and managers within the organisation, and that the establishment and maintenance of effective and efficient relationships between these groups is the focus of internal marketing efforts.

The first part of the paper discusses the development and conceptual definition of IM. It considers the objectives and different approaches of IM in the views of different writers. The second part of the article describes the broad classes of variables which are central to this review, namely corporate cultural change and internal organisational communication, and their relationship to internal marketing, which, it is argued, are critical for the implementation of any QM programme.

The notion of 'internal marketing'

The concept of IM is a relatively recent departure from more traditional notions of marketing. IM has been addressed by a number of authors including Berry (1985), Grönroos (1985) and George (1990). In fact, the study of IM dates back only some thirty years. Conceptually, 'internal marketing' had its origins in a desire to extend and refine the more traditional external orientation of marketing theory to the organisation itself (Berry, 1985; Helman and Payne, 1992).

Quite early in this development, internal marketing theory was proposed as an approach to service management that entailed the application of traditional or classical notions of marketing (Palmer, 2000; Helman and Payne, 1992). This application embraced the marketing concept and the associated marketing mix as being relevant to the exchanges, which necessarily occur within an organisation, between employees and between functional divisions. It was suggested that these individuals and groups could collectively be regarded in much the same way as external 'customers' of the organisation. The logic was appealing, in that IM was therefore to be regarded as a means for improving corporate effectiveness and efficiency in service delivery by improving 'internal market' relationships and processes. For instance, Lewis (1996) argued that IM is an appropriate vehicle or approach for promoting the firm and its products or services to the firm's employees.

Sasser and Arbeit (1976) were among the first to use the term 'internal marketing' to refer to their assertion that employees are the first market of the firm. Employees are essential and central to delivering the services that are provided, thus they must be knowledgeable and motivated. In addition, they must be trained by the organisation to be aware of the firm's policies and strategies. Corrall and Brewerton (1999) argued that employees of the firm are the cheapest and most effective way of marketing an organisation. Grönroos (1985) has long described this important dimension of services marketing.

Bowen and Schneider (1988) have identified what they believe are the responsibilities of the employee in spanning the gap between what they variously called the 'internal environment' of the organisation and the 'external environment'. They, too, stressed the importance of training and motivating employees, in order that they can effectively carry out their duties to the firm in dealing with customer needs. Indicative of the level of interest in IM, at least within the academic realm, was the fact that a significant portion of the American Marketing Association and Services' marketing annual conference programme has long been devoted to IM. Similar levels of interest have also been in evidence in the practical domain. Having introduced the nature and described some of the impacts of IM, we turn our attention to a more rigorous conceptual definition of IM.

Conceptual definition of IM

As has been shown, considerable attention in the literature has been and continues to be paid to the potential benefits of IM programmes. The IM concept is a complement to the traditional marketing concept and holds that an organisation's internal market of employees can be influenced most effectively and hence motivated to customer consciousness, market orientation and sales mindedness flowing from a marketing-like internal approach and by applying marketing-like activities internally (Grönroos, 1985).

McGuire (1999) described the concept of IM as a philosophy, strategy and process. IM as a *philosophy* describes a customer-orientated culture in which everyone understands the strategic intent or purpose, and is motivated to participate in implementing the strategy. Integrating 'front- and backstage' (McGuire, 1999) activities requires a shared and common understanding of objectives and desired outcomes, as well as clarity of the roles of these activities in the service delivery process. Further, Ewing and Caruana (1999) suggest that at the strategic level

IM should create an environment that fosters customer consciousness amongst employees. Thus, the concept is concerned with challenging the attitudes and behaviour of employees to make them more customer conscious.

Grönroos (1996) defined the IM concept as a *statement of strategy* for the IM process that identifies a 'product', 'target customers' and 'capabilities'. The *products* are jobs and the work environment that influence employees' motivations. The *target customers* are top management, supervisors, contact personnel and support personnel. Further, Grönroos argued that IM requires two *capabilities* – *communication* and *attitude management*. The first relates to customer orientation and what Grönroos describes as 'service-mindedness'. *Communication management* is the more traditional realm of marketing and the second capability, *attitude management*, is arguably more the traditional realm of personnel or human resources management (ibid.: 7–18). IM as a *process* is a set of functions or activities. The list of IM activities is usually defined very broadly to include 'almost any function or activity that has an impact on the service-mindedness and customer consciousness of employees' (McGuire, 1999).

Despite the attention that the subject of IM has received, a review of the literature shows that there is still no single compelling or clear conceptual definition of IM. This remains an area of considerable confusion, despite the fact that numerous alternative definitions of IM have been proposed over the past decade. There is still debate over the nature and application of the subject. Some authors view IM as either a concept, a philosophy or a management practice (Grönroos, 1988; George, 1990; Wilson, 1991), as either relating to human resource management, service marketing, or change management (Berry and Parasuraman, 1991; Van and Maanen, 1995; George, 1990). Rafiq and Ahmad (2000) suggested there are three phases of the evolution of IM: (1) employee satisfaction; (2) customer orientation; and (3) strategy implementation and change management.

On the one hand, (George, 1990) has proposed that IM is simply a 'philosophy for managing the organization's human resources based on a marketing perspective' (p. 63). IM is an holistic management process aimed at integrating the multiple functions of organisations. George described the IM concept as follows:

> Internal marketing starts from the notion that employees are a first, internal market for the organization. If goods, services and external communication campaigns cannot be marketed to this internal target group, marketing to the ultimate, external customers cannot be expected to be successful either.
>
> (p. 63)

Further, George (1990) asserts that IM creates an inspiring climate characterised by a framework of targeted communication aimed at everyone in the organisation, and in which, as a consequence, motivation and morale thrive. According to this view, IM ensures that both the internal 'people relationships' and the resources of the business are working in harmony to achieve the organisation's strategic and tactical goals (pp. 63–70).

On the other hand, Hales (1994) debates whether IM offers a new perspective on the management of human resources or whether it is a 'metaphor too far'. Hales is sceptical of the 'utility and relevance' of the use of marketing principles and the components of exchange and transaction inside organisations. However, there are some commonalities and overlaps, which have been considered in the literature. Hales (1994) suggests that the normative aspects of 'people management', which relate to the management of employees as a resource, should be aligned with the strategic direction of the firm. Hales (1994) stresses that the key physical, human and organisational internal resources of the firm together influence the development and maintenance of competitive advantage in the external marketplace. As far as human capital is concerned, Hales highlights the critical nature of 'training, experience, judgment, intelligence, relationships and insight of individual managers and workers in the firm'.

The term 'internal marketing' has been used to describe a variety of internal management activities, which, although not new in themselves, have 'offered a new approach to developing a service orientation and an interest in customers and marketing among all personnel' (Grönroos, 1990). As mentioned earlier, there is no single unified notion of what is meant by IM, however, it is a concept that offers a 'philosophy for managing the organization's human resources based on a marketing perspective' (George and Grönroos, 1990; Foreman and Woodruffe, 1991; Rafiq and Ahmad, 1993).

For the purpose of this chapter, IM is defined as the management process whereby exchanges and transactions within the organisation are managed in order to implement quality management programmes. Further, it is considered that the process of managing and improving IOC and CCC to ensure everyone in the organisation understands the organisational goals. Therefore, IM requires the commitment of strategic management in order to ensure it receives sufficient importance within the organisation (Preston and Steel, 2002). The idea of IM originates at the top management and can be communicated down to the very bottom of the firm (Greene *et al.*, 1994).

Such exchanges and transactions as above are decidedly two-way exchanges, as the managers in the human resource management department could benefit from a more market-oriented approach inside the organisation. Christopher, Payne and Ballantyne (1991), in broadening the boundaries for IM, applied the term to any form of marketing within an organisation that focuses attention on the internal activities that need to be changed in order for marketing plans to be implemented. Adding to the clarity of the concept, Ballantyne *et al.* (1995) have since refocused these earlier views of the domain of inquiry with the following definition:

> internal marketing is any form of marketing within an organization which focuses staff attention on the internal activities that need to be changed in order to enhance external market place performance.

> (pp. 19–44)

Quality management approach

Lings (1997) described this approach to IM as being based on the existence of internal customers and suppliers within the organisation. An internal supplier is any person or group who passes a product to, or performs a service for, another person or group within the firm, thereby effecting exchanges with these internal customers. While failing to critically evaluate the applicability of the notion of exchange in this setting, this approach proposes that internal suppliers should strive to provide quality outputs for their internal customers. Pitt *et al.* (1999) and Kotler (2000) described that an organisation cannot promise to provide an excellent service before the employees committed to such service delivery.

The rationale of this approach is that QM is built into the system, resulting in service quality to the external customer. This approach is based on the concept of internal customers and suppliers and the internal supply chain, which has found considerable support in the literature. Lee and Billington (1992) focused on the notion of internal suppliers within the organisation and the quality problem associated with this notion. In addition, Barret (1994) discussed the need for internal customer programs, and Denton (1990) suggested that the supplier–consumer relationship should become the focus within the organisation. Bhote (1991) proposes an improvement cycle within the organisation, based on the concept that in viewing the 'production process as a chain, the next operation is a customer of the one which precedes it' (pp. 11–12). This concept of internal suppliers and internal customers, also known as the internal customer model, is not without its critics. Guaspari (1993) has elaborated several criticisms of the internal customer model, namely:

1   the internal customer model addresses only continuous improvement and not breakthrough improvement. Evocatively, he asserts that this approach can lead to the world's best and most efficient bucket brigade when a fire hose may be far more useful;
2   it sets up a series of dominance-subservience relationships within an organisation, which are antagonistic to the delivery of sustained service quality; and
3   it reinforces insular thinking, particularly with people who do not come into contact with external customers.

The above approach of IM is presented by different authors. They suggest the role of IM is either that provided by the service marketing approach – employees' jobs and employees are the customers of these jobs; quality management approach-focused – internal suppliers must serve their internal customers; or IM-focused – selling a strategy to the groups within the organisations. The review of the literature relating to IM suggests that the employment of such a strategy may help overcome resistance to change and departmental conflict within the organisation (Preston and Steel, 2002; Morgan 2001).

Linkage between QM and IM

The purpose of IM in this study is to serve as an instrument to generate enthusiasm through IOC and cultural change in employees for the implementation of a QM programme. The IM concept and the procedures to implement the concept are ongoing processes with feedback mechanisms to incorporate dynamic elements, such as environmental trends and changing customer needs (Kane and Kelley, 1992). According to Kane and Kelley (1992):

> this dynamic aspect of the marketing concept recognised as the marking concept cycle, through its nature, embraces the notion of quality deliverance to enhance customers utility and value.
>
> (p. 26)

The QM movement has progressed by focusing on two areas, namely, better ways of producing need-satisfying products/services and improvement of internal operations (Kane and Kelley, 1992). Thus, there is a strong similarity in the dynamic focus of the marketing concept and the QM movement, which may provide for interfaces to yield fresh insights.

The common theme of QM and IM can be exploited when IM is offered as a mechanism for achieving the necessary customer-orientation and quality culture (Atkinson, 1990). All employees in the quality culture must be formulated with the notion of their own customer–supplier relationships (Morgan and Piercy, 1998). According to Varey (1995), QM and the IM concept have a strong affinity. However, the common themes of QM and IM are largely ignored by marketing and quality management writers. Phillips *et al.* (1983) provided a persuasive assessment, which showed that the role of the marketing department in implementing quality management has been widely neglected.

The literature shows the emphasis of QM programmes has generally been on the improvement of internal business processes, through techniques such as flow charts, pareto charts, cause and effect tables, control charts, scatter diagrams and histograms, rather than on focusing on creating internal awareness and motivation to QM programmes within the organisation. The initiative of QM programmes in creating employee awareness and motivation has been accorded little attention in the literature.

This study contends that the links of IM with other factors (e.g. IOC and CCC) are important factors for the implementation of QM programmes within the firm. Oakland and Dotchin (1994) suggest that QM 'starts' with marketing, and the link is formalised in IM. However, if a better link between marketing and quality is established, methods of market research could be used internally (e.g. internal customer surveys; focus group techniques; in-depth interviews; and brainstorming) to develop QM programmes within the organisation.

The notion of IM in this study is considered as a management philosophy that provides a systematic framework for managing employees towards the implementation of QM programmes. For an organisation to develop a culture in which the implementation of QM is the primary doctrine, it requires the support of employees at all levels. These employees must recognise the importance of the implementation of QM programmes and be willing to adopt the appropriate behaviours and function in a cohesive manner. Little research has been undertaken linking the concepts of IM and the implementation of QM programmes.

Corporate cultural change

CCC has received substantial attention from practitioners and researchers alike, including Deal and Kennedy (1982), Kilmann *et al.*(1983) and Saee (2005), as well as the periodic collections of articles published, which appears in the special issues of *Administrative Science Quarterly* and *Organisational Dynamics*. Several different conceptualisations of CCC exist in the organisational theory literature and some common threads run through the various conceptualisations, which have been summarised as follows:

> corporate culture change refers to the unwritten, often unconscious message that fills in the gaps between what is formally decreed and what actually takes place; it involves shared philosophies, ideologies, values, beliefs, expectations, and norms.
>
> (Kilmann *et al.*, 1983: 239)

There is substantial agreement among researchers about the importance of CCC as the pattern of shared values and beliefs that help members of an organisation to understand why things happen and thereby to teach them the behavioural norms in the organisation.

As Schein (1985) notes:

> because culture serves the function of stabilising the external and internal environment of an organization, it must be taught to new members. It would not serve its function if every generation of new members can introduce new perceptions, language, thinking patterns, and rules of interaction. For culture to serve its function, it must be perceived as correct and valid, and if it is perceived that way, it automatically follows that it must be taught to newcomers.
>
> (p. 10)

There have been numerous approaches to the definition of corporate culture, and these have often employed different terminology. Allaire and Firsiruto (1984) point out that adopting a particular definition of culture is a commitment to specific conceptual assumptions and ways of studying culture. Further, Allaire and Firsiruto (1984) argued that the various definitions adopted by different researchers in the study of CCC could be categorised into three types: *social interpretation, behavioural control* and *organisational adaptation* definitions. *Social interpretation* definitions focus on the interpretation schemata, meanings or frames of references of individuals as indicators and components of culture. *Behavioural control* definitions focus on patterns of interaction or activities that define shared organisations' behaviour. *Organisational adaptation* definitions emphasise habituated solutions to common encountered organisational problems, such as integration and adaptation.

This view is expressed by Wilkins and Patterson (1985), who indicate that:

> culture consists of the conclusions a group of people draws from its experience. An organization's culture consists largely of what people believe about what works and what does not. A group's beliefs range from conventional practices (for example, particular ways of making decisions or of recognizing and managing low performers), to values (judgments about what is good and bad; for example, 'you should always be thorough in preparing to make a recommendation'), to assumptions ('maps' in people's heads about what the world is like and how to get things done in it; for example, 'if you take risks and fail, you will be fired', or 'all problems are basically marketing problems').

> (p. 267)

Accordingly, CCC is defined in this study as 'the pattern of beliefs, values, rituals, myths, and sentiments shared by members of an organization' (Harrison and Stokes, 1992). It is

> made up of those aspects of the organization that give it a particular climate or feel. Culture is to an organization what personality is to an individual. It is that distinctive constellation of beliefs, values, work styles, and relationships that distinguish one organization from another.

> (p. 13)

CCC and QM

In 1986 the Australian Society Quality Council (ASQC) surveyed 600 managers across the country, asking the importance of several contributing factors in developing QM programmes within the organisation. Ten per cent responded that CCC was the most important ingredient contributing to QM programmes. In 1988 they performed a similar study of 600 different managers. This time, 40 per cent replied that CCC was the most important component producing quality (Covey and Keith, 1992).

In a quality culture, the organisation must have a common vision that is shared by all members of the organisation (Carr and Littman, 1993; Johnson, 1993; Saee, 2005). Sirota *et al.* (1994) view defects and problems as opportunities for improvement (Carr and Littman, 1993; Robson, 1988); reward and recognise employees when results are achieved (Johnson, 1993); use quality information for improvement rather than judging or controlling people (Sirota *et al.*, 1994); and must base its decisions on objective data (Carr and Littman, 1993). The quality culture must replace the 'test and fix', and 'if its not broken do not fix it' values with a detect and prevent culture (Robson, 1988). The 'way we do things around here' and 'cover yourself' values are incompatible with the quality culture and must be replaced with a quality culture that views continuous improvement as essential to the success of the organisation and problems as opportunities for improvements.

According to the CCC perspective, QM initiatives fail when an organisation fails to create a QM culture that is compatible with the elements of QM programmes. The literature indicates, prior to the implementation of QM programmes, that an effort to change the existing culture must be undertaken, otherwise failure is inevitable. To avoid the culture trap, organisations must assess their existing corporate culture, determine the extent to which it is compatible with the elements of QM and create a quality culture that focuses on values and the elements of QM, otherwise organisations would only be adding to the existing culture that will not prevail. People will revert to the old ways of doing things and QM will fail. Failure to seriously take the cultural factor into consideration when implementing QM has resulted in disasters (Crosby, 1992; Alloway, 1994; Atkinson, 1990; Townsend and Joan, 1988). Atkinson (1990) attributes the failure of many QM initiatives to failing to establish a quality culture.

The above review of the literature implies that CCC is a potentially powerful explanatory variable in the implementation of a QM programme. CCC in this study can be conceptually defined as the patterns of shared values, beliefs and organisationally relevant policies, plans and structures that shape how people should behave at work and determine what tasks and goals are important. In this respect, communication and IM play pivotal roles as the processes by which organisational members interpret and understand the various symbols and patterns of behaviour in their environment.

CCC and IM

Broadly speaking, IM is a strategy of applying marketing philosophy and principles within the organisation and a process of encouraging employees to accept changes in company philosophy. Recently, IM has been defined as a multifaceted construct that encompasses the importance placed on service quality, interpersonal relationships, the selling task, organisation, internal communications and innovativeness (Westbrook, 1995). For example, a type of IM culture is one that stresses professionalism among employees from top management to operational positions.

Westbrook states that employees, as well as customers, should be able to detect or 'feel' such a culture both directly and indirectly (e.g. by observing the apparent importance placed on punctuality, professional dress and conduct, and organisation). Further, he says, another type of marketing culture is one that concentrates on implementing the most recent innovations relevant to that particular industry. Yet, another might focus on the continuous monitoring and improving of the quality of established practices. In other words, an IM culture can stem from any combination of differential weights placed on these various dimensions (Westbrook, 1995).

This chapter contends that CCC process cannot be accomplished by concentrating only on culture. It suggests IM is based on the philosophy, more than listening to the employees and staff of a company and telling them what is happening and what your company is going to do. All organisations have a culture, which is either a positive or negative force in achieving effective performance. This study argues that 'organisations that have supportive internal CCC of their strategies are more likely to be successful in the implementation of quality management programmes'. For instance, Smircich points out that executives ought to consider the 'cultural risk' when adopting new strategies. They suggest that the organisation change implied by new business strategies should be compared to the cultural orientations of the organisation in order to determine the degree of potential resistance. In general, the research agenda arising from the view that culture is an organisational variable is how to mould and shape internal culture in particular ways and how to change culture, consistent with managerial purposes (Smircich, 1983).

IOC

The concept of IOC has been around since the 1930s. Serious attempts to define and study the concept began with the laboratory experiments of Bavelas and Barrett (1951). At various times IOC has been treated as synonymous with listening, honesty, frankness, trust, supportiveness and a variety of similar concepts. Redding (1972) attempted to clarify and systematically describe the dimensions of IOC. He argued that IOC included both message-sending and message-receiving behaviours, with the observation that superiors' message-receiving behaviours were especially important. Redding's model (1972) of the dimensions of IOC appear in Table 17.1.

Focusing on task-related activities, Baird (1973) and Stull (1974) supported the notion that communication within the organisation involves both message-sending and message-receiving behaviours. Baird (1973) also noted that similar behaviours described IOC in both superior–subordinate and peer–peer dyads. Baird, however, found IOC behaviours more related to task than to non-task communication activities. Earlier studies by Argyris (1990) identified non-task activities, such as personal opinions, suggestions and new ideas, as a characteristic of IOC.

Table 17.1 Dimensions of internal organisational communication

	Message sending	**Message receiving**
Superiors' behaviour	From superior to subordinate (downwards)	To superior from subordinate (upwards)
Subordinates' behaviour	From subordinate to superior (upwards)	To subordinate from superior (downwards)
Peers' behaviour	From peer to peer (horizontal)	To peer from peer (horizontal)

Source: Redding, 1972: 405.

Thus, while there is no commonly accepted definition of IOC, the concept seems to incorporate the message-sending and message-receiving behaviours from the superiors, subordinates and peers with regard to task, personal and innovative topics. In the organisational, communication literature, internal corporate communication has been defined as face-to-face, meaning-centred interaction conducted as part of the managing role by managers in their organisations (Ticehurst *et al.*, 1991).

Mastenbroek (1991) argues that communication within the organisation aims 'to establish mutual understanding and trust between employees and functional departments. Cooperation is a critical success factor in building the necessary organisational culture and capability' (p. 27). Further, he says it develops a clear conceptual framework, which combines thinking on integrated internal and external communications and relationships among organisational members. Ticehurst *et al.* (1991) defined:

> internal corporate communication as being broadly concerned with managing and administering communication resources and processes to facilitate communication within the organisations and between organisations and their communities.
>
> (p. 81)

In the light of the literature review, IOC in this study can be defined as an individual who will attempt to share accurately his or her views, feelings and intentions with another, on matters pertinent to organisational objectives. IOC is a vehicle for achieving and maintaining a level of cooperation among organisational members by providing them with knowledge and skills that create and maintain a CCC in which all members are enthusiastic for and committed to the implementation of new ideas. This is especially pertinent for present purposes since QM can be regarded as a new idea in contemporary organisations.

IOC, like CCC, is a contested term that has been subject to a multiplicity of definitional formulations (Dance and Larson, 1976). Here IOC consists of two types of actions: (1) those that create messages or displays; and (2) those that interpret messages or displays. A display consists of information not necessarily intended as a message but from which one can derive meaning. IOC, like other forms of communication, involves making and interpreting message displays. According to Fisher (1983), it forms part of an

> ongoing process that includes patterns of interaction between an organization's members that both emerge from and shape the nature and actions of the organization and the events within it.
>
> (p. 4)

In summary, to understand the cultural and communicative phenomena in the abstract is relatively easy: tracing the specific interrelationships for any given organisation in any plausible and convincing manner is, however, a considerable interpretive task, as we will demonstrate in this chapter.

IOC and IM

The importance of IOC as a motivational device within the IM campaign has been identified by several authors (Morgan and Piercy, 1998; Piercy, 1995). IOC is a vital link between success and failure of any good idea in which the human factor plays a critical role (Lovelock and Wright, 2002). Both verbal and non-verbal communications are to be used by management to clearly, consistently and continually communicate the goals and objectives of the organisation to employees.

Leonard (1983) argued,

> internal organisational communication and their relationships to all employee groups are critical to the success of the implementation of any new programs. Failure to consider these types of relationships result in a 'quick fix mentality' and has contributed to a high rate of failure among any new ideas.
>
> (p. 98)

Ingle (1982) espouses the necessity to bring together the employees for planned communication regarding the assessment and evaluation of each component of the new programmes/ideas (Payne, 1992).

An exhaustive review of the literature suggests that IM provides all employees with the means to improve internal communication processes through the development of individual work functions. The premise of IM is that the internal exchange between the organisation and its employee groups must be cooperating effectively before the firm can be successful in achieving its goals and objectives (Grönroos, 1990). Payne (1992) argues that IM involves a communication programme throughout the organisation, thus involving everyone in the organisation in IM. Further, he says, IM is concerned primarily with internal communications, with developing responsiveness, responsibility and unity of purpose.

Summary

Many researchers have dealt with the implementation of QM programmes but no previously published research has presented evidence of the effectiveness of IM in enhancing the IOC and cultural change within the organisation. While there is some consideration in the literature about the linkage of IM and QM programmes, little research has been done in the area of QM implementation and the effectiveness of IM programmes. This study provides a theoretical ground that is based on a synthesis of the work of various authors in the field of marketing, IOC and culture.

Management's role is to create a supportive environment that respects freedom of action and nurtures the creative energies of organisational staff, and to manage the relationship of the unit as a whole with its environment (Geranmayeh and Bartol, 1993). Geranmayeh and Bartol (1993) argue that every organisational unit is a business in its own right, having its own customer, suppliers, competitors and responsibility for the profitability of its operations. Success or failure of the unit will depend on how well it serves its customers' needs.

Success in QM implementation requires knowledge of whether organisations understand the QM concepts previously discussed and whether they are utilising this knowledge to formulate QM strategies. Evidence from the field regarding the implementation of QM programmes will help the researcher in studying how QM is implemented. The review of the literature shows there is no clear approach that considers IM as a management tool for the generation of CCC and internally communicate the new ideas within the organisation. This study conceptually argues the concept of IM as a process by which service organisations and their personnel understand and recognise not only the values of the marketing programme but their place within it. It also contends that the adoption of IM will facilitate improved IOC and bring about desirable CCC, which collectively enhances the successful implementation of QM programmes. The relationship between these factors may be causal, and the direction of causation is a matter for further theoretical and empirical investigation.

Bibliography

Allaire, Paul A. (1991) Quality: where it has been and where it is going. *Journal of Quality and Participation* 14 (March), 64–66.

Allaire, Y. and Firsirotu, M. E. (1984) Theories of organisational culture. *Journal of Organization Studies* 5(3), 193–226.

Alloway, J. A., Jr (1994) Laying the ground work for total quality. *Quality Progress* 27.

Arggyris, C. (1985) *Action Science: concepts, methods, and skills for research and intervention.* San Francisco, CA: Jossey-Bass.

Argyris, C. (1990) *Integrating the Individual and the Organization.* New Jersey: New Brunswick Transaction Publishers.

Atkinson, P. E. (1990) *Creating Culture Change: the key to successful total quality management.* Sann Diego, CA: Pfeiffer and Company.

Australian Coalition of Service Industries (ACSI) (1996) *Annual Review.*

Baird, J. W. (1973) An analytical field study of 'open communication' as perceived by supervisors, subordinates, and peers. *Unpublished doctoral dissertation,* Purduce University.

Ballantyne, D. *et. al.* (1995) What goes wrong in company-wide service quality initiatives?. *Asia–Australia Marketing Journal* 2(1), 19–44.

Barrett, C. (1994) Co-workers are customers too. *Sales and Marketing Management.* July, 31–32.

Bavelas, A. D. and Barrett, D. (1951) An experimental approach to organisational communication. *Personnel* 27, 366–71.

Berman, E. M. *et al.* (1995) Municipal commitment to total quality management: a survey of recent progress. *Public Administration Review* 55(1), 57–66.

Berry, L. L. (1986) Big ideas in service marketing. *Journal of Consumer Marketing* 3(2), 47–51.

Berry, L. L. and Parasuraman, A. (1991) *Marketing Services, Competing Through Quality.* New York: Free Press.

Bhote, K. R. (1991) Next operation as a customer. *Executive Excellence,* July, pp. 11–12.

Bowen, D. E. and Schneider, B. (1988) 'Services marketing and management implications for organisational behaviour. *Research in Organisational Behaviour* 6(4).

Bream, T. L. *et al.* (1992) Beyond the ordinary image of nursing. *Nursing Management* 23(12).

Carr, David K. and Littman, Ian D. (1993) *Excellence in Government: total quality management in the 1990s.* 2nd edn. Arlington, VA: Coopers and Lybrand.

Christopher, M., Payne, A. and Ballantyne, D. (1991) *Relationship Marketing: bringing quality, customer service and marketing together.* Oxford: Butterworth-Heinemann.

Compton, F., William, R. G., Grönroos, C. and Karvinen, M. (1987) 'Internal marketing' in John A. Czepiel, Carole A. Congram and James Shanahan (eds), *The Service Marketing Challenge: integrating for competitive advantage.* Chicago: American Marketing Association.

Corrall, S. and Brewerton, A. (1999) *The New Professional Handbook: your guide to information services management.* London: Library Association Publishing.

Covey, S. R. and Keith, A. G. (1992) Principle-centered leadership. *The Journal for Quality and Participation* 15, 70–78.

Crosby, P. B. (1992) The Baldrige as a negative. *Quality Progress* 24, 41–44.

Dance, F. E. X. and Larson, C. E. (1976) *The Functions of Human Communication: a theoretical approach.* New York: Holt, Rinehart and Winston.

Deal, T. E. and Kennedy, A. K. (1982) *Corporate Cultures.* Reading, MA: Addison-Wesley Publishing Company.

Denton. D. K. (1990) Customer focused management. *HR Magazine,* August, pp. 62–67.

Ewing, M. T. and Caruana, A. (1999) An internal marketing approach to public sector management the marketing and human resources interface. *The International Journal of Public Sector Management* 12(1).

Fisher, D. (1983) *Communication in Organisations.* St. Paul, MN: West Pub. Co.

Foreman, S. K. and Woodruffe, H. (1991) Internal marketing: a case for building cathedrals. *Proceedings of the Annual Conference of the Marketing Education Group,* Cardiff Business School, 404–421.

George, W. R. (1990) Internal marketing and organisational behaviour: a partnership in developing customer conscious employees at every level. *Journal of Business Research* 20, 63–70.

George, W. and Gibson, B. (1991) 'Blueprinting – a tool for managing quality in service', pp. 73–91 in S. Brown, E. Gummesson, B. Edvardsson and B. Gustavsson (eds), *Service Quality – multinational and multi-disciplinary perspectives.* Lexington, KY: Lexington Books.

George, W. R. and Grönroos, C. (1990) 'Developing customer-conscious employees at every level-internal marketing' in Carole A. Congram and Margaret L. Friedman (eds), *Handbook of Services Marketing.* New York: AMACOM.

Geranmayeh, A. and Bartol, J. R. (1993) 'Corporate integrity and internal market economies' in W. E. Halal, A. Geranmayeh and J. Pourdehnad (eds), *Internal Markets: bringing the power of free enterprise inside your organization.* New York: John Wiley and Sons.

Greene, W. E. *et al.* (1994) Internal marketing: the key to external marketing success. *Journal of Services Marketing* 8(4).

Grönroos, C. (1981) 'Strategic Management and Marketing in the Service Sector.' *Swedish School of Economic and Business Administration research report.*

Grönroos, C. (1988) Internal marketing: een theorie in die praktijk toegepast. *Marketing van diensten* 4(2), 1.2.

Grönroos, C. (1990) Relationship approach to marketing in service contexts: the marketing and organisational behaviour interface. *Journal of Business Research* 20, 3–11.

Grönroos, C. (1996) Relationship marketing logic. *Asia–Australia Marketing Journal* 4(1), 7–18.

Guaspari, J. (1993) Total quality management in health care. *Hospital and Health Care Service Administration* 36(1).

Gummesson, E. (1987) Using internal marketing to create a new culture: the case of Ericsson quality. *Journal of Business and industrial marketing* 2(3), 23–28.

Hales, W. E. (1994) From hierarchy to enterprise: internal markets are the new foundation of management. *Academy of Management Executive* 8(4).

Harrison, R. and Stokes, H. (1992) *Diagnosing Organisational Culture.* San Diego, CA: Pfeiffer and Company.

Helman, D. and Payne, A. (1992) Internal marketing of a service. *Industrial Marketing of Management* 21(4).

Ingle, S. (1982) *Quality Circles Master Guide.* Englewood Cliffs, NJ: Prentice-Hall.

Johnson, R. S. (1993) *TQM: Management Process for Quality Operations.* Milwaukee, WI: ASQC Quality Press.

Kane, E. J. and Kelley, E. J. (1992) Implementing the marketing concept: linking quality, marketing and value. Working paper no. 2, CSMM, Florida Atlantic University, Florida.

Keesing, R. M. (1974) Theories of culture. *Annual Review of Anthropology* 3, 73–97.

Kilmann, R. H., Saxton, J., Serpa, R. and associate eds. (1983) *Gaining Control of the Corporate Culture.* San Francisco, CA: Jossey-Bass.

Kilmann, R. H., Saxton, M. J. and Serpa, R. (1985) 'Five key issues in understanding and changing culture' in R. H. Kilmann, M. J. Saxton and R. Serpa (eds.), *Gaining Control of the Corporate Culture.* San Francisco: Jossey Bass.

Kotler, P. (2000) *Marketing Management: the millennium edition.* London: Prentice-Hall.

Lee, H. L. and Billington, C. (1992) Managing supply chain inventory: pitfalls and opportunities. *Sloan Management Review,* Spring, 65–73.

Leonard, J. F. (1983) Can your organisation support quality circles? A practical model. *Training and Development Journal* 37(9), 667–672.

Lewis, B. R. (1996) *Customer Care in Services. Understanding Services Management.* New York: Harper and Row.

Lings, I. (1997) Internal marketing: a new approach to building in quality. Working paper (RP9706), Aston Business School, Aston University, Birmingham.

Lovelock, C. and Gummeson, E. (2004) Whither services marketing? In search of a new paradigm and fresh perspectives. *Journal of Service Research* 7(1), 20–41.

McGuire, L. (1999) *Australian Services: Marketing and Management.* South Yarra: Macmillan Education Australia Pty Ltd.

Mastenbroek, W. F. G. (1991) 'Co-operation as a critical success factor: functional quality and corporate culture' in W. F. G. Mastenbroek, *Managing for Quality in the Service Sector,* Oxford: Blackwell.

Morgan, N. A. and Piercy, N. F. (1998) Interactions between marketing and quality at the SBU level: influences and outcomes. *Academy of Marketing Science Journal* 26(3).

Morgan, N. A. (2001) Strategy and internal marketing, in M. Warner (ed.), *International Encyclopaedia of Business and Management.* London: Thomson.

Oakland, J. S. and Dotchin, J. A. (1994) Total quality management in services part 2: service quality. *International Journal of Quality and Reliability Management* 11(3), 27–42.

Ouchi, W. G. and Wilkins, A. L. (1985) Organisational culture. *Annual Review of Sociology* 11, 457–483.

Palmer, A. (2000) *Principal of Service Marketing.* 3rd edn. London: McGraw Hill.

Payne, A. (1992) Internal marketing: myth versus reality. Working paper series, Cranfield School of Management, Cranfield.

Phillips, L. W. *et al*. (1983) Product quality, cost position and business performance: a test for some hypotheses. *Journal of Marketing* 47(2), 26–43.

Phillips, N. and Brown, J. L. (1993) Analysing communication in and around organisations: a critical hermeneutic approach. *Academy of Management Journal* 36(6), 1547–1576.

Piercy N. (1995) Customer satisfaction and the internal market: marketing our customers to our employees. *Journal of Marketing Practice and Applied Marketing Science* 1(1), 22–44.

Pitt, M. *et al*. (1999) A framework for research in internal marketing and the study of service quality: some propositions. *Management Research News* 2(7).

Preston, J. B. and Steel, L. (2002) Employees, customers and internal marketing strategies. *Library Management* 23(8/9), 384–393.

Rafiq, M. and Ahmad, P. K. (1993) The scope of internal marketing: defining the boundary between marketing and human resource management. *Journal of Marketing Management* 9(3), 219–32.

Rafiq, M. and Ahmad, P. K. (2000) Advances in the internal marketing concept: definition, synthesis and extension. *The Journal of Services Marketing* 14(6).

Redding, W. C. (1972) *Communication within the organisation: an interpretive review of theory and research.* New York: Industrial Communication Council.

Robson, M. (1988) Excellence through quality. *The Journal for Quality and Participation* 11 (March), 50–54.

Saee, J. (2005) *Managing Organisations in a Global Economy: An Intercultural Perspective.* Ohio: Thomson – South Western Learning.

Sasser, W. E. and Arbeit, S. (1976) Selling job in the service sector. *Business Horizons* 19 (June), 61–65.

Schein, Edgar H. (1985) *Organizational Culture and Leadership.* San Francisco, CA: Jossey-Bass.

Schneider, B. *et al*. (1988) 'Managing climate and cultures: a future perspective' in J. Hage (ed.), *Future of Organisational.* Lexington: Lexington Books.

Sirota, D. *et al*. (1994) Breaking through the culture wall. *The Journal for Quality and Participation* 17.

Smircich, L. (1983) Concepts of culture and organization analysis. *Administrative Science Quarterly* 28.

Stull, J. B. (1974) 'Openness' in superior–subordinate communication: a quasi-experimental field study. Unpublished doctoral dissertation, Purdue University.

Ticehurst, B., Walker, G. and Johnston, R. (1991) Issues in communication management in Australian organisations. *Australian Journal of Communication* 18(3).

Townsend, P. L. and Joan, E. T. (1988) A quality beginning. *The Journal for Quality and Participation* 11 (March), 26–27.

Van, H. R. and Maanen, B. (1995) Marketing of change: the added value of internal marketing to change management. *24th EMAC Conference Proceedings,* 1243–1261.

Varey, R. J. (1995) Internal marketing: a review and some interdisciplinary research challenges. *International Journal of service Industry Management* 6(1), 40–63.

Westbrook, J. D. (1995) Organisational culture and its relationship to TQM. *Industrial Management,* January/February.

Wilkins, A. L. and Patterson, K. J. (1985) 'You can't get there from here: what will make culture-change project fail' in Ralph R. Kilman, Mary J. Saxton, S. Roy and associates (eds), *Gaining Control of the Corporate Culture.* San Francisco: Jossey-Bass.

Wilson. A. (1991) The internal marketing of services – the new surge. *Management Decision* 29(5), 4–7.

18 Effective strategies for conflict management

Managerial conflict resolution approaches across the globe

John Saee

> The natural philosophers believe that if the forces of conflicts and discord were eliminated from the universe, the heavenly bodies would stand still, and in the resulting harmony the processes of motion and generation would be brought to a dead stop.
>
> Plutarch

Introduction

Since the beginning of time, conflict has always been part and parcel of human life. Globally speaking, some cultures have praised the virtues of conflict for its capacity to drive progress and innovation in their societies, whereas others, mainly collectivist cultures, have lamented that conflict is destructive for social harmony and a cohesive community life and should, therefore, be avoided at all costs. Meanwhile, philosophers and social scientists have, in different epochs, been grappling with this complex issue of conflict. For example, philosophers, including Plutarch, Hegel and Marx, have been interested in the paradox of conflict and its role as an impetus of progress, innovation and development.

On the other hand, the noted German philosopher Hegel propounded the notion of dialectical idealism, which is predicated on the thesis that new ideas are created as a result of the inner conflict occurring within the mind. It was dialectical materialism, declared Marx, that was the impetus of change and progress in human civilisation. In other words, class conflict in society is the main engine of change, which could ultimately pave the way for a better and fairer society with unfettered opportunities and prosperity for all.

Within the domain of managerial discipline, the question arises as to how conflict is viewed by management in an organisational context and what the possible managerial strategies are in dealing with conflict. Moreover, how is conflict dealt with internationally, with particular reference to multicultural organisations?

In response to the foregoing organisational questions dealing with conflict and conflict management strategies, an attempt is made in this research paper to provide a systematic explanation and analysis of conflict and conflict management within an organisational context across cultures. However, prior to discussing how conflict is perceived and dealt with within an organisation, it is important here to examine some definitional aspects of conflict.

Conceptualisations of Conflict

Conflict occurs because of disagreements or incompatibilities between individuals, or between groups and entire organisations (63).

Conflict also results from perceived or experienced differences over essential or emotional issues.

Other scholars, including Pondy (46) and Thomas (56), identified the stages of the entire conflict process, rather than attempting a definition, which may be confined to any one stage, such as conflictful behaviour. Thomas has, for example, conceptualised the process model of conflict, in terms of the following components: antecedent conditions; thoughts and emotions; behaviour; and outcomes.

Under antecedent conditions, they represent goal incompatibility, differences in judgement, or a combination of the two, where judgements differ because of incompatible goals. Members' concerns for satisfying personal needs, achieving delegated responsibilities or obtaining scarce resources all contribute to goal conflicts. Cultures differ in the degree to which they allow goal conflicts and related differences of opinion by restricting competition among organisational members or units. For example, research studies (44, 53) have shown that Japanese and Chinese organisations are different from American organisations in this regard.

Conflict is associated with various, mostly negative, emotions, which may also be felt and expressed differently across cultures. Emotions are affected by culture due to different interpretations and appraisal of the same situation, hence, by thought processes. Also, different behavioural modes and regulative mechanisms are open to each culture for the expression of emotions (43, 35).

Traditional managerial perspective and strategies on conflict

Traditional managerial perspective suggests that all conflict is bad, and therefore it must be avoided and/or eliminated where possible. The traditional perspective views conflict as a malfunction within an organisation, which is also seen by management as a disincentive to labour's productivity and organisational life. In this type of organisation, historically at least, conflicts between workers and managers were not tolerated. If overt conflict erupted between individual workers and/or between workers and managers in some organisations, the likely outcome was to ignore conflictual situation and/or ultimately dismiss the individual worker(s) involved in a conflict with the management over certain issues.

Since the early days of management, there has been an evolution in managerial thought, which increasingly gave rise to a new appreciation of conflict and its place within the contemporary organisational life.

Contemporary managerial perspective and strategies on conflict

Within a contemporary organisation, conflict is seen as neither good nor bad, but a fact of life, which is inevitable, given the differing personalities and cultural dimensions of employees involved in a contemporary organisation. However, managers perceive that too much conflict in an organisation can divert energy and precious resources, whereas having too little conflict in an organisation can lead to apathy and lethargy amongst its employees.

The inescapable conclusions that can be drawn from the foregoing explanation are essentially two distinct points of view:

- conflict can have positive results, which would in turn stimulate creativity within the workforce. Thus, primary managerial concern should focus on the management of conflict, and not the elimination of conflict; and
- conflict is inevitable in organisations. The critical concern is not conflict itself, but how it is managed. For managerial purposes it helps to define conflict in terms of its effect.

Viewed in this way, it can spawn either functional conflict or dysfunctional conflict, as described below.

Functional conflict

Functional conflict would normally occur when the employees disagree on the best means to achieve a goal, not on the goal itself; and it typically leads the way for the selection of a better means of alternative. The end effect is that it can play an essential role in preventing group or organisational stagnation and resistance to change. Moreover, it can lead to increased awareness of problems that need to be addressed. It can also result in broader and more productive searches for solutions whilst facilitating innovation and adaptation to new solutions. Some companies deliberately encourage competition between separate teams to create innovation and improve sales performance, etc.

Finally, conflicts are constructive when they:

- bring up rather than hide issues over which there are differences;
- force individuals to be direct, and to accelerate problem solving; and
- attack issues rather than individuals (10).

Dysfunctional conflict

It occurs whenever managers perceive that a conflict hinders achievement of organisational goals. Thus, management is prone to seek to eliminate such conflict.

Generally speaking, dysfunctional conflict takes place when:

- the participants refuse to collaborate to find a solution;

- a superior is unwilling or unable to arbitrate;
- one or both of the participants refuse to accept the superior's arbitration;
- rules and dispute-resolution procedures are inadequate, ambiguous or contradictory; and
- communication is poor – the participants are unable to communicate essential information or disagree on how it should be interpreted.

On balance, a moderate level of conflict is deemed healthy by contemporary managers, as they believe that, like stress, it can enhance achievement. What managers need to be mindful of, however, is that too much or too little conflict can lead to negative and even unethical results and destructive behaviours within an organisation.

Viewed in this light, the responsibility of the manager is to decide to what extent and how much functional conflict is needed in order to create, enhance and sustain the productivity and to make sure it does not degenerate into dysfunctional conflict.

Sources and types of conflict

Conflict manifests itself in a variety of ways in an organisation, due to the presence of certain conditions. These conditions can be a number of actions and non-actions that would trigger conflict, and they may include the following:

- *Structural conflict:* occurs because of the cross-functional departmental differences over goals, time horizons, rewards, authority, status and resources. For example, there may be a clash between the research and development department and the finance department over the allocation of financial resources and time-line.
- *Intrapersonal conflict:* occurs within an individual. This can be expressed in a number of distinct ways:
- *intra-role*: this is when an employee is receiving conflicting information about his or her performance over a particular role. For example, an employee would, in recognition of their outstanding performance, receive a reward in the form of a bonus or promotion from the management. Meanwhile, the same employee may receive complaints from customers over for an alleged inability/incompetence to respond quickly to customers' needs;
- *inter-role*: this comes about as a result of pressure over the need to perform several roles by an individual employee. For example, a working mother who has to reconcile her differing roles of motherhood and career, all at the same time; and
- *person-role*: an individual finds their values clashing with the job requirements. For example, a practising Muslim employee working for a bank, where, contrary to his/her Islamic belief system, interest is charged on loans to customers.

- *Intrapersonal value conflict*: individuals experience a gap between the values they believe to be important and conflicting values held by coworkers or managers. For example, employees who hold religious values about not working on a certain day of the week, such as Friday for Islamic workers, yet their employers insist that the employees show up at work on that day, irrespective of the employee's religious values. The end-result is that it can give rise to intrapersonal conflict, which can manifest itself in a number of ways, such as tension, distress and even work behavioural difficulties, such as absenteeism, and that is ultimately a cost to the employers.
- *Cognitive dissonance*: this occurs when an individual perceives inconsistencies in their own thoughts and/or behaviours. The existence of considerable and unrecognised inconsistencies can be stressful and it may motivate an individual to reduce it: (a) by changing thought or behaviour or (b) by obtaining more information about the issue that is causing the dissonance (19).
- *Interpersonal conflict:* occurs between two or more individuals. The nature of interpersonal conflict in organisations can be emotional- or content-based and is caused by many factors, such as personality differences, values, judgements, perceptions, competencies and management styles. Cross-cultural misunderstandings based on stereotyping and prejudice can also play a role in an interpersonal conflict. The end-result would be stress for the employee(s) concerned, because of uncertainty and anxiety caused by cross-cultural misunderstandings in the workplace.
- *Interorganisational conflict:* occurs between enterprises and external stakeholders (28). It is often a result of mergers and acquisitions.

For example, Microsoft has recently been accused of monopoly by its competitors and even the US government, who later filed charges against Microsoft in the US Court for its alleged breach of anti-competitive behaviour in the marketplace.

Understanding the types and sources of conflict is seen across cultures as the first step towards its resolution.

Factors that influence perception and tolerance of conflict in different cultures

Research (42) identified a number of factors as having influential roles on human perception and tolerance levels of conflict across cultures. These include:

- industrial and occupational factors. Some industries are regarded to be more tolerant than others. For example, political system in a democratic society is more tolerant than its army in that society;
- organisational culture. Some organisational cultures tolerate and even encourage competition amongst its employees as a way of stimulating creativity and innovation, whereas other organisational cultures demand strict compliance with its organisational rules and value system by the employees;

- urgency: A military command tolerates conflict amongst its members less in time of war than during peacetime.
- personal interest and the threat that conflict represents;
- individual psychology. It is a known psychological fact that some personalities are more tolerant of conflict than others; and
- culture. This is an important indicator of how conflict is tolerated in different countries.

The meaning of conflict within cross-cultural dimensions

Culture is pivotal in shaping people's perceptions, attitudes and appraisals of conflict and its management (e.g. Jandt and Pedersen (31); Leung and Tjosvold (40); Ting-Toomey (59). According to Hofstede's (22) influential research, East Asian societies are classified as collectivist, whereas those from the West, including Australia, USA and Great Britain, are associated with individualism. The well-documented individualist-collectivist dimension (e.g. Hofstede (24); Hui (26) and Triandis (62)) describes those in individualist cultures as focusing more on individual goals, needs and rights than on community concerns. By contrast, those from collectivist cultures value in-group goals and concerns, with priority given to obligations and responsibilities to the group. Collectivist societies in East Asia including people of Chinese ethnicity are usually characterised by a tendency to avoid conflict (e.g. Chen (5); Chi-Ching (6); Gao (14); Hwang (27); Leung (38); Leung, Koch and Lu (41). Conflict avoidance behaviour is adopted in those Chinese societies where many traditional Chinese values such as thrift, respect for authority, building trust and community harmony are still pervasive (Chen (5); Chi-Ching (6)). Conflict avoidance leads to passivity and lack of skills in persuasion and communication (Chi-Ching (6)) or to communication behaviour that promotes interrelations rather than conveying opposing opinion or information (Gao (14)). For the Chinese, in situations where affective relationship and instrumental reciprocity (*guanxi*) are salient (Hwang (27)), and where the influence efface in social interactions leads to fear of shame or retaliation (20), the value of harmony is emphasised over candid speech acts. More pragmatically, Leung, Koch and Lu (41) have proposed that people in collectivist societies, including Chinese societies, are motivated by harmony that is more instrumentally inspired rather than as a moral or traditional value, in order to achieve their goals by avoiding the disintegration of a relationship that is crucial for their well-being (3).

Managerial strategies on conflict across cultural frontiers

Conflict is a fact of organisational life in the contemporary global economy, but what is important to note is that the ways in which conflict is appreciated and handled by management varies across cultures. Hofstede (23, 24), in studying cultural differences, considered four dimensions that relate to fundamental values of any: individualism versus collectivism; large power distance versus small power distance; high versus low uncertainty avoidance; and masculine versus feminine cultures. Understanding of these cultural dimensions can help us to analyse the style of conflict management in different countries.

In a collectivist culture representing most Asian countries, harmony amongst its members is maintained and direct confrontation is avoided, and this is also evident amongst workers and managers in Asian enterprises. Individualist culture, on the other hand, regards individual liberty and freedom of expression as of paramount importance and maintains that an honest person should speak one's mind and, thus, confront the situation head-on.

Meanwhile, large power distance presupposes that latent conflict between ranks is normal, and therefore conflict is always expected. As such, peers are reluctant to trust each other. On the contrary, small power distance values harmony between the powerful and powerless and, thus, peers are willing to cooperate with each other.

In high uncertainty avoidance culture, conflict in an organisation is considered to be highly undesirable. It is emotionally disapproved of and readiness to compromise with opponents is low. In low uncertainty avoidance culture, though, conflict in an organisation is considered to be natural, and competition between employees can be fair and right. Also, there is a far greater degree of readiness to compromise with opponents.

Masculine culture, such as Anglo-Celtic culture, encourages competition and, therefore, conflicts are resolved by fighting them out, whereas a feminine culture, such as in Scandinavia, places a high premium on quality of life for the community and tends to resolve conflicts by means of compromise and negotiation.

Concept of face and managerial strategies in different cultures

Conflict is *face*-related in that the face appears to be a predictor of what conflict strategies are being used. Research (48) exploring this issue was conducted across five countries – USA, Japan, South Korea, China and Taiwan.

What the research discovered was that the concept of face across these cultures was at variance. For example, Americans' concept of face was based on self-face preservation and maintenance. Americans tend to equate saving their own face, that is, pride, reputation, credibility and self-respect. For them, face is more individualistic. Thus, Americans focus on self-face issues. This meant that Americans raised in an individualist culture were primarily motivated to preserve their self-face at the expense of their opponents, and therefore they are prone to adopt a more confrontational conflict strategy with their opponents. This implied a strong win-lose orientation.

On the other hand, Asians understand the notion of face to be related to honour, claimed self-image and the family/organisation. For them, there is an awareness of relational dynamics in the concept of face saving.

Individuals raised in a collectivist culture are thus motivated by the mutual preservation of face and therefore they are adopting a more face-smoothing strategy or a mutual face preservation strategy with their opponents. Thus, conflict avoidance is common amongst Asian managers.

Research (37) showed that strategies used to protect own's face in a collectivist culture include:

- asking someone to else to transmit a message (mediated communication);
- talking to a third person in the intended hearer's presence (refracted communication);
- acting as if a delegate – 'pretending' to be a messenger from a third person;
- not expressing wishes explicitly, but expecting the other person to understand (anticipatory communication); and
- corresponding by letter, so avoiding meeting face to face.

Generally speaking, confrontation occurs in a collectivist culture only when it carries little risk of losing face or the other side is a powerless outsider, and an open disagreement does not threaten the loss of face between the parties involved in a conflict.

In conflict-avoiding cultures, such as Asian cultures, the manager is expected to show strength and authority to deal with conflict and to impose his or her will. If the threat of face loss is high, conflict avoidance strategy may be chosen as an option.

It is important here to note that people from collectivist cultures, such as Chinese and Korean, tend to be aggressive and confrontational only when the other party to the conflict is a member of an outgroup (38, 32).

On the other hand, people from individualist cultures are more likely to use integrating, compromising and obliging conflict-resolution styles when dealing with members of an outgroup. One possible explanation is that individualist culture has a high concern with the task accomplishment that overrides national cultural predilections.

Notable is the fact that cultural disapproval of conflict in a collectivist society, such as Asian society, does not mean that conflicts do not take place. Conflict is contextually conveyed in a different manner across cultures. Therefore, an international manager has to be able to spot expressions of disagreement by members of the other culture and recognise that conflict has emerged, and to avoid communicating messages that can be interpreted as confrontational by the other culture. For example, in collectivist cultures with large power distance and high uncertainty avoidance expression of disagreement with a superior is avoided. Any action that may cause the superior to lose face is avoided. Disagreement will be communicated non-verbally rather than verbally. Therefore, the manager has to restrict any opportunities for the argument and competition among workforce by making clear demands that do not require clarification and will not lead the subordinate to make a mistake or to conflict with others.

Managerial conflict resolution approaches

The main goals of conflict management in modern organisations are principles of conflict mediation manifestly expressed in the following ways:

- to prevent negative (dysfunctional) conflict from occurring in an organisation;
- to encourage healthy conflict as a way of stimulating innovation and creativity in an enterprise; and
- to minimise and/or eliminate the dysfunctional conflict within an organisation, as it is seen to be destructive to the workings of an efficient organisation.

A model of conflict management styles (2, 33, 54) identifies the following five conflict-handling styles that can be adopted by management. The styles for handling conflict were differentiated on two basic dimensions – the concern for self and the concern for others:

- the *integrating style* involves high concern for self as well as the other party involved in the conflict. It is concerned with collaboration between parties;
- the *obliging style* involves low concern for self and high concern for others. It involves smoothing over differences and focusing on areas of agreement;
- the *dominating style* involves a high concern for self and a low concern for the other party involved in the conflict. It has been described as forcing one's viewpoint at the expense of others;
- the *avoiding style* is associated with low concern for self as well as the other party. It has been associated with withdrawing from the conflict situation; and
- the *compromising style* involves moderate concern for self as well as the party involved in the conflict. It is associated with give-and-take or sharing the search for a middle-ground solution.

A number of studies have since been conducted to explore the use of different interpersonal conflict-handling styles (7, 48, 49, 50, 51, 11). In general, they maintain that management tends to use collaboration more often than other styles, whereas forcing and avoidance tend to be associated with decreases in the constructive use of conflict, negative feelings from others, and unfavorable self-evaluations of performance and abilities. The effects of accommodation and compromise tend to be mixed. Research (34) showed that managers in Turkey and Jordan demonstrated a resemblance to each other and to their American counterparts in reporting a clear preference for the collaborative style in handling conflicts. Some evidence that national culture influences the style of handling interpersonal conflict was demonstrated by Ting-Toomey *et al.* (58). The results of a field study conducted in five countries indicated that American respondents reported greater use of the dominating style than Japanese or Korean respondents. In addition, the Chinese and Taiwanese respondents reported greater use of the obliging and avoiding styles than the American respondents.

Mediating conflict across cultural frontiers

In a collectivist culture, such as Asian culture, where conflict is seen as undesirable and potentially face damaging, involvement of a third party is seen as a favourable option. A neutral third party does not impose the decision, and parties decide for themselves; however, it creates a better opportunity for the parties involved in a conflict to achieve a harmonious win–win solution. This method of handling conflict is becoming increasingly popular in Western countries.

According to Fisher and Ury (13), management ought to consider principles of conflict mediation strategies while dealing with conflict by:

- separating the people from the problem;
- focusing on interests, not on positions;
- insisting on objective criteria (and never yielding to pressure); and
- inventing options for mutual gain.

Concluding remarks

In this chapter, the notion of conflict was discussed in different cultures with important implications for multicultural and international organisations. Various sources of conflict were examined. Managerial strategies dealing with conflict in different cultures were discussed. The phenomenon of mediation and its role in different cultures were explained, which has considerable implications for global management.

Finally, it was argued that multicultural organisations, irrespective of their geographical locations, must minimise interpersonal and intergroup conflict related to group/cultural identity and instead should promote a better understanding of cultural differences prevalent in their organisations. More importantly, international managers need to provide a systematic training programme for their respective culturally diverse workforce that focuses on identifying stereotypes whilst eliminating stereotypes and inaccurate assumptions about outgroup members representing minority cultures within their respective workplace.

Bibliography

1   Ben-Ari, E., Moeran, B. and Valentine, J. (eds) (1990) *Unwrapping Japan: society and culture in anthropological perspective.* Manchester: Manchester University Press.

2   Blake, R. R. and Mouton, J. S. (1964) *The Managerial Grid.* Houston, TX: Gulf.

3   Brew, F. P. and Cairns, D. R. (2004) Styles of managing interpersonal workplace conflict in relation to status and face concern: a study with Anglos and Chinese. *International Journal of Conflict management* 15(1), 27–56.

4   Brislin, R. (1993) *Understanding Culture's Influence on Behavior.* Fort Worth: Harcourt Brace.

5   Chen, G. M. (2001) 'Towards transcultural understanding: a harmony theory of Chinese communication', pp. 55–70 in V. H. Milhouse, M. K. Asante and P. O.

Nwosu (eds), *Transculture: interdisciplinary perspectives on cross-cultural relations.* Thousand Oaks, CA: Sage.

6   Chi-Ching, E. Y. (1998) 'Social-cultural context of perceptions and approaches to conflict: the case for Singapore', pp. 123–145 in K. Leung and D. Tjosvold (eds), *Conflict Management in the Asia Pacific: assumptions and approaches in diverse cultures.* Singapore: Wiley.

7   Cosier, R. A. and Ruble, T. L. (1981) Research on conflict handling behavior: an experimental approach. *Academy of Management Journal* 24, 816–831.

8   Cox, T. and Blake, S. (1991) Managing cultural diversity: implications for organizational competitiveness. *Academy of Management Executive* 5(3), 45–56.

9   Deutsch, M. (1973) *The Resolution of Conflict.* New Haven, CT: Yale University Press.

10 Dunford, W. D. (1992) *Organizational Behaviour.* Reading, MA: Addison-Wesley.

11 Elsayed-Ekhouly, S. M. and Buda, R. (1996) Organizational conflict: a comparative analysis of conflict styles across cultures. *International Journal of Conflict Management* 7(1), 71–88.

12 Fatehi, K. (1996) *International Management: a cross culture and functional perspective.* New Jersey: Prentice Hall.

13 Fisher, R. and Ury, W. (1981) *Getting to Yes.* New York: Penguin.

14 Gao, G. (1998) 'Don't take my word for it.' — Understanding Chinese speaking practices. *International Journal of Intercultural Relations* 22, 163–186.

15 Guirdham, M. (1999) *Communicating Across Cultures.* London: Macmillan Business.

16 Gulbro, R. and Herbig, P. (1995) Differences in cross-cultural negotiation behavior between manufacturers and service-oriented firms. *Journal of Professional Services Marketing* 13, 23–29.

17 Hellriegel, D., Jackson S. E, and Slocum J. W. (1999) *Management.* 8th edn. Ohio: ITP Publishing.

18 Hellriegel, D., Slocum, J. and Woodman, R. W. (1995) *Organizational Behavior.* 7th edn. New York: West Publishing House company.

19 Hellriegel, D. and Slocum, J. (1996) *Management.* 7th edn. Cincinnati, OH: South Western College Publishing.

20 Ho, D. Y. (1976) On the concept of face. *American Journal of Sociology* 81, 867–884.

21 Hofstede, G. and Bond, M. H. (1984) Hofstede's culture dimensions: an independent validation using Rokeach's value survey. *Journal of Cross-Cultural Psychology* 15, 417–433.

22 Hofstede, G. (1980) Culture's consequences: international differences in work-related values. Beverly Hills, CA: Sage.

23 Hofstede, G. (1984) *Culture's consequences: international differences in work-related values.* Beverly Hills, CA: Sage.

24 Hofstede, G. (1991) *Cultures and organizations: software of the mind.* London: McGraw Hill.

25 Hofstede, G. (1995) 'The business of international business is culture', in T. Jackson (ed.), *Cross-cultural Management.* Oxford: Butterworth-Heinemann.

26 Hui, C. H. (1988) Measurement of individualism-collectivism. *Journal of Research in Personality* 22, 17–36.

27 Hwang, K. (1997–1998) Guanxi and mientze: conflict resolution in Chinese society. *Intercultural Communication Studies* 7(1), 17–42.

28   Ivancevich, J., Olekans, M. and Matteson, M. (1997) *Organizational Behavior and Management.* Sydney: McGraw Hill.

29   Jackson, T. (1993) *Organizational Behavior in International Management.* London: Butterworth-Heinemann.

30   Jackson, T. (1995) *Cross-cultural Management.* London: Butterworth-Heinemann.

31   Jandt, F. E. and Pedersen, P. B. (1996) *Constructive Conflict Management: AsiaPacific cases.* Thousand Oaks: Sage.

32   Khoo, G. P. S. (1994) The role of assumptions in intercultural research and consulting: examining an interplay of culture and conflict at work. Paper presented at Pacific Region Forum on Business and Management Communication, Simon Fraser University at Harbour Centre, 10 November 1994.

33   Kilmann, R. H. and Thomas, K. W. (1975) Interpersonal conflict-handling behavior as a reflection of Jungian personality dimensions. *Psychological Reports* 37, 971–980.

34   Kozan, M. K. (1989) Cultural influences on styles of handling interpersonal conflicts: comparisons among Jordanian, Turkish, and U.S. managers. *Human Relations* 42, 787–789.

35   Kozan, M. K. (1997) Culture and conflict management: a theoretical framework. *International Journal of Conflict* 8(4), 338–360.

36   Laurent, A. (1983) The cultural diversity of Western conceptions of management. *International Studies of Management and Organization* 13(1–2), 75–96.

37   Lebra T. (1971) The social mechanism of guilt and shame: the Japanese case. *Anthropological Quarterly* 44(4), 241–55.

38   Leung, K. (1988) Some determinants of conflict avoidance. *Journal of Cross-cultural Psychology* 19(1), 125–136.

39   Leung, K. (1997) 'Negotiation and reward across cultures', pp. 640–675 in P. C. Barley and M. Erez (eds), *New Perspectives on International Industrial/Organizational Psychology.* San Francisco: New Lexington Press.

40   Leung, K. and Tjosvold, D. (1998) *Conflict Management in the Asia Pacific: assumptions and approaches in diverse cultures.* Singapore: Wiley.

41   Leung, K., Koch, P. M. and Lu, L. (2002) A dualistic model of harmony and its implications for conflict management in Asia. *Asia Pacific Journal of Management* 19, 201–220.

42   Mead, R. (2000) *International Management: cross-cultural dimensions.* 2nd edn. Cambridge, MA: Blackwell.

43   Mesquite, B. and Frijda, N. H. (1992) Cultural variations in emotions: a review. *Psychological Bulletin* 112, 179–204.

44   Moran, R. T., Allen, J., Wichman, R., Ando, T. and Sasano, M. (1994) 'Japan', pp. 33–52 in M. A. Rahim and A. A. Blum (eds), *Global Perspectives on Organizational Conflict.* Westport, CT: Praeger.

45   Phatak, A. V. (1997) *International Management: concepts and cases.* Cincinnati, OH: South-Western College Publishing.

46   Pondy, L. R. (1967) Organizational conflict: concepts and models. *Administrative Science Quarterly* 12, 296–320.

47   Rahim, M. A. (1983) A measure of styles of handling interpersonal conflict. *Academy of Management Journal* 26, 368–376.

48   Rahim, M. A. (1985) A strategy of managing conflict in complex organizations. *Human Relations* 38, 81–89.

49   Rahim, M. A. (1986) Referent role and styles of handling interpersonal conflict. *Journal of Social Psychology* 125, 79–86.

50   Rahim, M. A. and Blum, A. A. (eds) (1994) *Global Perspectives on Organizational Conflict.* Westport, CT: Praeger.

51   Rahim, M. A. and Magner, N. R. (1995) Confirmatory factor analysis of the styles of handling interpersonal conflict: first order factor model and its invariance across. *Journal of Applied Psychology* 80(1), 122–132.

52   Redding, G. (1995) *International Cultural Differences.* Aldershot: Dartmouth Publishing.

53   Redding, S. G., Norman, A. and Schlander, A. (1994) 'The nature of individual attachment to the organization: a review of East Asian variations' in H. C. Triandis, M. D. Dunnette and L. M. Hough (eds), *Handbook of Industrial and Organizational Psychology.* 2nd edn. Palo Alto, CA: Consulting Psychologists Press.

54   Saee, J. (2005) *Managing Organizations in a Global Economy: an intercultural perspective.* Mason, OH: South Western Thomson Learning.

55   Saee, J. and Saunders, S. (2000) Intercultural communication competence and managerial functions within the Australian hospitality industry. *Australian Journal of Communication* 27(1), 111–129.

56   Thomas, K. W. (1992) 'Conflict and negotiation processes in organizations', pp. 651–717 in M. Dunette (ed), *Handbook of Industrial and Organizational Psychology,* 2nd edn. Palo Alto, CA: Consulting Psychologists Press, 3.

57   Thomas, R. R. (1994) 'From affirmative action to affirming diversity', in R. R. Thomas (ed.), *Differences that Work: organizational excellence through diversity.* Boston: Harvard Business Review Book.

58   Ting-Toomey, S. and Korzenny, F. (1991) *Cross-cultural Interpersonal Communications.* Newbury Park: Sage.

59   Ting-Toomey, S. (1985) 'Toward a theory of conflict and culture', pp. 71–85 in W. B. Gudykunst, L. P. Stewart and S. Ting-Toomey (eds), *Communication Culture and Organizational Processes.* Beverly Hills, CA: Sage.

60   Ting-Toomey, S. (1988) 'Intercultural conflict styles: a face-negotiation theory' in Kim and Gudykunst (eds), *Theories of Cross-cultural Communication.* Newbury Park: Sage.

61   Ting-Toomey, S. *et al.* (1991) Culture, face maintenance, and styles of handling interpersonal conflict: a study in five cultures. *The International Journal of Conflict Management* 2, 275–296.

62   Triandis, H. C. (1995) *Individualism and Collectivism.* Boulder, CO: Westview Press.

63   Weiss, J. (1996) *Organizational Behavior and Change: managing diversity, cross-cultural dynamics, and ethics.* Minneapolis, MN: West Publishing Company.

19 Managing the potential conflict with an external advisor within the acquisition process

Angeloantonio Russo and Francesco Perrini

Theory, research model and hypotheses

Agency theory and transaction cost economics

Bidding and target firms invocating an external intervention to the extent of protecting their interests face the need for managing a new relationship with their advisor. It is easy to comprehend that such a relationship generates what scholars interested in the theory of the firm generally call agency problems (Berle and Means, 1932; Jensen and Meckling, 1976; for a complete review on agency theory see Eisenhardt, 1989). Acquiring and acquired companies usually have divergent interests that can be considered as the cause of the difficulties related to the acquisition process. Moreover, both the bidding and target firms can hold opposite concerns strictly depending on their own acquisitive objectives.

Considering the acquisition as a two-way exchange of resources and competences associated with both the acquiring and target firms, a twofold consideration can be suggested. First, the bidding firm will intend to pay the lowest price compared with the target value; second, the target will try to earn as much as possible from the transaction, considering that it will probably lose part of the control on its main resources and competences after the acquisition, as well as that it is probably trying to survive a critical condition before the acquisition. Of course, bidding and target firms implicitly show their opposite interests related to the acquisition, and hiring an external advisor might represent an opportunity for sidestepping those problems for both the involved firms.

On the other hand, it is crucial that new potential divergences will come out that are the conflict of interest between the bidding firm and its advisor, as well as between the target firm and its advisor. In particular, prior research has emphasised the agency problem associated with the acquiring side of the deal. This is because the bidding firm's goal of minimising the premiums paid conflicts with their advisor's objective of maximising fees for consulting services (Kesner *et al.*, 1994). Opposite logic can be easily suggested with reference to the target side of the acquisition. Kesner and her colleagues (1994), in fact, found a positive relationship between premium and compensation for investment bankers of both target and bidder firms. This result indicates alignment between the goals of the targets and their representatives, but suggests misalignment, and hence conflict of interest, with reference to the bidders. Given the above considerations, the agency theory of the firm (Berle and Means, 1932; Jensen and Meckling, 1976) provides the theoretical base which scholars as well as practitioners might focus on in order to untangle the relation between the external advisory activity for the acquisition process and the acquisition success, that is to comprehend whether or not the external advisors might be useful for the transaction (Hunter and Walker, 1990).

Agency theory suggests only a set of insights through which the relationship between bidding and target firms and their advisors might be investigated and explained. It is also important to note that prior research also referred to alternative perspectives emphasising crucial aspects of the above relationship. In particular, the transaction cost economics (Coase, 1937; Williamson, 1975) suggests the existence of asymmetric information among the actors competing for a specific economic advantage. Transferring this issue to the acquisitions allows us to identify other antecedents of the above relationship between those companies involved in the acquisition process and their advisors. Moreover, the transaction cost economics can provide alternative explanations to the mentioned agency problem among those actors. Prior research found that transaction costs are the main determinants of investment banking choice (Servaes and Zenner, 1996) whereas investment banks represent one of the possible advisors bidding and target firms can eventually appeal to. In particular, following a transaction cost approach Servaes and Zenner (1996) hypothesised that investment banks can analyse acquisitions at a lower cost than other firms. This means advisors can be generally considered able to reduce the asymmetric information between the bidding and target firms. By a different point of view, they might be able to provide their client with interesting and useful information. This can be true if we don't forget the specific self-interest leading the advisor to its own objective generally related to the conclusion of the acquisition at the higher possible price (McLaughlin, 1990).

What we would underline in the present study is that a combination of agency theory and transaction cost perspective can provide a theoretical base upon which scholars and researchers can propose a new comprehension of the acquisition process. As briefly described above, agency theory and transaction cost economics highlight interesting research questions and insights which, if deepened and answered, might contribute to afford new pieces of knowledge strictly related to the acquisition process, and to the reasons of its success or failure. In particular, prior research referring to agency theory and transaction cost economics emphasised the antecedents of the relationship between bidding and target firms and their advisors that means researchers tried to comprehend why and when such a linkage has reasons to be made. For instance, firms choose advisors when the acquisitions are more complex, when they have less prior acquisition experience, and when the acquisition involves the takeover of another company. Furthermore, acquiring firms having low insider ownership are more willing to hire an advisor, as well as those firms which are completing unrelated acquisitions or which are acquiring firms operating in several industries (Servaes and Zenner, 1996).

This chapter will deepen the nature of the relation between the acquiring and target firms and their advisor, trying to emphasise the managerial implications of such a relation. In particular, as financial research has particularly focused the attention on this phase of the acquisition process, strategic management research has rarely taken into account the role an external advisor can play in managing or intervening in the acquisition process (Hayward, 2002 and 2003). Controlling for the presence of an external advisor within the acquisition process, Hayward (2002) found a negative influence of the presence of an external advisor on the acquisition performance. He suggested that this result might reflect a self-selection bias: less capable firms seek investment bank help, or in general the help of an external advisor, and these advisors are not able to overcome these firms' poor acquiring skill. He also argued, following other financial research (Kesner *et al.*, 1994), that banks face some incentive to recommend offers that are highly priced to complete deals and this results in higher premiums and lower acquisition performance. Successively, Hayward (2003) found that relative to cash-financed acquisitions, stock-financed acquisitions more intensively apply investment banks' expertise. This means that acquiring firms generally hire external advisors, that is investment banks, when the acquisition is financed through stock instead of cash. What is important to note at this point is that both strategic management and financial literature generally took into account just the presence of an external advisor; furthermore, when a specific category of advisor has been considered in the analysis most of the time it was a financial advisor generally represented by an investment bank. This point is crucial for the aim of our analysis through which we would investigate whether different categories of external advisors might have a different influence on the acquisition performance. In other words, not only the presence of a financial advisor, typically investment banks, but also the hiring of equity advisors, legal advisors, or a combination of those and other different categories might determinate the success or failure of the acquisition. Of course, we would investigate the hypotheses in which both the acquiring and target firms, as well as just the former or the latter might hire an external advisor. Our research model is presented in Figure 19.1.

Hypotheses of the study

Given the above different agency problems related to the bidding side of the acquisition relative to the target side of the acquisition (Kesner *et al.*, 1994), we argue that acquiring firms which diversify the type of external advisor might reduce the probability of agency problems. This means that different categories of advisors might have a different impact on the acquisition performance. Hence, the following two hypotheses are proposed:

> Hypothesis 1: Acquiring firms diversifying the type of external advisor gain above-normal economic performance of the acquisition.

> Hypothesis 2: Acquiring firms diversifying the type of external advisor obtain a premium savings of the acquisition.

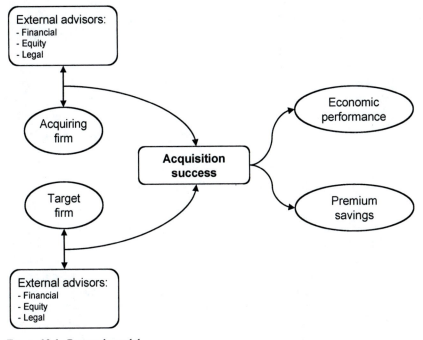

Figure 19.1   Research model

On the other hand, target firms can benefit from the similarity in terms of interests with their advisors, usually consisting in the maximisation of the premium paid for the acquisition. Therefore, the absence of agency theoretical problems between the target firms and their advisors can be transferred to the possibility of increasing the acquisition performance. Furthermore, the acquisition performance might also be related to the different categories of advisors the target firm can hire. Hence, the following hypotheses:

Hypothesis 3: Target firms diversifying the type of external advisor gain above-normal economic performance of the acquisition.

Hypothesis 4: Target firms diversifying the type of external advisor obtain a premium savings of the acquisition.

Methodology

In order to test the hypotheses of this study, an OLS regression model has been used. Alternative models have been implemented aiming to investigate the acquisition success by several points of view. First, the control variables have been entered in the equation, then the predictors. Each model considered one of the two dependent variables analysed. We based the analysis on a sample of 77 Italian acquisitions completed in the period since 1998 throughout 2002.

The acquisition success has been computed through two different measures. Using alternative measures of the acquisition performance has been widely suggested by prior research (Bergh, 1995; Hoskisson *et al.*, 1994; King *et al.*, 2004) with the extent to broadly explain how acquisitions success can be described. First, we measured the economic performance of the acquisition considering the *return on assets* of the acquiring firm. Second, we computed an alternative measure of the acquisition success that we called *premium savings* of the acquisition (Russo, 2004; Russo and Perrini, 2004).

The dependent variables

The return on assets of the acquisition. In order to investigate the economic performance of the acquisition, the return on assets of the acquiring companies has been taken into account. A variable called ROA has been computed throughout a five-year period; this period is usually considered long enough to the extent to which it provides information about the post-acquisition effects (Datta and Grant, 1990). Then, the average return on assets has been computed. Data about the simple accounting measure of the economic performance of the acquisition have been collected from the *AIDA* database for the industrial and commercial companies, and from *BANKSCOPE* database for the acquiring and acquired companies.

The premium savings of the acquisition. Looking at how expensive an acquisition could be has always been considered a crucial issue by both scholars and practitioners. Little effort has been done to the extent to investigate the implications of paying the right price for the right acquisition. On this matter, prior research has generally suggested the role of the premium assessment on the overall acquisition success (Barney, 1988 and 2002; Bruton *et al.*, 1994; Datta *et al.*, 1992; Harrison *et al.*, 1991 and 1993; Hitt *et al.*, 1990 and 1998; Jemison and Sitkin, 1986; Lubatkin, 1983).

In order to explore the relationship between the price the acquiring companies pay for the target and the acquisition success, we created a new variable called premium savings (PRS) of the acquisition.

Premium savings has been computed as the difference between the deal value of the acquisition and the book value of the assets being acquired. Furthermore, we preferred to consider a relative measure of this difference, whereas it has been divided again by the book value of the assets being acquired. For all these measures the logarithm has been considered in order to reduce the variance within the specific interval. Information about the deal value of the acquisitions was collected from Zephyr database. Data about the book value of the total assets of the target firms were collected from the AIDA database for the industrial and commercial firms, and from BANKSCOPE database for the acquired banks included in the sample.

The predictors

The bidder and target's external advisor. This study analysed the relationship between the influence an external advisor might have on the acquisition success. Both the bidder and target companies' external advisors have been considered in this study, aiming to deepen whether the presence of an external advisor and especially the nature of an external advisor might have implications on the acquisition process.

Two category variables have been used to measure the nature of an external advisor: *bidder external advisor (BEA)* and *target external advisor (TEA)*. Considering our sample, we identified all the categories of advisor supporting the bidder and target companies' acquisition process. In particular, seven different categories and combinations[1] have been taken into account: financial advisor, equity advisor, legal advisor, equity and financial advisor, equity and legal advisor, financial and legal advisor, and financial and transaction advisor. Therefore, the variables bidder external advisor and target external advisor were coded 0 if no one of the above categories was in each operation; otherwise, we built a scale in which each category was coded as follows: 1, financial advisor; 2, equity advisor; 3, legal advisor; 4, equity and financial advisor; 5, equity and legal advisor; 6, financial and legal advisor; and 7, financial and transaction advisor. The logic of this scale was not to give more importance to one instead of other categories, but to find a statistically significant relationship between the performance of the acquisitions and the different advisor categories. Information about the advisor categories was collected from Zephyr database, which provides information about how many and what kinds of advisors are supporting each operation.

The control variables

Looking at prior strategic management research on the acquisition process, several control variables have been included in the analysis. Typical control variables included in this study were the *relatedness (REL)* of the acquisition (Haleblian and Finkelstein, 1999; Hayward, 2002; Hoskisson and Johnson, 1992; Morck *et al.*, 1990), the *relative size (RSIZ)* of the involved firms (Bergh, 2001), and the *previous acquisition experience (PAE)* of the acquiring company (Bergh, 2001; Haunschild, 1993; Kesner *et al.*, 1994). Moreover, we decided to control for other factors that might have some influence on the acquisition success and which were not often investigated by prior research. In particular, we considered the *percentage acquired (DTP)* (Fowler and Schmidt, 1989), the *deal value (DVA)* of the acquisition (Kesner *et al.*, 1994), and the *survival (SUR)* of the acquisition.

Results

Table 19.1 reports descriptive statistics and correlations for the variables. The strongest correlates with the return on assets are the presence of an external advisor for the bidding firm ($r = 0.233$) and with the premium savings of the acquisition

Table 19.1 Mean, standard deviation and correlations

	Mean	SD	DTP	DVA	REL	RSIZ	PAE	SUR	TEA	BEA	PRS
1 Percentage acquired	0.51	0.349									
2 Deal value	17.28	2.508	0.291[a]								
3 Relatedness	0.23	0.426	0.229[a]	0.319[b]							
4 Relative size	1.75	1.294	0.098	-0.423[b]	-0.002						
5 Previous acquisition experience	5.32	4.569	0.001	0.043	-0.141	-0.086					
6 Survival	1.91	1.310	-0.184	-0.027	-0.268[a]	-0.008	0.012				
7 Target external advisor	0.43	1.093	0.009	0.335[b]	-0.105	-0.157	-0.018	0.037			
8 Bidder external advisor	1.10	1.586	0.007	0.324[b]	0.212	-0.319[b]	0.313[b]	0.125	0.369**		
9 Premium savings	-0.08	0.090	0.375[b]	0.227[a]	-0.130	0.099	-0.040	0.013	0.080	0.015	
10 ROA	1.90	6.473	-0.329	-0.050	-0.039	-0.214	0.065	0.180	0.042	0.233*	-0.270*

Notes
a $P<0.05$
b $P<0.01$, $n=77$

($r=-0.270$). In particular, the second correlation shows that acquiring firms with an increasing return on assets are those who bought more valuable target firms, or at least those who paid the least for the higher value of the target. Each of these correlations is statistically significant at the $P<0.05$ level. The strongest correlates with the premium savings of the acquisition are the percentage acquired ($r=0.375$), which is statistically significant at the $P<0.01$ level, and with the deal value ($r=0.227$), which is statistically significant at the $P<0.05$ level.

The correlation matrix also shows other consistent results. The deal value of the acquisition is statistically related to the presence of an external advisor for both the bidder and target firms (respectively $r=0.324$ and $r=0.335$) at the $P<0.01$ level. This result suggests that acquisitions are completed at a higher price if an external advisor of the bidding as well as the target firms is supporting the deal. Paying a higher price when the target firm receives its advisor's support is a logical consequence of the acquisition bargaining. On the other hand, this correlation reveals the agency problem occurring between the acquiring firm and its advisor; it can happen that the latter should be interested in reaching the conclusion of the acquisition at the higher price because so often its remuneration is linked to the price of the acquisition. The deal value is also positively ($r=0.319$) and significantly ($P<0.01$) related to the relatedness of the acquisition. This means managers are more willing to spend more money for target firms operating in the same industry or market, being those firms more similar to their firm in terms of managed resources and competences. Finally, correlations show that those acquiring firms supported by an external advisor prefer to acquire different sized target firms ($r=-0.319$, $P<0.01$). Furthermore, an external advisor supports the acquiring firms when those have a consistent previous acquisition experience ($r=0.313$, $P<0.01$), and also when the target firm is advised by an external advisor ($r=0.369$, $P<0.01$).

Results of hypothesis tests

Table 19.2 provides information about the test for hypotheses related to the economic performance of the acquisition. Table 19.2 includes three different models. In each of those first the control variables have been considered, then the predictors. This criterion has been used also for the second dependent variable, the premium savings of the acquisition (see Table 19.3).

Hypothesis 1 links the different categories of external advisor for the acquiring firm to the economic performance of the acquisition. Results reported in Table 19.2 show the bidder external advisor is statistically significant ($P<0.05$) and positively related ($r=0.255$) to the return on assets of the acquiring firm. Therefore, this result supports Hypothesis 1.

Hypothesis 3 suggests a positive relationship between the different categories of external advisor for the target firm and the economic performance of the acquisition. Results presented in Table 19.2 do not support Hypothesis 3. The target external advisor is positively related to the return on assets of the acquiring firms ($r=0.057$) but statistically not significant.

Table 19.2 Coefficients for the dependent variable: ROA

		Model 1	Model 2	Model 3
1	Percentage acquired	-0.276[a]	-0.275[a]	-0.272[a]
2	Deal value	-0.094	-0.180	-0.120
3	Relatedness	0.104	0.172	0.118
4	Relative size	-0.220[b]	-0.180	-0.222[b]
5	Previous acquisition experience	0.063	0.000	0.067
6	Survival	0.151	0.137	0.153
7	Target external advisor			0.057
8	Bidder external advisor		0.255[a]	
	R^2	0.170	0.216	0.173
	Adjusted R^2	0.099	0.136	0.089
	F	2.393	2.713	2.061
	$P<$	0.037	0.015	0.60

Notes
a $P<0.05$
b $P<0.10$

Table 19.3 Coefficients for the dependent variable: PRS

		Model 4	Model 5	Model 6
1	Percentage acquired	0.338[a]	0.338[a]	0.335[a]
2	Deal value	0.315[b]	0.349[b]	0.333[b]
3	Relatedness	-0.319[a]	-0.346[a]	-0.329[a]
4	Relative size	0.192	0.176	0.193
5	Previous acquisition experience	-0.082	0.057	-0.085
6	Survival	0.001	0.006	-0.001
7	Target external advisor			0.040
8	Bidder external advisor		-0.100	
	R^2	0.262	0.269	0.263
	Adjusted R^2	0.199	0.195	0.188
	F	4.138	3.625	3.521
	$P<$	0.001	0.002	0.003

Notes
a $P<0.01$
b $P<0.05$

Table 19.3 presents information about the test for hypotheses related to the premium savings of the acquisition. Hypothesis 2 states that acquiring firms diversifying the type of external advisor obtain a premium savings of the acquisition. Results presented in Table 19.3 does not support our hypothesis. Even if the bidder external advisor is negatively related ($r=-0.100$) to the premium savings of the acquisition, the coefficient is statistically not significant.

Hypothesis 4 suggests that target firms diversifying the type of external advisor obtain a premium savings of the acquisition. Again, results presented in Table 19.3 do not support our hypothesis. Even if the target external advisor is negatively related ($r=-0.040$) to the premium savings of the acquisition, the coefficient is statistically not significant.

Discussion

The results presented in the above pages offered alternative considerations. In particular, these considerations can be referred to different insights provided in this study. First, a new idea of acquisition performance has been provided, that is based on the use of different measures of the acquisition performance (Bergh, 1995; Hoskisson *et al.*, 1994; King *et al.*, 2004). Second, our results partially do not confirm what prior managerial and financial research argued, with reference to the presence of an external advisor within the acquisition process. In general, our results provide new insights that must be exploited in order to stimulate the debate related to the crucial role the external advisors of both the bidding and target firms can play within the acquisition process. Surprisingly, the bidding firm's external advisors seem to drive the acquisition success, whereas such a success is partially obtained in terms of the above-normal economic performance the bidding firms gain through the acquisition. Target firms, on the other hand, do not benefit of an external intervention in the acquisition process, even if it seems they might experience a better agency theoretical position than the bidding firms relative to the external advisor's self-interests. Given the above considerations, the results presented in this study have several implications for research on the managerial process leading to the acquisition success.

First, the results indicate that the bidding firms hiring an external advisor can be allowed to reach above-normal economic performance. This can be true if we consider the specific categories of external advisor that should support the acquisition process, with special emphasis on the acquiring side of the operation. In fact, not just the presence, for instance, of a financial advisor (i.e. an investment bank) is required to reach positive results, but a combination of more categories of advisors. In other words, we found those acquisitions which led the acquiring firms to obtain an above-normal economic performance were the acquisitions in which a combination of advisor was found. For example, financial and legal advisors, as well as financial and transaction advisors were two alternative combinations through which a potentially successful acquisition could be completed. This result confutes what prior research suggested about the negative relationship between the presence of an external advisor and the acquisition performance (Hayward, 2002). What we suggest here is the need for considering the opportunity in charge of the bidding firm to diversify the risk related to the presence of just one external advisor. Hiring a combination of external advisors might represent for the acquiring firm an opportunity for improving the acquisition process.

Second, the presence of one or more advisors supporting the bidding process of the acquiring firm does not seem to influence the premium savings of the acquisition. This means that bidding firms hiring an advisor as well as a combination of different categories of advisors are not paying the right price for the right target firm. Again, it does not seem that bidding firms supported by one or more external advisors can pay the right price that is even lower than the value of the target firm. Even if the result we found suggests a negative relationship between the different advisors supporting the bidding process and the premium savings of the acquisition, this result is not statistically significant. That means, a significant relation linking these two factors has not been found. What we believe is really interesting is that our result provides empirical support to the agency theoretical problem existing between the bidding firms and their advisors (Kesner *et al.*, 1994). In fact, we are emphasising the problem that bidding firms are not allowed to obtain a premium saving even if they asked for an external support which might lead to this objective. Once again, external bidding advisors are seeking their self-interests that are strictly related to the higher price to be paid by the bidding firm. In this way external advisors will earn the higher revenue from a specific acquisition.

Third, opposite considerations can be in general argued with reference to the target side of the acquisition. In particular, our results do not provide statistically significant evidence that the target firms are gaining an advantage that is possible to associate with the presence of an advisor or a combination of different advisors. This is true with reference to both the measures of the acquisition success we exploited in our analysis that are the economic performance and the premium savings of the acquisition. Looking at the economic performance of the acquisition, we did not find that target firms are able to gain above normal economic performance related to the consulting service they required. This means that external advisors supporting the target firms during an acquisition are really interested just in concluding the deal at the higher price (Kesner *et al.*, 1994; Servaes and Zenner, 1996). On the other hand, those advisors do not support the target firm after the acquisition, that means any form of advising is not provided throughout the most important and complicated phase of the acquisition process, that is the post-acquisition integration process. Therefore, first of all acquired managers might better do to link the advising remuneration not to the price of the acquisition, that is the conclusion of the deal, but to create an incentive mechanism through which external advisors must be related and guarantee a continuous support to the target firm, especially during the integration process after the acquisition.

Looking at the premium savings of the acquisition, our result does not confirm the agency theoretical perspective suggesting that target firms and their advisors hold the same specific interest, which is the maximisation of the premium to be paid for the acquisition. Once again our result is not statistically significant, even if we found a negative relationship between the target external advisor and the premium savings of the acquisition. Such a negative relationship, in fact, might suggest that the external advisor supporting the target firm is going against its parent's interest, because it is not seeking the premium maximisation. This is especially true if a combination of external advisors is committed in the acquisition. Different consideration might be done if just one advisor (i.e. a financial advisor) should be involved in the acquisition process.

Finally, our results can provide additional insights with reference to the analysis of the management of the acquisition process. In particular, investigating the influence the presence of an external advisor and especially a combination of external advisors can have on the acquisition success or failure, we provided opposite findings that can deny what both strategic management and financial research rarely investigated. Many questions still remain without answers, but this contribution can stimulate the debate around the external support some firms require and receive during the acquisition process.

Note

1 Herein, we refer to combinations as the presence of two or more different categories of advisors within the same operation.

Bibliography

Barney, J. B. (1988) Returns to bidding firms in mergers and acquisitions: reconsidering the relatedness hypothesis. *Strategic Management Journal* 9 (special issue), 71–78.

Barney, J. B. (2002) *Gaining and Sustaining Competitive Advantage.* 2nd edn. New Jersey: Prentice Hall.

Benston, G. and Smith, C. W. (1976) A transactions costs approach to the theory of financial intermediation. *Journal of Finance* 31, 215–231.

Bergh, D. D. (1995) Size and relatedness of units sold: an agency theory and resource-based view perspective. *Strategic Management Journal* 16, 221–239.

Bergh, D. D. (2001) Executive retention and acquisition outcomes: a test of opposing views on the influence of organizational tenure. *Journal of Management* 27, 603–622.

Bergh, D. D. and Wrafter, E. (2003) *The influence of management consultants on client firm market value: evidence from the U.S. and U.K.* Academy of Management Annual Conference, Seattle.

Berle, A. and Means, G. (1932) *The Modern Corporation and Private Property.*, New York: Macmillan.

Bruton, G. D., Oviatt, B. M. and White, M. A. (1994) Performance of acquisitions of distressed firms. *Academy of Management Journal* 37(4), 972–989.

Cannella, A. A. and Hambrick, D. C. (1993) Effects of executive departures on the performance of acquired firms. *Strategic Management Journal* 14 (special issue), 137–152.

Capron, L. (1999) The long-term performance of horizontal acquisitions. *Strategic Management Journal* 20, 987–1018.

Coase, R. H. (1937) The nature of the firm. *Economica* 4, 386–405.

Datta, D. K. and Grant, J. H. (1990) Relationship between type of acquisition, the autonomy given to the acquired firm, and acquisition success: an empirical analysis. *Journal of Management* 16(1), 29–44.

Datta, D. K., Pinches, G. P. and Narayanan, V. K. (1992) Factors influencing wealth creation from mergers and acquisitions: a meta-analysis. *Strategic Management Journal* 13, 67–84.

Dyer, J., Kale, P. and Singh, H. (2001) How to make strategic alliances work. *Sloan Management Review,* Summer, 37–43.

Eisenhardt, K. M. (1989) Agency theory: an assessment and review. *Academy of Management Review* 14, 57–74.

Fowler, K. L. and Schmidt, D. R. (1989) Determinants of tender trade offer post acquisition financial performance. *Strategic Management Journal* 10, 339–350.

Greenwood, R., Hinings, C. R. and Brown, J. (1994) Merging professional service firms. *Organization Science* 5(2), 239–257.

Haleblian, J. and Finkelstein, S. (1999) The influence of organizational acquisition experience on acquisition performance: a behavioral learning perspective. *Administrative Science Quarterly* 44, 29–56.

Harrison, J. S., Hall, E. H. Jr. and Nargundkar, R. (1993) Resource allocation as an outcropping of strategic consistency: performance implications. *Academy of Management Journal* 36(5), 1026–1051.

Harrison, J. S., Hitt, M. A., Hoskisson, R. E. and Ireland, R. D. (1991) Synergies and post acquisition performance: differences versus similarities in resource allocations. *Journal of Management* 17(1), 173–190.

Haspeslagh, P. C. and Jemison, D. B. (1991) *Managing Acquisitions. Creating value through corporate renewal.* New York: The Free Press.

Haunschild, P. R. (1993) Interorganizational imitation: the impact of interlocks on corporate acquisition activity. *Administrative Science Quarterly* 38, 564–592.

Hayward, M. L. A. (2002) When do firms learn from their acquisition experience? Evidence from 1990–1995. *Strategic Management Journal* 23, 21–39.

Hayward, M. L. A. (2003) Professional influence: the effects of investment banks on clients' acquisition financing and performance. *Strategic Management Journal* 24(9), 783–801.

Hitt, M. A., Harrison, J. S., Ireland, R. D. and Best, A. (1998) Attributes of successful and unsuccessful acquisition of U.S. firms. *British Journal of Management* 9(2), 91–114.

Hitt, M. A., Hoskisson, R. E. and Ireland, R. D. (1990) Mergers and acquisitions and managerial commitment to innovation in M-form firms. *Strategic Management Journal* 11 (special issue), 29–47.

Hoskisson, R. E. and Johnson, R. A. (1992) Corporate restructuring and strategic change: the effect of diversification strategy and R&D intensity. *Strategic Management Journal* 13(8), 625–634.

Hoskisson, R. E., Johnson, R. A. and Moesel, D. D. (1994) Corporate divestiture intensity in restructuring firms: effects of governance, strategy, and performance. *Academy of Management Journal* 37(5), 1207–1251.

Hunter, W. C. and Walker, M. B. (1990) An empirical examination of investment banking merger fee contracts. *Southern Economic Journal* 56, 1117–1130.

Ingram, P. and Baum, J. A. C. (1997) Opportunity and constraint: organization's learning from the operating and competitive experience of industries. *Strategic Management Journal* 18 (special issue), 75–98.

Jemison, D. B. and Sitkin, S. B. (1986) Corporate acquisitions: a process perspective. *Academy of Management Review* 11(1), 145–163.

Jensen, M. C. and Meckling, W. H. (1976) Theory of the firm: managerial behavior, agency cost, and ownership structure. *Journal of Financial Economics* 3(4), 305–360.

Jensen, M. C. and Ruback, R. S. (1983) The market for corporate control: the scientific evidence. *Journal of Financial Economics* 11, 5–50.

Kesner, I. F., Shapiro, D. L. and Sharma, A. (1994) Brokering mergers: an agency theory perspective on the role of representatives. *Academy of Management Journal* 37(3), 703–721.

King, D. R., Dalton, D. R. and Daily, C. M. (2004) Meta-analyses of post-acquisition performance: indications of unidentified moderators. *Strategic Management Journal* 25(2), 187–200.

Lubatkin, M. (1983) Mergers and the performance of the acquiring firm. *Academy of Management Review* 8, 218–225.

McLaughlin, R. M. (1990) Investment-banking contracts in tender offers. *Journal of Financial Economics* 28, 209–232.

Morck, R., Shleifer, A. and Vishny, R. W. (1990) Do managerial objectives drive bad acquisitions?. *Journal of Finance* 45(1), 31–48.

Pablo, A. L. (1994) Determinants of acquisition integration level: a decision making perspective. *Academy of Management Journal* 37(4), 803–836.

Russo, A. (2004) *Managing the post-acquisition integration process. Determinants and value creation.* Unpublished PhD dissertation, Bocconi University, Milan, Italy.

Russo, A. and Perrini, F. (2004) The choice of controlling and financing the acquisition for acquiring and acquired stakeholders. *Academy of Management Conference*, New Orleans, LO, USA, 1–40.

Servaes, H. and Zenner, M. (1996) The role of investment banks in acquisitions. *The Review of Financial Studies* 9(3), 787–815.

Singh, H. and Zollo, M. (2000) Post-acquisition strategies, integration capability, and the economic performance of corporate acquisitions. Working paper, The Wharton School, University of Pennsylvania, 1–41.

Walsh, J. P. (1988) Top management turnover following mergers and acquisitions. *Strategic Management Journal* 9, 173–183.

Walsh, J. P. (1989) Doing a deal: merger and acquisition negotiations and their impact upon target company top management turnover. *Strategic Management Journal* 10, 307–322.

Williamson, O. E. (1975) *Markets and Hierarchies: analysis and antitrust implications.* New York: The Free Press.

20 Managing innovation and learning in dynamic environments

The role of rapid response capabilities

Christoph Grimpe, Wolfgang Sofka and John Saee

Introduction

A broad stream of management literature has focused on resource-based firm strategies for achieving competitive advantage (Barney, 1991; Conner, 1991; Peteraf, 1993; Wernerfelt, 1984). However, relatively little is known on when and how these strategic resources can and should be activated. Gaining a head-start over competitors requires timely responsiveness, reaction to market intelligence as well as rapid and flexible product innovation (Kohli and Jaworski, 1990; Brockhoff, 1997). At the same time, competitive pressures from globalisation have forced firms to make every effort to streamline and rationalise their workflow (Franko, 1989). This has often led to outsourcing and offshoring strategies, that is, the shift of labour-intensive manufacturing to countries with significantly lower labour costs in order to decrease product prices (Teece *et al.*, 1997). Some – and not by coincidence the most successful – companies in their sector, however, have created their own approach to coping with this situation. Spanish fashion retailer ZARA, for example, has been the prototype for a new kind of competitive strategy. It competes within the market in a dynamic manner through its rapid launch of new products. We call this a *rapid response capability*, which is also referred to in the literature as dynamic capabilities (Eisenhardt and Martin, 2000; Hoopes *et al.*, 2003). More precisely, we explore its roots and antecedents to discover how firms may create and take advantage of employing such capability. This is particularly interesting as the development of rapid response capabilities is an important way to overcome competition based on price/cost advantages through speed and flexibility (Berger, 2006). Building on Nelson and Winter's (1982) view of organisations as a nexus of operational and administrative routines, we define rapid response capabilities specifically as a result of learning mechanisms directed at matching internal strategic resources with the external strategic context (Zollo and Winter, 2002).

The goal of this analysis is twofold. First of all, we aim to develop a theoretical framework dealing with this particular type of capability whilst testing it empirically. As Helfat and Peteraf (2003: 997) argued, 'it is difficult to fully explain how firms use resources and capabilities to create a competitive advantage', we provide some initial indications for management on the understanding of rapid response capability development. Our study is designed to, first of all, provide a conceptual framework with accompanying hypotheses. It also presents our empirical study that validates our hypotheses. In addition, the results of this quantitative analysis are also provided here.

Based on these results, we discuss our findings on rapid response capabilities and, finally, we offer our concluding remarks.

Theory and hypotheses

Deliberate learning and dynamic capabilities

The resource (and capability) based view of the firm complements traditional industry analysis. It combines internal and external factors to understand the sources of competitive advantage (Amit and Schoemaker, 1993; Sirmon *et al.*, 2007). Several studies argue that capabilities cannot be investigated without considering their relevant context (Atuahene-Gima and Haiyang, 2004; Brush and Artz, 1999): the 'when, where and how' resources and capabilities translate into competitive advantage (Priem and Butler, 2001). We follow this stream of literature by discussing the roots of rapid response capabilities and their relevant context.

First mover and follower advantages have been the centrepiece of research investigating timing in innovation activities (see, e.g. Jensen, 2003; Lieberman and Montgomery, 1988; Shankar *et al.*, 1998). It implies that market novelties appear and firms find themselves either on the pioneering or catching-up side. As our concept of rapid response capabilities is dynamic in nature, it combines innovation and imitation. Rapid response firms like ZARA do not innovate once and reap the benefits from temporary entry barriers for competitors afterwards (first mover). They keep offering new products and services while constantly adjusting to changing market pressures and opportunities. Their competitive advantage stems neither exclusively from innovation nor from imitation but from a combination of both, through short feedback and reaction cycles. We define rapid response capabilities as a form of dynamic capability. It addresses dynamics in the competitive environment through continuous changes in organisational routines. It is specific in the sense that competitive advantage arises not primarily from these readjustments but from achieving them significantly faster than industry rivals. This constant time compression provides additional flexibility which reduces the exposure to two fundamental risks in innovation: strategic blind spots and technological lock-ins.

The mechanism behind the build-up of rapid response capabilities can hence be regarded as a continuous and deliberate learning process (Zollo and Winter, 2002). This process describes the systematic methods by which firms modify their operating routines. Such routines constitute stable patterns of organisational behaviour and reaction to internal or external stimuli. On the one hand, routines define predictable, interrelated organisational actions, for example, order processing for new fashion. On the other hand, a routine may also initiate the introduction of a more demand-focused order processing system. Routines of this second type are typically referred to as search routines (Nelson and Winter, 1982). They deal with changes in the existing set of operating routines and can hence be perceived as a dynamic capability constitutive for rapid response capabilities.

In a relatively stable environment, operating routines superior to those of competitors can already be a source of sustainable competitive advantage (Zollo and Winter, 2002). A tacit accumulation of experience resulting in incremental changes and improvements in the set of operating routines may be sufficient. However, when the environment turns turbulent and involves rapid changes in customer demand, technology or competition, a stable set of routines might no longer be sufficient. Systematic efforts are needed to track the environment and dynamically adjust routines. This is where rapid response capabilities become crucial. A failure to develop such capabilities could turn once established core competencies into core rigidities (Leonard-Barton, 1992). An accumulation of experience resulting from a repeated execution of routines combined with a trial-and-error procedure is enough for developing rapid response capabilities. There are two further constitutive steps within the process, which are referred to as knowledge articulation and knowledge codification.

Knowledge articulation evolves from discursive actions between individuals and groups in the execution of organisational tasks (Levitt and March, 1988; Levinthal and March, 1993). Expressing opinions and individual viewpoints, challenging them and mutually understanding causal linkages – especially in the presence of ambiguities – are prerequisites for making implicit or tacit knowledge explicit and hence for enabling collective learning efforts. Knowledge from relevant customers and the environment has to be made available throughout the company in order to adjust operating routines accordingly and to spread successful action-performance links within the whole organisation. Sirmon *et al.* (2007) suggest that the effectiveness of this step also depends on environmental munificence. The varying munificence of environments might critically affect the potential value of a firm's resources and capabilities. Moreover, munificent environments can support the growth of resources within firms by providing access to complementary, external resources (Baum and Wally, 2003). This aspect directly leads to knowledge codification as a step beyond articulation. It is central to the capability-building process as it facilitates the diffusion of existing knowledge through written guidelines, manuals or process charts (Zander and Kogut, 1995). To transfer changes in one operating routine to other routines, the knowledge required to make the changes must be codified. Besides the benefits that codification has for organisational knowledge creation, there are most certainly considerable costs associated with it, for example, time, resources or managerial attention. These costs have to be balanced with the expected benefits from building and maintaining rapid response capabilities. Those companies that have the most efficient learning mechanisms will reap the benefits in terms of competitive advantage in a given environmental context.

Finally, a firm's ability to identify promising strategic resources in its environment and integrate them into the existing resource and capability portfolio for superior performance can be considered a capability in itself. We hence define rapid response capabilities more precisely as deliberate and specific organisational processes for generating superior customer value (and hence competitive advantage) based on time compression in these activities.

Antecedents of rapid response capabilities

The previous argumentation suggests that rapid response capabilities arise from a combination of internal competencies and external opportunities. In the following, we develop an evaluation scheme that explores the antecedents of rapid response capabilities leading to our hypotheses.

Absorptive capacities as internal drivers of rapid response capabilities

Based on our understanding, rapid response capabilities are built around a firm's ability to extract relevant market knowledge and integrate it quickly into new products and services as well as into the whole organisation. While market impulses are available to all competitors, firms can differentiate themselves through their expertise in synthesising this information, integrating and combining it with existing knowledge (Henderson and Cockburn, 1994; Kogut and Zander, 1992). An important stream of literature has summarised these capabilities as absorptive capacity (Cohen and Levinthal, 1989, 1990): a firm's ability to identify, assimilate and exploit knowledge from the environment. This differentiation corresponds with the three learning mechanisms in organisational capability development – experience accumulation, knowledge articulation and knowledge codification – but puts a stronger emphasis on exploiting and capitalising acquired knowledge. Several studies have linked absorptive capacity to superior firm performance (Landry, 2006; Love and Roper, 2005; Nadiri, 1993). Absorptive capacities are typically accumulated through experience by performing innovation activities. Hence, they are difficult to acquire, imitate or substitute (Amit and Schoemaker, 1993). We extend this view by focusing on the cycle time through all three stages, knowledge identification, assimilation and exploitation, and argue that a higher turnover rate can constitute a capability in itself by increasing the efficiency of the whole process, that is, rapid response capabilities.

Jansen *et al.* (2005) have recently argued along similar lines by differentiating between potential absorptive capacities (identification, assimilation) and realised absorptive capacity (exploitation). They find that a unique mix of organisational measures is required to balance a broad screening process for valuable ideas with a structured approach towards exploiting them. In conclusion, we derive the following hypothesis:

> Hypothesis I: Existing absorptive capacities enable firms to achieve time compression in their learning engagements and hence develop rapid response capabilities.

Environmental dynamism as external driver for rapid response capabilities

As previously mentioned, rapid response capabilities connote change as they inevitably aim at improving operating routines (Collis, 1994; Winter, 2003). This change is necessary to the extent that competitive conditions change. Competitive conditions in turn are largely given by the environmental dynamism that a firm faces (Miller and Friesen, 1983). Environmental dynamism describes the rate of change resulting from the market environment. It centres around three major driving forces: competitors, customers and technology. Dynamism increases to the extent that these three forces provide stimuli for change. A rapid change of the dominant technology paradigm, for example, paired with the emergence of new competitors entering the marketplace as well as shifting customer demands will obviously cause a high level of environmental dynamism. However, it is important to note that the environmental dynamism is not completely external to the firm but also a result of a firm's actions and interactions. Firms can use their position within an industry to influence the industry structure and take advantage from it. It depends on the resources and capabilities of the firm to what extent rents can be appropriated and rivals are motivated to imitate this strategy and subsequently detract from its advantage.

Their ability to imitate strategies determines the degree of rivalry among firms in an industry. When the industry structure is characterised by stable rent appropriation with only minor changes in the competitive environment, the pressure on firms stays also at rather low levels. When the industry structure, however, is continuously altered, firms typically feel under a great deal of pressure, which affects potential value creation (Sirmon *et al.*, 2007). But this pressure also forces firms to learn and develop capabilities to deal with environmental dynamism. The higher the rate of change the more capabilities to cope with it are rewarded. Firms unable to do so will ultimately disappear or pull out of the market. Hence, this pressure can also be a learning opportunity to develop rapid response capabilities. This will lead to sustainable competitive advantage to the extent that a firm disposes of rapid response capabilities that cannot be imitated by rivals. Our second hypothesis can thus be divided into three facets that capture the driving forces of the market environment:

Hypothesis IIa: Firms develop rapid response capabilities as they respond to dynamism from their competitor environment.

Hypothesis IIb: Firms develop rapid response capabilities as they respond to dynamism from their customer environment.

Hypothesis IIc: Firms develop rapid response capabilities as they respond to dynamism from their technology environment.

To sum up, rapid response capabilities may evolve based on absorptive capacity and/or environmental dynamism. Given the previous discussion, a combination of internal capabilities and external pressures can easily be envisioned as the strategic fit for rapid response capabilities. In fact, Jansen *et al.* (2005) find that potential absorptive capacities enhance performance as markets become more dynamic. Following this line of thinking, rapid response capabilities would be especially beneficial in dynamic environments. They would consequently be constituted as a form of dynamic capability (Eisenhardt and Martin, 2000).

Method

Data and estimation strategy

For the empirical part of this analysis we use cross-sectional data from a survey on the innovation activities of German enterprises called the 'Mannheim Innovation Panel' (MIP). The data is collected annually by the Centre for European Economic Research (ZEW) on behalf of the German Federal Ministry of Education and Research. The methodology and questionnaire used by the survey, which is targeted at enterprises with at least five employees, are the same as those used in the European Union's Community Innovation Survey (CIS). For our analysis, we use the 2005 survey, in which data was collected on the innovation activities of enterprises during the three-year period 2002–2004. About 5200 firms in manufacturing and services responded to the survey and provided information on their innovation activities. The sample was drawn using the stratified random sample technique. A comprehensive non-response analysis showed no systematic distortions between responding and non-responding firms with respect to their innovation activities (Spielkamp and Rammer, 2006). We utilise this data to operationalise the concepts presented above.

Our data set without missing values contains data on 3360 firms located in Germany. Very few companies collect data on the cycle time of their innovation activities. We therefore rely on the self-assessment of heads of R&D departments and innovation management on whether they established rapid response capabilities. To narrow down the complexity of the question we focus on two central stimuli from the environment: customers and suppliers. More precisely, we ask: 'Did your organisational innovation activities lead predominantly to a reduction in response time to customer or supplier requirements?' From the total sample, 779 firms responded in the affirmative and we interpret this approach as the establishment of rapid response capabilities. This indicator is the dependent variable in all subsequent steps of the analysis; the remaining 2581 serve as the comparison group. We will subsequently estimate two probit models since our dependent variable is binary in nature. This allows us to identify factors which significantly increase a company's probability of pursuing rapid response capabilities while controlling for contextual aberrations (e.g. industry effects).

Exogenous variables

Measuring absorptive capacity

Absorptive capacities are developed by performing R&D activities. We capture their effect in line with the literature (Cohen and Levinthal, 1990; Rothwell and Dodgson, 1991) through variables on the two major inputs for innovation activities: R&D expenditure (as a share of sales) and the expertise of employees (share of employees with college education divided by industry average). Given our analytical framework, we are especially interested in the accumulation process of absorptive capacities. We therefore add an additional dummy variable to indicate whether R&D activities are performed on a continuous basis. Hypothesis I will be supported if the coefficients of the absorptive capacity variables are positive and significant.

Measuring environmental dynamism

Environmental dynamism has been most prominently structured by Miller and Friesen (1983). We rely on a conceptualisation which rests upon the items proposed by these authors. Environmental dynamism resulting from the competitors is measured by the difficulty of forecasting competitor behaviour as well as the threat from market entry of new competitors. Dynamism resulting from customers is addressed by the difficulty of forecasting demand and the quick obsolescence of products and services. Finally, dynamism that stems from technology is measured by rapid changes in technology as well as an easy substitution of products. Respondents were asked to rate the prevalence of each of these factors for their business on a four-point Likert scale. We will use each variable separately as a dummy indicating that the particular form of pressure is high.

Control variables

We control for several other factors: regional differences between East and West Germany, company size (number of employees in logs and in squared terms to control for the effect of especially large firms), industry effects (grouped NACE2, see Appendices 20A and B for details) and technological stability (through the share of sales generated by unchanged products). Table 20.1 shows the descriptive statistics.

Rapid response firms are on average twice as large as the control group and operate more frequently in medium–high tech manufacturing (e.g. automotive industry) and less frequently in distributive services (e.g. transportation). Interestingly, they are more likely to perform R&D continuously but invest lower shares of their turnover on it. Finally, they are exposed to higher levels of environmental dynamism especially from technology changes and product obsolescence. A multivariate analysis is warranted.

Table 20.1 Descriptive statistics

Variables	Full sample		Rapid responders		Control group	
	Mean	SD	Mean	SD	Mean	SD
Employees (no.)	442.44	5082.74	725.64	5328.91	356.96	5003.98
Share of sales from existing products (%)	86.77	22.71	80.67	25.84	88.61	21.35
Employees with graduate education (%)	19.80	24.29	20.01	23.08	19.74	24.64
Employees with graduate education divided by industry average (ratio)	0.97	1.10	1.01	1.02	0.96	1.12
R&D expenditures as a share of sales (%)	7.49	149.92	5.11	37.71	8.21	169.80
Continuous R&D engagement (dummy)	0.26	0.44	0.37	0.48	0.22	0.42
Competitor moves are hardly predictable (dummy)	0.17	0.37	0.17	0.37	0.17	0.37
New competitors threaten market position (dummy)	0.15	0.35	0.16	0.36	0.14	0.35
Product technology changes rapidly (dummy)	0.09	0.29	0.14	0.35	0.07	0.26
Products rapidly become obsolete (dummy)	0.07	0.25	0.10	0.30	0.06	0.23
Easy substitution with competing products (dummy)	0.25	0.43	0.27	0.44	0.24	0.43
Demand forecasting is difficult (dummy)	0.21	0.41	0.23	0.42	0.20	0.40
Location East Germany (dummy)	0.34	0.47	0.31	0.46	0.34	0.48
Medium–high tech manufacturing (dummy)	0.13	0.34	0.17	0.37	0.12	0.32
High tech manufacturing (dummy)	0.07	0.26	0.08	0.27	0.07	0.25
Distributive services (dummy)	0.18	0.39	0.14	0.35	0.19	0.40
Knowledge intensive services (dummy)	0.12	0.32	0.11	0.31	0.12	0.32
Technological services (dummy)	0.13	0.33	0.12	0.33	0.13	0.33
Observations	3360		779		2581	

Results

The analysis is split up into two separate model specifications, shown in Table 20.2. While model 1, our baseline case, only estimates the main effects of absorptive capacity and environmental dynamism on the development of rapid response

Table 20.2 Results of the probit models

Variables	Model 1 Coef.	Model 2 Coef.
Employees with graduate education divided by industry average (ratio)	0.02(0.02)	0.02(0.02)
R&D expenditures as a share of sales (%)	0.00(0.00)	0.00(0.00)
Continuous R&D engagement (dummy)	0.23c(0.07)	0.23c(0.07)
Competitor moves are hardly predictable (dummy)	0.00(0.07)	0.00(0.07)
New competitors threaten market position (dummy)	0.10(0.07)	0.09(0.07)
Product technology changes rapidly (dummy)	0.31c(0.09)	0.41c(0.11)
Products rapidly become obsolete (dummy)	0.14(0.11)	0.15(0.11)
Easy substitution with competing products (dummy)	0.07(0.06)	0.07(0.06)
Demand forecasting is difficult (dummy)	0.13b(0.06)	0.17c(0.07)
Interaction product technology changes and demand forecasting		−0.30a(0.17)
Location East Germany (dummy)	−0.05(0.05)	0.05(0.05)
Employees (no. in logs)	0.12b(0.05)	0.12b(0.05)
Employees (no. in logs, squared)	0.00(0.01)	0.00(0.01)
Share of sales from existing products (%)	−0.01c(0.00)	−0.01c(0.00)
Industry dummies	yes	yes
Constant	−0.75c(0.17)	−0.76c(0.17)
Observations	3360	3360
R2	0.09	0.09
Wald chi2(14)	170.37	172.16
P>0	0.00	0.00

Notes
a significant at 10%
b significant at 5%
c significant at 1%
Robust standard errors in parentheses. Industry dummy results are available in the appendix.

capabilities, model 2 includes an interaction term between the two significant environmental dynamism variables. This interaction term is intended to capture the effect of an almost turbulent environment which results from simultaneous changes in more than one of the three forces of environmental dynamism.

Generally speaking, our results show a high stability across the two models. Starting with the main effects in model 1 we observe no significant impact of two of the variables that make up absorptive capacity: formal education of employees and R&D intensity. In contrast to that, continuous R&D engagement, our third indicator of absorptive capacity, is positive and significant. Obviously, there is a strong emphasis on the experience effect with its long-term accumulation of knowledge. This seems to shape absorptive capacities in a way that is relevant for building rapid response capabilities. We can hence confirm our first hypothesis. Regarding the impact of environmental dynamism we can observe a positive and significant effect for the items 'product technology changes rapidly' and 'demand forecasting is difficult'. Therefore, Hypotheses IIb and IIc are supported.

Model 2 includes an interaction of both significant environmental factors. Here we can even observe a negative significant coefficient. This means that a simultaneous existence of both highly pronounced environmental factors would lead to an overextension of company resources resulting in an inability to develop rapid response capabilities.

Furthermore, we include several control variables in our analysis. Their effects vary only to a very limited extent across the four models. The results show that particularly large firms, measured in terms of the number of employees, are more likely to develop rapid response capabilities. An explanation might be that as firms grow larger they have to be more goal-oriented in improving their speed and flexibility while smaller firms are – at least to some degree – flexible anyway. Moreover, there is a negative significant effect of sales of existing products which serves as a measure for technological dynamics. Evidently, the lower this share of sales and consequently the higher the technological dynamics, the more rapid response capabilities are propelled. This is in line with our previous argumentation. Finally, we included industry effects in the analysis. These are hardly significant with the exception of high-tech manufacturing companies, which exhibit a negative effect on the build-up of rapid response capabilities. Detailed results are available in Appendices 20A and B.

Discussion

Our empirical results suggest that rapid response capabilities are developed through persistent R&D engagements as well as high environmental pressures from the technological and customer side. The effects of these internal and external drivers are additive in nature, although a combination of external pressures leads to negative results. We discuss these results in more detail.

Absorptive capacities as drivers for rapid response capability

The positive effect of absorptive capacity on rapid response capabilities stresses the importance of prolonged R&D commitments. Current investments in R&D projects and personnel have no significant impact. This supports the general accumulation aspect of absorptive capacity (Cohen and Levinthal, 1990). What is more, we find that firms that engage consistently in innovation activities develop routines and capabilities that cannot be readily acquired on factor markets (Amit and Schoemaker, 1993). This supports our view of capability development as a continuous and deliberate learning mechanism. Firms with established competencies and routines find it easier to reduce cycle times for individual innovation projects. This is achieved by streamlining the knowledge accumulation, articulation and codification steps within the learning process. In other words, capabilities need to be 'tightened' to ensure their efficiency (Sirmon *et al.*, 2007). Hence, this facet of rapid response capabilities is born out of efficiency gains from experience effects.

Environmental dynamism as drivers for rapid response capability

We find that environmental dynamics propel the development of rapid response capabilities. Interestingly enough, competitors are not a significant source for this capability development process. Technological volatility as well as uncertainty about future demand trends are the dominant drivers. Firms deal with these uncertainties in their environment by developing rapid response capabilities that allow flexible solutions and prevent strategic blind spots as well as 'betting on the wrong horse'. When implemented effectively, this can produce a series of competitive advantages (Sirmon *et al.*, 2007). Hence, rapid response capabilities are necessitated and potentially rewarded by dynamics in the environment depending on its munificence (Baum and Wally, 2003). There are limits, though, to the degree of organisational flexibility for coping with external volatility. If upstream (technological) and downstream (demand) uncertainties interact, firms are less likely to respond with the development of rapid response capabilities. We argue that the more diffuse the environmental pressures are the more difficult and costly is the assessment of potential risks and opportunities and the subsequent translation into rapid response capabilities. This is in line with Sirmon *et al.* (2007), who propose that under extreme environmental uncertainty it might not be enough to rapidly respond but may also be necessary to direct capabilities at the development of a new technology that might itself create environmental pressure for competitors. This implies an entrepreneurial leveraging strategy.

Concluding remarks

The goal of this research study was to detach the topic of rapid response capabilities from specific cases (like ZARA), and embed it into the literature and test its antecedents empirically. We acknowledge important limitations which may suggest promising routes for future research projects. There are issues concerning the data but also regarding conceptual development. First, we can only report empirical results for Germany. While we are confident that this is a fitting research setting, comparative results for other established (e.g. USA, Japan) as well as emerging economies could provide important additional insights. What is more, although we work with a comprehensive data set, it is only available as a cross section. As time has been shown to be an important factor in this context, longitudinal studies could shed more light on the build-up process of capabilities over time. Regarding our conceptualisation it has to be noted that we do not address performance effects of rapid response capabilities. Although we raise the importance of gaining competitive advantage from such capabilities we do not analyse the impact on firm performance. Future research should hence focus on the performance effect of rapid response capabilities. This short overview makes it clear that the development of rapid response capabilities will be an interesting topic for further research.

Appendix 20A Industry breakdown

Industry	NACE Code	Industry Group
Mining and quarrying	10–14	Other manufacturing
Food and tobacco	15–16	Other manufacturing
Textiles and leather	17–19	Other manufacturing
Wood / paper / publishing	20–22	Other manufacturing
Chemicals / petroleum	23–24	Medium high-tech manufacturing
Plastics / rubber	25	Other manufacturing
Glass / ceramics	26	Other manufacturing
Metal	27–28	Other manufacturing
Manufacture of machinery and equipment	29	Medium high-tech manufacturing
Manufacture of electrical equipment and electronics	30–32	High-tech manufacturing
Medical, precision and optical instruments	33	High-tech manufacturing
Manufacture of motor vehicles	34–35	Medium high-tech manufacturing
Manufacture of furniture, jewellery, sports equipment and toys	36–37	Other manufacturing
Electricity, gas and water supply	40–41	Other manufacturing
Construction	45	Other manufacturing
Retail and motor trade	50, 52	Distributive services
Wholesale trade	51	Distributive services
Transportation and communication	60–63, 64.1	Distributive services
Financial intermediation	65–67	Knowledge-intensive services
Real estate activities and renting	70–71	Distributive services
ICT services	72, 64.2	Technological services
Technical services	73, 74.2, 74.3	Technological services
Consulting	74.1, 74.4	Knowledge-intensive services
Motion picture/broadcasting	92.1–92.2	Knowledge-intensive services
Other business-oriented services	74.5–74.8, 90	Distributive services

Appendix 20B Probit results: industry dummies

Variables	Model 1 Coef.	Model 2 Coef.
High tech manufacturing (dummy)	−0.17[a](0.10)	−0.18[a](0.10)
Medium-high tech manufacturing (dummy)	0.00(0.08)	0.00(0.08)
Distributive services (dummy)	−0.10(0.07)	−0.10(0.07)
Knowledge intensive services (dummy)	−0.02(0.08)	−0.03(0.08)
Technological services (dummy)	−0.10(0.09)	−0.10(0.09)

Notes
a   significant at 10%
Robust standard errors in parentheses. For full regression results see Table 20.2.

References

Ai, Chunrong and Norton, Edward C. (2003) Interaction terms in logit and probit models. *Economics Letters* 80, 123–129.

Amit, Raphael and Schoemaker, Paul J. H. (1993) Strategic assets and organizational rent. *Strategic Management Journal* 14(1), 33–46.

Atuahene-Gima, Kwaku and Haiyang, Li (2004) Strategic decision comprehensiveness and new product development outcomes in new technology ventures. *Academy of Management Journal* 47(4), 583–597.

Barney, Jay B. (1991) Firm resources and sustained competitive advantage. *Journal of Management* 17(1), 99–120.

Baum, J. Robert and Wally, Stefan (2003) Strategic decision speed and firm performance. *Strategic Management Journal* 24, 1107–1129.

Berger, Suzanne (2006) *How We Compete: what companies around the world are doing to make it in today's global economy.* New York.

Brockhoff, Klaus (1997) *Industrial Research for Future Competitiveness.* Berlin *et al.*

Brush, Thomas H. and Kendall, W. Artz (1999) Toward a contingent resource-based theory: the impact of information asymmetry on the value of capabilities in veterinary medicine. *Strategic Management Journal* 20(3), 223–250.

Cohen, Wesley M. and Levinthal, Daniel A. (1989) Innovation and learning: the two faces of R&D. *The Economic Journal* 99(397), 569–596.

Cohen, Wesley M. and Levinthal, Daniel A. (1990) Absorptive capacity: a new perspective on learning and innovation. *Administrative Science Quarterly* 35(1), 128–152.

Collis, David J. (1994) Research note: how valuable are organizational capabilities?. *Strategic Management Journal* 15(8), 143–152.

Conner, Kathleen R. (1991) A historical comparison of resource-based theory and five schools of thought within industrial organization economics. Do we have a new theory of the firm?. *Journal of Management* 17(1), 121–154.

Eisenhardt, Kathleen M. and Martin, Jeffrey A. (2000) Dynamic capabilities: what are they?. *Strategic Management Journal* 21(10/11), 1105–1121.

Franko, Lawrence G. (1989) Global corporate competition: who's winning, who's losing, and the R&D factor as one reason why. *Strategic Management Journal* 10(5), 449–474.

Helfat, Constance E. and Peteraf, Margaret A. (2003) The dynamic resource-based view: capabilities life cycles. *Strategic Management Journal* 24, 997–1010.

Henderson, Rebecca and Cockburn, Iain (1994) Measuring competence? Exploring firm effects in pharmaceutical research. *Strategic Management Journal* 15(8), 63–84.

Hoopes, David G., Madsen, Tammy L. and Walker, Gordon (2003) Guest editors' introduction to the special issue: why is there a resource-based view? Toward a theory of competitive heterogeneity. *Strategic Management Journal* 24, 889–902.

Jansen, Justin, Frans, J. P., Van den Bosch, A. J. and Volberda, Henk W. (2005), Managing Potential and Realized Absorptive Capacity: How Do Organizational Antecendents Matter?, Academy of Management Journal 48 (6), 999–1015.

Jensen, Richard A. (2003), Disclosure and licensing of university inventions: 'The best we can do with the s**t we get to work with'. *International Journal of Industrial Organization* 21, 1271–1300.

Kogut, Bruce and Zander, Udo (1992) Knowledge of the firm, combinative capabilities, and the replication of technology. *Organization Science* 3(3), 383–397.

Kohli, Ajay K. and Jaworski, Bernard J. (1990) Market orientation: the construct, research propositions, and managerial implications. *Journal of Marketing* 54(2), 1–18.

Landry, Réjean (2006) Why are some university researchers more likely to create spin-offs than others? Evidence from Canadian universities. *Research Policy* 35, 1599–1615.

Leonard-Barton, Dorothy (1992) Core capabilities and core rigidities: a paradox in managing new product development. *Strategic Management Journal* 13(5), 111–125.

Levinthal, Daniel A. and March, James G. (1993) The myopia of learning. *Strategic Management Journal* 14, 95–112.

Levitt, Barbara and March, James G. (1988) Organizational learning. *Annual Review of Sociology* 14, 319–340.

Lieberman, Marvin B. and Montgomery, David B. (1988) First-mover advantages. *Strategic Management Journal* 9, 41–58.

Love, James H. and Roper, Stephen (2005) Innovation, productivity and growth: an analysis of Irish panel data. *Proceedings of 32nd Conference of the European Association for Research in Industrial Economics (EARIE)*, Porto.

March, James G. (1991) Exploration and exploitation in organizational learning. *Organization Science* 2(1), 71–87.

Miller, Danny and Friesen, Peter H. (1983) Strategy-making and environment: the third link. *Strategic Management Journal* 4, 221–235.

Nadiri, Ishaq M. (1993) Innovations and technological spillovers. NBER working paper no. 4423, Cambridge, MA.

Nelson, Richard R. and Winter, Sidney G. (1982) *An Evolutionary Theory of Economic Change*. Cambridge, MA.

Penrose, Edith Tilton (1959) *The Theory of the Growth of the Firm*. Oxford.

Peteraf, Margaret A. (1993) The cornerstones of competitive advantage: a resource-based view. *Strategic Management Journal* 14(3), 179–191.

Porter, Michael E. (1980) *Competitive Strategy. Techniques for analyzing industries and competitors*. New York, London.

Porter, Michael E. (1985) *Competitive Advantage*. New York, London.

Porter, Michael E. (1991) Towards a dynamic theory of strategy. *Strategic Management Journal* 12(8), 95–117.

Priem, Richard L. and Butler, John E. (2001) Is the resource-based 'view' a useful perspective for strategic management research?. *Academy of Management Review* 26(1), 22–40.

Rothwell, Roy and Dodgson, Mark (1991) External linkages and innovation in small and medium-sized enterprises. *R&D Management* 21, 125–137.

Sapienza, Alice M. (2005) From the inside: scientists' own experience of good (and bad) management, *R&D Management* 35(5), 473–482.

Shankar, Venkatesh, Carpenter, Gregory S. and Krishnamurthi, Lakshman (1998) Later mover advantage: how innovative late entrants outsell pioneers. *Journal of Marketing Research* 35, 54–70.

Sharma, Subash, Durand, Richard M. and Gur-Arie, Oded (1981) Identification and analysis of moderator variables. *Journal of Marketing Research* 18, 291–300.

Sirmon, David G., Hitt, Michael A. and Ireland, R. Duane (2007) Managing firm resources in dynamic environments to create value: looking inside the black box. *Academy of Management Review* 32(1), 273–292.

Spielkamp, Alfred and Christian Rammer (2006) Balanceakt Innovation – Erfolgsfaktoren im Innovationsmanagement Kleiner und Mittlerer Unternehmen. Unpublished manuscript.

Teece, David J., Pisano, Gary and Shuen, Amy (1997) Dynamic capabilities and strategic management. *Strategic Management Journal* 18(7), 509–533.

Wernerfelt, Birger (1984) A resource-based view of the firm. *Strategic Management Journal* 5(2), 171–180.

Winter, Sidney G. (2003) Understanding dynamic capabilites. *Strategic Management Journal* 24, 991–995.

Zander, Udo and Kogut, Bruce (1995) Knowledge and the speed of the transfer and imitation of organizational capabilities: an empirical test. *Organization Science* 6(1), 76–92.

Zollo, Maurizio and Winter, Sidney G. (2002) Deliberate learning and the evolution of dynamic capabilities. *Organization Science* 13(3), 339–351.

Index

Note: Page references in italic type refer to Tables and Figures. Appendices are not indexed.